DAVID JACKSON with NICOLA JACKSON

SURGEON
IN THE
RAW

A MEMOIR

Mereo Books

Mereo Books 2nd Floor, 6-8 Dyer Street,
Cirencester, Gloucestershire, GL7 2PF

An imprint of Memoirs Book Ltd. www.mereobooks.com

SURGEON IN THE RAW: 978-1-86151-966-5

First published in Great Britain in 2020
by Mereo Books, an imprint of Memoirs Books Ltd.

The address for Memoirs Books Ltd. can be
found at www.mereobooks.com

Typeset in 11/15pt Times New Roman
by Wiltshire Associates Ltd. Printed and bound in Great Britain

We dedicate this book to the armed forces personnel who have been physically injured, emotionally damaged or killed during battle campaigns. We also devote this work to the innocent civilian bystanders who have been caught up in the physical or emotional crossfire of war, be that military or domestic.

CONTENTS

Acknowledgements
Foreword
Introduction
They shall grow not old

PART 1: NHS 1967-1978

PART 2: ARMY 1978-1995

PART 3: NHS 1995-2012

Acknowledgements

I could not have completed this memoir without the support of my family, friends and colleagues. They have given me constructive criticism when needed, praise where due, and general encouragement. I was often told, during the early writing and editing process, to stop procrastinating and just get on with it. Indeed, 'Get On With It' was the first working title.

Firstly I would like to thank Belinda and 'Smiffy', our animal-mad neighbours in Spain, for taking time out from their daily rounds of feeding Turre's feral cat colonies to scrutinise the early draft of my manuscript. I assured them I was not precious, and they could be ruthless. They were, and Belinda struck out great swathes of unnecessary passages, with a metaphorical red marker pen, arguing that they were either inappropriate, futile or plain boring – she was right, and the manuscript is all the better for it.

My thanks also go to my neighbour Martin Benson. He strengthened my resolve to confront the reader and risk being controversial by including the graphic details of war, rather than resorting to mere discussions about the moralities of conflict. He reminded me that if my readership was to extend beyond those who are medically qualified, I might need to consider providing a better explanation of some surgical procedures and decode the terminology; I have taken his advice. He also caused me to re-examine my motives for including certain case studies, and to include only those that served a purpose or illustrated a valid point.

Martin's observations about my wife Nicki caused me to reflect on the strength of our marriage. He described her as the rock around which I have been able to rebuild the Jackson family life. Would we have survived as a couple if we had not been such tenacious types, or less committed to each other and the children's future?

Both my children are now adults. Martin reinforced our conviction that they need to know the inconvenient truths and unpalatable facts about my life and therefore theirs. For far too long we have been denied the opportunity to explain and defend our actions, in trying to ameliorate the unhealthy and dysfunctional circumstances we found ourselves in. I hope they can regard what I have written with retrospective benevolence and an appreciation of the many sacrifices made for their welfare.

My thanks also go to Professor Len Scott, a Cold War historian and expert on military conflicts, making him the ideal person to correct some of the detail I had included concerning historical matters. I learned from him that I must have been asleep whilst being taught the rudiments of the English Language.

He reinforced my decision to include plenty of humour in the book, which in his view, provided it with essential seasoning throughout and was a welcome contrast to the darker and more tragic situations I discuss.

Although the personal anguish of my family life is integral to my story, Len quite rightly advised me to resist letting it dominate or define my memoir, or let it detract from all the good I have achieved. His advice caused me to re-hash the introduction and deal with the 'hotchpotch' ending, bringing the focus back to a more deserving subject. Thank heavens for 'cut and paste'.

Dr Frances Gerrard, Len's wife, my GP and a colleague in Aberystwyth, was forensic in her assessment of an early manuscript. Her advice was relevant, succinct and to the point, in direct contrast to some of my text she was reviewing. She provided perspective from a medical point of view and advised against, shall we say, some of my more earthy observations, though not all.

Vivien Green, an ex-librarian and neighbour in the UK, provided some very good advice about publication. On the other hand, she cautioned me to tone down some of the more distressing passages and consider removing a lot of the harrowing photographs. I was extremely grateful for this piece of advice, as it caused me to re-evaluate the absolute need for them. I defended my position to include them and the importance of not sanitising the realities of war, or hardships in undeveloped countries. In pandering to the sensibilities of the reader/ viewer to make the truth less distasteful, I would be doing a huge disservice to my fellow servicemen. They are prepared to go to war and die, or sustain physical and emotional trauma for their country, so the civilians they protect should not shy away from the uncomfortable feelings that harsh reality provokes.

John Edwards, my surgical colleague and good friend for many years, checked the veracity and accuracy of relevant parts of the manuscript regarding the surgical descriptions, and I have incorporated his opinions. When he had finished reading it, he said I had had 'a hell of a life'. His comment made me realise that with the passage of time and as a coping mechanism, I had adopted a blasé attitude to some of the events of my past.

My thanks must also go to Chris Newton of Mereo Books and his editorial skills. If I had thought the manuscript I gave him was polished, he buffed it up considerably. My attempts at punctuation were quite frankly dyslexic. He has the patience of Job.

Lastly I pay tribute to Nicki, my wife, friend and co-author, who, with her relentless pursuit of detail and accuracy, challenged me over the inclusion and approach of many topics, when she felt they were valueless, unsuitable, or made no sense. She was forthright with her opinions, having no hesitation in telling me when she considered certain passages were sub-standard and demanding a rewrite. Her contributions were wise, well thought out and of course extremely irritating, until I had pondered sufficiently to grudgingly conclude that she was right. However, if she had been a scrub nurse in my operating theatre, I would have cheerfully strangled her.

Foreword

These memoirs span the 40 years of my experience as a doctor and surgeon in the Army and the NHS. I was eventually persuaded to write them after my younger daughter, whom I shall refer to throughout as A, aided and abetted by her stepmother, badgered me for years to write down my story before it became either forgotten at the onset of my inevitable senility, or lost when I died, also inevitable. Now they can both leave me in peace, knowing that they succeeded. My wife maintains that though I am very stubborn, she has more stamina. I guess that as I have finished this story of my surgical life, she must be right.

A career in surgery is challenging at the best of times, even when operating in optimal circumstances, with all the necessary equipment available and properly-trained support staff on hand. However, oftentimes, especially in the army, there are external influences beyond the surgeon's control which can add an additional layer of pressure to an already demanding situation. Most patients imagine their operation will take place in a state-of-the-art operating theatre, with an abundance of expensive and shiny-looking equipment laid out on immaculate sterile surfaces, but this is not always the case. I have had to operate in many difficult situations throughout my surgical career in several far-flung parts of the world and under the most trying conditions. At times it has not been the physical challenges that have tested me, but the psychological ones.

However, although the narrative thread, in this account, is that of my surgical life, there is much more to my story than just that. I found myself in dark places, both professionally and domestically. Years after her affair with Bill Clinton became public, Monica Lewinsky wrote in an article entitled 'Shame and Survival'. *'It is time to stop tiptoeing around my past—and other people's futures. I am determined to have a different ending to my story. I've decided, finally, to stick my head above the parapet so that I can take back my narrative and give a purpose to my past[1]*. As I progressed with my own story I realised that in the main, I had the same motive.

Me with my youngest daughter (A)

The first part of these memoirs deals with my time at medical school and my early surgical training. I have relied on my memory, photographs and surgical notes, and it has been written for those who may have a general interest in how surgeons are trained and exactly what they have to do. I have given some idea of the teaching of medical students in the late 1960s, totally different from how it is today, and I have also detailed my experiences in self-financing most of my student existence, as well as a few predicaments I got myself into.

The second part is an account of the years I spent in the Army undergoing further surgical training and my experiences in N. Ireland during the troubles, the Falkland Islands War and the war in the former Yugoslavia. I have included patients that I have treated in other near and faraway places and illustrated the injuries and other conditions I have had to deal with, to inform the reader about the human costs of conflict and other illnesses. In this part I also relate details of my personal life, specifically my disastrous second marriage when I finally

---

1. https://www.vanityfair.com/style/society/2014/06/monica-lewinsky-humiliation-culture

began to realise that the mother of my two daughters was not whom she appeared to be. I discovered that beneath the superficial charm of the woman who had asked me to marry her lurked an altogether different personality. Slowly her true persona emerged, one with a breath-taking capacity for infidelity, dishonesty, betrayal and deceit. It became her intention to destroy me and my Army career.

In the third part I describe my return to the NHS in Wales. The surgical theme is maintained throughout in tandem with an account of how I tried to protect myself, my children and my new family from an ex-wife whom I had divorced with considerable relief. However, neither I nor the judicial system would be able to prevent her emotional abuse of our two young daughters R and A and by employing innuendo and the fabrications which were second nature to her, she would try to erase my role as their father and further, attempt to sabotage my new marriage and my second career.

This part of my story will appear to cross the line between fact and fiction. Nonetheless it is true, based on evidence in the form of diary entries, tape recordings, newspaper articles, letters, court transcripts[2] and photographs, the complete details of which I have never revealed to anyone, apart from my present wife and certainly not to my children. In writing this account I have had to be mindful of any residual legal boundaries of the Family Division of the High Court and the Office of the Official Solicitor (OS) to the Supreme Court, and to that end, I have sought their guidance before proceeding[3].

Where necessary and appropriate, names have been changed or abbreviated to protect identities.

---

2   94 D 0723 Judgement/Order Judge A M Kenny 25 August 1994, Transcript proceedings MR/0167 Mr G Arthur/Miss Clements 25 August 1994 (Reading County Court) D L Sellers & Co. Case 6667 of 1994 Royal Courts of Justice, Judgement Mr Justice Ewbank 24 February 1995, Judgement Justice Douglas Brown 14 August 1995, Appeal 3245/95 Lord Justice Butler-Sloss & Lord Justice Simon Brown 12 October 1995, Judgement Mr Justice Johnson 14 February 1996 & 13 June 1996, Report of court psychiatrist 30 August 1996 & 26 February 1997, Report of the OS 11 March 1997 (LTM14530), Judgement Mr Justice Johnson 16 December 1997, Report of the OS 12 February 1999, Judgement Mr Justice Hughes 5 March 1999, Report of the OS 28 September 1999.

3. Letters 13 Mar 2019 and 28 Feb 2019. Telecon 9 Aug 2019

Introduction
They shall grow not old

"Sorry sir. I cannot survive this. It's too much; it's too bloody much". The anguished young Guardsman had interrupted me as I explained what I proposed to do in order to try and save his life.

On the morning of 13 June 1982, the Scots Guards were moved by helicopter from their position at Bluff Cove to an assembly area near Goat Ridge, west of Mount Tumbledown in the Falkland Islands. Guardsman C.C.T., a dispatch rider from the 1st Welsh Guards, was mortally wounded by Argentine shellfire directed from Tumbledown. He was brought into our Field Surgical Team (FST) in a terrible state. He was still alive when he arrived, but had lost both feet, his legs were at unnatural angles and he was bleeding to death internally. It was a very severe blast injury. There was some hope for him, if I could arrest the bleeding, but this young, brave soldier knew there was no hope. He knew that better than I did.

His haunting words are not ones that I can ever forget, nor do I really want to, because they epitomised the spirit of the soldiers, who know when they have been injured beyond recovery and can accept their own death, even at their tender ages, with the same courage that they had faced the enemy. He was right. He had massive intra-abdominal and pelvic bleeding. His vena cava, the main vein in the body, had ruptured beyond repair and he died on the operating table.

As I closed his abdomen, I realised that I was never going to be as immune to the injuries of these young men as I hoped to be. I could divorce myself from the sufferings and the injuries whilst I had to do something about them, but in the dark moments, in the quiet moments, it got to me. It may be the case that his parents or family read this account and recognise this young Guardsman, who I have anonymised. He died bravely, with no hope, but no pain, on my operating table.

When I had finished sewing him up, I went on to my next casualty, who fortunately would recover from his comparatively light wounds. This patient was a young Argentinian and he looked about 15 years old. He had been wounded by a fragment which had entered his upper right abdomen, and he was stable as I opened him up. Fortunately, the fragment had missed all the important anatomy; there was no bile, faeces or much blood for that matter. He had a small hole in the substance of his liver which I closed with a circular suture, and no exit wound that I could ascertain. I assumed that the penetration of his abdominal wall had taken the sting out of this injury. I left a drain in for safety's sake and closed him up. He was shipped off back to Argentina. The padre knew the Spanish word for liver, so I wrote a note to accompany him, saying *"Higado – OK"*.

Damage to Argentine soldier's 'Higado' Falklands War 1982

I would dwell many times on these surgical cases throughout my life and even now, nearly 38 years later, the impact has not significantly diminished. Indeed, as I have grown older, the emotions are harder to contain, as my resistance to the awfulness of the human cost of this and other conflicts I have been involved in has been markedly degraded with the passage of time. Having now retired from a busy civilian surgical practice, which occupied me almost to the exclusion of what had gone before, I have had more time to think and reassess, sometimes relive a little of my past, and it is not a place that I am altogether happy about revisiting. These recollections and others have been compartmentalised for many years, but now that they have been reopened, I don't think I will ever be able to fully close them again. I have heard too many agonised screams and cries of despair and attended too many funerals, burials and remembrance services.

I have got on with my life, with my career, with my family because I have had to, but that is not to say that I have not been afflicted, like so many of my service colleagues, with that other described cause of mental anguish, 'survivor's guilt'. This is an insidious thought that resurfaces now and again, to punish me and others who came back, whole and healthy, though never the same. Why did I survive when 255 servicemen didn't? What marked me as different? I have had 38 years more life than them, 38 years more experience of the ups and downs of this world, the good and the bad, the pleasures and the pain. I did not have to fight for my life (medics are non-combatant but will fight to protect their patients). I just had to rely on serendipity and in truth, the fighting skills of those that I was there for, to try and save.

They shall grow not old, as we that are left grow old: Age shall not weary them, nor the years condemn. At the going down of the sun and in the morning, we will remember them[4]*'*. I know that I will.

---

4. Robert Laurence Binyon, CH (August 10, 1869 – March 10, 1943)

PART 1

NHS 1967-1978

CHAPTER 1

The Biggest Balls

Liverpool School of Medicine, 1967

Medical school was looming, and I had been allocated shared digs in a house in Gateacre near Speke airport, a few miles out from the city centre where the Liverpool School of Medicine was located on Brownlow Hill. It would later become an affluent area, but not whilst I was living there, which, as it turned out, would not be for long, due to an unfortunate incident involving the landlady's daughter.

I intended travelling there in my old 1938 Morris 8, registration GFC 42, but in those days without the benefit of satnav and our present motorway system, my grandfather and I agreed that I should do a dummy run prior to the start of my first term, in his car, an MG 1100 which I had jumped at the chance to drive. My father was indifferent and unhelpful in his usual way, but I suppose he was still trying to recover his equilibrium from the shock of having to financially contribute towards my university grant, which had been assessed on his gross income and not that of his post repayment of gambling debts income. The prospect of having to rely on my father to provide a stipend for me that would allow me to live and eat was not a reassuring one, but to be fair he started well, by supplying me with the full whack for the first semester – an occurrence never to be repeated.

My father had joined the Royal Artillery after expensive schooling at St Paul's in London, from which he emerged with relatively paltry academic credentials, though this did not stop him from thinking he knew everything. He left the Army whilst at Gunnery School in Wales in the mid-1950s and started a business with my grandfather selling high end hi-fi equipment in Abingdon. My grandfather, who had also served in the Army, had settled my father's gambling debts.

The journey to Liverpool was uneventful, and when I arrived Mrs Jones, the landlady, showed me around my new lodgings, where I would be sharing a small bedroom with another medical student. The third student, who was not studying medicine, was in a box room which he would share with a vacuum cleaner, other household utensils and family bric-a-brac. There was no Mr Jones on the scene, but my landlady did have a daughter who worked in a local factory and shared the double bed with her in the small master bedroom. I couldn't understand a word she said, as her Scouse accent was so thick that she might just as well have been speaking a different language. If the lecturers in the medical school were going to speak like that, I was unlikely to learn anything. However, I was adaptable and after a couple of years I could speak Scouse like a native, which was essential if I was going to get anywhere with the 'Judys' in Seffie Park. Fortunately, the lecturers did speak English.

I took my leave from Mrs Jones, not knowing at that time that our acquaintance was going to be short-lived, and drove into the centre of Liverpool to find the medical school. The city centre was grimy and busy. I drove back home and reported my findings to my grandfather, who was quite excited for me, in contrast to my father, who was not and who still regarded me as a drain on his diminished resources.

It may have been prophetic, but prior to starting medical school, I had a tenuous first introduction to a surgical procedure that I would later do many times in my career. It was when I had been employed on a building site working as a casual labourer with my best friend

Richard Coulbeck, whose nickname was 'Dog' because of his peculiar canine-like gait when he ran.

One morning there was no sign of the building foreman, Mick, which didn't initially bother us as he was generally unreliable, only being punctual at knocking off time. However, he had been missing all day and again the next morning. Mick appeared at lunchtime as we were eating our sandwiches and apologised for his absence, explaining that he lived with his girlfriend in a caravan and that she had been having a lot of 'toilet troubles'. He went on to say that the doctors had decided to operate on her and had "moved her arsehole" to the front. He had been looking after her whilst she recuperated. Dog and I were absolutely horrified, as we both assumed that our anuses would always remain where they started off. Now as I look back, with the wisdom of a 40-year surgical career, I would surmise that Mick's girlfriend had suffered from Inflammatory Bowel Disease and that she had had a bowel excision with the formation of a colostomy or ileostomy bringing her bowel end through her abdominal wall to the surface for discharge into a (stoma) bag.

So in September 1967, I loaded up my car with a large trunk precariously strapped to the rear luggage rack and left my home in Abingdon for my first semester at medical school, armed with a packed lunch and lots of water both for me and the car. My departure was accompanied by tearful waves from my mother Clarice, who had been born in Alexandria, Egypt, where she had met my father whilst he was posted there. She spoke fluent Italian, Arabic as well as English, but we generally conversed in French, which had been her first language. Seven hours later I arrived in Speke, Liverpool, exhausted but triumphant, although Mrs Jones didn't hang out any bunting to celebrate my arrival. I was the first of the students to arrive, so I took the bed by the window and almost all the meagre storage space where I would also have to study.

Richard, my new roommate, hailed from an ancient settlement called Sheffield, which as far as I could gather, had only just got electricity, and Tony, the occupier of the box room, was apparently from London and had a relative who was rich enough to provide him with the money required to buy a new Vauxhall Viva car for his start at university. He had already fitted air horns to it that played 'La Cucaracha' and he managed to annoy just about everybody right from the outset, when he turned up for registration in it.

There were about a hundred or so students in my year and the attrition rate was around 10% for second MB (Bachelor of Medicine), the first professional exam I would take. This would mean that I had to remain 85th in my year or better, to leave some margin for error. We were advised to have nothing to do with Engineering, Arts or Social Sciences students, the engineers being mortal enemies of the medics and the other two faculties being regarded as recruitment centres for long haired, handbag swinging lefties, all devoted to Marxism and troublemaking. Little did I know that 28 years later, I would end up marrying an Arts graduate who is remarkably normal.

We all had to join, and therefore pay to be members of, the Liverpool Medical Students' Society (MSS). I had navigated Fresher's week reasonably well, but the freshers' meeting of MSS was an eye opener. It was the prerogative of the fifth-year medical students to introduce the freshers into MSS, and its rituals. There was a President, Treasurer and Sports Secretary. No one could speak at the meeting without wearing a hat which would be thrown to them from the front, or from the last speaker. The President would open the meeting and introduce the guest speaker. The Treasurer would report on the finances and the Sports Secretary would report the successes or failures of the various sports teams representing the Medical School.

However for fresher's week, there was always something different going on and on this occasion as we filed into the old lecture hall for the meeting, we were told that following a random selection of participants, Freshers of each sex would take part in a competition to find out who had the biggest balls and who had the most widely-spaced nipples. Eight freshers were selected, the girls who had the biggest busts and the boys who were the skinniest. Fortunately, I was not selected, and I just looked on in awe that something like this could take place in a learned society. The girls stood in the front of the lecture hall to the wolf whistles of the audience, protectively clutching their bosoms, whilst the boys had hands on crotches of rapidly diminishing size.

The President announced that the competition could commence, and the eight contestants were told to step forward, which they did with snail-like reluctance. The audience were asked whether the girls or the boys should go first and the shout for the girls was unanimous with cries of 'Get'em off!' The tension became unbearable and the girls were white as sheets, though none tried to escape.

Suddenly the fifth year Master of Ceremonies asked the girls to remove their shoes. This caused more agitation amongst them, as to whether this was the start of the striptease to find the girl with the most widely-spaced nipples. However, and with much relief all round, it emerged that the competition for the biggest balls applied to the girls, measuring the diameters of the balls of their feet, which were duly taken with callipers and noted down on the blackboard. When the boys realised that the distance between nipples was the required measurement they had to provide, shirts were ripped off and torsos puffed out as the dimensions were taken and recorded. A winner from each side was declared, to go down in the minutes for posterity, and the meeting was closed to be followed by drinks in one of the local pubs. This was an excellent introduction to the social side of being a medical student, but the academic side was going to be hard work, endless rote learning and bookwork, coursework and regular viva voce examinations.

Our introduction to the academic side of medicine was in the form of a lecture by a senior medical consultant, Dr Baker-Bates, who held the position of Honorary Senior Lecturer (universities and medical schools often make these appointments when they harness the expertise of others). Dr Baker-Bates was introduced to the freshers and expounded on the merits of the most rewarding career in the world. He outlined some of the history of medicine and as was his custom, produced patients for clinical demonstrations.

The first patient he brought in was a brittle diabetic, and he told us of the clinical signs to elicit, for example to smell the patient's breath for the sickly-sweet smell of ketoacidosis. To confirm the diagnosis, it was necessary to test the (glucose) sugar levels in the patient's blood and urine. He solemnly produced a bottle of urine that the patient had just passed and showed us how to test it. He stuck his finger in the golden liquid and then put it in his mouth, stating the urine tasted sweet and that the patient was indeed diabetic. The lecture room was eerily quiet. He then invited a student in the front row to similarly test the urine, (never sit in the front row at medical school). This was a test of character; this was medicine in the raw. There was some tittering from the back and the student, wriggly lipped, approached the poisoned chalice.

Dr Baker-B took the student under his arm and whispered some words of encouragement. The student nodded, put a finger in the urine and then put it in his mouth and agreed that it did indeed taste sweet. This was a stunning demonstration of what was expected of us medical students and I predicted a mass walkout. However, the tension was alleviated when Dr Baker-B explained to us what he had said to the student and indeed what he had done himself (every year to an audience of freshers since the year dot), which none of us had noticed. He had put his forefinger in the urine and his middle finger in his mouth.

Over the year, we students would be required to dismember a donated, preserved corpse in the dissecting room in order to obtain a smattering of anatomical knowledge. We trooped into the dissection room which stank of formalin. There were six of us to a cadaver, armed with our forceps, scalpels and anatomy books and wearing our white lab coats. We were to be supervised by young doctors who were studying anatomy prior to their surgical training. Anatomy and most of medicine/surgery uses Latin nomenclature, and as I had studied Latin at school, I was comfortable with learning something like Flexor Digitorum Profundus (Deep muscle finger flexor), but finding it on the cadaver was another matter entirely.

As an aside, donating one's body to science in those days inevitably meant having six medical students pouring over one's carcass, clumsily groping around for elusive anatomical bits and generally, ignorantly, dividing and removing said bits before identification. The cadavers were divided into anatomical sections, and each week we had a viva voce test to pass before we could progress to the next phase. Removing any anatomical parts from the dissecting room was strictly forbidden, but that did not stop the hand from one such cadaver being used to summon a barman in a pub, somewhere in Liverpool.

Medical books are notoriously expensive and therefore almost always bought second hand. I had dutifully purchased a copy of 'Gray's Anatomy', but its usefulness was limited after I was forced to use it to prop up my bed in digs, because the side spar had become broken when my irritated roommate had shoved me causing me to land heavily on my bed. My landlady was none too pleased, and even less so with subsequent events.

I struggled with my academic studies despite conscientiously attending lectures and copying lecture notes for any I had missed; I would then go to the library stacks and learn very little. As well as anatomy, the other two subjects for the first year were biochemistry and physiology and these too were hard going. They had to be learned by studying incomprehensible second-hand tomes with well-thumbed pages that had been extensively underlined and stained by the tears that reflected the cerebral agonies of previous owners. I never failed a semester examination, or a viva, or professional exam. However, I doubt if anyone would have written that I was a bright student; I just had dogged determination.

I was coming to the end of the first semester, working and playing hard, but I was homesick. One evening I decided to phone my mother to indulge in a bit of a 'miss fest' with her and after the phone call I went to the local pub to have a pint of Tetley's bitter or two. Being slightly pissed, I then returned to my digs, rather unwisely loaded with more beer. After I had consumed the lot, I called it a night and went to bed. In the night, I got up drunk and confused to go to the loo. In my defence, it was quite an easy mistake to have made. On returning to what I assumed was my bedroom, I collapsed on top of the landlady's daughter. She screamed blue murder.

Mrs Jones came rushing up the stairs and hauled me off her bed, yelling a stream of Scouse expletives. However she soon realised that she was dealing with a bumbling slurring idiot, completely under the influence and oblivious to what all the fuss was about. When I eventually realised the actual gravity of my offence, I apologised profusely, but it was not enough. I got my marching orders first thing in the morning. However, as luck would have it, accommodation had just become available in one of the university halls of residence, called McNair. Though expensive, I grabbed the opportunity and went mainstream, in a better-behaved sort of way – but not for long.

CHAPTER 2

Learning to Walk

Abingdon, 1968

I drove back home for the vacations and settled back into my previous employment as an orderly at the Fairmile Hospital in Cholsey, which was part of the network of pauper lunatic asylums. There I would work and save my wages, ready for the beginning of the next semester at medical school. Though now an embryonic doctor, what I was employed to do there bore no relation whatsoever to medicine. Being physically of a reasonable size, I became part of the staff on the locked ward housing violent, mentally-ill males, though their behaviour was for the most part placated by industrial doses of sedatives. The charge nurse issued me with a large bunch of keys and I think, or at least I hoped, with tongue in cheek, advised me to always have my back to a wall and consider carrying a hammer. I had also been issued with a short white lab coat to give me an air of authority. I then cheerfully commenced an eternal round of bed-making, mainly for incontinent inmates, and cleaning and polishing the lino floors.

However, whilst at home tragedy would strike. I became ill with symptomatic sequelae that still affect me to this day. I had been working on GFC 42, as its MOT was due, and a tyre needed changing. I was penniless and elected to do the job myself with old tyre levers. It was hard work and was compounded by the fact that over the preceding few days and throughout the job of changing the tyre, I had felt off colour, feverish, sweaty, and just generally wimpish. I washed up, explained to my mother that I must have caught something and decided to go to bed. She was worried, as I was almost always in outrageously good health.

The next day I woke up feeling terrible. I noticed that the (lymph) glands in my neck and armpits were swollen and tender, and when I attempted to get up my body did not work, refusing to obey any of the commands from my brain. The world spun sickeningly out of control. My balance had gone, my coordination had vanished and I fell over. I had to crawl on my hands and knees to the bathroom to have a pee, whilst the carpet and the ceiling perpetually changed places and waves of nausea overcame me.

My mother heard the commotion and ran upstairs to ask me what was wrong. Crawling on the floor, I tried to tell her, but I couldn't form the words. My speech was so slurred it was incomprehensible. I later realised with the knowledge that I have now that I had developed a full-blown cerebellar ataxia (lack of muscle co-ordination). The cerebellum is that part of the brain that synchronizes all muscular movements. Every action that requires a series of movements, like staying upright or speaking or picking something up, or fine movements like writing, is supervised by the cerebellum. My cerebellum was basically screwed up.

My mother helped me back to bed, where I lay in a spinning vortex, whilst she called our local GP for an emergency visit. He came later that afternoon and though sure of the neurological diagnosis, he did not know what the next move should be for me. He suggested that he would ask a local consultant for a domiciliary visit and in the interim told my mother to keep giving me plenty of fluids with electrolytes in them, especially potassium. My father bought me a crate of bottles of pineapple juice, and my mother sourced bananas, which all contain potassium. My appetite was not good anyway, but I made the effort whilst awaiting the consultant. I could do nothing. I just lay in bed with my eyes shut, to keep the world on an even keel.

I was not to know this, but the consultant's opinion was guarded. They needed to establish the cause of my neurological illness, so I was transferred to the Slade Isolation Hospital in Headington, Oxford, by ambulance, where I could be investigated and nursed if, or until, my damaged cerebellum recovered – or didn't.

My biggest problem was that the rest of my brain was functioning normally. My thought processes were all fine, most of my senses seemed to be okay, I just couldn't do anything, and I was bored stiff. My mother, bless her, visited every afternoon and read the newspapers to me; she would also read letters from my girlfriend, which arrived weekly without fail. I also asked for a radio, which substantially improved my morale. My mother later confessed that my slurred speech was so bad that she rarely understood a word I said; days of listening to BBC newsreaders with perfect diction absolutely wasted.

I had a plethora of tests and the Epstein-Barr virus, a nasty little bastard and the cause of glandular fever, was isolated from one of my bodily fluids and was held to be the cause of my cerebellitis (inflammation of the cerebellum). It was found in my cerebro-spinal fluid extracted by a lumbar puncture, a procedure that I would not like to undergo again. As a junior doctor I performed it many times and believe me, each of my patients had my deepest sympathy as I proceeded with a gentleness born of my own experience.

I had to get better. I just could not bear the indignity of sitting on a bed pan to empty my bowels, stimulated by liquid paraffin, the de rigueur laxative of the time, whilst being propped up by two female nurses. I decided to take small bites at recovery, which I now knew to be possible, and concentrated on trying to sit up in bed without keeling over. I fell over the first time I tried it and was unceremoniously put back in bed with a lot of harrumphing from the nursing staff and the clanging of cot sides being elevated. I tried to improve my diction by speaking slowly, but even though I knew what I had just said, what I heard was unintelligible. Writing anything was out of the question as

I couldn't hold a pen, and if for example I had to scratch my nose, it took an age for my fingers to lock onto it, as my hand travelled and wavered unsteadily around my confined world. But there was good news; the world had stopped spinning. I almost cried with relief.

One day whilst I was in hospital listening to the radio and idly staring out of the window, my father came flying down the road in my beloved car, GFC 42, and parked it where I could see it. I was flabbergasted. He had decided, in his own way, to contribute towards my recovery by getting my car repaired and putting it through its MOT. He came to the ward to see me and suggested that I could now get better, following this grand gesture of paternal generosity. I thanked him and vowed that I would recover as fast as I could, if only for his sake, as it would not suit his lifestyle to have a permanently ill son on his hands and anyway, I owed it to him, as he had also brought me another crate of pineapple juice. My mother was warned that if my recovery was going to be complete, it might take up to a year. The Medical School was informed that I was ill and would not be returning in time for the second semester, but they kept my accommodation for me in McNair Hall.

I needed to demonstrate to the hospital medical and nursing staff that I would be able to undertake some of the mundane tasks of daily living before discharge, as my recovery required no specific treatment. I couldn't walk unless my legs were splayed apart like the base of the Eiffel Tower, a classical wide gait (and I still kept falling over), though I was pretty nifty with a handy supporting wall to lean against or slide along. Pouring a glass of water reasonably accurately took many attempts, but I was stymied by the fact that getting it to my mouth was near impossible with my poor hand-eye coordination. I would have sailed through the test if I could have drunk water through my ear, which seemed to be the endpoint of the default direction my hand was taking under the supervision of my recovering cerebellum, which had yet to rediscover the position of my mouth. For much of my hospital stay, I had been spoon-fed by a nurse.

I could eat eventually with a fork, after a fashion, and my unintelligible gobbledegook improved to relatively passable speech. I did a 'going to the loo' test on my own and avoided crashing into the stacks of bedpans which live and reproduce in hospital toilets. In my mind, though not in anyone else's, I was ready for discharge.

I had been in the Slade Hospital for what seemed like a lifetime, though it was only around a month, and although I have generally made light of this episode in my life, it was a very worrying time. When discharged, my recovery phase was extremely slow and I had to practise walking and making fine movements (like picking up a pencil, which eluded me for months). My speech was still slurred and those who didn't know about my illness thought I was drunk. In the early days I tried to improve my balance by riding my old bicycle, but after a series of collisions and the damn near demolition of a garden hedge, my mother made me promise never to do it again and confined me to staying inside the house, where at least there were walls and furniture I could hold onto. I had lost a lot of weight, especially muscle mass, and getting around from one place to another was arduous.

My mother had returned to work as the bookkeeper in my father's business, so I was pretty much unsupervised during the day. I started to have a go at reading again and though I could manage a sentence, I had lost the automatic knack of dropping down to the next line of prose. It was all unbelievably frustrating. I was stuck with just the radio for company and got to know the schedule of the Home Service (now Radio 4) pretty much off by heart, a very sad state of affairs. It was obvious that I would not be returning to medical school for the immediate foreseeable future and having lost so much time, I would have to repeat the year. Everyone else with whom I had started my first year at medical school was soon to sit their 2nd MB examinations.

I looked into changing course to Genetics, which I was quite interested in, but the truth of the matter was, having had a personal demonstration of what selfless medical personnel could do for the sick, my determination to join their ranks was as resolute as ever and my vocation was even stronger. I would do this, and repeating a year was not the end of the world. One thing I had noticed though was that I seemed to be detached from my immediate world. My GP diagnosed this as a manifestation of depression. I was akin to a prisoner on his release to the outside world, who had to catch up with the progress that had taken place whilst he was incarcerated.

In any event the feeling passed, and I was ready to take another step in my recovery. My car was languishing unused and it was time to resume driving. However, my ambitious attitude totally outweighed my abilities, and the words "definitely not", and "learn to walk before you can drive" were the universal responses I received. I held back with my demands, as the first foray back into the motorised world would require someone brave enough, and who cared enough, to sit beside me and supervise, and this was going to have to be my mother. However she had only recently passed her driving test and was not confident in her own skills behind the wheel, let alone mine. So until I was medically signed off by my GP, I had to content myself with just starting my car and re-familiarising myself with where the controls were.

I was passed fit at the beginning of what would have been the summer vacation at the end of the first year of medical school, though I have retained one slight defect. I am very hesitant and almost unbalanced in the dark when without the assistance of my eyesight, I have to rely on my cerebellum to be exclusively responsible for my correct orientation. I always wait several minutes for my eyes to adjust to the dark and I have torches… everywhere.

I started driving again with my mother in the passenger seat. GFC 42 was a joy to drive, accelerating on demand to nearly 40 mph, but tragedy was to strike again. At a roundabout on the A34 near Oxford, I was correctly waiting to join the traffic when a Transports Internationaux Routiers (TIR) lorry failed to stop and rear-ended my car. My mother went flying, but was unhurt, as was I, but GFC 42 was mortally wounded, now being about a foot shorter than prior to the impact. I was heartbroken, GFC 42 was finished and I had lost my wheels. She was just about driveable to the scrapyard.

Still, when one door closes another one opens and demonstrating the true fickleness of car owners, whilst temporarily reduced to two-wheeled transport (though in a much more stable sort of way than before), I came across an old Ford Consul Mk1 for sale at the BP garage where I had previously worked the pumps.

Though the job in the lunatic asylum was not available during the summer, I had gained employment as a general labourer on a building site a few miles away in Benson, near Wallingford, where a new supermarket was being built. The pay was excellent, and it would mean that I could save for the new medical school year and stop relying on my father (he would use the word sponging) for meagre financial handouts. As time went by, he became less and less enamoured of being the parent of a 'nearly' doctor, particularly as I had flunked the first year, regardless of the justifiable cause. He therefore encouraged me all the way in this new employment.

I had felt that it would be good for me to regain my strength with a bit of honest hard labour, and that's what I got. My job was to dig the foundations to the depth stipulated by the foreman, of about 3 feet. I attacked the ground with the unbridled enthusiasm of youth and after about 20 minutes I was knackered and blistered. Fortunately, digging the foundations was just a way of keeping me busy until after a couple of days the JCB they had booked arrived, much to my relief. Soon the concrete foundations were laid and lorry loads of bricks were delivered, not in packages for unloading by crane, but loose, requiring manual unloading by labourers, throwing, catching and stacking, ready for the bricklayers. I was a catcher and stacker of four bricks at a time and this activity certainly tested the recovery of my coordination. I was employed there for about six weeks and by then I worked and swore like a navvy. On Friday afternoons we all adjourned to the local pub to be entertained by the foreman, recounting his sexual exploits.

One Friday he took me to his car, an old Ford Zephyr, and showed me two holes in the roof lining above the front passenger seat. He asked me if I knew what had caused them. I shook my head. I hadn't the faintest idea. He then explained that his girlfriend was so tall that her stilettos had made the holes in the roof when he was shagging her. I was full of admiration. The roof lining of my old Ford Consul was virgo intacta, and I hoped to follow my leader's example at some stage in the future, but if the truth be told, my car was not going to last that long. However, 26 years later as a consultant surgeon, I damned nearly ended up with two stiletto marks in the leather dashboard of my prized Mercedes S Class, whilst dating the woman who became my third wife. The Ford Consul had cost me £12.50p; the Mercedes had cost me £25,000. I was happy to acquire evidence of sexual success in the old Ford, but not quite so keen in the Merc.

By now I was much fitter and if I had been working on a railroad, I could have 'hoisted a jack, laid a track and learned to pick and shovel too', in the way outlined in *The Legend of John Henry*'s *Hammer* as sung by Johnny Cash. However, whereas John Henry challenged and beat the steam drill, I was not going to take on the JCB. I will refer to Johnny Cash and the relevance of his songs and music in my life as this story progresses. I put aside a tidy pile from my wages for the start of the new academic year, when I would be a sort of seasoned fresher on my return. I was anxious to get back to it. I had the career I wanted, waiting five years away for me.

On my last day at the building site I was driving to work past the Culham Laboratory, just a few miles east of Abingdon when suddenly, from out of nowhere an OAP on a bicycle appeared and turned right across my side of the road. I swerved to avoid him, but this manoeuvre resulted in the Consul hitting a kerb at high speed and ploughing on, leaving parallel furrows in the pristine lawn at the entrance to the Science Lab. The OAP cycled on, blissfully unaware of his brush with death. Within a few minutes I was approached by security guards, who had seen what had happened. As they pointed to my car with the ruined undercarriage, they said, "Bad luck mate, but you can't leave it here. This is a secure place, so hop it". Luckily, just as with GFC 42, the car was drivable, despite being a write off. Once again, I got it to the local scrapyard and accepted the 10 shillings sale price for the scrap. I then walked to the same garage I had bought the Consul from and promptly bought an old A35 saloon with my last week's wages. My insurance file with my broker was getting thicker by the minute. My father was quite frankly disbelieving when I told him what had happened.

I was soon to return to Liverpool, so I arranged a goodbye pub crawl with my friends Dog and Andrew. As we would be having a few pints, we resolved to go on two wheels, which was a mistake in hindsight, in view of my precarious night-time balance, and after visiting a couple of pubs, I predictably came off my bike and gravelled the right side of my face. This meant that when I returned home I would have to say

"I'm home" and "goodnight" to my mother whilst avoiding revealing the whole of one side of my face to her.

In the vacations, we – that is Dog, Andrew and many of our other friends – used to meet up at the Nag's Head, a pub on Abingdon bridge, and then at the Barley Mow in Clifton Hampden, where we often attracted an entourage of interested females. The breathalyser was still in its infancy at this stage and nothing to be feared, as it would be several years before people's freedom to severely maim or kill themselves or others through drunken driving was to be curtailed.

We were at a party one night when I was knocked across a stream in the garden of the host by a jealous husband whose wife had taken a fancy to me. I was entirely innocent and not interested, as I had my own girlfriend at the time, but his soon to be ex-wife Sheila had started playing around and had latched onto our group. Sheila had taken my rejection of her rather badly and had grabbed a pint of beer and poured it over me in a fit of pique. Bemused, I left the kitchen where this had occurred and was just having a smoke in the garden outside when I caught this great right hook, leaving me literally and metaphorically seeing stars as I gazed into the night sky, wondering what on earth had just happened. It turned out to be a case of mistaken identity, which the husband grudgingly admitted sometime later.

I decided to leave the party and adjourn to the Barley Mow. There I was to find my girlfriend Valerie sitting on the bar counter weeping and being caressed and plied with drinks by the publicans. She had been telling them that I had abandoned her at the party for another woman. On seeing me, she pointed and squealed "There he is!" and then asked where the hell I had been and what on earth I saw in 'that' woman. I was speechless.

Then to cap it all, one of the partygoers, whom I knew vaguely, came rushing into the bar and said in a loud voice that David Jackson had been knocked out by a man for having an affair with his wife. My girlfriend let out another haunting wail, as her cuckolding, though untrue, was now public knowledge. Just as I was about to open my mouth and give my version of events, for what it was worth, the bar room door was flung open again and another partygoer came in to spread the news that I had been knocked out cold, quite oblivious to the fact that I was standing right beside him. I was soaked in beer, had a sore jaw and had lost my girlfriend, all for an affair which I did not have in the first place.

I returned to Liverpool and took up residence in McNair Hall, a re-fresher as it were. Living in Hall was expensive at £7 per week out of my budget of £10, and there was a tutor system for the students on each floor of the building. Though they meant well, ours was an ogling interfering busybody, tolerated by some students but disliked by most. He was forever checking our rooms for members of the opposite sex and alcohol, and I found this intrusive, not that I was ever caught and was unlikely to be, as I only resided in the Hall for a matter of weeks. I suppose bricking up this tutor's door one night didn't help my cause. I found myself homeless once again.

I packed all my worldly possessions into the A35 and looked for somewhere else to live. I found my next accommodation after an uncomfortable night in the car. A mature medical student fresher called Gary Clarke had rented a flat in the Lark Lane area of Liverpool and needed a flatmate. I was in. Gary was about 26 years old and had bummed around America after leaving school, working as an odd job man here and there, before finally settling as a beach dweller somewhere on the West Coast, driving speedboats for his employer's water-skiing business and singing folk songs in various cafés and dives during the evening. He was a good guitarist and indeed taught me how to play "Cocaine Blues" in the same style as Keith Richards of the Rolling Stones. So I started my first year again, and time passed.

Gary and I studied and learnt together, testing each other in the evenings, or occasionally socialising with our friends. He had an agile brain but a poor memory, and I was the reverse. I often say that I am not a "thick quinker". I suppose that combined into one, we would make a good doctor.

Liverpool is where the "Mersey beat" was born, music that would be popular throughout the world. It was the setting for the legendary Cavern Club, dark, dingy and sweaty, and where The Beatles and many other pop groups and singers had started their paths to fame, such as Gerry and the Pacemakers, Billy J Kramer and the Dakotas, The Searchers, the Fourmost, the Swinging Blue Jeans and of course

Cilla Black. The booze flowed freely and the bands playing on stage almost spilled out into the audience. The atmosphere was electric and the music deafening, such that any attempt to pick up a member of the opposite sex had to be conducted in sign language. I was not a rake during this period of my life, nor was I a sexual saint, but the reader must understand that the prevailing attitudes towards boy meets girl had changed dramatically during the 60s and women were far more empowered about expressing their sexuality and independence, especially with the arrival of the new contraceptive pill.

It was around about this time that I considered joining the Royal Army Medical Corps (RAMC) and if accepted continuing my studies as a commissioned officer, which of course, had the benefit of a salary. I weighed up the pros and cons and decided that even though I had always been attracted to the idea of service life, I would wait and see what sort of employer the NHS would be after my graduation and then decide.

Before we left Liverpool for the summer, Gary and I had to secure our flat in Lark Lane, whilst unoccupied, i.e. preventing the landlord from re-letting it. He naturally wanted a deposit, and we agreed to pay some of it, with the balance on our return. The landlord in the meantime would have all our possessions as security and the deal was done.

During the summer vacation, I resumed working back at the lunatic asylum. As a seasoned hand by this stage I was moved to the elderly demented patients' ward. I had to assume that in addition to my usual duties, being allowed to dispense food from the hospital trolleys and then wash up 50 patients' plates and utensils was a form of promotion. However the upside was that though against hospital rules, the Charge Nurse turned a blind eye to us, the menial staff on the ward, eating anything left over from the food trolley. The remainder would normally go to the pigs on the farm. I was happy, as it saved me from the daily task of making sandwiches for my packed lunch, and I don't suppose the pigs begrudged us our share.

One thing that was beginning to worry me was that my parents' relationship seemed to be deteriorating badly. My father was spending even less time at home, though this was fine by the rest of the family, as he was becoming more irritable and objectionable, with frequent rantings at just about everything.

I drove back to Liverpool for the start of the new academic year only to find that my key did not unlock our shared flat. I rang the bell and the landlord opened the door. He did not look amused. Gary had arrived a few days earlier and promised the landlord he would get half the agreed retainer out of his bank account. Then, whilst the landlord was at work, he had done a runner, taking all his stuff with him, but not mine. I had no idea where Gary had gone to, but I would see him at the start of the semester. But what to do now? The landlord possessed everything I owned, held hostage in lieu of the money we owed him. I spent another night in the car outside the flat, hoping that he would have pity on me and fortunately, the next day he did. He accepted my half of the money, in exchange for my possessions.

"I've got nothing against you Dave" he said, "but if I find your mate, I'll string him up by the balls".

I agreed that that would probably be equitable in the circumstances and drove to 9 Percy Street, Toxteth, Liverpool 8, where there was a room going.

CHAPTER 3

Harry's Consumables

School of Medicine, Liverpool, 1969

Number 9 Percy Street was a large three-storey Georgian terraced house, with attic rooms and a cellar which housed nine medical students. The kitchen was rank, the gas cooker rarely cleaned, and any personal food left there was invariably stolen. Short or long-stay girlfriends were resigned to cleaning the toilets, and ablutions were carried out for free in the University swimming pool showers. Rent and rates amounted to 30 shillings (£1.50p) a week.

Although I did not know it at the time, number 9 had a famous connection. A few years before I moved in, it had been home to Stu Sutcliffe, an art student at Liverpool College of Art, who studied alongside John Lennon and their mutual friend Bill Harry. Stu became the original bass guitarist for The Beatles (their fifth member), but unfortunately died of a cerebral haemorrhage due to a ruptured aneurysm at the age of just 21 in 1962[5]. Our landlady was called Beryl Williams, wife of Alan Williams, the Beatles' first manager when

---

5. https://www.beatlesbible.com/1962/04/10/stuart-sutcliffe-dies/

9 Percy Street (white door), in modern times

they started out playing in Hamburg. Unfortunately he fell out with them over his commission payments. He told Brian Epstein who would become their manager also in 1962, "Don't touch them with a fucking bargepole, they will let you down." Subsequently he wrote a book entitled 'The Man Who Gave the Beatles Away'[6].

Around 50 years later, after I had retired, I would return to 9 Percy Street to survey my old bedroom on the ground floor at the back of the building, which had since been converted into a rather stylish kitchen and upon going up to the front attic room, I was shown letters etched around the window frame, allegedly by John Lennon. If only I had known when we lived there that a piece of history was already sitting amongst us.

Acceptance at number 9 was by vote of the remaining occupants and as I had recently become the Liverpool Medical School Society (LMSS) sports secretary, played rugby, and was male (no women permitted in number 9, except as long-term or temporary visitors), I was accepted, and here I would stay until I qualified.

Percy Street was within walking distance of the medical school; thus, my car fuel costs were low, but my old A35 was by this stage smoking away and burning a lot of oil. The engine was worn out, with complete wear of the piston rings, and had developed a rattling noise which I assumed was piston slap. As it was obvious it needed a change of engine, I would need a part-time job during evenings and weekends and preferably one that paid well, to cover the cost.

The latter stipulation was pie in the sky, but I found what I was looking for, not far away in Back Percy Street. There a gentleman

6. https://en.wikipedia.org/wiki/Allan_Williams

(pretty loose description) called Harry Phillips ran a small garage business, servicing cars, mainly those run by Anchor Taxis. He was also the caretaker of a block of flats in Gambier Terrace. As he was not paid for his caretaking duties, he was given exclusive use of the basement flat, where he told me he stored his business consumables. He agreed to employ me on an ad hoc basis, and I started pretty much straight away, changing oils, replacing brake shoes and other servicing requirements on the taxis.

I discussed the possibility with Harry of getting another engine for my A35, as the blue smoke trail was now comparable to that of the vapour trail from a Red Arrows display team and its oil consumption matched that of an old cruise ship. Harry said he knew where one was available which would cost me about £5, and I could use his garage for the changeover in lieu of pay. Despite Harry's engine hoist not being available and him saying he had a bad back, the job got done and I fired up the engine to take it for a spin. Cruising along Queen's Avenue the car seemed to perform well, but I was a little alarmed to see that I still had a blue smoke trail, in fact quite a large one, if the truth be told, and worse than the one I had had before the engine change. I pulled up at a red light and the driver of the car beside me wound down his window and yelled, "Hey mate, your fuckin' engine's knackered". I was not best pleased with Harry, but accepted that he had acted in good faith in getting hold of the clapped-out engine for my A35. I would now have to insist on actual money in return for my services and soon found myself on first-name terms with the Anchor Taxi drivers.

All the drivers would leave their cars with me and then go through the rear of the lock up, across the derelict garden and into the back entrance of Harry's basement flat; none of them seemed to be in a hurry to get their cars back. Often, I would just be tasked with checking the tyres on a car that had not long been in the garage. As the drivers dropped their cars off with me, they would invariably say something along the lines of, "Hello Dave. You arrright? Look, just check the tyres will youse, she seems to be pulling to the left. I'll pop up to see Harry, so no hurry, know wha' I mean? I see (so-and-so's) car's here (the name of a cab driver); is he up with Harry now?"

I need to say at this point, that it is impossible to get a Scouser to call anyone David; it just isn't in their DNA. The use of 'Dave' as a greeting by anyone towards me still rankles, which only serves to encourage my stepson Karl to test my patience, by calling me "Dave-id" with a deliberate hiatus. Anyway, on this particular day, the taxi driver trundled off and I thought little of it, except to vaguely wonder what he was up to. I did the tyres and the next job was an oil and filter change on a Ford Cortina. I couldn't find the correct filter for the car, but knowing that Harry stored his consumables in the flat, I too trundled up the garden, to ask him for one. The back door of the flat was wide open and I heard a song playing on a stereo from within and some female voices in the background. The song was *I Walk The Line* by Johnny Cash, and I was hooked from the minute I heard his bass-baritone voice and the melodic sound of the music. This was the first time I had heard Cash sing and it was the start of a lifetime interest for me in Country Music and The Man in Black.

I keep a close watch on this heart of mine
I keep my eyes wide open all the time
I keep the ends out for the tie that binds
Because you're mine, I walk the line[7].

I called out Harry's name, to which his response was, "Come in Dave, and shut the fuckin' door". I shut the door and went into the next room, which was a large lounge of sorts, with a kitchen off to one side where Harry was standing. The music was coming from somewhere in there. The lounge was furnished with some old chairs and cheap screens between a few beds occupied by ladies of the night, except that it was daytime and several of the taxi drivers whose cars I was servicing appeared to be getting serviced themselves. Harry was running a knocking shop. All the girls were in various stages of undress and two were performing what would be called a 'sex act' these days. Harry must have seen the look on my face. "Come on Dave, you've seen it all before and anyway you're a doctor". One of the girls looked up from her compromising position and said, "He's too fuckin' young to be a doctor".

---

7. *I walk the line* by Johnny Cash

In a voice pitched several semitones higher than normal I told Harry that I needed an oil filter, and he said he would get it while I made everyone some tea. How quaintly civilised, I thought. I made about 10 cups of tea in the kitchen, using mugs and milk that had seen better days, and delivered them, trying not to interrupt those still 'active'. Harry came in with the filter and asked how much he owed me in pay. "About 15 shillings" I replied. He turned to an unoccupied whore and said, "Terri, that's what you charge. How about giving Dave one on the 'ouse for me?" Still somewhat flustered, I declined, saying that I needed the money instead and that anyway, I had a serious girlfriend. I did not add "One with teeth", but I had certainly thought it when Terri had smiled her agreement to Harry's financial proposition. Johnny Cash was still singing when I left the flat and from that day until now, 'I Walk the Line' reminds me of that episode in my life.

My studies continued apace, and I was beginning to grasp the details of the normal workings of the human body, the essential knowledge, before being taught what can go wrong with it and how to manage patients. This is lifelong learning, and I can honestly say that on an almost everyday basis of my 40-plus years as a doctor I learned something new, or if not, was reminded of or had to investigate something that had slipped my mind.

One night whilst at a loose end, I and one of the other students in the house called Alan decided to go out for a few bevvies. No one else was interested, but it had been suggested that we go to a new strip club, which I seem to remember was in Duke Street, to assess it. We made our way there, sat down in the front row and ordered our drinks. We were the only ones in the club. The show was due to start at around 10 p.m. but still nobody else arrived.

At about 9.30 p.m. a plump, heavily made-up woman of indeterminate years walked onto the stage and surveyed the almost deserted room. When she noticed Alan and me, she came down from the stage for a chat and we bought her a drink after she proudly informed us that she was the stripper for that night's show. She introduced herself by her stage name 'Maria d'Alsace' (she came from Huddersfield) and told us she had started stripping because her husband, a lorry driver, had lost his job. He had driven her to the venue and was waiting in their car outside.

We clucked our sympathies and Alan mentioned that we were medical students, which provoked a never-ending list of her and her husband's illnesses. Eventually the time for her act approached and she went back-stage to put on the clothes that she was going to take off. For what it was worth we had our own private strip show, unfortunately robbed of any possible eroticism by Alan pointing out Maria's appendicectomy and caesarean section scars and the sight of her pendulous breasts (adorned with nipple pasties) which, when she revealed them, preceded by a poorly-recorded drum roll, undulated not far above her knees. She finished her act with a flourish, jiggling around to try and make her pasties rotate in opposite directions. We dutifully clapped, and with her clothes back on and her appearance and sexual appeal much improved, Maria joined us for another drink prior to her return to Huddersfield. "Ta-ra lads" she said, as she waddled out of the door.

We reported back unfavourably on this venue and as a house returned to the Gaslight Club in Cumberland Street as the watering hole of choice, which had extended opening hours, a juke box/disco with a dance floor and a flexible attitude to licensing hours by the owner, whose name was Mac. It was a handy place to go when the landlord of the Grapes pub called last orders. We had a lot of good times in the Gaslight Club and Mac tolerated our occasional wayward ways with good humour. He did however take exception to us poisoning a new shoal of tropical fish that he had just acquired and installed in an ornamental fish tank to liven up the décor. Several of us had sat around the tank one night, and each time a round of drinks was bought we had "one for the fish", which was ceremoniously poured into the tank. Not a particularly clever stunt, just a light-hearted attempt to see if we could get the fish drunk. Mac banned us for three months.

On another night at the Gaslight, the bar staff had continued to serve drinks beyond its extended licensing hours and the club was raided by the local police, who took our names and addresses. They asked each one of us what we were drinking, to which the reply should have been, "Just finishing off my drink officer", or something similar, implying that whatever we were drinking had lasted a long time and had not been recently purchased. However, one of the house members, Richard Sloka, was in the loo at the time of the raid and unfortunately on his return, when asked what he was drinking by the policeman, he cheerfully replied, "I'll have a pint of Guinness please". Mac rolled his eyes, and about seven of us were done for drinking after hours.

We were summoned to appear before magistrates, but in the interval between charge and trial we had all qualified as doctors, as at the time of the arrest we were doing our final exams. We had a think and the group consensus was that we should use our new titles as 'doctors' when summoned before the magistrate, as this might persuade him or her to go easy on us. This might indeed have worked as about seven new doctors (all yet to be employed) were summoned into the courtroom. Notwithstanding the circumstances, I was quite pleased to be called in as "Doctor David Jackson". The charges were read out and we all pleaded guilty, our extenuating circumstances being that at the time we were nearly at the end of our exams. The magistrate gave us a minor bollocking, hoped that as doctors we would behave more responsibly in the future and adjourned the case "sine die", which means no future date is given for a review.

That night in the Grapes the mood was sombre as we discussed the next stage of our training, the dreaded house jobs. For 12 months we would be the sleep-deprived drudges of the medical hierarchy, at all and sundry's beck and call, but we would be fed, housed and moreover paid. Not that long ago, house officers only received food and accommodation. The 'pay' was the privilege of being taught by one's master. It took the medical profession a long time to cotton on to the fact that slavery had been abolished.

In Percy Street, 21st birthdays, as the only coming of age landmark in those days, were treated as something special to celebrate in the house and all members turned out for the evening's revelries. These events were noisy and bawdy, but generally uneventful, except mine. I am hazy about the actual conversations of the night, though very clear about the accuracy of what happened and the repercussions. I still inwardly cringe when I remember this episode.

As usual the celebrations started in the Grapes with a drinking game and by the time we left about closing time, I was quite merry. So far so good. Next in the order of affairs for celebrating a 21st birthday was a 'rat' curry in Joe's Café, also in Duke Street, within stomach-emptying distance of Percy Street. This establishment was located on the first floor of a block of flats and Joe could re-open it faster than the Public Health Department could close it down, which they did frequently. However, it had the advantage of only serving one type of curry (meat, you just specified how hot you wanted it) with rice, and it was very cheap. There was no vegetarian option, as vegans had yet to arrive from Mars. At a push Joe would cook up some Indian bread, if you really felt like eating something similar to a heated copy of the local *Liverpool Echo*. Almost everybody who ate the hottest version of Joe's curry ended up in A & E.

We had a table in the centre of the room (I just can't bring myself to use the term restaurant), where nine of us sat with Sam Smith at the head. Surrounding us and a bit close for comfort, were a few tables occupied by the unsavoury types who would 'dine' there on a Saturday night, those who were obese, tattooed and smelling of Old Spice, with wives of a similar ilk, also freshly shaven, apart from their legs and armpits.

The curry arrived and we tucked in, calling for more beer. I admit that we were a bit boisterous and none of us had noticed the dark looks we were receiving from the other diners. Sam, who was head of house at the time, called for quiet and told a revolting joke, alcohol having completely removed his ability to control the volume of his speech, so though he may have thought he was only telling us the joke, the whole of Liverpool 8 could have heard it, not to mention everybody else in the room along with the enhancing swear words. I should mention at this point that Sam was pretty extrovert. He played guitar and harmonica Bob Dylan style and had performed in a few nightclubs, entertaining huge audiences of three or four people.

There were a few titters and mutterings as Sam sat down laughing uproariously and looking as if he had just auditioned favourably for a talent show, but he clearly hadn't and one of the patrons, who was undoubtedly the biggest bloke in the room, probably a bouncer on a night off, let him know it. Stretching the seams of his Paddy's Market suit as he stood up, he said "Hey youse, don't tell fuckin' jokes like that 'ere and don't fuckin' swear in front of me fuckin' missus, you fuckin' gobshite". Sam ignored him, but unfortunately another senior house member, John Searson, piped up and offered Sam his support. John told the objector that we were celebrating a birthday and he could just "Fuck off".

John was a bespectacled, slightly obese character, who played piano to a high standard and trombone to a low one, the latter usually in the early hours of the morning next to my room, where I got the full benefit. He normally wouldn't say boo to a goose and very rarely swore, so why he chose this night of all nights to let rip is a mystery. Perhaps it was the irony of the bloke voicing his objections to Sam's bad language in front of his "missus", using language just as bad as Sam's; I will never know. Anyway, the whole room erupted into a massive drunken brawl. Punches were thrown and a chair went out of the window and landed in the street. Curry was all over the place as tables were overturned and I remember a leviathanic 'missus' breaking a plate over my head as I struggled to stay upright.

The police arrived quickly, but by then things had settled down. John Searson was left searching the curried carpet for his glasses with my help. The coppers instructed us to move against the wall, but John insisted he had to find his glasses and I rather unnecessarily repeated what John had just said. A copper went to grab him and not bothering to look or think, I threw a punch which fortunately for me, did not connect with the copper's chin. "Grab him!" yelled one of the coppers, and I was put into an arm lock, bundled down the stairs and thrown unceremoniously into the back of a Black Maria. I was going to be taken to the Bridewell. I was in deep shit.

Witness statements were made and written down and after about an hour, a police sergeant opened the back of the prison van and asked me what had happened. Being incarcerated in a Black Maria is a very sobering antidote to drunken behaviour in a medical student whose career could be on the line. I explained that I lived in Percy Street with the other medical students and we had been celebrating my 21st birthday when the other diners had taken a dislike to us and everything had kicked off. I was not sure who had started it, but I explained I was only trying to protect my friend who was as blind as a bat without his glasses and I was sorry, but I had not realised that it was a policeman whom I had taken a swing at. "So youse wouldn't 'ave been sorry if it hadna been a copper. Is that wha' your fucking sayin'?"

The sergeant slammed the back door of the vehicle, started up the engine and drove around Liverpool here and there until about 5 a.m. He then parked the vehicle, opened the back door and told me in no uncertain terms to get out. He said that the proprietor of the café had verified our story and that the other diners had started it. He had also been told we were regular customers (only as regular as our stomachs could take) and had never caused any trouble before. As dawn was breaking the sergeant pointed his finger in the direction of the city centre. "You live five fuckin' miles that way" he said and promptly drove off. There have only been a few occurrences in my life that have given me such a profound sense of relief.

I started walking, but fortunately managed to hitch a lift into the city centre and was back in Percy Street by about 8 a.m. Everybody else had congregated in the kitchen nursing their battle wounds. Black eyes abounded and a head wound had required a few stitches. I had a tangerine-sized lump on the top of my head, the pain from which had been masked by sky-high anxiety levels, but which now hurt like hell. After each one of us had related our heroic actions in the Upper Parliament Street fracas, whilst consuming copious amounts of toast to mop up any residual curry lurking dangerously in our stomachs, we went to bed. As I went to sleep with a throbbing headache, I resolved to be law abiding in future and never cross the Liverpool coppers ever again. It was a resolution that lasted about a year.

My studies were progressing nicely, in tandem with my misdemeanours, and soon I was to begin the clinical terms, when several sessions would be spent in one of the surrounding hospitals assisting the house officer, refining our techniques and learning the clinical duties which would be required of us whilst still under supervision. For the clinical terms we had to purchase a stethoscope, patella hammer (for eliciting nervous reflexes), a tuning fork and a tourniquet. A necktie was compulsory for clinical attachments, as consultants were highly conservative. What is more, with a mere questioning arch of an eyebrow, a withering look, or a miniscule lip curl of disapproval, they could turn 4th year medical students into blithering idiots. It was a game they had honed well over the years.

As I came into contact more and more with patients, my vocation, my desire to help these people, increased. During a neurological attachment I was being taught on a patient who had developed a cerebellar ataxia like mine, but unfortunately had not fully recovered as I did. Through my own experience I could demonstrate every clinical finding and my heart wept, for I knew of the devastation caused by a dysfunctional cerebellum and although mine was now in rude health, coordinating the neural messages it was receiving and instantly allowing my body to respond appropriately (apart from my balance deficit in darkness, or when my eyes were shut) this patient's cerebellum had basically shrivelled away. I thanked my lucky stars once again, or God, depending.

CHAPTER 4

The Making of
a Surgeon

Liverpool Royal Infirmary 1971

Surgery was well known to be a very difficult career path, from getting on a training scheme to passing the primary FRCS (Fellow of the Royal College of Surgeons). This examination distinguished the men from the boys, as the pass rate in those days was around 5-7%. This would be followed a few years later by sitting the final FRCS. There are four surgical colleges in the UK; London, Edinburgh, Glasgow and Dublin. Then there was the difficulty of getting on a four or more years post-fellowship senior registrar training scheme, accreditation at the end by a College, finding a vacant consultant post and being appointed after gruelling interviews. Medical staff planning was non-existent at the time and a newly-appointed consultant could be in post for 20 to 30 years, resulting in hospitals being awash with time-expired, fully-trained senior registrars. It was a truism that if a learned meeting was being held abroad and a planeload of UK consultants were attending it, then collectively and independently, accredited (qualified to apply for a job as a consultant) senior registrars in that surgical speciality throughout the country would pray fanatically for a plane crash.

Consultants of course, had a vested interest in having a time-expired senior registrar on their firm, because as an experienced operator, he (or even she, though that was very rare in those days), could deal with a lot of the surgical burden, especially at night. Often these characters were far more surgically experienced and competent than the consultants they worked for, as even then it was not unusual for a new consultant to be appointed based on academic attainment, rather than surgical ability. Now, as the training has been politically meddled with out of all recognition, a new generation of consultant surgeons is being produced to satisfy consultant target numbers rather than based on experience, as they should be, and many are far too sub-specialised to be useful, particularly in the emergency context, with regulations confining them to specific areas of the body. The general surgeon of old, as I was, one competent to deal with most areas of the body, as I would like to think I was, has disappeared entirely. I was probably one of the last of these surgical dinosaurs.

So what made me decide to become a surgeon? Well, I was on my first of two student surgical attachments at the old Liverpool Royal Infirmary and I had been allocated to the firm of Helsby and Brewer. Mr Helsby was a general and vascular surgeon and Mr Brewer was a general and breast surgeon. Mr Brewer was usually quiet and away for a lot of the time, whereas Mr Helsby was a surgical tyrant, brash, condescending and assertive. However, he did encourage his students to go into the operating theatre rather than sit in the dome (observation room) to watch procedures, which was usually near impossible anyway, as all the theatre personnel were hunched over the patient, totally obscuring the surgical field.

Every so often, we would see a diseased organ being removed and held up like a trophy for examination by the dome dummies, with a commentary that was superfluous, as the intercom never worked. Helsby wanted his students to be on the spot, near the action, part of the team, clinically involved. His reputation for the poor treatment of medical students was legendary and I expected a bit of stick and sarcasm, which I got in spades, having to scrub up four times for example in order to satisfy the demands of just his scrub staff.

With my gloved hands locked firmly together in front of me, so that I could not come into contact with anything that was not sterile, gowned, capped, masked, and wearing Wellington boots, I was led into the hallowed operating theatre. In Helsby's theatre the atmosphere was electric. Nobody dared say a word. I couldn't see anything much, but I felt enthralled by being part of the team.

I went carefully into the adjoining theatre, where Helsby's senior registrar was operating. He was undertaking a femoro-popliteal bypass graft on a leg in order to increase blood flow. Here I could get much closer to the action. As I watched him work, deal with bleeders and finally suture the graft in situ to bypass the blockage in the patient's leg, I was fascinated, absolutely fascinated, particularly as this patient would leave hospital 10 days later, able to walk a good distance without the calf pain (claudication) that he had had prior to his operation. I wondered, could I do something like that? I reckoned I could. The road to travel would be hard, but I was not short of determination. I would have to be able to take a few knocks, but I considered myself quite experienced in that aspect of life already. So there it was: with more than two years to go before qualification, I had already decided on my specialty, though at this stage I did not know whether I wanted to remain in the NHS. However, one thing was for sure, I was going to be a consultant surgeon and I would climb that mountain, no matter what.

Despite my occasional wayward ways, I was still attracted to the idea of being an Army doctor. The discipline, the structure, the travel and adventure, the emphasis on sports and the encouragement to develop those skills that would be useful to the Army appealed to me. I knew several students at the medical school who had accepted a commission in one of the three services, and these were available to the right candidates, after they had passed 2nd MB, which was considered a potential stumbling block and following a successful Commissioning Board. If an applicant passed this first professional exam, then it was most likely that they would qualify. The main advantage of this course of action was that as a commissioned officer (2nd Lieutenant) in the Army, all expenses would be paid, in addition to receiving a salary and those who had opted for this choice seemed very wealthy compared to the rest of us, especially me.

The main disadvantage was that the payback for this generosity was five years of service; two years as a Regimental Medical Officer and then the start of specialty training and further service, say a Regular Commission, or discharge back into civilian life. I was always broke and constantly having to work during the vacations, which during the clinical terms were much shorter, as so much had to be learned. I had a long think, weighing up the options, a solution to my financial woes balanced against the five-year enlistment. I decided against it, worried that if I disliked the Army way of life, I would be straining at the leash to be released, and in any event, I wanted to go straight into surgical training following my house officer year. There was no point in discussing the dilemma with my father, as he would never have considered me to be the right material. I would review the situation after my house jobs and a couple of years in surgery in the NHS.

One evening, whilst idly checking my balls, as one does, and simultaneously reading about what can go wrong with them, I noticed that my right one was a touch painful. It was not excruciating, so I resolved to ignore it and confine my checking examinations to longer intervals, say, once every three seconds. I went to bed, but next morning I awoke in a lot of pain with the supersized scrotum of every boy's dreams. With all the diagnostic skill I could muster, I concluded that unless I obtained a quality medical opinion (which excluded all my colleagues), I would die of a testicular detonation.

I was still on Helsby's firm at the time and I thought I would ask his registrar. Though I could drive to the Liverpool Royal Infirmary, walking to the clinic was certainly going to test my mettle, or lack of it. I had to adopt the wide gait of my cerebellar ataxia days to avoid having the tops of my thighs come into contact with my scrotum and shuffled along what seemed like, the longest bloody corridor in the whole world, where I met the nurse doing the clinic and tried to explain my predicament.

"Could I see the registrar please? I have a severe pain in my… err", I trailed off as my mind went blank. "In my testiballs", I blurted out. She went to relay this information to the registrar and through the open door I heard, "There's a medical student asking for you. Says he's got pain in his balls". The registrar sighed resignedly and wearily replied, "They are all a pain in the balls. Put him on a couch".

Very slowly and carefully, I inched myself onto the couch and lay back. I revealed my tackle (freshly washed in a less than pristine Percy Street sink and powdered with stolen talc) and awaited my fate. The registrar came in, took a general history, fixated on to my preceding cerebellar ataxia, which he found interesting, and finally getting to my right testicle, which he did not. No, not testiball I thought; at least my brain was back on track. "Could be a torsion" (a twist that obstructs the blood supply that often leads to the loss of the testicle), said the registrar, "maybe too late to save it. I'll ask the boss to have a look when he gets here".

If I hadn't been lying down, I would have needed to, with that news. I licked my lips nervously and the nurse asked if I would like a drink of water, but before I could reply, the registrar chipped in, "No drink please, he may need to have an emergency anaesthetic".

Mr Helsby breezed in. "What have we got here then? Aren't you a student on my firm?" he enquired. "Yes sir", I squeaked.

He grabbed my testiball; my mind had gone again, but at least I now knew where it resided. "Looks like an epididymo-orchitis" he pronounced. "It'll settle. We needn't operate. Put him in a bed with some intravenous antibiotics and I'll review him on my ward round tomorrow".

I had been given a testicle-saving diagnosis. It would settle, he said. No operation necessary and free hospital food for a day or two, which had to be better than gravy and chips in digs. My spirits soared, but not for long. I was put in a single room where I stripped very slowly, gingerly got into the hospital gown, which was so starched it could stand up on its own, and idly flicked through the patients' menu. I was given some antibiotics to eat (not intravenously as Mr Helsby had said), and to my horror found that I was made 'nil by mouth' with a card stuck at the bottom of my bed confirming it. But hang on; hadn't Helsby said there was no need to operate?

The registrar reviewed me later in the evening and decided that it would be better to 'look and see', rather than 'wait and see' and I was pre-medded, consented, whisked up to theatre and anaesthetised. My testicle was exposed in all its glory, nestling in the registrar's hands as he examined it carefully.

I was in a lot of pain after the operation, but a shot of morphine certainly helped. It was almost worth having the surgery just for that, and I was happily euphoric when, early in the morning, the registrar appeared. He told me my testicle was fine, very swollen as a response to infection, but it would soon be back in working order. I was being discharged. I would recover at home, the stitches would dissolve, the ward would get me transport, but I had to go, like right now, immediately and certainly before Helsby's ward round when he would discover that, contrary to his instructions, I had been operated on.

The registrar's course of action had certainly been clinically justified and I was quite happy to have had the exploratory operation to prove that Helsby was correct in his diagnosis. The registrar would have preferred that I did have a torsion, but without that justification for his having taken me to theatre against Helsby's wishes, I had to be disappeared. I was transported back to Percy St., back to the land of chips and gravy. I had not had the benefit of one hospital meal. I should have asked for a takeaway.

Gradually I recovered, but of course my fellow medical students could not lose this opportunity of taking the piss unmercifully. The get-well cards I received were unprintable and in spite of the fact that I offered to demonstrate that I still had a pair, "Jackson has only got one ball" was sung frequently. In LMSS one of the senior medical students asked the President if the Sports Secretary should be replaced, as he had not 'got the balls' for the job.

Nowadays, ultrasound will help in the diagnosis of this condition and to the experienced surgeon, distinguishing between an infection and torsion of the testicle is possible on clinical examination, if a little uncomfortable for the patient, or in my case very uncomfortable.

By this time, after driving, repairing and scrapping a succession of old cars on their last legs, I had acquired, on a more infrequent visit home, a red series 2 Sunbeam Alpine convertible sports car. It had done a couple of lifetimes' worth of miles, but the paintwork was good, and the cancerous rust had not yet metastasised to the chassis. It was the dog's bollocks with the registration number 66 FOF. If only I could have forecast the huge appeal of personalised registration plates that was to come and the potential value of that number plate a few years down the line.

Percy Street 1972, my car 66 FOF under the lamppost[8].

My next brush with the law involved this car. When engaging the gears and driving off, I noticed a rather ominous clunking noise, which was getting worse. I went around to see Harry, and after crawling under the car he diagnosed either a worn universal joint where the prop shaft is bolted to the differential or a worn-out differential. Either option would be a financial disaster, but luck was on my side. A friend of mine told me that he had seen an old Sunbeam Alpine parked in Penny Lane – the Penny Lane made famous by The Beatles. It looked derelict and had a council notice on it, threatening removal and disposal.

8. Photo courtesy of Gallery Press *Liverpool. This is my city* by Richard Whitting-Egan 1972

I made my way there, crawled underneath it, being a lot thinner in those days due to starvation and stress and examined the prop shaft and the differential, both of which seemed pretty solid with no play in the universal joint. This seemed the answer to my prayers, though I would have to tow the car back to Percy Street. The trouble was that it was not my car, even if it wasn't being claimed by anyone else, and if I was going to just take it, there might be some legal issues if I was caught. But on the other hand, its owner had abandoned it, the council were due to remove it anyway and then no doubt they would crush it. That would be a complete waste, would it not? My reasoning oscillated between outright car theft and doing the council a favour, though I had not actually considered what I would do with the remainder of the car once I had stripped it of the parts I needed.

I engaged the help of my friend Mike and his disco van, the only vehicle I could have access to with a towing hitch, no questions asked. He refused to let me drive his van but said he would drive it himself. I had an accomplice. I found a tow rope and we were off at dusk, having sunk a few pints for courage. Borrowing (which was the term I settled on) a derelict car has its drawbacks in addition to the legal issues, as the handbrake, or foot brakes could have seized, and it might not steer, or respond to any controls.

I sat at the wheel of the Sunbeam as Mike towed me along, his old van puffing and wheezing with the strain of it. This wrecked sports car had no hood, so when it started to pour with rain I got completely soaked; perhaps it was some sort of moral justice for the deed I had undertaken. We had aimed to get the car when the evening rush hour was over, but in the event, it wasn't. The traffic was clogged up nose to tail and of course I had forgotten to make an 'On Tow' sign in my haste. I do not know how we did it, but eventually we got the car to Percy Street and then hid it in Back Percy Street. The next day, with Harry's guidance, I would start to take the prop shaft and differential out. I would cure 66 FOF of her malady.

I was up early and with some help and wooden props, at Harry's suggestion, we turned the car on its side against one of the walls of Back Percy St, giving full access to the parts I wanted. I had thought of taking the whole back axle and prop shaft, but Harry said it would be impossible to move the two-wheeled remains of the donor car afterwards. This was good forward thinking and prophetic, as when I was halfway through the job and had cut the brake pipes for ease of access, a police constable appeared, ambling along towards me. I must have been shopped, because we had never seen a policeman patrolling Percy Street, let alone Back Percy Street. He came over to where I was working and asked me what I thought I was doing and where I had got the car from. I answered his first question, saying that I was dismantling part of the car for spares and deliberately failed to acknowledge his second. "I can see what youse fuckin' doing" said the PC, "but where did you get the car from?" "Er, Penny Lane", I eventually replied, to which the PC said, "What, you just took it did ya?"

I could have simply and truthfully answered "yes" and then thrown myself at the mercy of the law, but instead I explained that the council had put a notice on the car, which had now expired, and the car was due for removal and destruction. It had been my intention, I said, to 'borrow' the car for a few hours, salvage some parts and return it to where I had found it. I showed him the council notice. In summary, the PC then said, "So you stole a car, under the jurisdiction of the council, to nick the parts you wanted and then you were going to return the car to them?" I agreed that it could perhaps be construed that way, though I still preferred the word 'borrow'. He asked me for my full name, address and occupation. When I said that I was a medical student, I prayed that we hadn't met before at the incident in Joe's Café on my 21st birthday. He looked at me sideways whilst noting my details and then said with incredulity, "So you're going to be a fuckin' doctor, are you? God fuckin' save us all" and then added, "I'm going to speak to my sergeant".

I could hear him outlining the case against me on his radio and he kept repeating, "No, he fuckin' stole it". In a few moments he was back. "Everton won the derby this year and my sergeant's an Everton supporter, so he's in a good mood. He said that unless this STOLEN car is back in Penny Lane by 5 pm tonight, exactly where you fuckin' found it, you'll be charged with car theft". With that he turned on his heels and walked off muttering.

My mood improved considerably. Harry, who had disappeared at the first whiff of the copper (he claimed he could smell them), to go and empty his basement of any evidence of working girls or taxi drivers, suddenly reappeared. For once, he was in the clear and not the person of interest. I had another thought. I had been told to return the car to where I had found it, but not exactly as it was when I found it. I remarked to Harry, "If I am going to get done, I might as well take the diff and the prop shaft anyway", which I did, but I still had to get the car back to Penny Lane, and that was another problem.

Although Mike agreed to tow it back, I had cut the brake pipes at the rear. Pressing the brake pedal just produced two puddles of brake fluid and no retardation of movement whatsoever. It was going to be a difficult tow, and though his van was old and quite beaten up, Mike was not keen on having a ton of Sunbeam Alpine crashing into the back of it when he braked. We tried putting some rope down an iron pipe, to get a solid tow bar, but this only worked if the Alpine was in a direct line with both the tow bar and van, otherwise the two vehicles jack-knifed.

The only way we could get the car back to Penny Lane was to either push it all the way (I ran out of friends with that suggestion), allow it to crash into Mike's van, or to tow it very slowly with a house member walking on either side of the Alpine, with a brick in each hand to chock the wheels when necessary, at traffic lights for example. We decided we also needed other house members walking alongside, ready to push the Alpine backwards when the van slowed down. This was eventually the course of action we took, and I think we caused the worst traffic jam in the history of Liverpool, but despite this and just in time, we manoeuvred the Alpine back into the space in Penny Lane from which I had taken it. We had accomplished this by the stipulated time, and for good measure and in the spirit of honesty, I slung the worn parts from my car into the boot of the 'borrowed' car, so that the council could destroy a complete vehicle, if not exactly the original one. I cannot hear The Beatles singing 'Penny Lane' without remembering this escapade.

Meanwhile I had passed the pathology exams, a subject that was tedious as a student, but fascinating a few years after qualification when I really got to grips with it. That was another exam out of the way.

During the vacations prior to my final year, I stayed in Liverpool and looked for casual work. Unemployment in Liverpool was high, but casual, no-questions-asked labour was not difficult to find, and this led me to the Ford gearbox factory in Halewood, where a 'specialised' cleaning firm were recruiting labour to clean the pipework in the roof space above the machinery, as over time all the pipes get filthy and covered in oil. My friend John Tappin and I applied for a job and we were both taken on. We should have run a mile.

The roof spaces were divided up into bays and we would work in pairs with buckets, rags and solvent fluids. When the bay was inspected and passed by a supervisor, we would move onto the next bay. We were paid a good amount for this, but there was a big problem. To do the job, we would have to be high off the ground, swinging like apes through a metallic and asbestos jungle canopy. The cleaning company engaged several specialised 'riggers', one to each pair of cleaners, who would rig up duckboards for the cleaners to walk along, as a token degree of 'elf an' safety', in order to comply with local regulations. The cleaning would be a night job and would take about 10 days.

However, our appointed rigger looked about 70 years old, was not keen on heights, and said rather indignantly, "I'm not fuckin' climbin' up there, I've got an 'eart condition you know", and that was the last we saw of him. I nearly went with him, as the thought of holding onto a metal roof truss with one hand whilst cleaning with the other, using a rag dipped in a type of Swarfega, did not appeal. However, needs must, and John and I concentrated on just cleaning those pipes and structures that were easily visible and therefore likely to be inspected, having decided to rope ourselves to the pipe work. It was tedious work and when dawn came around and we knocked off, we were ready for bed, to start again the next night. We passed all our inspections and I think that this was because the contracted time was so short for the job to be done that the supervisors just waved us on. After all, who in the Ford Motor Company was going to climb into the roof space and discover that the top halves of the pipes concerned had never been touched?

I could not rely on my father at all by now. He and my mother were at complete loggerheads and their marriage had crumbled after 30 years together, resulting in him eventually moving out of our home in Abingdon. I would never meet my father's new woman, later to become my stepmother, ironically also called Clarice.

I needed another job. Nothing was in the offing for quite a while, but then in the nick of time, two financial opportunities arose simultaneously. John discovered that they needed workers at the Lavrock Bank depot of the Liverpool Cleansing Department, and I fortuitously discovered that the landlady of the Queen's Head in North Hill Street was looking for help in the bar of her pub, as she couldn't manage on her own. Her husband, who could not be appointed a licensed victualler due to a bit of previous dishonesty, worked night shifts as a switchboard operator at the nearby GPO exchange in South John Street.

The landlady's name was Big Kath and she was a powerful woman. She had to be if she was going to throw troublesome drunks and dockers out of her pub. She must have weighed about 20 stone and a roll-up cigarette was continuously stuck to her lower lip. She ruled her pub with a rod of iron.

When I went to see her as part of the 'interview', I was asked if I liked dogs. I told her I did. We had had many family dogs, mainly bumptious boxers of varying levels of obedience and blighted by a poor judgement of human beings, as they always seemed to take to my father. She asked if I had any experience of bar work. "Yes", I replied, stretching the truth considerably. Well I could pour beer from a four-pint tin from the off licence. Big Kath told me I would be behind the bar and she would do the cellar work and help me out if needed. She said I had to get to know the punters, as they liked their drinks poured out and handed to them as they reached the bar. The interval between them entering the pub and reaching the bar was about four seconds.

She then disappeared and returned with a large Alsatian dog. I can't remember its name, but I reckoned that with that canine by her side, Big Kath was the safest woman on the planet. On the other hand, it was a lovely dog and one of my duties would be to walk it for half an hour along the Dock Road by the Tate & Lyle sugar factory at closing time, while she locked up.

Big Kath then showed me the secret knock on the door or window of the pub used by friends or punters who wanted to have a drink or several outside the licensing hours. She called these occasions a 'sesh' and I could remain behind to serve at the bar, which was blacked out to prevent detection. She then mentioned my next and last task. Her husband had Thursday nights off and he usually went on a pub crawl, also along the docks. My job was to bring him back to the pub. "It doesn't matter what fuckin' state he's in, just make sure you bring him back, before midnight" she said.

So, on Thursday nights I babysat a GPO switchboard operator whilst he drank himself shitless, and when he was completely incoherent and unstable in every regard, I returned him to the arms of his 'loving' wife, who threw him into bed. Usually he just sang his way back home, but one night he would not cooperate and I had to sling him up over my shoulder in a fireman's lift and carry him back to the pub, whilst he dribbled saliva down the back of my coat, and simultaneously burnt a hole in it, with a cigarette he had somehow managed to light whilst hanging upside down.

In any event I always got him back on time and Big Kath would give me a free pint, cluck her thanks and tell me to walk the dog, whilst she and the others in the bar got ready for their 'sesh'. Once, when there was nobody about, I made the mistake of letting the dog off the lead for a wander around. He spotted a rat (there were thousands along the docks) and shot off like a bat out of hell. It took me about half an hour to coax him back and try tentatively to remove the rat from his jaws. I gave up in the end and let him eat the damn thing. If I had lost the dog, I would be dead, more dead than if I had lost Big Kath's husband.

John and I signed up with the Cleansing Department at Lavrock Bank. We would start work at 7.30 a.m. next morning, when we would meet the foreman and be allocated our barrows, brushes, bins and notebooks giving the details of the streets we had to sweep and which sides. This varied according to which way the wind was blowing, as all the rubbish would generally be blown to one side or one end of the street and therefore this was the only side, or end, that needed to be done. My allocated employee number was 006, John was 007 and of course, he loved that. Next day we were at the depot. I was bog-eyed, because Kath had had a session the night before, which had gone on until 3 a.m. I had served the drinks, as she was pretty much away with the fairies when I returned the dog from its walk. She did not do it often, but when she decided to lay one on, she could almost drink her own pub dry.

The Lavrock Bank foreman was a small middle-aged man with a clipboard. There was only John and I there. He called out 001 to 005 with no answers and each time he noted the absences, getting to 006 and 007, when John and I braced up and shouted "here!". He could see that there were only the two of us present and accounted for, but he superfluously kept calling out numbers until about 015, at which point he put his clipboard down and led us to a storage shed, where we were issued with our equipment.

We were allocated a hand cart with two large bins on it, a shovel and a stiff broom. We were taught how to spread the bristles of the broom (by standing on it basically) for more effective sweeping. We were given our beats, told where to dump the rubbish when the bins were full, for collection later by motorised dust cart and we were off. Percy Street was on my beat, so I swept the street I lived in, clearing away the cigarette butts and all the other rubbish thrown in the road by my house mates as they passed me on the way to the medical school. The latest property information I can find informs me that the last house sold in Percy Street went for £557,000 in 2016. A lot happens in nearly 50 years. I wonder who is sweeping it now.

There is a balcony above the front door of 9 Percy Street. It was there that we used to sun ourselves and occasionally throw super-heated coins to the tramps and beggars shuffling by below, having fired them up on the kitchen gas hob. When they picked up the burning hot coins, we explained that they had just been minted. Not very clever or kind, but it amused us at the time.

One summer evening, a couple of us were on the balcony of number 9, having a beer. It was hot and the window curtains of the flat opposite, which belonged to the 'Greek whore' as she was known, had been left ajar. We noticed through the gap, that she was in her room with Lennie the Jew. He was a cellist in the Liverpool Philharmonic Orchestra and a horny little bugger. She and Lennie were at it, going hell for leather. Word spread quickly and soon we were all on the balcony, enjoying the view, well, up to a point. It took our resident extrovert to spoil everything by shouting "Way hey!". This had the effect of stopping the two of them in mid-shag and the curtains were swiftly wrenched closed. We did wonder if this could be a money-spinning opportunity, with an invited paying audience, but even though we watched very carefully after that, the chance never arose again.

I had a very good friend at medical school, though he could be a bit weird. His name was Edward C, otherwise known as Nod. His parents lived in North Wales and his father was a retired baker. Nod wanted to be a psychiatrist, and even as a medical student, he tried to attribute every symptom of any illness known to man to a manifestation of a mental disorder. Nod's other interests in life were shooting (cameras and guns) and fishing. I used to go shooting with him and his father on the farmland where they lived, blowing apart clay pigeons and the odd duck.

Anyway, we in the house collectively decided to go on a deep-sea fishing expedition. Nod would arrange it for us, all the tackle would be provided, and we would eat everything we caught, like true hunters. Early one morning we arrived at the embarkation point, on the North Wales coast. The weather was foul, raining with occasional squalls and the white horses indicated a sea swell of about six feet. The fishing boat looked tiny, with a small wheelhouse, seating for six (there were seven of us, eight including the captain) and an outboard engine that had seen better days. There should have been no way we could have gone out into the high seas under these circumstances, but we did. The Captain was quietly confident that the weather would turn, and it did, becoming worse by the hour. When we were about 2-3 miles out, the little boat was heaving all over the place. However, the Captain insisted we could start fishing, so we baited the hooks and tossed the lines, immediately pulling up fish by the dozen.

Fortunately, the seating problem had been solved by Nod having a disabling attack of sea sickness, spewing his breakfast overboard into wind, the idiot, while I held him by the collar. He then collapsed moaning and groaning onto the deck of the vessel. This was where our catch was being tossed and where our bait (cut up strips of mackerel) had fallen. Nod was covered in plaice, cod, mackerel, and fish guts, as well as some of his own stomach contents. Most of the rest of us were okay, perhaps just a bit of queasiness, but certainly well enough to eat our packed lunches in front of Nod, offering him the odd cheese and pickle sandwich, and laughing at his pained expression as he retched into the face of a suffocating mackerel.

Transporting our catch back to Percy Street would have been a problem, except that Nod had a little A40 estate car. Gamely he loaded the fish in cardboard boxes into his car and when back in Percy Street we unloaded them and put them in the ground floor bath, and there the fish stayed for about a week, until the smell was so bad that we had to do something about it. They were laid to rest in the back garden in a shallow grave and nobody would ever use the bath again. Nod gave up sea fishing and stuck to tranquil rivers, fly fishing from dry land.

I was very fond of Nod, and despite his peculiar thought processes and habits, he was popular in the medical school and he would frequently attend events, both formal and social, camera in hand, recording for posterity. He had an Irish girlfriend, a student nurse called Mary, who resolutely refused to surrender her virginity, though I gather persistence paid off in the end. Nod was very good at failing exams and he had to re-sit most of them. I think he failed final MB ChB and the resits, but passed a conjoint exam, or the Licensed Apothecary exam, did his house job and went off to train in psychiatry. This did not work out, so he became a GP, treating his patients for depression regardless of whether they were depressed or not. He eventually married a nurse called Debbie and had two children with her, and I hope for their sake that Debbie contributed more to their genetic make-up than Nod did.

I was still working in the Queen's Head and on the streets, but I was exhausted, not getting more than about six hours' sleep at best and three at worst. Good training for a house officer I suppose, but I needed to do something about it and on my beat there were a couple of unoccupied old houses where I could bunk down for a short kip during my shift.

I had been advised (by a real road sweeper, when he eventually returned to work) to always have one full bin on the barrow, as the foreman did a twice daily check, lifting the bin lids. This meant that if my plan to sleep on the job came to fruition, I would have to have one bin unemptied when I started my round. This made pushing the barrow up Upper Parliament Street a real test of strength. Fortunately, the foreman did his morning and afternoon rounds at the same predictable times and he wasn't worried if the streets looked untouched, as any wind change negated our efforts anyway. So long as there was some rubbish in the bins, he was happy.

The first couple of days my scheme worked well. I'd sleep for an hour or so under an old donkey jacket, and then resume sweeping until the foreman arrived. On about the third day, after a snooze, I took up my barrow and started off, only to be confronted by a scouse harridan, for want of a better word. She was about 40 years old, looked 90, and was dressed in an old pinafore with thick brown stockings which stopped at mid-calf and slippers. She had her hair in curlers under a headscarf and the customary filter-less cigarette hanging out of her mouth.

She started haranguing me. "I know wha' youse a' doin' you lazy bastard. My old man never had a day on the sick before he died an' we had three kids" she said. I looked closely at her and concluded that I wouldn't have to ask her what her husband had died of. He had probably taken the easy way out.

"Youse a' fuckin' skivin'. Arthur an' me old man were mates" she continued (I assumed she was referring to our foreman, as he had never told us his name). "He'd like to know what youse ar' fuckin' doin'". So far, I hadn't said a word. It would have been pointless anyway. She told me to follow her and led me to the back entry of her terraced house, which was full of rubbish. "Clear up this fuckin' mess and come back every few days to keep it clear" she demanded, "or me an' Arthur are going to have a few words".

With that parting shot, she shuffled through the back door into her house and I meekly started clearing up the yard for her. I stuck to the deal, clearing away her rubbish when necessary. I did not mind as it was all in one place, rather than spread out along the street and it was a good source of rubbish if one of my bins needed an emergency top up. Everyone was happy and I continued to sleep in the old house, until one day I arrived to find it had been demolished and my old donkey jacket was covered in several tons of rubble.

Three or four nights a week I was behind the bar in the Queen's Head. I had developed a rapport with the regulars and as Big Kath had instructed, I started to pour their drinks out for them as soon as they arrived. I was frequently treated to a pint – "Youse 'avin' one Dave?" – but I was not allowed to drink during licensing hours, especially as the big lolloping Alsatian needed his walk without me staggering all over the place or stopping for a pee, and Big Kath's husband required a sober and strong hand to ensure his safe return to the pub on time. I got to know him quite well, as alcohol loosens the lips and the inhibitions, but he never revealed his criminal past. So I charged each customer for a drink for myself, wrote it in a notebook behind the bar and drunk on the house on my nights off.

I got to know life in the raw with these down-to-earth, generous men and women and tried to advise them on their various ailments. Many were on the dole, others were dockers or low-grade tradesmen and all had good stories to tell. By this stage I could speak Scouse with the best of them and I like to think that I am a good listener, so I partook in a culture, albeit temporarily of course, that few people in my profession would have any experience of, and I am a better man for it.

One morning, after roll call at Lavrock Bank, the foreman approached John and me. He said that we would not be going on our usual beats, because there were two derelict houses that required clearing out prior to demolition, or refurbishing. He gave us directions and told us that the houses were in a terraced block of three, the middle house of which was still occupied. He suggested that we inform the occupant of what we were going to do. He would call in on us sometime later to see how we were getting on.

John and I trudged to the houses in question and knocked on the door of the middle house. We were met by the furious barking of what had to be more than one enormous dog, followed by the shouts of a male voice trying to silence them. The front door opened a few inches and the occupant, a man of about 60 years old, took in the scene of John and me with brushes, shovels and bins, and told us to "Fuck off". We tried to explain, but he retorted that every time "the fuckin' council" tried to clear out the houses, the rats were disturbed and made their home in his house, "And I don't like fuckin' rats" he said. He then told us that if we went near the adjoining houses, he would set his dogs on us.

We had our orders, and undeterred we went to one of the other houses regardless. He set his dogs on us, as he had warned, and we had to quickly scramble up a nearby wall with our legs tucked up, so that the snarling hounds, which were bouncing up and down like demented pogo sticks, couldn't reach us. The occupant whistled his dogs back and we sat where we were, until we heard his front door slam shut. Just then the foreman arrived and asked us, "what the fuck are youse doin' on tha' wall?" I told him about the rats and that the occupant of the middle house had set his dogs on us to stop us clearing out the houses on either side of him. The foreman was not having it. "We'll fuckin' well see about tha'. He can't obstruct the Council or their employees from goin' about their lawful business".

He marched off and banged on the middle door. Thirty seconds later he too was up on the wall with us. The dogs were called off again and the three of us dismounted after a suitably safe interval. I picked up my shovel, just in case. The foreman said that he would report back to his boss and they'd get the police involved, but meanwhile we could have the rest of the day off. He told us to take our barrows back, then go to a place called the Greek club and have a pint. We were to say that we were on the bins and they would let us in for free.

He gave us directions and we found the establishment, which looked very run down, and knocked on a heavily-reinforced door. It had a peephole hatch in it, just like a prison door, and when the hatch eventually opened, a huge black face appeared, peering through the hole. "Wha'?" the face demanded. I explained that we were on the bins and that our foreman had said we could have a drink. We could hear three bolts being slid across and then the door opened.

John and I both whistled as we viewed the inside of this club. It was lavishly, if completely tastelessly, decorated with chintzy curtains, plumped up imitation silk cushions in armchairs and a thick shag pile carpet that consumed our feet as we traversed it and even though I had little experience of knocking shops (Harry's being the only one), I knew this had to be the real deal. It was early evening, we were the only punters and neither of us wanted to be there much longer. We had noticed the size of the black doorman and although John was a big bloke, he was dwarfed by him.

A long-legged, scantily-clad, bottle-blonde girl came in and went behind the bar. In the base levels of male bar room titter, she was shaggable, at a push. "Wot youse 'avin'?" she said. John threw caution to the wind and asked for two pints of Guinness. I flinched and wished he had said halves instead. "Will youse be wantin' anythin' else?" she asked. "No ta" we both chorused, far too loudly and a little too enthusiastically, as it dawned on us that the Guinness that she had just poured could end up being very expensive.

We sipped for a long time, under the unflinching gaze of the doorman. We needed to pay up and leave as quickly as possible, and there was a potential problem. Neither of us thought we had enough money on us for the drinks and the only way to get the doorman to shift would have been to use weapon-grade explosives.

"Drink up" I hissed to John. He obliged and we drained our pints. I picked up both glasses and took them to the bar. "Ta-ra love" I said, whilst motioning John to walk with me to the door. I asked the doorman to open the door so that we could get back to work. He was dumbfounded, as we were blatantly leaving without paying, but I summoned up an air of casual confidence. "When Arthur comes in, tell him we only had the one pint each, like he said, and he'll pick up the tab when he's in later, and don't tell him any different, cos' we'll be seeing him soon, and he's not paying for more than we had". With that, the doorman opened the door and we nonchalantly walked out seemingly without a care in the world. As soon as we were out of sight we legged it. John had left his cigarettes behind, but that was a small price to pay, and Arthur never did raise the matter with us.

The time had come to say goodbye to Big Kath and the Queen's Head. My final year, 6th year, was about to start. I loved my job there, but needs must. She was very gracious about my departure, thanked me and wished me well. However, I stayed on for a couple of weeks or so at Lavrock Bank, as the pay was better than the pub and I needed the money to get me through the whole year. In the evenings I would catch up with the lecture notes of my fellow final year students.

The foreman announced that I was to be promoted to the bins, but prior to this, I had to do a week as a sweeper behind the dustcart. My purpose was to clean up the spillage from the bins, as when the lids were taken off and the bins hoisted onto the shoulders of the wiry bin men, half the rubbish fell out onto the pavements or into the back entries. A couple of times the bin men missed the lorry altogether, which made me suicidal as I swept up the detritus of the poor in mind, spirit and income. That week was one of the worst so far, in my employment life, even if we did all bunk off on Friday lunchtime, the lorry having been hidden away, for an afternoon of drinking, 'arrows' (darts) and sharing the spoils of the week, i.e. saleable rubbish. Then it all became too much, and I had to leave my employment at Lavrock Bank. The foreman said that if I ever fell on hard times, there would always be a job for me there. I treasured that statement. I had made a good impression, and if I failed in my medical career, I had a future with the Liverpool Corporation Cleansing Department.

It was about this time that Sheila reappeared in my life (just for a long weekend). I had seen her at the Barley Mow when I went back to Abingdon to talk with my mother about the way things were going with my father, and to visit my grandfather who was very frail, but still managing to live independently. Sheila was sassy and flirtatious, which I ignored for the most part. She said she intended to go up to visit some relatives near Liverpool and she would like to call in on me whilst there. I murmured my agreement and gave her my phone number, knowing that it was unlikely that this would lead to anything, even if I wanted it to, and in any event I did not want another public beer soaking.

However, when she proved me wrong and the phone call did unexpectedly materialise, the thought of no-strings-attached sex stirred my loins briefly. I agreed to meet her at Lime Street Station and then we journeyed to Percy Street. She was not impressed with what she saw there, and neither were my housemates when they saw her. "What were you doing Dave? Wiggling a woodbine in the Mersey Tunnel?" was the kindest comment I elicited from them later. Comparing my member to a woodbine was hurtful to say the least, although I wasn't overly concerned about the Mersey Tunnel comparison. But to be fair, though Sheila was not as attractive as she thought she was, she wasn't bad and certainly back then, she had all the attributes and requirements of a modern-day MILF.

We went to Blackpool for a long weekend and stayed in a B & B. The landlady looked distinctly uncomfortable when we signed in as a couple and looked on the verge of collapse when Sheila made sure that we had a double bed, rather than two singles. She then crooked her finger, beckoning me towards her and said, "Come on dahhhrling, let's go to our room and have a quick… (I immediately blushed a deep crimson red and prayed, don't say it, please don't say it)… freshen up" she continued, "and then explore the town". I remained flushed and sheepishly followed her mischievously swinging bottom as she turned on her heel and headed for our room. Even though she was in front of an audience of only one, excluding me, she just could not resist playing to the gallery. I wondered if "freshen up" was a euphemism for something else. It was, and then we went out for a drink.

Sheila was rediscovering herself, looking for the meaning of life. She had become a vegetarian, started smoking pot and socially and politically seemed to have lurched to the liberal left. She wore a collection of beads and carried a handbag made of hessian, decorated with peace emblems. We got pleasantly tipsy, ate fish and chips along the pier and went back to the B & B, where she wanted to "freshen up" again, but I was not keen. I am not sure why, as normally a couple of beers and a willing woman would have been conducive to a successful evening and a good night's sleep. Maybe I thought that what we were doing was wrong, as she apparently had some children knocking around somewhere, which she never mentioned, or maybe I was just developing a better moral compass as I grew older. We may have parted in Blackpool, or after I drove back to Liverpool, I can't remember, but she went off to visit her relatives and I never saw or heard of her again. I suppose I was an amusing interlude for her, and I hope she eventually found what she was looking for. I was just glad that I was merely a stop en route and not the final destination of her journey.

One night at around midnight I was driving back to Percy Street in 66 FOF, having just left a miserably boring party at number 6 Sefton Park, where our rival medical students resided. We were number 9 and the best, they were number 6 and mediocre, most of them being studious nerds, in our parlance (but conscientious medical students as far as the Deanery was concerned). I had had a skinful, but as all car drivers will tell you when they are drunk and foolishly get behind the wheel, I felt quite capable at the time. I did not drive at break-neck speed, but according to the policeman who pulled up in front of me, with blue lights flashing and siren blaring, I was weaving all over the road along Queen's Drive, which was a dual carriageway, so I had plenty of room to weave.

He asked me to get out of the car, which I did whilst holding onto the roof to stop myself from keeling over. He said he suspected I was drunk, which wasn't a difficult assumption, and he produced one of the brand-new breathalysers for me to blow into. It was of the early variety which required him to look for a change in the colour of some crystals in it. I took a deep mouthful of fresh air and blew it straight out again into the bag, hoping that the air had not had enough time in my lungs to be marred by alcoholic fumes and register a damning result. I crouched down obscuring what I was doing and did the same thing a few times.

The copper had not noticed that I had just blown mostly Liverpool city air, which was contaminated with just about everything apart from alcoholic products, into the bag. The crystals resolutely did not turn green as they should have done and the copper was furious, holding up the bag against his car headlights to get a better look. He could not cope with the mismatch of his senses; his eyes, nose and ears telling him I was completely pissed and the breathalyser telling him I was not. He threw the bag to the ground in a fit of temper, stamped on it, picked it back up, chucked it into his patrol car and then said to me, in no uncertain terms, "Leave your car where it is and walk. Pick it up when you're fuckin' sober, you fuckin' pillock" and with that, he drove off angrily. I had sufficient presence of mind, albeit befuddled, to do exactly as I was told. I walked back to No. 9 and picked 66 FOF up the next day, relieved to find that it still retained all four wheels.

In my final year in Percy Street I met two of the nicest girls, very attractive, tall and slim with dyed blonde hair. They were identical twins, Annie and Sheila, from the Wirral. Annie was an ECG technician and Sheila was a nurse. They were great fun, often went out with the Percy Street crowd and they would be instrumental in introducing me to my first wife, Beverley.

The final examinations were rapidly approaching and I had to become a teetotal monk for a time, in order to cram in all that I needed to know to remain in the top 85 percent. There would be some written papers, but the main focus would be on the clinical and then the oral examinations, the viva voces. There was a short interval between the written and the clinical examinations and in Percy Street, there were about six of us doing finals at the same time. Each evening in the Grapes, we held post-mortems on the answers to the written questions. The clinical examinations were held at different hospitals and patients were usually dragged in each year from a bank of mainly incurables or retrieved from recent clinics. We were allotted one long case for a full history, examination and demonstration of clinical signs, and several short cases for spot diagnoses in medicine or surgery. The more correct diagnoses you obtained, the greater the chance of success.

Our surgical clinicals were first, and Alan Harris, Simon Lewin and I were to attend the same hospital. I would be last to be examined. Did the Medical School know that we all lived under the same roof, I wondered? Alan's long case was the first patient on the left in the ward, and he diagnosed a duodenal ulcer. Medical treatment had not been successful, and he had been listed for surgery. Next day Simon went in and was allocated the same patient. He flew through the history and noticed in addition that the man had severe varicose veins. It should be noted that every patient had been told not to assist the examinees, but let's face it, they were on our side. Simon returned to Percy Street triumphant, in that he had diagnosed the varicose veins in addition to the duodenal ulcer. Next day it was my turn and I was allocated, you guessed it, the first patient on the left. I introduced myself and couldn't help asking, "Er, have you got a duodenal ulcer and varicose veins?" "Yes," he replied, "and these", demonstrating Dupuytren's contractures (thickened tissue) in the palms of both hands. I was elated, but not too keen on discussing his hands, as I knew very little about the condition. However, for the sake of appearing to be an observant clinician, I added it in when relating the clinical findings to the examiner. The examiner then asked the dreaded question "What do you know about Dupuytren's contracture, now you've mentioned it?" "Nothing" would have been the honest answer, but I fortunately remembered the 'how to answer a medical question on a condition about which you have no idea' advice.

I looked at the patient and said, "It is a fairly common condition, though probably less common than thought. It affects both sexes (the patient was a middle-aged man), although it is slightly more likely to occur in men, at around middle age. The cause is not fully understood, but the effect is a nodular thickening of the tissues of the palms". I carried on feeling and demonstrating the nodules. I then went on, "that treatment was either medical, surgical, or expectant (wait and see)" and that was all the treatments covered. The examiner seemed quite impressed, even though in truth I had said absolutely nothing of real note. I got through quite a few short cases, and as I trudged back to Percy Street I was quite sure I had earned a distinction in surgery, which of course I had not.

My medical clinical exams were hard work and I did not excel myself at all. I have always regarded medical diagnoses as intuitive and uncertain. The treatments the physicians employed were simply a hodgepodge of antibiotics, steroids, insulin and voodoo.

In 1973 we did not have many investigations which were any more sophisticated than X rays, blood and urine tests at our disposal, and the elicitation of clinical signs as the indicators of a disease process was extremely important. Ultrasound technology, in its infancy when I was a house officer, was only at the stage of measuring the various diameters of prenatal (before birth) babies' heads. Then came the endoscopes followed by Computerised Axial Tomography (CAT), Magnetic Resonance Imaging (MRI) and Positron Emission

Tomography (PET) each offering their own particular image of the human body, which were routinely available in almost every decent-sized District General Hospital (DGH). Clinical acumen was less necessary, as decision making often centred on which specialised investigation to order first; usually the cheapest. On the other hand, there is no substitute for clinical experience, especially in surgery.

Prior to finals we, the soon-to-be-qualified young doctors, had applied for the various house officer posts in the region. It was generally accepted that the Liverpool Royal Infirmary consultants had already made their choices from the students who were attached to their own firms and the further you went from the centre, the less prestigious the post, and therefore the less likely your career would be fast tracked. Thus, if you worked for the "professor" you would generally have an advantage, even if you had learnt or done absolutely nothing. It was traditional amongst the Percy Street graduates to go to Clatterbridge Hospital on the Wirral, and to this end, the outgoing houseman on a firm already there would arrange for the prospective new houseman to do his week's holiday locum as a student, just to get to know the routine of the jobs, the layout of the hospital and where the hospital actually was, as well as the peccadilloes of the bosses. I had done a seven-day locum (paid, eventually) with two medical consultants. Occasionally a Percy Street graduate would get a more prestigious post, but this was certainly the exception rather than the rule. Working in a peripheral DGH had its advantages, as the consultants were all generalists with a subspecialty and the clinical work and thus, the experience obtained, was huge.

CHAPTER 5

Undescended Testicle

Clatterbridge Hospital, 1973

With finals over, we had a nerve-racking wait for the results. No plans could be made for the summer, as it might have to be spent hitting the books again. On 14th July 1973, I was admitted to the degrees of Bachelor of Medicine and Bachelor of Surgery. I became Doctor D S Jackson MB ChB, now a person of substance and responsibility, the transition having been made in the time it took to find my name on the list pinned to the Medical School notice board. Social class 5 to social class 1 in 20 seconds.

I was chuffed to bits; it had taken me six years to rise to the very bottom of the medical ladder, but my pride was tinged with sadness. My father would attend my degree presentation, but he expressly forbade my mother and my grandfather, whom he now hated, from being present. I hired the cap and gown, marched up and shook the Medical Dean's hand at the appropriate moment, got some photos taken to mark the occasion and went for an early supper with my father. Perhaps I am being unkind, but he seemed to be more proud of his newly-acquired Audi 200 than his son's achievement.

During supper we discussed his prostate, which was troubling him, and he patronisingly explained to me that I would get to know all about the prostate as I progressed in my career, as it was unlikely that I knew anything about it yet. Despite his condescending manner, he was right in a way, as I did a few open prostatectomies later during my career. However, I wish that I could go back in time with the knowledge I have since acquired and rip his out there and then on the bloody restaurant table, as I was so angry with the way he had treated my mother and his father. At the end of the meal he paid up, said goodbye, with a muttered "Well done" and left to drive back to his fancy woman, my mother's namesake, the other Clarice.

My surgical consultants would be Mr Raphael Marcus and Mr W B Ashby. This firm would provide me with the clinical surgical experience I wanted. It was by far the busiest firm in the hospital as Mr Marcus was a complete workaholic, his only interests really being surgery and some surgical research. He was never off-call as such, and would phone the duty house officer, generally me, at all hours of the night to enquire after the wellbeing of some or all of his patients, whilst sipping a whisky, which was his tipple. The local police knew better than to stop Mr Marcus if he was driving to a surgical emergency, no matter how much he had had to drink. If I was not on call, but still around in the hospital, Mr Marcus would insist on speaking to me regardless. I can remember being phoned many times in the early hours of the morning and trying to give some sort of coherent update on a patient that I had last seen about 10 beers ago. It did teach me one thing, and that was the concept of care and responsibility for one's patients always, no matter what. Even if you were out of the country and had devolved care to a colleague, the clinical responsibility as the consultant remained yours, and even when retired, complaints from patients whose cases had not gone to plan could be raised, as I was to find out many years later.

Mr Ashby was the better technical surgeon, but he was overshadowed by Mr Marcus, who had lots of referrals from the local GPs, as he had a reputation for getting things done, or their patients done, or even done in. Mr Marcus and Mr Ashby did not get on at all and Mr Marcus had quite a temper, with a recent heart attack to add to it. Thus, if Mr Marcus came on the ward whilst Mr Ashby was doing a ward round, he was abandoned whilst Marcus's requirements were met. Mr Ashby lived in North Wales and brewed beer a lot.

There was another slight problem. The firm, in addition to the two consultants, consisted of a senior house officer (SHO) called Dr Singh, who was from India, a Surgical Registrar called Mr Shah, who was from Pakistan, as well as the two house Officers, Dr Simon Lewin and me. Shah was a high caste Pakistani and Singh was a low caste Indian, and Shah would not interact with Singh directly. They were on call separately with one of us house officers, but during the day, Shah would only communicate with Singh through an intermediary, usually either Simon or me, along the lines of "Dr Jackson, please tell Dr Singh to…"

The situation was manageable, but the farce of this all came to a head when Shah's wife came to visit him from Pakistan and he would reconnoitre anywhere she and Singh were likely to meet, such as the doctors' dining room, to make sure Singh was not around to look at his wife, as that was a cultural no-no. I had little time for all of this, as I felt the practise of medicine should not be influenced by religion, culture or ideology, but this was the early 1970s. Does it still happen today? One hospital where I worked employed an Iraqi locum registrar from Baghdad. He would demand that the nursing staff on my ward round always walked behind him, and he was rude and dismissive of the scrub nurses in my operating theatre.

My contract of employment stipulated that I was in a compulsory resident post with free board and lodgings. I would work every weekday and be on call on alternate days, nights and weekends. This amounted to about 104 hours out of the available 168 hours in a week. Any hours worked beyond those contracted would attract a payment of one third time (not time and a third), provided at least four hours had been worked and the payment was authorised by the responsible consultant. Of course, this was never asked for, because of the possibility of receiving a bad reference, and in any event, would never have been sanctioned. In 2003 the European Working Time Directive came into play, limiting the working week to 48 hours with specified rest periods, The Government and NHS managers went into collective collapse.

My annual salary would have been around £1200, or £100 per month after deductions of income tax, National Insurance and pension payments, which worked out at around 25 pence/hour (decimal currency having arrived in the UK in 1971). As a student I had managed to survive on £10 per week and with £25 per week in my bank I considered myself rich, and what's more I had no time to spend any of it. When I wasn't working, I was sleeping, and when I wasn't sleeping I was working.

Though there were emergencies at night requiring admission and urgent surgery by the middle grade surgeons, or rarely the consultant, many of the night calls to the house officer involved prescribing night sedation to the inpatients who could not sleep. In those days, the night nursing staff could not act on a telephone prescription by the house officer and therefore he, or she, had to attend in person to prescribe and sign up even the most innocuous of sedatives. This resulted in the patient enjoying a drug-induced sleep, whilst the fuming house officer inwardly ranted and raved against the system until he or she eventually fell into a comatose sleep, at what seemed like one minute before having to get up again to start the next day's work.

Marcus phoned me up one night to ask how a female patient was. On the operating list that morning he had removed her gall bladder after a Teutonic struggle, with much blood loss and a bit of liver damage. I had been called to attend her as she was short of breath with a little bit of chest pain. The most obvious conclusions were that she had suffered a heart attack or a pulmonary embolism (clot on the lungs). I explained to Mr Marcus that I had asked for an electrocardiogram (ECG, heart test) and a chest X-ray and I could find no evidence of either occurrence, so I had just prescribed some light sedation to help her through the night. There was a slight and ominous pause from Mr Marcus and then he exploded. "She's bloody dead!" he yelled and slammed the phone down.

Mr Marcus was Jewish and had an irritating adenoidal tone of voice, especially noticeable when he was in a foul mood, which he was with me the next day. However, even our eminent medical colleagues could find no evidence on the ECG and Chest X-ray of the pulmonary embolism which they all agreed, in their wisdom, had killed the patient, and therefore I was exonerated. In any event, there probably would have been nothing to be done. Postoperative pulmonary embolism was more prevalent in those days, when modern preventative strategies were not routinely used, and it will feature more than once in this memoir.

The patient underwent a post mortem, which revealed she had actually died of a heart attack. When the physicians, those with huge brains and limited treatment options, had a closer look at the ECG, they agreed that there was evidence of a heart attack in the tracings, too subtle for an inexperienced house surgeon to spot (or themselves, first time around until their critical reading of the ECG improved with the benefit of the post mortem diagnosis).

I was not sure how well I was getting on with Mr Marcus, but I was reliably informed by the nursing staff that if he liked one of his house surgeons, at some stage he would compare their qualities and capabilities to those of an undescended testicle. This was the term of endearment he used for a house surgeon whom he considered good enough and tough enough to be derided by him, without committing ritual suicide, i.e. not a snowflake, in today's vernacular.

Sometime later, on a ward round, when I was a mere minute late, having been tied up admitting a patient through A & E, Mr Marcus greeted me with these welcome words. "Jackson, you're always late, you are no bloody good where you are, and you are no bloody good when you get to where you should be. You are about as much use as an undescended testicle". I was thrilled. I had received the highest accolade of my career so far. Later, as a trainee and then consultant surgeon, I was to re-site hundreds of little testicles, as paediatric general surgery became part of my repertoire. During these procedures whilst I was operating, the theatre scrub nurse or my assistant, would often ask me what I was chuckling about, as I recalled Mr Marcus's description of me.

Mr Marcus was not very tall, not much more than about 5 feet 6 inches, if I'm kind, and both Simon Lewin, the other house surgeon and I were well over six feet. This made assisting in theatre very uncomfortable and required us to hold retractors and other instruments at waist level whilst Mr Marcus ceremoniously excised a diseased organ, usually managing to deprive the patient of half of his or her blood volume in the process. Once during a difficult stomach operation, Mr Marcus had been standing on a foot stool in front of me, whilst I held retractors around either side of him. It was an excruciatingly difficult position to maintain. I gritted my teeth and tried to amuse myself by counting the blackheads on the back of his neck. At the end of the operation I walked away from the operating table with my arms outstretched and fixed apart like the horns of a Highland bull.

During these six months I was taught how to perform an appendicectomy and undertook around 20 of them. It was not that unusual at the time for house surgeons to do this and as I had professed my aspirations for a surgical career, I was encouraged to develop "surgical hands" by practising the various methods of dissection and other surgical techniques. It is lifelong learning.

Mr Marcus will reappear in my memoires a little later, but before I leave him, I will relate the time he brought his son Sammy into the operating theatre. Sammy had started medical school, or was just about to start, and was to receive a taste of what his father did for a living (turning live patients into moribund ones). I was introduced to mini-Marcus and he was exactly as I had expected, thick glasses, small, skinny, with a limp handshake and a voice like his father's. He would never have got into Percy Street, or survived if by some miracle he had.

The next case arrived. "Jackson, get scrubbed!" barked Marcus. I prepped and gowned the patient, while Sammy and his father chatted together and then I watched as Marcus supervised his son scrubbing up, with an unheard of and nauseating benevolence, whilst little fucking Sammy violated all the principles and techniques of acquiring and maintaining sterility. If I had scrubbed up like that, Marcus would have cut my (undescended) balls off.

"Well done Sammy" he said in encouraging tones. "Now come and join Daddy at the table". 'Team Marcus' sauntered into the theatre like surgical royalty. With Sammy at his side, Marcus made the incision and I started to dab away the blood, as I had done many times before, but no, Marcus wanted his son to do it, so I was rebuffed. Sammy tentatively wiped a swab across the wound, obscuring the whole surgical field of view in the process, and looked as if he was about to faint. God, I wished he had. "Now Sammy" Marcus said patiently, "just hold this retractor here so I can see what I am doing", and then to me he snapped, "Jackson, put your retractor in and hold the bowel out of the way. Not there, there" and he moved my retractor about an eighth of an inch to make his point. Sammy's retractor could have been on the moon for all the good it was doing. "Sammy", his father said gently, "let me get you into a better position". Marcus moved his son's retractor about six bloody inches. "Can you see Sammy?" he asked, and then to me "Jackson, adjust the light so Sammy and I can see!" The table was at its lowest to accommodate the vertically challenged father and son, and my lower back had started to seriously ache.

Marcus continued to mollycoddle Sammy, who could do no wrong, in contrast to berating me, who could do no right. By the end of the procedure I was mentally sticking cocktail sticks into their eyes. Marcus told me to close the skin and left the table with his arm around Sammy's shoulders for a freshly-made pot of tea before driving back to 'Marcusland', somewhere on the Wirral. I went to the doctors' mess and drowned my homicidal thoughts in Guinness. Next day my affability rating was back to normal, but thanks to Team Marcus, I had a life-threatening hangover.

At the end of six months with Mr Marcus and Mr Ashby, I had a week's leave before I started my medical job with Drs Robinson and Aitken in General Medicine and Geriatrics, but I hung around the doctors' mess, as there was nowhere I really wanted to go to.

Dr Robinson was a tall angular man, whom I only saw once a week on his ward round. These were interminable affairs when I presented new patients and the progress, if any, of the old ones which were then up for discussion between Dr Robinson and his registrar. Medical registrars are an odd species, sharing few traits of normality with their medical colleagues outwith their speciality. They were desperate readers of books and journals and painstakingly memorised rare and implausible diseases with which to impress the boss on a ward round, rather than consider the more common and obvious diagnoses afflicting patient populations. I was usually mute during these drawn-out discussions. Most of the time I did not have the faintest idea what they were talking about. Dr Robinson would always enter some sort of conclusion, or treatment plan, in the patient's case notes himself, using an ink pen with a nib about a foot wide. On his ward rounds, I was forever handing him extra case sheets, as he only managed to fit about three lines to a page of foolscap. However not many consultants bothered to write in the notes themselves, preferring to leave it to their house officer to record their words of wisdom for posterity. Robinson referred to me as 'Dr... er'. He would not have recognised me in the street.

The other medical consultant, Dr Aitken, specialised in Geriatrics, and like Mr Marcus he was very popular with the GPs. This was because he responded quickly to their requests for a domiciliary visit, admitted their problem elderly patients onto his ward and got them treated and out again, either in a box or into a nursing home, usually the former and normally in record time. In those days it was unfashionable for the elderly incurables, or just plain wornoutables, to die at home.

There was a lucrative spin off to his practice. If a patient who passed away was going to be cremated, then I could sign the first part of the cremation form, which reaped a payment. With a high turnover this could constitute quite a tidy sum of money. 'Crem' form fees (or 'ash cash') were counted as one of the few positive attributes of an otherwise very tedious house officer post in Geriatrics. Did I regard the patients I clerked in for Dr Aitken as potential financial contributors to a new set of wheels? No, I did not. Did the thought ever cross my mind? Possibly, once or twice. In any event I followed Dr Aitken's treatment plans.

The on-call house physician and registrar would each carry the cardiac arrest bleeps. The medical wards (old Nissen huts) were a good 15-minute walk away from the doctors' mess (20 minutes with a hangover), which made all attempts at resuscitation pretty pointless, unless the nursing staff on duty had been trained to perform the pretty brutal cardiac massage as advocated in the early 1970s. This logistical problem was solved by the use of the dedicated medical moped and during my tenure, if the cardiac arrest bleep sounded, my registrar and I would fly out of the mess, mount the bike and wobble dangerously quickly overland to the specified ward, where we would crash to a stop and arrive as merciful medical angels on their coughing, spluttering steed, dispatched to try and almost inevitably fail to prevent a patient from going to the afterlife. We would take over any resuscitation in progress and after about 15 minutes of futile activity, the patient would be pronounced dead at the given time, the porters would be summoned to cart the corpse off to the morgue and we would return to the mess at a more sedate speed. The one positive outcome from this was that a medical bed would now be available, and my boss, Dr Aitken could send in another patient for recycling.

On the one occasion when we did manage to successfully bring a female patient back from the brink, someone pointed out the 'DNR' (Do Not Resuscitate) notice on her case notes. This elderly patient was terminal with irreversible kidney disease, so our efforts were then abandoned, and the patient succumbed as she should have done in the first place, if but several minutes later, with cracked ribs, severe bruising and the inevitable breathing tube in her oesophagus, not her windpipe, as my intubation skills were rudimentary. The moped did not in any way reduce the mortality of cardiac arrests, it just ensured that the whole process was over more quickly.

One Christmas, everyone in the Doctors' Mess got wrecked, except of course the religious fanatics, who were delegated to cover the hospital. An electric ambulance was hijacked from its recharging bay and with all aboard, we went on a tour of the hospital, stopping at each ward to raid the donated alcohol and wish everyone a Merry Christmas. Once back in the ambulance and speeding along, we were flagged down by an old man who was limping quite badly, having injured one of his feet. He was trying to find A & E. I stopped the ambulance, gave him directions and took off again, unfortunately running over his good foot in the process. The ambulance (where of course the blame lay) had rendered this poor old man immobile, so I reversed the vehicle, loaded him on board and deposited him in A & E. The ambulance was quickly returned, reconnected to its electrical supply and all the surfaces were wiped clean to eliminate any obvious evidence, like fingerprints, especially mine on the steering wheel. We were back in the mess listening to carols on the TV when the inevitable phone call arrived, at which point the accusations were firmly denied.

There was a partially heated swimming pool in the grounds of the hospital. Of course, it was locked at night, but that was no barrier to midnight skinny dipping. One night there were four of us house officers with some nurses, just noisily enjoying ourselves, though with the presence of the nurses bathing costumes or underpants were in order, not only to save their blushes, but also ours as the water was not warm enough to stave off penile shrinkage. At that time there was no hospital security to speak of, and if there was a security guard on duty, he spent his time in the hospital avoiding being called by not answering his bleep and conveniently claiming to be on patrol at any given moment. No, in reality, the security was provided by the local police if it was needed and it wasn't long before our frolics in the pool were interrupted by a local policeman. "'Ello, 'ello, 'ello, what's goin' on 'ere then?" By this time the girls had scarpered back to the nursing home to sneak back in, having seriously broken their curfew.

The police had received a report that vandals had wandered into the hospital, broken into the swimming pool and were disturbing the patients, many of whom were desperately ill. This last bit of information had stirred the conscience of the usually indifferent plod, and a patrol had been dispatched to apprehend the criminals. We were ordered out of the pool and asked who we were. I replied shivering beneath a hospital towel the size of a postage stamp and with the consistency of fine grade sandpaper. I told him that we were all hospital staff, indeed we were doctors. "Show me some ID then. How do I know youse are who you say youse are?" said the copper. We had no means of identifying ourselves. Who goes swimming with their IDs around their necks? I explained, again at great length, that we were employees of the hospital and were perfectly entitled to unlock (break the lock of) the swimming pool for our use. The copper was unmoved. "If youse are fuckin' doctors, and you don't look like it to me, then who can identify you?" It was well past midnight, but I had a brainwave. "The switchboard operator", I replied.

We were marched, dripping pool water everywhere, to the switchboard office. The night duty operator was busy knitting and the ineffective security guard was asleep in a chair. "Can you identify these persons?" the copper asked the operator. "They say they are, er, 'doctors' and they claim they all work 'ere". "No" she said unequivocally, "I have never seen them before". "Aha!" The copper nodded and produced a self-satisfied and knowing smile. His instincts had been correct and four arrests in one night should get him a commendation.

There had to be a reason why we, the doctors of the hospital, could not be identified, and then it came to me. The switchboard operator had never actually seen us, just heard our voices on the phone. I suggested this was the reason and asked if we could phone in from an adjoining office, and the switchboard operator could then identify us from our voices. It went perfectly. As soon as she heard my voice, she identified me. "That's Doctor Jackson" she asserted, "works for Dr Aitken". The smug expression slid from the copper's face. I went back into her office and all my colleagues were identified in the same manner. Thank goodness for good old-fashioned voice recognition technology. We were in the clear, but the copper gave us a bollocking anyway, to hide his disappointment, and returned to his duties. The security guard was still asleep.

I had been signed up by all the supervising consultants of my house jobs and my registration with the GMC (the organisation that protects patients and persecutes doctors) had been converted from provisional to full registration, making me street legal. I was to subscribe reluctantly to the GMC for forty years. It was like that other tax, paid to the BBC. If you didn't subscribe to the GMC you could not practise medicine, and if you did not subscribe to the BBC, you could not watch television. As I sit here typing this, I do not subscribe to either of them.

I had to consider my next post, and for some extraordinary reason I thought I might apply for Mr Marcus's SHO post. He was a known quantity, and if he refrained from introducing me to any more of his children, I would stand a good chance of keeping my hands off his neck and learn some surgery. I must have developed Stockholm Syndrome.

During my house year in Clatterbridge, I met Linda Williams, who was the junior nursing sister on two other surgical wards, run by another two surgical consultants. We got on well and went out together for a considerable time. It was then that I decided to spend my two weeks annual leave on a trip to Morocco with her and two others, Alan Harris (from my Liverpool days) and his long-term girlfriend Cindy, and soon four of us were planning the trip.

By now I had my grandfather's MG 1100, which he had left to me in his will, though he wasn't dead at that point. However, he couldn't drive any more, and it was pointless leaving it unused in a garage. I had a towbar fitted and scrounged the family trailer tent, which had been unused for years, except as a place for my father to sleep in the garden of our house in Abingdon, when he and my mother no longer slept together and prior to his moving to Kennington with his fancy woman. We bought a two-man tent for Alan and Cindy and a few cooking utensils and went for a dummy run with everything packed, to see if the car could handle the load. It couldn't, there was absolutely no way. We needed much more power, and anyway the clutch broke.

Dr Keith Parkes, a couple of years ahead of me in the junior doctor hierarchy, and his similarly qualified wife, had decided to go "off-piste" for a couple of years and they had applied for and got jobs as medical officers on the remote island of Tristan da Cunha, in the mid-Atlantic. Tristan da Cunha is part of the British Overseas Territory, which also includes St Helena, where Napoleon was exiled until his death, and Ascension Island, which was used as a staging post for British ships and aircraft during the Falkland Islands War. Ascension Island was just a volcanic rock with the official worst golf course in the world and was rumoured to be where the Americans had tested their moon buggy[9]. Anyway, the point of this digression is that Keith Parkes needed to sell his 2-litre Triumph Vitesse convertible, which would suit our purposes admirably, so I bought it, later selling my MG

---

9. https://en.wikipedia.org/wiki/Tristan da Cunha

1100 to my bank manager (Midland Bank, now HSBC – having been with them since 1967, I am nothing if not loyal).

Our plans were not complicated. Drive to Dover, catch the cross-channel ferry to somewhere in France, drive through France using the camp sites on our Michelin map, then through Spain to Algeciras and cross by ferry to Ceuta, then into Morocco and try to get to Marrakesh before returning. 'How hard could it be?' to quote Jeremy Clarkson, who would have been 14 years old at the time.

Our first problem manifested itself on the roundabout approximately 100 yards from the hospital. The Vitesse had oversize wheels and tyres and with the weight we were carrying, they rubbed on the bodywork of the car, so we needed to change them. Fortunately, Alan and Cindy had bought a Triumph Spitfire a couple of years previously and the wheels were the same size as those on the Vitesse, with a nearly new set of normal-sized tyres on them. We swapped them over and set off again. Our colleagues came to see us off yet again, with shouts of, "have a great trip, see you in 20 minutes". I had taken the precaution of obtaining AA five-star travel cover and have been a member of the AA ever since 1973 (loyalty again, or just too lazy to cancel the direct debit). I have probably never made a wiser decision, before or after, regarding my motoring career.

Our journey was completely uneventful for all of about three hours, after which time I noticed a noise coming from the engine, the sort that sounded like it could be very expensive if you didn't do something about it. When I looked under the bonnet in a lay-by about 50 miles outside Dover, I could see and hear that it was coming from the tappets, the parts responsible for opening and closing the valves in the engine and vital to travel. I called the AA, and the excellent AA man found that an oil feed screw had come loose. He retrieved it and refitted it, so that the oil-starved tappets were now lubricated in the way that the engine manufacturers had intended.

We were too late to catch the ferry, so Alan was dispatched to inform the ferry company from a public telephone box (mobile phones were at least 20 years away at that stage) and the crossing was rearranged for the next morning. We spent the night in the lay-by, and next morning I drove to the port, where we were loaded on board. The rest of the journey through France and Spain was relatively uneventful, apart from two punctures in the trailer tent tyres, both repaired by artisans in small villages, and then with me gaily setting off driving on the left hand side of the road for a short period of time, whilst the rest of France drove on the right.

Travel through southern Spain was too hot to have the car hood down, and to compound this, the engine temperature was above normal, such that not only did the hood have to remain up, but I had to put the heater on to aid the engine cooling. Alan and I roasted in the front and the girls gently broiled in the back. We carried water, but often we would stop in a small town and drink the local bar dry. If we were on the coast road, then a cool dip in the Mediterranean kept us going.

At the end of the fourth day we arrived in Algeciras, dirty, dusty and knackered. We found the ferry booking office and booked our crossing, found a campsite and crashed out after eating something unrecognisable with *patatas fritas* in a local restaurant. In the morning I checked the car over. It was fine and I had no worries about it, but I was not to know that the nearside rear wheel bearing was pretty much on its last legs. It was just a matter of time before it collapsed and when it did, it couldn't have been at a more inconvenient moment.

We crossed from Algeciras to Ceuta next day into Tangiers and ate some Moroccan food at a street stall, which was composed of oily lamb and couscous, with a whole load of herbs added to it, giving it a very odd taste to my mind. Driving through Tangiers, we were continually preyed on by locals wanting to sell us tourist paraphernalia. We did go to a couple of Aladdin's cave-like places, where I bought a silver curved ceremonial Berber dagger, after protracted bargaining, all the while worried that my car was being dismantled and sold for spares on the black market. The dagger wasn't silver, but both the vendor and I knew that. Next, we traversed the Rif Mountains down to Fez. The views were spectacular, but Fez wasn't. It just seemed full of wailing noises and Morocco's poor.

Moroccans can speak some French as well as Arabic, so we did manage to communicate with the locals, but they were always wanting to sell us something, even their daughters, or offering camels in exchange for Cindy, or Linda, as both had blonde hair; an apparently irresistible feature for a male Moroccan Muslim.

From Fez we drove west to the coast road and stopped at a beach in Mohammedia for a swim and cool down. When we were walking down to the sea, Alan started muttering to himself and began to wander off. He seemed very confused, and in a flash, I had my doctor's hat on and diagnosed heat stroke and dehydration. We got some water, which he would not drink, so we cooled him down by immersing him forcibly in the Atlantic Ocean until he was sufficiently normal and docile to drink some water and recover. We had water-boarded him into acquiescence, without any help from the Americans.

Back on the coast road, driving south towards Casablanca, the wheel bearing on the car finally gave up and the half shaft broke. We were in the middle of nowhere, but with the selflessness of a born leader, I volunteered to try and hitch hike to Casablanca and safety, taking Linda with me and leaving poor Alan and Cindy to guard our possessions in the heat. We left them some water and some cardboard-like sandwiches for sustenance and pointed out some shade. We promised to be back as soon as we could.

Fortunately we quickly managed to get a lift and were able to phone the AA travel helpline, who contacted the local Jaguar Rover Triumph garage (yes there was such a thing in Casablanca), and pretty soon we were in the back of their breakdown Land Rover with one of their drivers and a mechanic, heading at breakneck speed to the area in the trees where we had abandoned Alan and Cindy.

The Land Rover had seen better days. It now had to carry six passengers and tow my car with the trailer tent attached, after the broken half shaft had been removed. It struggled, but we made it back to the garage. It was going to take two or three days to get the parts and repair the car, so we had hotel accommodation courtesy of the AA, with meals included, and if the truth be told, this delay to our goal of reaching Marrakesh was most welcome. We vaguely explored Casablanca until the car was ready. I signed over the equivalent Swiss franc vouchers (AA supplied), for the car repair bill, which was in dirhams, and as we departed, we were waved off by the obsequious garage manager. However, we would no longer have enough time to get to Marrakesh, so we decided to go home. This should have been the end of it, but it wasn't.

We were back in the Rif Mountains returning to Tangier and following a battered and dented old lorry, laboriously climbing up the road, which was quite steep. My car was dangerously overheating again, in spite of the heater being on full blast, so I resolved to overtake the lorry. I hit the horn and pulled out when the road was clear, but just as I was alongside the lorry, the driver swerved over towards us to avoid a ditch. I slammed the car into first gear and surged forward, but not enough. The lorry clipped the side of the trailer tent, tearing the fibre glass on one side. I was furious, as the driver could have easily slowed down as we were passing. We were once again in the middle of nowhere. I stopped. The lorry stopped. The very large, fat driver only spoke Arabic and my yelling at him had no effect. He just kept pointing to the tiny dent on his front mudguard, the smallest of dents, on a lorry which was smothered in dents.

I had to get some sort of European accident form signed and whilst I was doing so, I noticed that this deserted part of Morocco, was now teeming with curious villagers, complete with camels, chickens and donkeys, who had appeared from nowhere. I told Alan to try and prevent the many inquisitive hands, from 'exploring' and then nicking our possessions from the trailer tent, through the gaping hole in the side. I went back towards the lorry, wondering how I could get the retarded driver to sign the form, probably a fingerprint in his own blood. At that point, fortunately, I was relieved to see that another car, which had been following the lorry, pulled up and the driver asked us, in perfect 'Franglais', if he could help.

I asked the him if he could explain to the gorilla of a driver that he had wrecked my trailer and ask him to fill in the accident form, or whatever, acknowledging guilt. I was not prepared for his reply, the gist of which, was, "I am the owner of the lorry and the man you called a gorilla is one of my drivers. I was behind the lorry and saw you do a dangerous overtaking manoeuvre and damage my lorry and the wing mirror of my lorry has been broken".

This was absurd. The wing mirror was a good two feet above the height of the trailer tent. Any further discussion was futile, so we patched up the hole in the trailer tent with some bungees and went on our way, pretty convinced that in spite of Alan's valiant efforts, some of our clothing had new Moroccan owners.

The rest of the trip was without incident. On my return to the UK, I abandoned the trailer tent and had to get the Vitesse into the garage as the new bearing was making a noise again. I was not surprised to be informed that the bearing replaced in Casablanca was either the wrong one, or an old one. At least the half shaft looked new.

I discussed my application for Mr Marcus's SHO post in surgery with him. He seemed agreeable, so I applied and was appointed. I had a vague idea of what I would be in for and in truth, Mr Marcus was very good to me. I don't think he had ever had a white SHO before, which gave him some sort of bragging rights. In 1974, a home-grown member of the surgical team between house officer and consultant was a rarity in a district general hospital.

An appendix/laparotomy was a frequent procedure undertaken as an excuse to explore the abdomen for the unidentifiable cause of severe symptoms. Taking the appendix en route if nothing was found was a means of lessening the impact of a negative laparotomy. Throughout my early surgical career, I did many of these, always remembering Mr Marcus's wise caveat; "Jackson, never open an abdomen if you can't deal with anything you find, unless you have access to someone who can". On the other hand surgeons must learn when not to operate, and though many decisions are far from clear cut, in the following case I had thought it was a no brainer.

An old lady had been found in her house several hours after having collapsed in her chair. She had fallen forward, obstructing the blood supply to her legs, which were then unsalvageable. Her only slim chance of survival required amputation of both legs above the knee, done in one go. Marcus elected to operate and give her that chance of survival, but she succumbed a few hours later. I thought that the better option would have been to let her pass peacefully with plenty of morphine or heroin on board, rather than indulge in surgical heroics, but I was wise after the event and mine was the opinion of a surgical tadpole. Without intensive care, specialised anaesthetists and informative investigations, the abilities and the decision-making of surgeons were often sorely taxed, as I would find out later in my own career.

This case was discussed in the doctors' mess, and most agreed that it was the wrong decision, apart from one of our staff members, who said, "He probably did it to reduce her funeral costs". Bemused by his remark, we asked for an explanation. "Well", he said, "with both her legs gone, she would only need a child-sized coffin". Sick humour often relieves the tensions of the day, and is rampant behind closed doors amongst junior doctors.

The orthopaedic middle-grade surgeons won my respect and that of the doctors' mess, due to the following case mismanagement. The patient in question had fallen and broken her neck of femur on the right side; essentially, but not anatomically, the hip joint. The standard treatment at the time was to reduce the fracture using a special operating table that could pull the corresponding leg out and twist it into position, and when the anatomical alignment was correct, confirmed by X-rays, firmly fix the fracture in place using a metal fixation device, generally a McLoughlin pin and plate.

The patient was clerked. An orthopaedic clerking is pretty truncated, just details of name and approximate age, and any examination would be solely to confirm that the patient had a heartbeat and at least one lung. Consent would be obtained with a limited explanation of the procedure, because the junior doctor doing all this had no idea of what the operation entailed, and even if he did, there was absolutely no chance that the patient would be any the wiser, after precious time had been wasted in a prolonged discussion.

Everything went quite smoothly. The patient was anaesthetised and with plenty of muscle relaxant on board, the leg was stretched in the apparatus and the fracture accurately reduced by rotating the foot inwards. X-rays were taken and examined, but there was no need for any adjustment; the displaced fracture had been reduced so perfectly that the fracture line had all but disappeared – in fact it couldn't be seen at all. Without more ado, an incision was made, the pin and plate were introduced and bolted together and the wound was closed. Pretty damn slick. The X-ray technician was recalled to theatre with his portable machine and check X-rays were taken and returned. The

X-rays were fine. They showed a perfect reduction and fixation, but with just one slight problem. The X-ray marking was LEFT. The fracture was on the RIGHT.

There was no option but to repeat the procedure on the other side, where the fracture could not be so perfectly reduced, due to the fact that there actually was one. Anyway, the patient woke up on the ward with both hips fixed as it were, and obviously a bit puzzled. An explanation was due, followed by a confession of the mistake, contrition, pleas for forgiveness, lessons will be learned and all that stuff, but far from it, our orthopods were more inventive than that.

"Good morning Mrs 'Smith' said the registrar.

"Mornin' doctor".

"How do you feel?" asked the registrar.

"I'm orright, but me good 'ip hurts" said the patient.

"Yes, well I need to talk to you about that," said the registrar.

"Wha' about it?" asked the patient.

"Well" said the registrar, "when we did your broken hip on the right, we noticed that your bones were very fragile. We made a decision, without waking you up and asking for your permission, to fix the other side as well, just in case you fell again and broke the other hip".

"Ta very much doctor" said the patient, "tha's very good of youse, I'm very grateful. When can I 'ave a fag? I'm bloody gaspin'."

Occasionally, but not often, orthopaedic surgeons can be inspired with genius. They now had a very satisfied customer, who thought her treatment had been excellent.

I gained a lot of experience in this job, but I felt that if I did not leave Liverpool at that point, I would never leave, and I had other things I wanted to do.

CHAPTER 6

Avoiding Effluent

Battle Hospital, Reading, 1974

Leaving Liverpool was an enormous wrench as I had been there nearly eight years and had had a fantastic time, some great adventures, and some wonderful relationships with my co-students, co-doctors and girlfriends, but there was more to life to explore than Merseyside. I needed experience in A & E, and where better to apply than at a hospital called The Battle, in Reading. It took in the casualties from drug abuse, those overdosing or users, or both, alcohol-related incidents, also both, domestic accidents, domestic violence, and accidental falls. We treated criminals, football hooligans and vandals. We dealt with the broken remains of the dead, or the just about to die, or the only just alive who would survive and those unscathed but in shock, retrieved from a long section of the M4 killing fields.

Other medical emergencies included children who had stuffed beads and other objects into their noses, ears and anuses and adults who just confined themselves to their anuses. There were those patients who were too lazy to see their GPs but would happily wait several hours in A & E. Frequently, after a two-minute consultation with a Casualty Officer who didn't look old enough to shave, they would be instructed to consult their GP in the morning. This led to huge arguments, resulting in the hospital porters or police, or both, being called.

I was appointed to the job without an interview. I like to think that it was due to the excellent references I had been given, but when I started working, I realised that nobody else in their right mind would do battle in The Battle. The fact that someone had applied for the job who spoke fluent English with a good old Anglo-Saxon surname must have put the hospital management into a frenzy of anticipation of my arrival.

The A & E department of the Battle Hospital was my first war zone. The shifts I worked were endless, though each A & E post rotated every six weeks with an orthopaedic SHO job, which was a sort of recovery period. I worked for a Mr C M Squire.

In addition to dealing with the routine injured, the duty Casualty Officer had to reduce simple limb fractures on a short-day case operating list, morning and evening. There were no consultants or registrars around, so the porter, who took the X-rays to check the reduction on a portable machine, would give some advice as to which direction in which to pull, bend, or twist the limb to get some form of anatomical correction. This was not as bad as it sounds, as the patients whose limbs were still at a nauseating angle, or whose broken bone ends were nowhere near each other, or those whose dislocated joints remained dislocated, were more skilfully treated at a fracture clinic the following day.

I have mentioned Annie and Sheila, who both left Liverpool around the same time as me to retrain as air stewardesses for British Airways, and I saw a lot of them as they rented a house near Slough. They introduced me to Beverley-Ann Wild, an ex-model, and an air stewardess when I met her, working in the first-class cabins of the jumbo jets and doing mainly long-haul flights. She was tall, slim and blonde, with a lovely nature, and our romance flourished. We decided to get married and did so in 1977, but it was the wrong decision, for both of us.

I was gaining lots of experience in Trauma and Orthopaedics, managing the severely injured, though the work itself could be tiring and tedious. I would often get little sleep for days on end, which sorely tested my vocation. Typically, I would return to my flat in the early hours of the morning only to be called 10 minutes later and woken from a deep sleep. I would then return, zombie like, to the Casualty Department. This was at the time when all patients presenting at A & E had to be seen by the doctor before discharge. Nowadays specialist nurses can handle most of the cases, so the A & E senior house officers can get all the beauty sleep they need; they don't know they are born!

I got a phone call from my father out of the blue asking me to meet him at a local pub. I had no idea what this was about, but agreed to meet him, nonetheless. I arrived at the pub in my newly-purchased Austin Healey 3000, a car I had always hankered after, to find him already there nursing a half pint of beer. It would have been nice if he could have greeted me with a cheery "Nice to see you", but instead, the first thing he said to me was along the lines of, "You should not be driving around in a car like that, you are an inexperienced driver and the car is far too powerful for you". He hadn't changed.

We chatted about inconsequential stuff for a short time and then he told me that he and my mother were getting divorced, which wasn't really a surprise and without further ado, he then got up, said goodbye and simply left; I never saw or heard from him again, but later learnt he had moved to France, where he died. How would I summarise my relationship with my father? It was distant, but notwithstanding his major gambling addiction, he did his best. I know he had a great affection for me and was proud of me; he just had difficulty showing it, though he had no difficulty in showing his affection for the family boxer dog, Sheba. He did however teach me a lot about self-reliance, mainly through neglect and determination, which I had in spades. Did I hate him? No. Did I regret being his son? No.

Back to the Battle. I remember a particular young man who, whilst completely drunk, had been involved in a road traffic accident and suffered a head injury. He was rude and obnoxious and halfway through my examination of him, he deposited a semi-digested madras curry all over the nearby sterile trolley. I was quite nimble at the time and avoided most of the effluent, though the nurse next to me did not, which made me furious. I would warn everybody who needs it to never deal with a patient in an angry frame of mind, because it does cloud your judgement.

This man's skull X-rays were normal, and I was just on the verge of discharging him to sleep it off when a warning bell ran in my angry brain. Was his obnoxiousness due to alcohol or to cerebral irritability following a closed head injury? As it was, I took the right decision and admitted the young man to the wards for neurological observations. Sensibly I followed the precautionary principle, which usually resulted in the drunken patient having a comfortable bed for the night and being discharged the next day, but not in this case. He suddenly became unrousable, with signs of raised intracranial pressure, and despite emergency surgery, where his skull was opened to relieve the pressure by removing blood and clots, he never recovered consciousness and died.

His parents were naturally upset, and the hospital received a solicitor's letter on their behalf. At that time, before the NHS indemnified its staff, every doctor joined a medical defence society and, in all cases where a complaint was lodged, the advice was to call them immediately. My Medical Defence Union (MDU) adviser said that there was no case to answer, and the parents were eventually satisfied with condolences, but a denial of responsibility. The outcome could have been very different for me had I discharged him. That would have verged on negligence. What could have happened if I had allowed my emotion to cloud my judgement troubles me to this day. It was a valuable lesson learnt, and when as a consultant I looked after head-injured patients, including my wife many years later, I always emphasised to my junior doctors that alcohol and a head injury presented a diagnostic dilemma and the two together were a toxic mix.

Luckily the conundrum faced in these circumstances has become more manageable with the advent of emergency CAT scanning. There are many traps for the unwary junior A & E doctor, and these can snare their hapless victims with monotonous regularity. Fortunately, in those days, more hospital beds were available, so the mantra 'if in doubt, admit' was a pretty good one to adopt, but it risked filling the hospital with the walking well, or even limping well, patients with indigestion rather than a perforated stomach ulcer and of course, the totally pissed.

CHAPTER 7

Sloan/Stansfield

Heatherwood, Ascot & Harefield, 1976

So, having had enough of the Battle Hospital and A & E and having gained a lot of experience in the process, I applied for a Surgery in General rotation, which would give me some experience at registrar grade and in Thoracic Surgery at Harefield Hospital. The base hospital was called Heatherwood, in Ascot. Ascot of course is famous for its racecourse and the week of Royal Ascot in the summer, attended by the Royal family, was the jewel in the crown of the horse-racing fraternity. I remember running around that racecourse on many occasions in the early mornings to keep fit. It was the 16th fence that was a killer.

As Heatherwood was the local hospital, we were on standby for emergencies, and as a result we were issued with free entrance tickets to Royal Ascot, when off duty, but not to the posh areas like the Royal Enclosure. We were ready for the influx of broken jump jockeys and other disasters, but the only casualties I remember being called to, were an old boy who was drunk on champagne and brandy and choked on a quail's egg from his Fortnum and Mason picnic hamper, with various gastric juices dribbling down the front of his morning suit and an old dear, at least a Duchess I would presume, who had collapsed with excitement when the horse she had backed came in a winner. Of course she had to be completely checked out to exclude the commoner causes of collapse, like heart attacks, brain haemorrhages, alcohol, diabetes etc before a diagnosis of "nervous exhaustion due to a horse winning a race" could be entertained and then she was sent on her way.

The rotation included another A & E module, but I refused to do it and somehow managed to get the hospital management to agree to allow me to attend a Primary FRCS course in London, in lieu. Not only that, they agreed that I could have free accommodation; they would cover the cost of the course and I would still be paid. How I wangled that lot, I don't know.

The course was known as 'Sloan/Stansfield' after the two elderly medical men who had conceived and then ran it and the examination success rate of those who attended and worked hard was relatively high. Sloan was a retired professor of physiology and Stansfield a retired anatomist. I had already had a shot at the primary FRCS at the Royal College of Surgeons in London, a 'sighter' as it were, and the questions and my performance in the examination made it quite obvious to me that I was going to need a lot of tuition and an intense uninterrupted period of hitting the books.

The Sloan/Stansfield course was held in Caxton Hall, Westminster, not far from New Scotland Yard on Wednesday evenings and Saturday mornings. The course would last three months, and I attended around August 1977. How do I remember? Well, I was on the course studying in the accommodation I had been given, reading R J Last's book *Regional and Applied Human Anatomy* in the bath, when Beverley, who was there at the time, told me that Elvis Presley had embarrassingly died whilst on the loo. Going to the loo can be dangerous, as it has been reported that there is an association between having a dump and fatal pulmonary embolus, and I remember a middle-aged female patient of mine, who three or four days following her operation did exactly that; she went to the loo and never came out again – well, not of her own volition that is. It was very sad. I will write still more about fatal pulmonary emboli.

I passed my Primary FRCS in Glasgow (the college recommended by Sloan and Stansfield). I had been nauseatingly knowledgeable and apparently nearly got the anatomy prize (missed by one mark). The Professor of Anatomy examined me in the viva and I had been told, "If he asks you about the ossification centres of the bones of the skull, then you have passed and he is looking to try and get you a distinction". The professor's first question was about the ossification of the sphenoid bone – in the skull. I started out, "There are two ossification centres in the sphenoid bone…. blah blah blah", and continued in that vein until I thought he had had enough. "All right" he said and waved me over to his co-examiner, who was a young consultant surgeon standing by a cadaver.

He pointed inside the abdomen and asked, "What is that?"

"That", I said, "is the splenic notch". "Hmm" he said, "that was actually the answer to my second question. The answer to my first question was spleen. Well done. What do you know about the spleen?" I was about to say pretty much everything, thanks to Professor Sloan and Dr Stansfield, but I held back and gave him both barrels of my knowledge slowly and kindly, so as not to overawe him. We moved down the cadaver to the knee joint. "Tell me about the knee joint". This time, I let him have it, and it was obvious that his surgical interest did not really include joints.

After a pause he said, "I suppose you know the blood supply of the knee joint too, do you?" "Yes, I do" I replied, "There are 16 named arteries that supply the knee joint, the left and right superior and inferior geniculate arteries…" By then he too had had enough of me and waved me out. I had become an absolute anatomy nerd. Another Liverpool graduate and friend of mine called Graham Croker also sat the exam but failed it. I will come back to Graham later, because he was in the RAMC and I would seek his advice about my career path.

I celebrated my success in time honoured fashion, as I had overcome the biggest hurdle in a surgical career, which led to a slight mishap on the way back to London, when my confused brain misread the information at Glasgow Central Station and I embarked on the wrong train. When I woke up, I was in Kilmarnock, which was and still is in Scotland and only 70 miles from Glasgow.

Beverley and I married in a small church in Woking and the reception was at her home, with a marquee. It was a special affair and I loved Bev very much, but her mother was very pushy, almost hinting that we should start on her first grandchild that very same night. This was going to be a bone of contention between Bev and me.

My next job on the rotation was at Harefield Hospital in Middlesex. Beverley and I lived in a small flat on site because, as my post was resident on call,

Beverley and I on holiday 1977

the hospital management were obliged to provide us with married accommodation. Harefield was one of the most notable cardiothoracic hospitals in the country at that time and I was there for six months working for an Irish man called Mr John Walter Jackson. There I learnt to open and close a chest and assist at pneumonectomies (removal of a lung) and oesophagectomies (removal of the gullet), almost always for cancers.

John Jackson was a meticulous surgeon and an oesophagectomy would often take him six hours, or even longer. He would sometimes do two a week and he showed me his technique for the hand-sewn, waterproof reconstructive anastomoses, which in his hands very rarely leaked – when it did happen, it was almost always disastrously fatal. Nowadays these anastomoses are invariably performed with reliable automatic stapling devices, which markedly reduce the operating time. Anyway, I puffed my chest out when the Jackson squared team went into theatre to metaphorically rip an oesophagus out. Much better than team Marcus.

John Jackson was a remarkable surgeon who taught me well, ensuring that I received a good grounding in chest surgery, but he died far too young aged only 62, just after his retirement. I am not sure what the cause of his death was, but he already looked way beyond his years when I worked for him. Having experienced just six months of his operating schedules, I reckon he was just completely worn out.

It was here I also met Sir Magdi Yacoub and watched him operate as he embarked on his glittering and unmatched career in cardiac surgery, resulting in Harefield Hospital becoming the UK's foremost heart transplant hospital. He always had a large retinue of foreign doctors, unpaid 'clinical assistants' with no clinical roles, but in that capacity, they were allowed into theatre to watch him operate. They were all over the place, from my point of view a bloody nuisance, and as a permanent member of staff, I had to demand that they got out of the way so that I could see what was happening. It seemed as though some of them were prepared to hang upside down from the operating lights like bats in order to observe the great man (and he *was* a great man), at work.

There was a story going around that following fame and fortune Sir Magdi developed a passion for exotic cars, which he kept crashing. The well-known saying amongst his admirers and jealous detractors was that "he arrived from the Middle East on a camel and now uses disposable Maseratis". I remember his calm operating and his ability to tie surgical knots at lightning speed whilst performing a CABG (a Coronary Artery Bypass Graft), known as a Cabbage, when narrowed arteries supplying the heart muscle were bypassed, using veins harvested from the patient's leg.. Often a CABG had to be performed in an emergency if the arterial obstruction was critical. (I will describe a case in detail when I had to employ the same surgical tactic following an assassination attempt.) Radiological stenting, the form of treatment used nowadays, would not be commonplace for many years. This involved special expandable tubes being inserted through the narrowed arteries via a patient's blood vessel and the development of this technique, performed in the X-ray department ensured that the cardiac surgeons were less stressed, got more sleep and lived longer.

It was at Harefield that I met and became friendly with a registrar called Mr Guvendik, who was from Turkey. He had a British Surgical

Fellowship but was thinking of taking the Turkish equivalent qualification. He told me that in this examination, part of it would be a practical, whereby the candidate would operate with the examiner as first assistant. This had no parallel in the British colleges. Guvendik told me he had to perform an abdominal procedure whilst the examiner assessed his abilities and general surgical technique. He passed the examination. I am relating this because I have met many surgeons who have had all the academic knowledge in the world, but have not got a good pair of hands, the surgeon's greatest attribute in the clinical setting. This form of assessment would have ensured that those who were all thumbs were kept away from patients until their techniques improved, if ever.

Beverley was keen that we should have our own place. I agreed, and we bought 2 Jubilee Cottage in Church Road, St John's, Old Woking. It was tiny but suited our purposes very well. Graham, the builder and vendor, lived next door in Number 1. He was very helpful in dealing with the usual teething troubles that arose with the conversion he had undertaken. We were very happy, even though circumstances contrived to keep us apart. Beverley was still on long-haul flights and would be away for several days, and I was working full time with a 1:3 on call commitment. This was manageable and we really had some good times, but there was an elephant in the room which would break both our hearts. Beverly's biological clock was ticking away quickly, and my surgical training had to simmer and take its time. She desperately wanted children and there weren't the options then, as there are now, to have them much later in life. I just could not agree to it at the time, as my work schedule was too frantic, and I did not want to be the sort of father who never saw his children. If we had had children then, I could not see my future being in surgery and I knew that Beverley wanted me to become a GP and be more settled. This career move would have been anathema to me, so there really was no solution.

Very sadly we agreed to part. I neither bore nor bear her any ill will. She was a lovely person both inside and out. The future each of us wanted drove us in different directions and she quickly got remarried to a relatively wealthy businessman and produced two little girls in quick succession. It took me a long time to recover after my divorce from Beverley, and I still get the odd pang of guilt from time to time.

CHAPTER 8

Interview Hara-kiri

King Edward 7th Hospital, Windsor, 1978

The last part of this surgical rotation was the Registrar post based in King Edward 7th Hospital in Windsor. As well as my duties in the King Edward, I did clinics in Heatherwood Hospital and my own operating list there once a week. I was on call every other night covering both hospitals, so I would drive from one to the other, sometimes by moonlight, whilst listening to Meatloaf on my car stereo at sound levels sufficient to wake up the Royal Household.

I found myself operating on lumps and bumps, hernias, varicose veins and then progressing to open cholecystectomies (gall bladder removal) almost inevitably for gallstones, assisted by the SHO who was doing the job that I had done a year earlier, with surgical cover from the next-door theatre where my consultant boss was operating. Removal of the gall bladder for gallstones is one of the commonest abdominal operations performed in the Western world and also in those countries where the population was susceptible to biliary disease. Laparoscopic (keyhole) cholecystectomies would not be commonplace for at least another 10-15 years, when keyhole surgery would explode in popularity. I was trained in laparoscopic cholecystectomy in 1992 by the Americans in Frankfurt, West Germany.

There are three points I would like to make about this surgical procedure. Firstly, cholecystectomy is a catch-all name for an operation that would sometimes take me about 15 minutes laparoscopically on a day case patient or in more difficult and dangerous circumstances (for the patient), about four hours as an open procedure with a list of complications as long as your arm. All patients requiring a cholecystectomy knew of a "friend" who had had the operation, had recovered in a couple of weeks and was soon back home enjoying the diet and lifestyle that had contributed to their gallstones in the first place! Thus it was bewildering for some patients to find themselves in intensive care post-operatively, with tubes coming out of their abdomens, draining bile and blood, whilst being transfused with blood themselves, with their urine collected and measured via a catheter in their bladder. These sorts of cases will always appear from time to time and are surgical nightmares.

Secondly, as laparoscopic cholecystectomy became the operation of choice, many consultant surgeons have little to no experience of the way to safely perform the open procedure when complications occur, nor the tricks and approaches needed and the reconstructive operations that may be required. Some call themselves laparoscopic surgeons only and will never open an abdomen. They therefore rely on calling the surgical dinosaurs of old like me when things do go wrong. I have performed hundreds of laparoscopic cholecystectomies in my time, but more importantly I had a wide experience of the open procedure, for when I needed a get out of jail card.

Thirdly, if a general surgeon is going to be sued, it will probably be over a gall bladder, which in my experience ranks as the number one cause of potential litigation. We should start a programme to breed gall bladders out of existence in human beings, which could have saved me and my surgical colleagues a lot of anguish, though with a substantial loss of private practice income if the truth be told. Perhaps not such a good idea after all.

I was working for Mr R J Luck and Mr John Blaxland, both fine competent surgeons, though if memory serves me correctly and in keeping with what I have expounded on above, I seem to remember Mr Blaxland getting into deep shit with a private gall bladder operation when I was assisting him. His exit strategy was to put in a big tube drain to safely channel leaking bile out of the abdomen and refer the patient to a specialised (hepato-biliary) surgeon. Quite right.

When my rotation came to an end, and my subsequent divorce from Beverley was finalised, I felt that I had procrastinated long enough and decided to apply for a commission in the Royal Army Medical Corps (RAMC). I was becoming bogged down in the NHS and wanted a bit more adventure, a bit more excitement outside the operating theatre, more sporting opportunities and the chance to have my surgical training directed more towards becoming the complete surgeon who could deal with most things that he would be faced with. The Army training would encompass this, as postings to isolated areas and conflict zones would require a broader level of skills, which appealed to me; in civilian life, one would generally specialise in a major surgical discipline, for example orthopaedic surgery, thoracic surgery, urological surgery or organ transplant surgery (early in those days) and one's training would be along those lines. To remain a generalist having been accredited in General Surgery, yet be required to go outside one's surgical territory when the situation demanded, really rocked my boat.

I consulted Major Croker, whom I have previously mentioned, with regard to his failing the Primary FRCS (I don't think he ever passed it) and we had a long chat about being an RAMC officer and the way of life. He certainly enjoyed it. He emphasised that it was essential to be able to 'take a joke', in the broadest of terms; never was a truer word spoken.

A little prior to all this, I was granted an interview for an orthopaedic registrar rotation, the 'Oxford rotation'. The difference between say, the teaching hospitals and the district general hospitals is that the staff of the teaching hospitals tend to regard themselves as la crème de la crème, whereas the staff of the district general hospitals just get on and do the job. As it was a post-Fellowship job and I had yet to pass my final Fellowship, though due to sit it soon, I was surprised to be asked for interview. Perhaps they thought my passing the Fellowship would be a no-brainer. Well, as I will recount, I proved them wrong about that!

My sponsor on the panel was Mr Mike Squire, my old boss from the Battle Hospital, who, unfortunately and rather typically, turned up late towards the end of my interview, which was not going at all well. He shuffled into his seat on the panel looking as if he had been dragged through a hedge backwards and asked me a couple of loaded questions, designed to put me in a good light, which was near impossible by this stage. I was getting fed up, as I was pretty sure I was in the running either to simply make up numbers or be the token ethnic minority DGH candidate, when one of the members of the panel asked me what would turn out to be the last question.

"Tell me Dr Jackson [with emphasis on 'Doctor', as I was not yet a post-Fellowship 'Mister'], are you involved in any projects that we should consider, anything that might be relevant to your appointment to this rotation?"

I did not hesitate for a second. "Yes I am, as a matter of fact".

"Good," he said, "tell me about it."

So I did, and immediately committed interview 'hara kiri'.

"I'm about to rebuild my Austin Healey."

When the coughing and spluttering had stopped and the smelling salts had been passed around, I was rapidly shown the door. Mike Squire had an amused smirk on his face. He drove a Triumph Stag with the 3-litre V8 engine, so he was a proper consultant. However as one door closes another door opens and soon after, I was interviewed by a Mr Kingsmill-Moore for his orthopaedic Registrar's post at Ashford Hospital. After mulling over my name, he asked "You're not the chap who told the Oxford rotation lot that you were rebuilding your Austin Healey are you?" I said "Yes", to which he replied, "You've got the job!"

But the shame of it was that even though this was a very good hands-on job, with lots of experience, it was the second string to my bow, should I need it, if joining the Army proved to be impracticable or not what I wanted. I was to go to the MoD and discuss this with the Director General of Army Surgery, Norman Kirby, known affectionately as 'Big Norm', which I did a couple of months after this interview. He was big, bluff and honest, and we had a far-ranging discussion. I outlined what I wanted to get out of the Army and my surgical training, and he pointedly reminded me that I "would be a serving officer, not a demanding one". He explained that on-call could be difficult and that in some isolated areas, even though the Army Medical Services tried very hard to get surgical back up from local civilian resources, this was not always possible, or they simply weren't good enough, and operative holding procedures might need to be considered whilst waiting for medical evacuation. I was to learn all about this; life and limb saving surgery in the metaphorical front line, and let the clever boys finish off in the comfort of a base hospital.

I had made up my mind. Mr Kingsmill-Moore said he was sorry to see me go and that I would have had a good future in the NHS – he was right about that bit as it turned out, but I wanted to dip my toe into a different life altogether. The surgery would be good and would come with the add-ons I wanted; sport, travel, adventure, and challenges. I proposed to apply for a three-year commission and review the situation after that. In fact, I stayed for over 16 years as a regular officer and would probably have stayed longer, in the absence of difficult personal circumstances. But I did have some adventures, both good and bad, exciting and gruelling, uplifting and heart breaking. I am the better person for all of that, and I am grateful to the Army for instilling in me some lessons of life (and death) that have stood me in good stead and still do.

PART 2

ARMY 1978-1995

CHAPTER 9

Vicars and Tarts

On Her Majesty's Service,
Cambridge Military Hospital, 1978

I passed the Commissioning Board, obtained a three-year commission and was posted to the Cambridge Military Hospital (CMH) in Aldershot, the home of the British Army, as an SHO, then Specialist in Surgery. I could stay in my cottage in Woking when not on call. I met the consultants I would be working with, all pretty much Lt Colonels and above. I had the rank of Captain but had been given several years seniority so that my majority (promotion to Major) would not be long. Pay was related to rank, with the addition of medical officer's pay and specialist pay.

The hospital was an imposing grade II listed building with a clock tower and a very long main corridor from which the wards, departments and operating theatres branched off to one side. It was nearly 100 years old. The officer's mess, "Mandora", was another fantastic old building with excellent accommodation, food cooked by Army Chefs and a busy bar, managed by a steward called Mr License.

The mess was named after a battle in Egypt and for accuracy's sake should have been Mandarah, where the French, under Napoleon, were routed in March 1801 by a British force which later won the Battle of Alexandria, near where my mother was born 119 years later.[10] I worked for Col Bob Parker, Lt Col John Carter (JC) and Lt Col Brian Mayes with occasional duties with a CILOM (Civilian In Lieu Of Military) orthopaedic surgeon called Smith (he preferred his name to be pronounced Smythe) and I kept fit by playing rugby, running (battle fitness test) and squash.

In the Army I had more time for these pursuits, as they very much encouraged physical activities and selection for an Army team. This was regarded as a "parade" and therefore participation was considered compulsory. I operated at mid-level on all the general and orthopaedic surgery cases, with occasional forays into other subspecialties such as basic urology or paediatrics. The hospital was staffed by QAs, (Queen Alexandra's Royal Army Nursing Corps or QARANCs), either trained in the Army or recruited fully trained from the NHS. They were a fine body of men and women, whom I greatly admired for their all-round general nursing skills.

This was a different life, and certainly a different way of doing things. Holding the Queen's Commission was a privilege and came with a raft of responsibilities outlined in the Military Manuals, Queen's Regulations and Military Law. There were rules and regulations, uniforms, ranks, esprit de corps and rivalries in inter Corps and inter Service competitions. It was just like being a prefect at public school again, only with a slightly greater risk of being killed or maimed.

I had to go to Sandhurst for what was called the "Vicars and Tarts" course, a residential block of about 8 weeks, followed by a 4-6 week course at the RAMC depot in Keogh Barracks, in Mytchett, Surrey. It was called the Vicars and Tarts course because it was a truncated module of the full Sandhurst course for regular officers, and catered for the Army specialised Corps. Thus medics, dentists, vets and chaplains were all lumped together, to be licked into shape by Non-Commissioned Officers (NCOs) instructors, who would have their work cut out.

---

10. http://www.friendsofthealdershotmilitarymuseum.org.uk/garrison.013.html

The Sandhurst module was excellent fun, with everything done at full pace. We were taught the history of the Army, weapons training, combat fitness and tactics as well as drill. Despite the enormous quantities we ate to sustain the pace, we all lost weight and even the portly vicars sent by their bishops for three-year stints as Army Chaplains were lean and mean at the end of the course. We also learnt how to wash and properly iron our kit and the art of bulling shoes and belts. Every item of kit or clothing was minutely inspected on parade and suitably derisory comments were made and endured. Being late for a parade was only excusable if you were dead. It was tough love. Field exercises were held during days and overnight, often with a local Gurkha battalion providing the enemy. We all got killed as such, as the Gurkhas are probably the best night fighters in the world.

We learned about battlefield tactics, patrolling, patrol attacks (left flanking, right flanking, laying down covering fire etc). We also had lectures which covered the role of the armed forces in the contemporary world, and the political perspectives regarding the function and capabilities of the Army.

Anyway, we all passed out and the medics moved to Mytchett for the Special to Arms training related specifically to the RAMC, especially during warfare. There we were taught the buddy-buddy principle of first aid, casualty evacuation lines and the roles, responsibilities and transport facilities at each echelon. We were also shown the kit we would have to use, which was robust, effective and soldier-proof. We learnt about the concept of a mobile Field Surgical Team which gave me some idea of my role in commanding one in the future and the limits of surgery, depending, for example, on the terrain and the casualty numbers. We also learnt about triage of the injured and only saving the salvageable, whilst also bearing in mind the requirement of the Army to have fit fighting men sent back to the conflict as soon as possible.

I was happy, as I truthfully believed my role would be at the Field Hospital, usually about 5-10 miles behind the battlefront; an illusion I was soon to be relieved of. My personal weapon was a 9mm Browning semi-automatic pistol, a bit of a popgun in the weapons of war hierarchy, but nonetheless I had to take and pass my personal weapons test on a yearly basis, or when the MoD could afford the ammunition. I never drew my sidearm in anger. I also had to maintain fitness in order to pass my Battle Fitness Test on a yearly basis, which I never failed. Much of our physical training involved orienteering competitions and my map and compass reading abilities learnt in the scouts, gave me a head start and sometimes I won even against the racing snakes amongst our intake.

Having done all this, I went back to my post at CMH. I had applied to sit the London final Surgical Fellowship examination for which I was preparing. I had attended a course of FRCS related lectures and I want to mention an excellent talk given by a lady surgeon of the cloth known as Sister Joseph. She spoke about the role of chemotherapy in the management of testicular teratomas (a form of cancer) and informed us of a new drug called cis-platinum, which was very effective and would revolutionise the treatment of widespread disease. Hot off the press.

I sat the exam, which cost a lot of money in those days, and passed the written papers and the operative surgery viva. The last hurdle was the pathology viva and I took my seat at a desk opposite the two examiners, an external examiner and a London-based surgeon who had been appointed to the Court of Examiners. I was ready. The first few questions were concerned with general pathology, as a sort of easy introduction, and then the London examiner handed me a pathology specimen in a pot. He asked me what it was, and I could see it was a testicular cancer, a variegated teratoma. I smiled inwardly. I could nail this one. We discussed the various described testicular cancers and then I was asked about the management of this particular tumour. Well I was in, or so I thought. I gave the textbook answer about staging the disease, orchidectomy (removal of the testicle) and deep X-ray therapy where possible and I was getting a few appreciative nods. I then recited Sister Joseph's words almost verbatim, that new chemotherapeutic agents like the cis-platinums were getting good results with complete remission in some cases of stage 4 disease.

I waited for a favourable response. Unfortunately my answer to the examiner's question had lit a fuse and the explosion was not far off; a flash to bang time of a couple of seconds. The internal examiner stood up, leaned over the desk towards me and growled "If you think that chemotherapy has any part to play in the management of testicular cancers, you will never pass this examination", and with that he walked out. The external examiner shrugged and motioned for me to leave the table. I was stunned. What had this guy had for lunch? He was clearly entrenched in the past, because chemotherapy had already had a part to play, before the arrival of cis-platinum. I did think of putting in a re-dress, because plainly what he had said was nonsense, but as I had arranged to sit the Edinburgh Fellowship, a much more surgically-centred exam, a few weeks later, which I passed with no trouble, I just put it down to experience. I was now able to call myself a Mister rather than just Doctor, in civilian speak, though still a Captain in military terms, with just a little more specialist pay for my trouble.

Now with a Fellowship, I was given more operative responsibility. I was still the same person with the same experience and abilities, but with my new qualification, I had been surgically enhanced. If for example a procedure went tits up, at least a somewhat qualified surgeon had been involved. I was revelling in my job doing basic orthopaedic procedures (knee surgery, fixing fractured wrists, forearms and necks of femur etc) as well as gaining experience in the routine general surgery on children and neonates. It was time for my Higher Surgical training.

I had discussed this with Big Norm, who would arrange my senior registrar rotation. Having looked at my experience, he suggested that I would be better obtaining accreditation in general surgery, rather than say orthopaedics, which had vaguely crossed my mind. The Army wanted general surgeons who could do orthopaedics, because as a rule, orthopaedic surgeons would not do general surgery. I agreed, because dealing with the most challenging injuries to soldiers, requiring immediate surgery, invariably falls within the remit of the broadly-trained general surgeon. Any concomitant difficult orthopaedic problem could be referred for more specialist help once the immediate threat to life (and limb) had been dealt with.

I went to a Mess party one Saturday evening and met a tall slim dark-haired Army QA nurse called Kathy; I thought she was fantastic. She came from Morpeth in Northumberland and had that wonderful

Geordie accent. She had been commissioned into the QAs about a year before I had joined the RAMC and she too was divorced and wanted to make the Army her career. She was sexy and straight to the point. We danced, we cuddled, we smoked and drank and in fact I liked her so much that I instantly forgave her when she sat on my new Ray Bans as she got into my car. She wanted to train as a theatre sister, and as I was in theatre a lot, we worked and played together.

Kathy and I at a dinner party. Circa 1981.

I had some adventures with Kathy, but I was unfortunately lured away from her under false pretences.

CHAPTER 10

Soldier Surgeons

Musgrave Park Hospital, N. Ireland 1979

In 1979 I was posted to Northern Ireland as the junior surgeon for four months. I would work with Col Kim Stephens, a charming, even-keeled consultant who liked the vascular work. I would be based in the Military Wing of Musgrave Park Hospital, which was closely guarded by the Ulster Defence Regiment.

The resident UK battalion would have their HQ Company in the hospital grounds on their Operation Banner tour. Some battalion tours were for two years, with quarters available for married officers and men. It was the year of Warren Point, when 18 British soldiers were killed in an IRA (Irish Republican Army) ambush, and the year that Airey Neave MP, was killed by the INLA (Irish National Liberation Army) with a car bomb planted outside the House of Commons. It was also the year Margaret Thatcher came to power.

In Musgrave Park, things were generally quiet. Most British casualties were treated locally in Northern Irish hospitals as the nearest hospitals to the point of injury, and were then transferred to Musgrave Park when stabilised. Serious casualties in Belfast were evacuated to the Royal Victoria Hospital, which obtained an unrivalled experience in the management of these very damaging missile and bomb blast injuries, as well as High Energy Transfer Wounds, or High Velocity Gunshot Wounds (HVGSW) as they were known at that time.

It was very claustrophobic in the Military Wing, as travel outside was generally inadvisable and we were encouraged to allow our hair to grow long. There were the usual Mess facilities, a squash court and of course inevitably a running route for fitness training. I ran three miles every day and played a lot of squash, but I never regained my Sandhurst leanness. The surgery was routine fracture work and the general stuff looking after the military personnel and entitled civilians. Occasionally we would operate on transfers in, with delayed primary suture wound closures, or in honesty, undoing some of the procedures inappropriately undertaken in remote Irish hospitals. I will relate more of this when I recount my experiences in Northern Ireland as a surgical consultant a few years down the line. I will also write about Professor John Gibbons, whom I met briefly on this tour and then again when I returned to Northern Ireland several years later. He was a soldier surgeon, which was exactly what I wanted to be, and if I became just half as good as he was, I would be a very happy man. I'd like to think that I did get to be half as good as he was – just.

CHAPTER 11

Rosie and Me

Belize, 1979/80

Having passed my Fellowship, I was posted to British Honduras, soon to become Belize following independence. I would be there for six months as the surgeon in the Field Surgical Team that worked out of Station Hospital, in Airport Camp, the HQ area for British Forces Belize. This was late 1979 and early 1980. There were full assets there, including the RAF with their Harriers and Puma helicopters, RAF regiment, and the resident battalion at the camp were two Royal Irish Rangers (2RIR) part of Battle Group North. King Edward 7th's Own Gurkha Rifles, provided Battle Group South, near the border with Guatemala. All the support corps were present too, such as REME, RCT and of course us, the RAMC. This force was maintained to discourage the Guatemalans from their incursions into Belize, as Britain was the colonising country and took responsibility for its security. The RAF Regiment guarded the airfields, aircraft and other installations. It was not true that their ranks were filled by those who could not get into the Army; however they were nicknamed 'Rock Apes'.

I would provide some elective services with clinics and the odd operating list, but I was mainly on hand for emergencies and my surgical back up was the Mount Sinai Hospital in Miami, Florida. With the agreement of the administrative command I could summon up a Learjet with an aero medical evacuation team. I just had to keep any desperately ill patients alive until the jet got to us.

Before I was due to depart, I received a phone call from a Major John Lovegrove, a fellow RAMC surgeon. I did not know him at the time, but I was to get to know him well as we were subsequently posted to the British Military Hospital in Hong Kong to run the surgical department together. He had done a tour in Belize recently and just thought he could give me some information about the place and ask for a favour.

The capital of the country was still Belize City but because it was on the coast, it kept getting flattened by hurricanes. The last one spread the city over several square miles, as the buildings were not exactly built to withstand more than a light breeze. The administrative capital of the country was now Belmopan, 50 miles inland. There were hospitals in Belize City where I could go for medical meetings and Belmopan (which had no resident doctors) where I could do clinics and operate using their facilities, if I felt so inclined.

He then said to me that if I decided to do clinics for the locals in Belmopan Hospital he would like me to look out for a Mennonite family. The father and mother had five children, two of whom had some sort of neurological (nervous) condition the symptoms of which, mainly progressive weakness, seemed to point to a diagnosis of a myaesthenic type syndrome, a failure of neurotransmitter substance (or neurotransmission) between nerves and muscles. He thought that these children would benefit from the drug Neostigmine or any other anticholinesterase, which could be used first as a diagnostic test and then treatment. Would I take a load of tablets out with me and give it a go? I agreed and asked John if he knew the name of the family. "No, but he's a wood cutter" was his response.

I asked John if there was any other advice he could give me and he said that the sand flies and mosquitoes would drive me mad, so I should take plenty of repellents. He then added that they didn't work anyway.

I packed my kit of brand-new light weight DPMs (disruptive pattern material) combats, shorts, shirts and all the other standard issue paraphernalia along with a load of tablets for the woodcutter's family, supplied from the CMH pharmacy, and hopped on the VC10 from Brize Norton. I had left a key to my cottage with Kathy to use and keep a weather eye on whilst I was away and I looked forward to a six-month holiday in the Caribbean, courtesy of HM Government. The flight was uneventful until we landed with quite a bump. The Military Air Traffic Controllers manned what was known as 'Butcher Radar' and they assessed each RAF landing with a score, rather like Strictly Come Dancing. I think our pilot achieved a 4 out of 10 for throwing the aircraft onto the tarmac.

Once at Airport Camp I went in search of the Officer's Mess and found I had been allocated a room sharing with a captain from the Army Education Corps. There were two single beds, a cupboard, a wardrobe and a creaking fan in the centre of the ceiling just vaguely moving hot air around a bit, with no actual cooling effect. My roommate promptly showed me his ankles, both scratched skinless. He pointed to them and said, "This is what you have to look forward to". He was due to go back to the UK and had clearly not enjoyed his tour.

I wandered along to the Station Hospital to meet the Field Surgical Team which consisted of a Sergeant Lab Technician, an X-ray technician, the usual complement of Operating Theatre technicians (OTTs) the male nurses, the dentist (a very accommodating Lt Colonel) and my soon to join us anaesthetist Lt Col John Restall, whom I would be very glad to see as we had worked together in the CMH. Not only was he a good golfer, he was the bee's knees at anaesthetics and resuscitation. We also had a couple of clerks, and I felt happy that these soldiers, my Field Surgical Team, would not let me down in the unlikely event of an emergency, or anything else I planned, in terms of fulfilling our potential in this developing country. I was not wrong.

I had liberally applied insect repellent to all areas of skin not covered by clothing, but within an hour I was hopping on alternate legs and scratching my ankles with unrestrained enthusiasm. The biting insects showed no mercy and my socks were no barrier to the little bastards. I would just have to wait until I developed some sort of immunity.

I wandered around the camp to get my bearings and was approaching the cook house when a Lt Col in a forces Land Rover stopped by me and told me to get in. It was the Commanding Officer of 2RIR. "You're the new doctor, aren't you?" he said. I agreed that I was. "Captain David Jackson - sir!" He then said, "Come and have a look at these drains". I tried to explain to the Colonel that I had nothing to do with drains, as he showed me around the open cookhouse, but I promised to send the Environmental Health Officer to take a look, as there was a hell of a smell. I soon found out that the whole of Belize City had an open drainage system known as the "Sweetwater Canal". A day later in Belize City I noticed a swollen decomposing pig floating down the waterway, as the sewage travelled at a snail's pace.

I decided to take stock of what we as an FST could do to make our presence more rewarding. The first thing of course was to re-establish the clinics and operating list in Belmopan Hospital, and to this end I drove with the FST senior non-commissioned officer (SNCO) to make contact. It was about an hour's drive along the Western Highway, which was dusty and unmade in those days. I met the matron and she confirmed the arrangements. She could supply the theatre/nursing staff – her and one other – and the instruments (sterilised, I hoped), and we would supply the FST personnel and equipment. As we left the meeting with the first clinic arranged in a week, I noticed the recycled theatre gloves and bandages hanging out to dry on a washing line. I decided we would bring our own.

Later that day I went to introduce myself to the staff at the Belize City Hospital and have a look at the facilities available, which even for a poor country were only just about adequate. I met the chief of the surgical department, who I was told was British trained, which was stretching the truth a bit. He had done a few SHO jobs in Ear Nose and Throat. However I was very surprised to meet one of their radiologists who had served in the RAMC. I never learnt the story as to why he was working in Belize of all places, the far end of the Caribbean gastro-intestinal tract.

Realistically, if push came to shove, I could not rely on host country resources for surgical assistance unless we had a mass casualty situation, but I would attend the City hospital monthly clinical meetings, as I was keen to learn as much as I could about the indigenous illnesses that prevailed and also the common surgical problems. These were much the same as anywhere else in the world; trauma of every sort, drunkenness and gallstones pretty much topped the list, with the odd snake bite thrown in. I also had the problem of the Mennonite woodcutter's children to resolve. Having carted about a million tablets for them half-way round the world, I would have to find him, if he didn't turn up in Belmopan.

The 'pox doc', Cpl Ed Sutton, asked to see me. He was responsible for the garrison's sexual health and he told me that there was a problem that needed resolving. There were two brothels in Belize City frequented by the soldiers, called the Big C and the Queen of Hearts, both of which were responsible for outbreaks of the clap (mainly chlamydia which can be asymptomatic in men, though they can spread it around a bit, and gonorrhoea). There was no point in putting these establishments out of bounds as the soldiers would use the girls on the streets, most of whom had syphilis in addition to the other two. The solution which had been suggested, but had yet to be fully implemented, due to objections by the padre, amongst others, or so I was led to believe, was that we garrison 'medics' should keep the girls clean and fit for purpose by weekly inspections and treatments. This was a bit out of my comfort zone, but I could see the sense in it, so we set about visiting both establishments.

There were about 10 girls from Mexico, Spanish Honduras, Costa Rica and El Salvador in addition to Belize working in each brothel. Some had children in tow, some were sending their earnings back home to their families, some were looking to earn a dowry, and others were keen on the idea of marrying a British soldier. This is one of the reasons that a soldier must ask his Commanding Officer for permission to marry, as it is in the nature of the British soldier to fall in love with the supplier of his first blow job, at 10 Belize dollars (£2). No Commander is going to allow a working girl entry into the Regiment without a very good reason and being the provider of a good commercial blow job is not one of them. We met the managers of both brothels. The actual owners were absent in America.

It is difficult to believe as I write this that I was stating the terms under which we, the army, would provide a genito-urinary service to local prostitutes. We (me) would examine the girls regularly with regard to their general and sexual health and if any of them were found to be infected, we would treat them for free. They would be taken off sex work until they were rechecked and clear. They could serve behind the bar, but not service behind the bar. Any girl caught working when off work, as it were, would be sacked. We also wanted Polaroid photographs of all the girls for contact tracing, as almost all of them were called Maria and "I got it from Maria" was not helpful unless we could identify which one. All conditions were agreed, and we would start in a couple of days. Cheap champagne brandy bottles were opened, and we drank to our future relationship. We would do the Big C on Mondays and the Queen of Hearts later in the week[11].

The Big C. Belize 1980

The rumour that these two establishments would be medically certified soon spread and they did a roaring trade amongst the soldiers, but of

---

11. https://www.youtube.com/watch?v=i7fSK-6QmqQ Four minutes in, is an interview with the manager of the Big C confirming our involvement in taking care of his girls.

course we had to take into account the wandering locals who dropped in for a beer, a quick shag and the spreading of whatever diseases they were carrying, so my colleague John Restall would hold the torch, I would introduce the speculum and Cpl Sutton processed the swabs and did the contact tracing. I became a part time gynaecologist, a 'specialist in the sex trade'.

Cpl Sutton and Lt Col Restall in one of the whore's cubicles. Belize 1980

The results were analysed, attributed and the disease-ridden treated, all part of the service, and our drinks in the brothels were always on the house. I can say with hand on heart that I never availed myself of anything else that was on offer. However, I did have a very close shave with one of the girls just before leaving Belize, though not of my own doing, as will become apparent.

In the evening all the officers of the battle group and support elements would gather round for pre-dinner drinks and a chat in the mess. There was always a little bit of resentment towards the RAMC officers as we would be on a higher pay scale, due to our professional qualifications and specialisms, compared to the officers of the Big Army, as they liked to call themselves. It would not be the first time I would come across this in my postings and it was understandable in a way, but Army pay had to compete with civilian pay for the purposes of recruitment and retention within the service.

One evening a young subaltern in 2RIR was sounding off in this regard. "Paid much more than us" he said, "and just out here for a holiday". I approached him and introduced myself as one of the overpaid holiday makers he was referring to. He was a bit sheepish and I tried to mollify his resentment by saying that I was the equivalent of the weapon he was carrying, as I hoped he would never have to use my services, but I was around 24/7 if need be. I am not sure how he took this, or even if he understood my point, and as I left the group of young officers, I got the impression they had resumed their conversation where they had left off.

About a month later this same young subaltern came to the medical reception and rather sheepishly asked me and Cpl Sutton, who I was with at the time, if a girl called Maria "was er... all right?" (I knew who he was referring to as this particular Maria was fancied by all the soldiers at Airport Camp, but I showed him her photo anyway). This girl worked in the Big C. and we were going to sign her off the following morning with her first dose of the antibiotic clindamycin. I looked at Cpl Sutton and said, "She's fine". The young officer muttered his thanks and got into civvies ready to travel on the 4-tonner transport lorry into Belize that evening, with other junior officers and soldiers. Cpl Sutton looked at me aghast. "Don't worry" I said, "I'll tell him".

I chose my moment carefully, just as the 4-tonner was about to sign out at the exit/gate barrier from Airport Camp. I ran up to the back of the lorry and yelled "Mr (whatever his name was), I made a mistake, Maria is NOT all right". Everybody on the lorry, from private soldier to junior officer, would have known what I was talking about and of course the intentions of the young subaltern, who looked like he would die of embarrassment. I didn't have any problem with the 2RIR officers after that. I would argue that it was a genuine mistake, but a degree of poetic justice was to come my way at the end of my tour, the close shave I referred to above.

Next day, we were going to do a clinic in Belmopan and the FST Land Rover and trailer were loaded up with just about everything we could foreseeably require, several packed lunches and lots of water. The station hospital was informed where we would be going, and we took off. My driver was a Cpl Chad. After a mile along the Western

Highway I took over the driving, as I wanted to arrive in Belmopan in one piece. Despite the occasional pothole the size of a bear trap and the crazy driving of the locals, we arrived safely and met the matron, and I started the clinic.

As I was to find and as others had before me, in countries where the medical service is poor, most of the local population will turn up either with genuine complaints, or out of curiosity, and there was a massive clinic list. There were no case sheets, little organisation and poor communication between the patients and me, until I got more used to their way of talking. As Belize was a former British colony, English was the official language, but many of the inhabitants did not know that and the usual interethnic language was Belizean Creole. I had to frequently ask the matron, who was doing the clinic with me, to keep some sort of order and help decipher the words of the patients, but I soon got fed up and slipped into vet mode for the first time in my surgical career, but not the last.

There was little I could do for the majority of those I saw in most clinics. There were lots of what seemed like cases of tuberculosis, tropical skin diseases and chronic incurable illnesses – kidney failure, anaemias, blood dyscrasias, serious abnormalities, diagnosed when I could get a blood test, which we performed and processed in the Station Hospital. Old, malunited fractures were in abundance and any X-rays I ordered took forever to be taken and when returned were still dripping with the development fluid. Cataracts were common and of course the old staple, gall bladder disease, was rife. This was something I could help with and I soon had three patients who would be booked in, a week later, for open cholecystectomy. In retrospect, I think I must have been completely off my head. That was certainly John Restall's opinion when he arrived.

The last local I saw in the clinic said to me, "Is you de soldier doctor man?" I replied in the affirmative. He said his name was – it sounded like Aldo Moro, the murdered Italian Prime Minister. I didn't ask him to repeat it; I called him Aldo in various conversations that we had, and he seemed to go along with that. He was very rotund and as I later found out, he had a bad Belikin habit (Belikin is the locally brewed beer). He opened his shirt and showed me an entrance wound in his abdomen. It turned out that he had been working on a lathe of sorts, grinding down a metal bolt for use on one of his farm machines, when the bolt flew out of his hand and straight into his abdominal wall, where it still was, and so had not entered his abdominal cavity, which was distended, with shifting dullness (free fluid in the abdomen), and an everted belly button. Coupled with his slightly jaundiced tinge and a few other signs, this pointed to early cirrhosis of the liver.

I prodded around and though he had a lot of belly fat, I thought I could feel something in his abdominal wall. I asked the matron for some local anaesthetic and without looking at the expiry date, injected a bucketful of the stuff in and around Aldo's wound. When the area was numbed, I enlarged the wound and shoved my finger in. I could feel the bolt and I managed to extract it along with a small piece of his shirt, and what looked like some oil and iron filings or 'swarf'. I then thoroughly cleaned the wound, saturated it with an iodine solution and stitched it up. I gave him the bolt, still bloody, and he was delighted. He could now repair his machine. I told him to come back the next week and mentioned in passing that his liver was knackered.

Back at camp we picked up the pox doc and did a clinic at the Queen of Hearts. Almost all the houses and businesses in Belize were built out of wooden slats, apart from some hotels and government buildings, and the Queen of Hearts was no exception. The girls' cubicles were on the ground floor and the bar was on the first floor. As the floor of the bar had contracted, expanded and warped over the years, it had left large cracks looking directly down into one or two of the cubicles. There most nights, for all to see and admire, would be a white, occasionally tattooed backside, going for it.

The following extract from the Army Rumour Service (ARRSE) could almost be read as a reference to the quality of our work:

Grand opening of the rose garden, knew Raoul from the hotel he worked at before branching out in business/pimping, memories a bit hazy but remember large crowd of drunken squaddies (a given) and only about 5 or 6 brasses on duty, some problem with inadequate bribes to immigration officials causing a hold-up with a posse of Salvadorean tarts.

Also a god [sic] bothering half-colonel who wanted names from the pox doctor's pecker parade published on orders as a deterrent to sin, this would have been around 1980-ish. Pre-Rose Garden, the Queen of Hearts was the place to be, club 102 having acquired a nasty rep for unlicensed taxi drivers with sharp machetes[12].

I have vague recollections of the God-bothering half-colonel. In any event what he wanted was not possible, due to patient confidentiality (yes, even soldiers are sometimes afforded that).

I drank the local beer, Belikin, from time to time but stayed away from the local rum. I had to casevac two patients with severe alcoholic pancreatitis, following a rum boozathon that lasted a whole weekend or more without pause, in San Pedro Town, on Ambergris Caye, where the soldiers went for convalescence or R and R.

I still had to find the woodcutter, but I was getting closer having asked where the nearest Mennonite settlement was in relation to Belmopan. It was a place called Spanish Lookout and so we got in the FST Land Rover, that is me, Cpl Chad, a young female RADC (Royal Army Dental Corps) dentist, my X-ray technician, and a Combat Med Technician from 2RIR and off we went. As I look at my photographs, I can see that it was early in my tour, as I was not wearing boots, because I too had shredded my ankles, due to the voracious mosquitoes and sand-flies which seemed to thrive on the strongest insect repellents.

We travelled along the Western Highway to a place past Belmopan known as Central Farm. We then took a dirt track north to a tributary of the Belize River and crossed, vehicle and all, by a rickety hand-cranked ferry.

The Mennonites are a religious sect who eschew the modern world. They are farmers and artisans and marry within their own community. In those days they did not use cars or phones, or even have electricity. All the men wore beards and both sexes dressed very conservatively. They were also not keen on being photographed. We drove through the settlement and after making enquiries were given directions to the woodcutter's house and workshop, where he carved the components

---

12. https://www.arrse.co.uk/community/threads/belize-retrospective.166276/samain11 Jul 21, 2011#17

of the furniture which he sold. I met him, his wife and the two affected children, who could hardly manage to breathe, let alone move about. I introduced my team and explained that we were there following Major Lovegrove's request and I had the medication that we hoped would improve his children's symptoms. Fortunately, his English was reasonable as the Mennonites normally converse in Plautdietsch, a sort of incomprehensible dialect of the incomprehensible language that is German.

John Lovegrove and I were being surgically trained, and ordinarily would have little to do with myaesthenic patients unless they were on the operating list, and even then, would know precious little about it. Certainly, nowadays disease management would be undertaken by specialist neurologists or endocrinologists. Myasthenia gravis is an autoimmune disorder, where the body's own defence system attacks and damages its own tissues. It is not hereditary, but there is a disease called Congenital Myaesthenic Syndrome, which is hereditary and would explain why only two of the woodcutter's children were affected and why they were affected as children.

I have used my trusty retrospectoscope a bit here. Their mother confirmed that her other three children were normal and that her two affected children had had symptoms from birth, with difficulty swallowing and ptoses (droopy eyelids) worse when they were tired. I suggested that with their permission, we try out the medication I had brought 6000 miles and following their agreement I gave each child a tablet to swallow. It took 30 minutes or so, but gradually both of them improved, walking and talking, breathing and then smiling almost normally and each of us in the FST felt an overwhelming sense of achievement. We had risked life and limb and the possibility of a drowned Land Rover, and we had done some good. I don't think I am being overdramatic. The woodcutter and his wife were amazed and thankful and they were hugging each other.

The father took me to his workshop and gave me four mahogany dining chairs and a mahogany rocking chair as a thank you present, all needing assembly, but I was delighted to have them. I did offer a chair to each of the other members of the team, but they were not really interested. We left the large jar of tablets with the family, and though they would last a long time, the father would have to get more medical help and more medication from wherever he could; I suggested America, rather uselessly. I also tried to explain that from my limited knowledge of the disease, he should not have any more children. There would be a 1:4 chance of another affected child. We waved goodbye and I never saw them again.

When I returned to UK after my tour, I picked up the Movements Forwarding Office (MFO) box load of furniture pieces, where they had been delivered to the CMH. I assembled the dining chairs and rocking chair, varnished them and used them in my cottage for quite a few years. I still have the rocking chair, which I have refurbished, repaired and re-varnished several times over the years, and at this moment, as I am typing these memoirs, it sits on the front porch of my villa in Spain nearly 40 years later. Apart from a bit of damage to one of the rockers caused by my dog Bevvy chewing on it many years ago, it is as good as new and I am sure it will see me out.

We returned triumphantly to Airport Camp and after a quick shower I was back in the Mess ready for a beer and then removed myself as the twice-daily swing fog machine was brought into action. This was operated by a local employee whose purpose in life was to asphyxiate the British Army with the foul smoky cloud it produced to keep the biting insects out. It did the trick for a limited amount of time.

Early the next day, I was called to the Station Hospital, as there was someone there who wanted to see the surgeon. I crunched my way through my usual breakfast of antimalarials and scrambled eggs and wandered down to meet a retired Warrant Officer who lived in Belize City. When he had left the Army he returned to Belize, married a local lady, and for the last 20 years or so, he had been living off his pension and his wife's wages – I could not bring myself to ask what her line of work was.

Most days he rocked himself in a hammock on his front porch, chain smoking King Edward cigars, drinking rum and growing the most enormous lipoma (benign fatty tumour) on the back of his neck. It was as if he had an extra head. He asked me if I could remove it. I was hesitant, as in some areas of the body, these growths can be very difficult to get out, and the back of the neck was one of them. I asked why he didn't go to the Belize City Hospital. He said he would only go there if he needed a post-mortem and even then, reluctantly. I asked John Restall, to have a look at him. It would be difficult to get a breathing tube into his trachea (windpipe) as his neck would not extend and he would need to be lying prone for the procedure.

John was his usual pragmatic self. "Should be all right" he said, after trying and failing to manipulate the patient's neck, "better get some blood cross matched". That was something I had never thought of. Where did we get blood from? "On the hoof", replied my lab tech when I enquired. In other words, snatch a passing soldier with a compatible blood group and tap him for a pint. This would be very useful information. The ex-Warrant Officer was instructed to present himself at the hospital next day, starved and if possible, sober. He was then anaesthetised, flipped on his front and after a titanic struggle I removed his second head, with surprisingly little blood loss. It was carried off in a bucket to be preserved in formalin and sent back to the Army pathologist in UK for analysis. I discharged the patient a day later. He could now lie flat in his hammock and contemplate the sky, rather than his navel.

One day whilst I was in the reception of the hospital, there was a screech of brakes and a lorry came to an abrupt standstill outside in a cloud of dust and gravel. The driver helped a man out of the vehicle who had an obviously badly injured right arm. The staff rushed out to help him into the hospital, as the driver then unloaded two crates of Belikin beer. He yelled that Ernesto had "got his arm caught" in some sort of machine in the brewery which was only a couple of miles away in Ladyville. The driver then got back in his lorry and drove off.

Ernesto was in considerable pain and we took the usual resuscitation measures with the addition of plenty of strong pain medications. I then had an opportunity to examine his arm carefully. It looked as though it had been dragged into the machine by his clothing.

His hand and forearm were fine with reasonable pulses, and a full neurological examination of his sensory/motor system seemed normal (no severe nerve damage). Most of the injury had been to the soft tissue of his upper arm and shoulder, where there was a large open wound with protruding muscle. An X-ray did not reveal any bony damage and his humerus was correctly located, eliminating the possibility of a dislocated shoulder. Following a period of starvation, John Restall anaesthetised him, so that I could explore the wound surgically. He seemed to have torn his triceps, part of his biceps and deltoid muscles. The wound depth reached the shoulder joint capsule, which had not been breached.

Essentially what could have been catastrophic fortunately was not. However, identification and repair of the damage took forever, and after about three hours I left the theatre to go and get myself a Belikin or two to drink. I opened the unit fridge, where I expected to find at least a couple of the beers alongside all the vaccinations, anaesthetic drugs, antibiotics, local anaesthetics, packed lunches and soft drinks, which normally occupied the fridge. Nope, not a beer in sight. My team had disappeared having drunk the lot. One of them said, "We were worried about you sir, and we were drinking to your health and inspiration." Yes, I'm sure they were, the buggers.

I kept Ernesto in for a few days, just to ensure he did not develop any vascular complications, as I had no doubt he had stretched his main blood vessels. He made a good recovery and six weeks later was back at work. The brewery did not send any more beer.

I was doing the next clinic in Belmopan when Aldo Moro turned up. His abdominal wound had healed, and he was so pleased that he invited the whole FST to a lunchtime BBQ at his home, Little Rock Farm, in San Ignacio, where he would prepare fresh lamb's liver. We agreed to arrange it in a week's time.

After the clinic I went to the operating theatre to do the list. In hindsight, I am relieved to say that only one patient had turned up. John Restall was relieved too. The lady whose gall bladder I was going to remove was a typical Belizean mama, very large and very fat. I nominated one of my operating theatre technicians (OTT) to assist and the matron would pass the instruments. The other OTTs checked the available equipment, the anaesthetic machine, drugs and gases – we had brought our own – and the most important item of equipment I would need, a foot-operated suction pump.

I went over the instruments available, which seemed to be a random mix of general surgical and obstetric clutter. I saw a pair of obstetric forceps on the trolley. Had she laid up the instruments based on her previous experience? How big was this gall bladder going to be? I did not expect any gallstones other than in her gallbladder as her history and liver function tests did not suggest it likely. In those days a stone which had migrated from the gall bladder and risked obstructing the flow of bile into the small intestine was a very difficult problem to deal with. The operation should have been straightforward, but I had to enlist help to keep the patient's wound apart so I could see something of what I had to do and attempt to identify the important anatomical structures. Memories of Marcus and his many tribulations flashed before me.

The air conditioning in the operating theatre was pretty much non-existent. I lost a gallon of sweat and had to be quickly mopped before the drops on my brow dripped into the wound. After two hours it was all over. I closed the wound and wrote up the operation notes and the post-operative instructions. When the patient was awake and responding, we left her to the tender mercies of the hospital and drove back to Airport Camp, leaving the Station Hospital telephone number, a pointless gesture as all phone calls within Belize seemed to take a minimum of two hours to get connected if at all. We would go back and check on her in a couple of days. She did recover, with a not unexpected wound infection, and eventually went back to having babies, which she carried four at a time balanced on her swaying hips.

Each Sunday a boat and captain would be hired for the weekly trips to one of the offshore Cayes; there are thousands of them. The boat was loaded with booze, food, ice, snorkels, masks and fins and about 30 participants for a 1-2 hour cruise to one of the Cayes, trolling fishing lines from the stern. The usual Caye we journeyed to was called Goff's Caye, just a small desert island with a couple of palm trees, rickety shelters, a small sandy beach, and a part of the coral reef not far away for the most superb unspoilt underwater exploring. Often the boys pitched a tent as the sun was searing. Goff's Caye had a small sand bar several metres away.

Once whilst snorkelling, I noticed that one of my team was far too close to a sting ray in the shallow water. I half stood up and yelled to him to move back to shore. I then promptly fell over, as fins make getting into the upright position very difficult in shallow water and in righting myself, I fell over again and scraped the back of my calf on the underlying coral. It was extremely painful and I assumed I had come into contact with some fire coral. I staggered out of the water and my predicament was noticed by Cpl Snowy Collins, one of my male nurses. Before I could stop him, he ran to the first aid box, picked up an aerosol of "op-site" surgical dressing and sprayed my bleeding open wounds. The pain of this, added to the pain of the coral grazes, was bloody near indescribable, but the wound was effectively closed.

Cpl Collins then led me to his hammock (he was well organised), which I collapsed into, and rushed to the large cool box of drinks we had bought. He picked up a bottle of coke, drank all of the contents bar the last half inch or so, then refilled the bottle with whisky and handed it to me. I drank the lot over about half an hour and the pain dissipated. I was cured. First aid in the raw, raw being a good way of describing my calf. I thanked him and hobbled back to embark on the boat which was now leaving the Caye.

I had sufficiently recovered to trawl off the stern and an hour or so later, I felt a pull on the rod. I started to reel in the catch, which felt like quite a big fish, when the rod suddenly bent double and the line went slack. The cadre of the wise after the event British Armed Forces professional fishermen on board, all rolled their eyes. "You lost it. Should have kept the line taut sir" etc etc. The advice kept coming as I reeled in the line to find the head and gills of a large barracuda, still on the hook, with a very surprised look on its face. The master of the boat said that it had probably been taken by a shark or grouper as I was hauling it in. I felt completely vindicated as I had still landed my catch, if only the front half. On a later occasion I caught a whole barracuda, which was cooked by the chefs in the Officer's Mess and consumed for supper. The consensus amongst my brother officers was that it tasted awful. I am not a great lover of fish anyway.

It was time for the BBQ at Aldo Moro's farm. The FST and a qualified civilian nurse would attend. By the FST, I should explain that only those members of it who were not on duty in the Station Hospital at the time accompanied me, not the full FST. I always left details of where I would be going, so that I could be retrieved in an emergency when out of camp. I will illustrate this point later.

We drove to St Ignacio, about 40 kms the other side of Belmopan, and eventually found Little Rock Farm. It was a bit of a shambles, unlike the cultivated farms in the Mennonite settlement we had visited at Spanish Lookout. Scrapped cars and old rusty machinery dotted the place. There were some scrawny cattle, a herd of sheep and lambs and two or three dogs crashed out under the family clapboard house, which sat on old and rickety stilts. A few trees grew wearily in the surrounding scrubland. An open-sided thatched wooden hut housed a bloodstained butcher's chopping block, which looked particularly gruesome. In preparation for our visit, half a rusty oil drum had been mounted on a wooden trellis, with a wire mesh grill ready for the BBQ. We opened the gate, hit the vehicle horn and slowly drove down a track to the house. The dogs barked frenziedly and fiercely for a second or two before flopping back to sleep.

Aldo Moro and one of his sons appeared; he was effusive in his greeting. I am pretty sure he had never expected us to turn up. "Hi doc, you dun come" he said. We had bought a cool box full of Belikin and we all had a drink and chatted. Aldo took me over to a rusty old bit of farm equipment and showed me the bolt I had extracted from his abdominal wall, which he had subsequently fitted in its intended, and certainly more appropriate, location. He then took me over to the lambs which he had corralled. "Which one you wan'?" he asked me. I was not prepared for this. I am one of those meat eaters who needs to be blissfully ignorant about how it gets on the plate. I asked how long he required to get the lamb and its liver prepared and he said about an hour, so I told him that we had to go to the hospital, and we would return in an hour. He was happy with this and so we all mounted up and left the farm.

We mooched around Belmopan Hospital and I gave my opinion, for what it was worth, on a couple of inpatients languishing and decaying slowly in the wards. An hour or so later we were back at the farm, the slaughter having been performed; half the lamb had been butchered and the other half hung in the thatched hut, occasionally being sniffed at by its relieved siblings and brethren.

The slaughter. Belize 1980

The BBQ had been lit, and Aldo cooked the liver, which was offered to us with other parts of the lamb. By this time the biting insects had descended on us in droves, so we ate the lamb and its liver, along with some bread, and drunk even more Belikin amidst a cloud of mosquitoes. It was delicious. We left the rest of the beer with our host, thanked him profusely for his hospitality and went back to camp. Little did I know that I was to meet Aldo again in late spring/early summer of 1981, under quite tragic circumstances.

BBQ at Little Rock farm. Aldo's lovesick son (explained later) is standing next to him, wearing a white shirt. Belize 1980

Quite a few of the Royal Irish Ranger soldiers were employing their appendages frequently and vigorously, it being so cheap, but one of the consequences of this, (apart from the odd dose of clap, which due to our efforts was infrequent unless they had used the whores outside the brothels we controlled) was that they developed quite severe foreskin problems. It was not so much a matter of hygiene, which can be difficult, living and soldiering in a tropical environment, but a matter of minor problems which had become more major in the environment of the brothels.

In medical terminology several were suffering from phimosis, paraphimosis and chronic infections. As this was early in their tour, I decided to do a circumcision list and about five soldiers underwent the chop. It was all uneventful and after their operation, each patient was given plenty of pain relief and sedation at night to try and ward off nocturnal erections, which would be extremely unwelcome post-surgery. The next day a junior NCO from the Battalion who had been detailed to visit the men and report on their well-being asked the ward staff if he could see them, which, following permission, he did. He should have been searched. As he chatted with each soldier, he surreptitiously handed out some pornographic magazines for them to peruse and while away the hours as they recovered, and then left to report on their state of health. Despite the sedation, the images in the magazines caused the tumescent effects that I was trying to prevent, and soon all the soldiers started moaning in discomfort, calling out for more pain relief. My ward staff retrieved the offending magazines and I prescribed industrial doses of Valium. I then detailed one of the staff to check all the men to see that the sutures I had put in had held under the strain (the sutures were made of part of a sheep or cow's intestine and were called catgut, or chromic catgut, but they had nothing to do with cats), and also that all the tented bedsheets had collapsed. Fortunately, no harm had been done, and I left my team happily thumbing through the pages of the confiscated magazines as they manned reception. The soldiers recovered, and well within the prescribed period of abstinence I had advised, they all got back into action, either with a paid and admiring companion or solo if they were broke.

Driving back from a clinic at Belmopan one day, we stopped as usual at JB's bar for a drink. We were just about to leave when an enormous local man appeared out of the jungle where he had been clearing the scrub with a JCB type of vehicle. He was built like a gorilla. He asked me if I was the "doctor fella" and when I said yes, he pulled off a heavy calf high leather boot and showed me his lower leg. Just above the ankle was a large granulating ulcer, about two inches in diameter. It looked clean and healthy and I asked him what happened. He said that a few weeks previously, he had gone to work without his boots, for the first and only time, and had been bitten by a snake "a Yella Jaw man" he said. This was one of the names given to the Fer de Lance, which means "spearhead", from the French.

I was amazed he was still alive, as this snake is very aggressive and has a powerful venom which destroys tissue and causes massive bleeding. Even with medical help and anti-venom a limb can be lost, in addition to brain bleeds and other horrible things. However, the sequelae will depend on the degree of envenomation. He carried on with his story.

"I kicked the snake off, I wrassled with it to the ground and killed it with ma machet'. I went to bed an' I pisse' blood, I vomited blood, I shat blood. I couldn't get up for days. I lost about 30 lbs", (that would have got him down to about 250 lbs then), "an' then I got better man". No medical help, no anti-venom. I was bloody amazed. He must have had a mighty constitution. I asked him where he lived. He said, "San Ignacio man, on a farm, de one where y'all had a BBQ with ma dad". It turned out that this jungle clearer was the eldest son of Aldo Moro.

I told him that his ulcer would eventually heal over, or if not, I could slap a skin graft on it, but he wasn't worried; he just went back into the jungle and carried on working, with his boot back on.

Snakes should be avoided. That is the general advice, as even the non-venomous species can cause very nasty infected wounds and worse, because of the bacteria they carry in their mouths and hence inject via their fangs. I was asked for my help in the case of another snakebite. A young Mayan Indian boy had also been bitten on the lower leg, a few weeks before, and was very ill. He had developed an acute osteomyelitis (infection) of his tibia, along the whole length of the bone, and he had also got fluffy changes on his Chest X-ray, a fever and an irregular pulse, suggesting metastatic infectious disease in his lungs and vegetations (infected blood components) on his heart valves. The ex-RAMC radiologist I had met working in Belize City Hospital confirmed the likelihood of this being the case when reviewing the X-rays of his tibia and chest. The lad was on antibiotics, but they were ineffective, suggesting that the causative bacteria were not sensitive to them. I took some time to think. I was to do this a lot during my surgical career.

There would have been no point in surgically debriding (clearing out the dead tissue and bone from) this little boy's tibia, if ever, until we had controlled the infection. I was pretty sure that the bacteria (bugs) that were causing this infection were a strain of staphylococcus aureus, though blood cultures had not revealed this. We needed to change his antibiotics or use a combination of different ones, but access to these was limited. Fortunately I knew of an antibiotic called fusidic acid which was effective against staph aureus, especially in bone and joint infections. There was no chance of this being available in Belize, nor indeed did we carry any in the Station Hospital. However, I was pretty sure it was available to our orthopaedic surgeons in UK, and enquiries confirmed this. I also seem to remember that it was very expensive. I could order the intravenous and oral preparations, but only on a named patient basis.

Untreated, this little Mayan was going to die, and we had to do something. We gave him the pseudonym Ranger M. Indian 2RIR or something similar, with a fictitious Army number, and sent a signal back to the UK. A few days later the drug arrived, and we immediately drove to Belmopan to start an infusion of the maximum dose his weight would allow and then some more. I had reckoned on seven days' intravenous administration, followed by six weeks of oral therapy.

In short, he had improved in 48 hours and was almost walking within a week. I was worried about a pathological fracture as his tibia was so diseased, so I put his leg in a full non-weight bearing cast and a local carpenter made some crutches for him. At about a month his X-ray changes were resolving, and he was discharged. He went back into the jungle to rejoin his family. He would need to have the cast removed after another month, though I doubted that the plaster of Paris would last that long in the intense humidity, and assuming that X-rays of his leg were normal he would not need any further treatment. I never saw him again, but he should have been all right.

I presented him as a clinical case of the management of widespread osteomyelitis at the medical/surgical meeting in the City hospital, extolling the effectiveness of fusidic acid, as I went through the details and showed the X-rays. At the end of my presentation, the only comment that I elicited was that I should have immobilised his leg sooner than I did. I had an uneasy feeling, which was soon borne out.

After the meeting, the Chief of Surgery came up to me. He congratulated me on the successful management of the case and then said something else. His words had the effect of making me question a lot of what I and others were doing regarding hearts and minds work. He said, "Belize is a poor, small, underdeveloped country and we are only just achieving independence from our rich colonial power. We do not have the resources available to us that you have, to provide any comparable treatment. It is all very well, but you raise the expectations of our population for a service to be delivered that is not possible at this time and therefore what we can provide is undermined and our people become dissatisfied".

I took his point, but on the other hand it was very hard to neglect the requirements of this young patient who would have otherwise died, when we had the resources to provide an effective treatment which was unavailable locally. The thought that this would cast the local medical services into a poor light had never occurred to me, though in any event I could not have permitted this rather churlish attitude to influence the way I had been taught to practise medicine. Should I have ignored the request for help and just let the young lad succumb to avoid the risk of demonstrating the inadequacies of the local medical services when independent of their colonial power? No, but perhaps I should have just kept quiet about it.

I was in a similar quandary when doing a locum in Nepal several years later. Again I would say that it is very difficult to withhold the techniques of modern medicine, surgery and the resources that were available to me, but in this case I should have done so and not undertaken the rather drastic but inevitably futile surgery that I did to try and save an infant's life.

I decided to hitch a lift on an Army Air Corps Puma helicopter to visit a friend of mine who was the medical officer for Battle Group South, in Punta Gorda, near the Guatemalan border. His name was Captain Lorenzo Pieri and we had been at Sandhurst together. The trip was uneventful until the helicopter developed a fault and the pilot made a rotating heavy landing on the helipad. He said something about the engine cutting out, so I should be glad to be alive. Anyway, I stayed with my colleague for lunch, then went with him to an observation post and had a look at Guatemala, which looked pretty much just like Belize.

On saying goodbye, I got into the return helicopter. I suppose it must have been the same one, as no sooner had we got into the air than the pilot bumped it down again. That was twice in one day. Another helicopter was sent to retrieve us and I determined never to voluntarily travel in one again, though I would abandoned this resolution when on a desperate search for alcohol a couple of years down the line.

The next event I describe rather proved the point that I made to the young 2RIR subaltern and demonstrated what a dangerous place Belize City was at night, so much so that soldiers were only allowed out in pairs. Violent crime and drugs were rife.

In the early hours of a Sunday morning I was awoken by the camp Motor Transport Officer (MTO) crashing into my room in the Mess. I was groggy, but soon awoke as he told me I had to get to the Hospital ASAP as Lt Col Restall was struggling to resuscitate a Corporal who had been stabbed. It was a desperate emergency. It transpired that a Cpl Billingham, a portly clerk at Airport Camp, had wandered half pissed into the Big C for another drink. He had been waiting his turn to be served when a Creole local, who had been working out in the jungle and was high on drugs, came in and pushed Billingham to one side to get to the bar. Billingham took offence at this (there was no love lost between some of the indigenous population, especially the Creoles and the soldiers), swore at him and shoved him out of the way, not noticing the machete that the Creole was carrying in his belt.

The Creole drew his weapon in front of everybody, stabbed Billingham in his left lower abdominal quadrant and ran out of the bar. Billingham collapsed, but was helped to the back of the building to lie on one of the whore's cots whilst someone went for help. The story gets a bit apocryphal here, but as related to me, it seemed that the girl and her next customer had need of the cot, so Billingham was thrown out. He went out of the building and collapsed again on the street. There he was found by a group of soldiers, who, thinking that Billingham was drunk, helped him to his feet but then noticed Billingham's small bowel, which had prolapsed (fallen out) through the machete entrance wound in his abdomen.

Remembering some first aid, they lifted Billingham onto the back of a flatbed truck, covered his small bowel with an item of clothing and also went off to find help, hopefully getting the RAMC Land Rover ambulance to come down from camp to collect him, or help from patrolling Royal Military Police (RMP). This is where Billingham got lucky, because the MTO, either of his own initiative or under routine orders, was patrolling all the soldier's usual haunts to pick up the drunk and injured. He spotted Billingham's inert body on the flat bed, tried to wake him, lifted the shirt or whatever, saw his injury and did the best thing, which was to get him into his vehicle and back to the Station Hospital at high speed.

John Restall had about four intravenous lines set up and he and a couple of the OTTs were squeezing bags of saline and Ringer's Lactate solution in order to get as much fluid as possible back into Billingham, who was now unconscious. We got his medical records and found out his blood group. As soon as Billingham had a blood pressure, he was anaesthetised and put straight onto the operating table. Under these circumstances it is better to stem the blood flow as far as possible and then continue resuscitation. When I opened him, I found he had a belly full of blood and that the weapon had sliced through a couple of loops of bowel and through the small bowel mesentery (the root through which its blood supply travels), which was bleeding heavily, and into the liver, which was also bleeding with some large attached clots. As there was no smell of faeces, I reckoned the large bowel was not perforated.

From what I could see and feel, I confirmed as best I could that all his other organs were undamaged. However, the blood loss was excessive and we really needed to get some blood into him. I asked my sergeant lab tech to phone the Battalion ops room and ask them to immediately send all the soldiers in camp who had Billingham's blood group, or who had O Rhesus negative blood (universal donor blood group), to the Station Hospital. I was having real difficulty controlling the blood loss, so I just packed his abdomen tight with abdominal packs and waited.

I have always been taught that the best way to deal with haemorrhage is patience and I followed that advice, resisting the temptation to peek under the packs to see if the bleeding had abated whilst I mentally rehearsed the operative procedures I would have to undertake. Later in my career this would be intuitive through experience, but in 1980 I was not that far along the learning curve.

Next, I heard an authoritative voice shouting, "Lef' light, lef' light, lef' light. HALT. Stand at - EASE". The blood had arrived. We could only give un-crossmatched group compatible blood, or O negative blood, which we did, and my lab tech bled the donors. When he had extracted a bagful or so, he would shake it to mix up the anticoagulant and toss it to John Restall, who would transfuse it, still warm, into Billingham, and Billingham began to look a lot pinker after a few pints.

Now it was up to me. Every Field Surgical Team has three Operating Theatre Technicians (OTTS) and I can tell you (I was later to be in charge of their school in Aldershot), that each one is highly trained and highly competent, whether they are acting as an anaesthetic tech, scrub tech, or surgical assistant. I started to tentatively remove the abdominal packs and at that precise moment, we had a power cut. I pushed the packs back in and one of the team went off to start the emergency diesel generator. He came back to say that there was no fuel in the generator and the battery was flat. It was supposed to be checked and started every week. John Restall had already started to ventilate Billingham by hand, as the electrically-powered anaesthetic machine had ground to a halt.

The whole camp was blacked out. As nobody knew where the fuelling point was and they would never find it in the total darkness of the night anyway, nor a battery for that matter, I did the only thing I could do. I stopped the bleeding, anastomosed (joined) the gut ends after removing injured segments, and using large hepatic sutures (liver stitches) repaired the liver, all under torchlight. The army issue torches were held by the team in relays, about an inch and a half from the tips of the instruments I was using. The minute I'd put the last skin suture in, electricity was restored to the camp and the lights came back on. We were all sweating profusely, because of course the air conditioning had been knocked out.

Billingham recovered and was stable. He had a fever and high pulse rate. There was no sign of further bleeding and as a bonus his brain was still working, in spite of his bleeding to the point of unconsciousness. I asked for permission to call up the Learjet and he was evacuated to the Mount Sinai Trauma Hospital in Miami. He would need a military doctor to accompany him and report back, so the RAF medical officer went with him on the grounds that he was in the RAF and therefore trained to deal with aeromedical evacuations and not because he wanted a couple of days in Miami. Billingham made it alive to the Mount Sinai, but he then developed a whole series of complications which required several further operative procedures, including a temporary colostomy (bowel brought out onto the abdominal wall) and a tracheostomy (a semi-permanent breathing tube into the larynx). He also developed a severe psychosis caused by his prolonged stay in their Intensive Care Unit.

Several months later he was well enough to be retrieved, back to his base in BAOR, where he had his colostomy closed. He was left with a severely scarred abdominal wall and a big incisional hernia. Whilst he was on sick leave, he had gotten married to a girl that he woke up in bed with after a party. How was I to know all this? Because I would meet him again.

I was lucky to have had the anaesthetist I did, with his experience and calmness under pressure, and though this washed over me on the outside, inside my heart was racing faster than Billingham's ever did. I was also pleased with the way we had all reacted to the difficult circumstances, and this reflected the can-do attitude in the Forces and the general camaraderie and discipline that it engenders. Did I save Billingham's life? No, the team did. Each of us contributed the skills we had acquired, the training we had undertaken and achieved the objective, in presenting Billingham with a fighting chance of survival under the specialised care of the American doctors and surgeons. Finally, Billingham would not have survived without the quick reactions of the 2RIR ops room and the blood donors who were marched in, in record time.

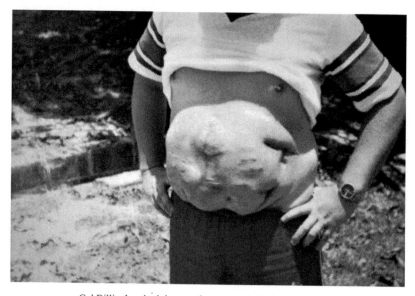

Cpl Billingham's abdomen after surgery in Belize and Miami.

I was on Goff's Caye one Sunday and was lounging about, chatting and catching a few rays. It was a beautiful day, the skies were blue, and I was just about to explore the reef after lunch. There were some American families on the Caye who were cooking a BBQ and getting out some sandwiches and beer. One of our number, whose ears were not filled with wax, sand and seawater, heard a helicopter approaching and soon enough a Puma was circling the Caye. I was pretty sure it was for me. One of the aircrew yelled down and signalled to confirm this was the case, whilst the helicopter started to hover and the winch to get me up into the aircraft was swung out. There was no way I wanted to do this, to be hooked like a fish and hauled into an alien environment i.e. go from land to air and then into a machine that had all the flying characteristics of an unpredictable bumblebee, and all of those in which I had travelled so far had landed with some sort of mechanical failure.

I signalled and pointed to a sandbank just off the Caye. The pilot landed the aircraft on this sandbank and I climbed aboard. Unfortunately, the sand displaced by the helicopter blades covered everything on the Caye, and the American's BBQ flew off somewhere. One of them shouted, "Gee, it's just like Vietnam" as I was flown away in this method of transport which I had grown, quite justifiably, to distrust.

There was no real emergency. A soldier had presented to the medical reception saying he was bleeding from his tail end. Apparently, the day before, in a rather half-hearted suicide attempt, he had eaten some broken glass. The boys had pre-empted my request and obtained an abdominal X-ray and I detected a small amount of glass, which would no doubt pass naturally. I debated whether I wanted to penalize the nursing staff by making them sift through the patient's faeces. I thought better of it and just kept the soldier in the ward until we could refer him back to the Regimental Medical Officer. No doubt his depression could be cured by a couple of days in jail.

There were a lot of questions in the Officer's Mess about why I had been choppered away and what the emergency was. I couldn't say anything because of confidentiality issues, so I just opted to say, that I had arranged for the medical reception staff to recall me to the Hospital for an emergency at a predetermined time, to save the two-hour boat journey (the helicopter took about 20 minutes). Of course, had this been true, I would have been in deep shit and probably made to pay the MOD for the costs of the trip, deducted from my pay for about 20 years.

I was coming to the end of my tour. As an FST, we had often gone out together in the evenings into Belize City for relaxation and a few drinks, at say the Bellevue Hotel, or the slightly posher Fort George, or even one of the brothels (though we usually visited both) to take advantage of their alcoholic hospitality and check that all was going smoothly as it were. We tended to stick together, as it cut down on any logistical problems retrieving us in an emergency, such as Billingham's.

On previous explorations of the City I had been very taken with the hand-worked carvings from driftwood that were sold usually in the backstreets. They looked exquisite and were very cheap, and I had found a delightful carving of a pirate ship complete with sails and rigging, which was slightly more expensive. I knew that it was traditional for the FST to buy 'the boss' a parting gift and present it to him on his last night's celebration and I had shamelessly told all those who would listen how much I liked that particular carving. I was pretty sure that they had got the hint.

When my replacement arrived, I was off call for the first time in six months, which in itself was a cause for celebration and having been very careful as to how much I drank before, I was determined to enjoy the evening in the company of the RAMC's finest, an FST that had proved itself up to the task. With no surgical responsibility that night, there would be no brake on the booze for me.

We all went downtown, where the Belikin and San Miguel beer, whisky, gin and elaborate cocktails, all slipped down well. As I was feeling quite light-headed fairly early on in the evening, I decided to throttle back a bit, though nonetheless, I was pretty pissed when we reached the Queen of Hearts, where I sat down in the bar and ordered another round of drinks. The senior rank then stood up unsteadily and in a slurred voice said, "Goodbye boss. We all wish you well (hic), it's been great (hic), and we've got something for you as a memento". The senior rank sat down and slurred to another member of the team "Go an' get 'er". Hang on a minute. If the wood carving was on its way, he would have said "Go an' get it" surely. Had I misheard?

Nope, I had not. One of the girls from the Queen of Hearts, plump but not unattractive, was led in. She had a ribbon tied under her chin, knotted in a bow on the top of her head. "Pox doc says she's all right and she's paid for all night".

My informer collapsed into a chair and she (I will call her Rosie) sashayed round and sat on my lap. I was almost speechless at their 'generosity', as an all-nighter must have set them back all of £15. I managed to murmur my thanks at their thoughtfulness whilst simultaneously trying to stop Rosie publicly fondling my crotch. It occurred to me that they must have paid her a lot more than the usual rate to ensure she got her way with me. She was absolutely determined, but the last thing I wanted to do was shag a girl whom I had instrumentally (literally) inspected once a week and even if I had wanted to, I did not have any condoms.

"Thanks lads" I said, "but I haven't got any...." I was interrupted. "Here you are sir, you'll need these. Can't 'ave you going bareback" and a packet of three was thrust into my hand. My team really were thorough, they had even thought of condoms to try and prevent the STI (sexually transmitted infection) that I would inevitably get if the pox doc had got it wrong.

Technically, Rosie was a patient, and the GMC forbids relationships between doctors and patients, even if the patients are willing, fully paid for sex workers. I didn't think that would hold much sway in these circumstances. The FST gradually broke away with a bit of sniggering and their parting comments were unprintable. I spoke to Rosie and explained that I was, "not in the mood, had had too much to drink, had a girlfriend, was married, preferred boys", and finally "that I'd just had a major operation". She was unmoved. "Oh, dey say you say all dat" she responded. Yes, I'm sure they did.

I said we could go for a drink and we changed bars. I bought her a drink, said I was going to have a pee, ran out, dived into another bar a few yards away and hid in a corner. The door swung open, and in she walked, seductively sidling over to me, accompanied by the wolf whistles of the other customers. I got up, gave her a quick kiss, waved goodbye, went outside, hailed a taxi (one of the very old American cars that were on their last legs in Belize) and went to somewhere I think was called Estelle's Bijoux just outside camp, which was full of 2RIR soldiers. There I stood at the bar with a large scotch, relieved that I had managed to escape. I felt confident that there was no way she would follow me in a taxi.

Halfway through my scotch a 2RIR lance corporal came in, ordered his drink and stood next to me and we sort of conversed in low tones. He was clearly curious as to why I, obviously an officer, was in this particular bar on my own and three sheets to the wind. I told him that I had had a slight problem, just as Rosie walked in. I was astonished by her persistence. Perhaps I would just have to grit my teeth and do the deed to get rid of her. I tried my best, through blurred vision, to see her in a different light as she stood beside me at the bar. The words "paid for all night" kept recycling in my brain.

Then a solution came to me. The bar was full of horny soldiers. Turning to the lance jack I asked, "Umm, how would you like to help me out with this young lady?" I explained that she was a parting gift from my team, the best in the Queen of Hearts and fully checked out. He looked her up and down and she looked him up and down. It wasn't love at first sight, but it was close. We agreed on 20 dollars, which he handed over to me and I gave to Rosie, which would go some way to satisfying her honour. She and her new companion went off for the night to consummate the deal, somewhere out in the bush – an activity described by the soldiers as 'swamping'. I breathed a sigh of relief, finished my drink and left the bar.

I woke up as dawn was breaking, all in one piece, but a little damp from the dew and the ditch I had fallen into and then subsequently slept in. I walked back to camp, ignoring the *sotto voce* comments from the guards at the gate, found my hut and fell into bed. It had been a hell of a night and I would have a hell of a hangover. Next day, feeling very much the worse for wear, I climbed on the transport for the airport, and the return VC 10 flight back to the UK. My team came to see me off, unable to resist making sexual gestures.

I arrived safely back in the UK and was keen to meet up with Kathy, as one can imagine. She was going to be posted to Hong Kong to work in the British Military Hospital, followed by a 12-month posting to Nepal. This was a prime posting and if the truth be told, one of the good reasons for joining the Armed Medical Services and therefore an opportunity not to be missed. I was heartbroken, and I think she probably was too, and although we discussed it at great length and she said she was prepared to forego the tour for the sake of our relationship, I felt that it would be unreasonable to expect her to, as no one could predict our future together, though we were a pretty strong couple. If she had stayed, future events might have been very different.

In the meantime, I went back to my job at the CMH, and worked with Kathy in theatre during my operating lists; she became a very good scrub nurse in a very short time. We were living together in my cottage in Old Woking, but the inevitable separation was drawing near.

My Higher Surgical Training had been arranged to begin in October 1980 and I would spend a year at The General Hospital in Birmingham, then a year at the Queen Elizabeth Military Hospital in Woolwich, London, followed by a year at CMH Aldershot and finally a year at St Peter's Hospital in Chertsey. I would be the first Army surgeon to go to the General Hospital in Birmingham and it was hoped I would set the standard; I tried, but had the odd lapse. In the meantime, I had been promoted to Major.

CHAPTER 12

The Oates Charcoal Manoeuvre

The General Hospital, Birmingham, 1980

The General Hospital was old and getting past its time, but it had an excellent reputation, with well-known and respected surgical consultants. I thought Birmingham was dark, dirty, dingy and drab, certainly not a city I would enjoy being in, though some of the surrounding suburbs were pleasant. I walked around the city centre and the Bullring, just to give Birmingham a fair crack, but in all honesty, as it stood in those days, visiting Birmingham was never going to be on anybody's bucket list.

For the first six months I would be working for Mr G D Oates and Mr N Dorricott. Geoff Oates tended to specialise in breast, thyroid and large bowel surgery and Norman Dorricott was developing one of the first colonoscopy clinics in the country, though he generally did not get too involved in the surgery of the large bowel. He was the junior consultant surgeon in the firm, and he was concentrating on developing a novel service to which he would get referrals.

My schedule was not too arduous and most of my time would be spent on ward rounds and in theatre. The General was a teaching hospital, accepting medical students from Birmingham Medical School, and teaching would also be an integral part of my duties, which I welcomed. I have taught medical students and junior surgeons for the whole of my surgical career, in the UK, Hong Kong, in the Chinese University of Shatin and in Wales. In addition, I would help with some papers for publication with regard to the optimum procedures in duodenal ulcer surgery, following long term follow up. Duodenal (stomach) ulcers were rife in those days, and I don't think one night on call went by without my having to operate on an ulcer that was either bleeding profusely or had perforated, contaminating the peritoneal (abdominal cavity). Nowadays this disease and the complications I have described are relatively uncommon, due to a better understanding of the aetiology (cause) and better medical treatment.

I would be on a 1:4 emergency rota, a luxury for me, and I would therefore be able to return to my cottage on my off-duty weekends.

I got on well with Norman Dorricott, a nice man, who had some pursuits outside surgery and drove an Alfa Romeo for a start, but I found it difficult to get close to Geoff Oates, who was single-minded with regard to his practice and extremely reluctant to distribute his cases for operation to the senior registrars, especially those patients requiring thyroid surgery. I assisted him in these procedures many times and credit where credit is due, he did the operations beautifully, and in my subsequent practice as a consultant I shamelessly emulated his technique. He was obsessively concerned with any operative blood loss and would attack minor bleeders with the diathermy machine (electric coagulation) in what I thought was a tissue destructive fashion and convert areas of the operative field into charcoal. I christened it 'the Oates Charcoal Manoeuvre'.

Geoff Oates' large bowel surgery was also meticulous, but each case always took at least four hours, with the faff index sometimes at stratospheric levels. Stapling instruments which have revolutionised bowel and other organ surgery were in their infancy at this time, but when I used them some years later as a large bowel surgeon, I found them to be reliable and fully developed, and they made short work of difficult anastomoses (joins), so I must not be unkind to Mr Oates.

I was to blot my copybook early on with him. Whilst I relate this, it must be remembered that I was in the Army, on their payroll, and not reliant as such, on job references from civilian consultant surgeons. Mr Oates had invited me round to his house for supper and I made sure I was on my best behaviour, at least for a while. We had a delightful meal cooked by his latest wife, and he gave me a potted history of his ascension to consultancy.

Birmingham born, Birmingham bred, Birmingham Medical School, Birmingham junior and senior registrar rotations, Birmingham consultant. I was not exactly fascinated. I wanted to tell him about Belize and other adventures, but I thought better of it. It might be a painful reminder that the world did not end outside the city limits of Birmingham, and my forays into sex worker gynaecology would seriously upset his equilibrium. He told me he did go skiing in Switzerland once a year, when he thought his senior registrar could be trusted to look after his patients, so he obviously knew that at least one other country existed.

At this point in the conversation I was bored stiff with Birmingham and then Mr Oates asked me a question. "Well David, you've been here a few weeks, tell me, what do you think of Birmingham? Be honest." He should not have asked me to be honest, and I should not have forgotten what I had been told about him. He did not have a sense of humour. 'Honest' he'd said, so I was. "To be frank Sir, it is not really my cup of tea. I live in the country and until I came here, I used to think Bracknell was the arsehole of the world".

There was a stunned silence. Mrs Oates went to the kitchen. "I was joking, of course", I added rather feebly and a little too late to be convincing. The damage was done. I glanced at Mr Oates and thought I might have detected a slight upward twitch in the corner of his mouth, which I hoped might be the result of his attempting to suppress a smile. The alternative was that this was his way of communicating to me that I had committed a professional gaffe so heinous, by deriding his city, that if ever I wanted a surgical post in Birmingham, the UK, or for that matter anywhere else in the civilised world, I would find it extremely difficult. The evening ended on this rather solemn note.

On the other hand, I think he was pleasantly surprised by my surgical and clinical experience, my patient care and my generally light-hearted affable nature. I was also meticulous, perhaps a facsimile of himself, only one with a sense of humour, which he found irritating. He did say once that if he asked me to do something he would bet his mortgage on the fact that I would get it done, and I don't think he even said it through gritted teeth.

One day he asked me to do the thyroidectomy on the operating list and said he would be available in the coffee room, if needed. This was unheard of, and soon the subject of the theatre suite scuttlebutt (gossip). Geoff Oates giving away a thyroid; never happened before. I am generally pretty sanguine under pressure, and so I just got on with the procedure. I did it exactly as Mr Oates had shown me, identifying all the important structures in the bloodless operative field, which he would have had, by doing 'Oates charcoal manoeuvres' if in name only. I did slip up by saying this out loud, just as Mr Oates came in to stand by my side. When he asked me what I had said, I replied, with a speed of thought that I am not renowned for, that I was using one of his "manoeuvres for dividing the thyroid isthmus". He seemed perplexed but satisfied. I completed the operation, closed the wound, wrote the notes and post-operative instructions and checked with the anaesthetist that the patient still had full use of the vocal cords. I reported to Mr Oates, who said, "You did that rather well". I had to sit down.

I was satisfying my vocational drive with a lot of patient care and theatre lists, quite happy to turn out at all hours if I was available to help, even when I was not on call. I was generally good humoured about the interruptions of normal life by hospital phone calls, as I had signed up to this way of life the minute I entered medical school and then the operating theatres. I was paid reasonably well, and truthfully, as long as I did not have to worry too much about the costs of living, I was quite happy with my salary.

There is a flip side to this, as on some occasions I came out of theatre after several draining hours and ruefully realised that I had not even earned enough to get my car serviced! There was an American paediatric heart surgeon who put his salary into perspective when he said, "There are times when I go into theatre and you wouldn't have to pay me. There are other times that I go into theatre and you couldn't pay me enough".

I think that Mr Oates and I had reached an understanding. I am sure he was happy with my developing clinical skills and my overall work rate without any major disasters, but he still remained suspicious of my sense of humour and did not believe it was an appropriate attribute for a career in surgery. Even though I was always courteous, I suspect that in his opinion, I failed to appreciate how powerful and respected he was in the profession. I did not, but my career was already mapped out in the Army as I had been accepted for a Regular Commission by the Army Board and therefore had the security of my job until retirement or disaster struck – or in my case, both.

Norman Dorricott and I were closer in age and shared many common interests. One day he told me that he had been invited to attend a sporting shoot and asked me if I had any experience of shotguns. I explained that I had done a bit of rough shooting and clay pigeon shooting in North Wales with my friend Nod, whose father had an extensive gun collection. Norman was late for the shoot (he was generally late for everything), and unfortunately crashed his Alfa driving to the meeting and never made it. Quite a disappointing day out for him really and it was the talk of the hospital for all of an hour. I liked Norman Dorricott, but he needed to calm down a bit. We were to meet again in West Germany in 1992 and he still hadn't calmed down.

The General Hospital was providing one of the few services in the NHS for bariatric surgery. Obesity was becoming a nationwide problem which was getting worse, and it seemed particularly prevalent in the Midlands. These were patients, often of gargantuan size, in whom the usual less invasive strategies had failed e.g. dietician's advice, weight watchers' clubs, followed by dental surgeons wiring their jaws together so that they could only eat and drink through a straw. However obese patients are cunning and manipulative and often they would get well-meaning relatives to liquidise the four Chinese take-away meals they would normally eat for supper into a bowl, which they could suck up like dredgers. Others were so driven to eat that they cut the dental wires themselves and then after eating, kept their teeth clamped together to give the impression that the wiring was still effectively in situ.

The surgery of obesity in those early days was open, as opposed to keyhole, generally involved a spaghetti junction-like rearrangement of the upper intestinal tract to bypass the food absorbing areas and was fraught with hazards. In the General, these patients were affectionately known as the "Fatties", which of course would be verboten nowadays. Some patients were so large that they required two operating tables in parallel and the surgical wards that housed them before and after their operations, had oversized beds, specially modified bathrooms and, I suspect, reinforced toilets. All the patients had multiple co-morbidities (additional illnesses) which substantially increased their complication rate and consequently their operative mortality, but this seemed to be cheerfully accepted by all concerned. I mention all this because this is a branch of surgery that I would pay not to get involved in. However, the spinoff for those surgeons that do is a large private practice, earning vast amounts of money (in their own time of course).

It was during this year that Peter Hawker, a senior registrar in medicine and future medical politician, and I did a combined upper gastro-intestinal inspection of the gullet, stomach and some small bowel, a flexible endoscopy list, once or twice a week. I also learned how to do flexible sigmoidoscopies (similar examination of the lower large bowel), so in the end I could 'top and tail' a patient if required under the same sedative.

After six months of working for the Oates and Dorricott firm, Geoff Oates implored me to encourage my new consultants, Mr John Alexander Williams and Mr Mike Keighley, to contribute patients with bowel cancers to a clinical trial he was involved in, the relevance of which will become clear a little later.

John Alexander Williams was an extremely attractive character and a master surgeon. Mike Keighley was a professor in waiting, with a huge number of published learned papers to his name (or at least with his name on them), and he led the field in the use of (prophylactic) antibiotics in surgery, to reduce post-operative infection rates. His main area of interest was the colon, rectum and anus, about which he was to write a book. I was very lucky to work with these two, as indeed I had been lucky to work with Oates and Dorricott, but this attachment gave me insight into the working of clinical trials.

Mike Keighley had his own research Registrar to run the various trials and write them up for publication, which, subject to Mr Keighley's approval, would be submitted to the various Journals with Mr Keighley's name added to the end of the list of authors, to provide more clout. Other trials were sponsored by pharmaceutical companies who wanted their products favourably independently tested, and financial contributions would be made per patient entered, and in turn these contributions would help fund the research Registrar.

This is a short, if slightly cynical, synopsis of how the system worked and I should stress, it was very important that every patient was fully utilised with regard to their possible contribution to keeping the General on the map, and of course the investigators and contributing consultants with them.

However, before I started with Alexander-Williams and Keighley, I took some leave in March 1981 and went to visit Kathy in Hong Kong. It had been a long time since I had seen her, and I had missed her very much. The time passed quickly and all too soon I had to return home. It was very sad, but Kathy would return to the UK on leave and I would be able to have more time with her then.

CHAPTER 13

Speaking Klingon

Belize revisited, 1981

I arrived back in the UK towards the end of March and on checking my mail, I came across what looked like a posting order from the Ministry of Defence. Indeed it was, back to Belize for a week. It transpired that the Belize police had caught the man who had stabbed Cpl Billingham and I had been summoned as a witness to the committal proceedings in the Magistrates court on the 4th of 'Arpil' 1981 (yes, that's exactly what was written on the summons).

I phoned the General Hospital and explained that I would be back a couple of weeks late due to military commitments and then packed for what I thought would be just a week. I deliberated about what I would have to say. I supposed they would want the details of the extent of Billingham's injury and the likely weapon. I used the rail warrant I had been issued with to travel to RAF Brize Norton and checked in for my flight. Who should I be standing behind in the check-in queue but Cpl Billingham himself and a young Royal Military Policeman

(RMP) who had been working as a liaison with the Belize Police Force and the British Forces.

I said hello to Billingham, though of course he could not remember me, which was to be expected as he had only seen me after his operation before he was carted off to Miami. I filled him in on exactly what had happened to him and the sort of surgery he underwent, including the contribution of the Royal Irish Regiment in saving his life. He was very grateful and then explained to me what he remembered happening in the Big C Disco up until the point when he had collapsed on the whore's cot.

The VC 10 landed after an uneventful flight. 'Butcher Radar' gave the pilot a surprisingly good score and I made my way to the officers' mess. I introduced myself to the resident surgeon, who was a Crab (RAF). I had no surgical responsibilities this time and was therefore truly on holiday, though I did cover his on-call for a night so that he could go out and get pissed, bladdered or wrecked in Army speak, or weave an uneven course for home, in Crab speak. I had a couple of days to fill in prior to the committal proceedings, so Billingham, the RMP and I went around the country visiting Mayan ruins and eating watermelons. It was still the hot season and the weather was beautiful, my tan was nicely topped up and I reshredded my ankles.

The 4th of 'Arpil' arrived and I presented myself to the magistrate's court, which was in an old rickety slat-board building, and sat down with a few other witnesses. The magistrate came in with his clerk, took his seat and called for the accused. As Belize was an old British Colony, its justice system was based on that of the UK. The perpetrator was brought in handcuffed between two policemen and faced the magistrate, looking surly and disrespectful. He identified himself with a nod of his head as his name was read out, and then the charge was put before him, "that on the such and such a day he did cause 'grievous harm' to a British soldier in the establishment called the Big C Disco".

I was not familiar with the term 'grievous harm', but was informed, "dat is murda boss, but de solda, he ain' dead" or put simply, it was one down from murder. I was asked if I agreed with the charge, to which I concurred, as it had been a pretty grievous injury. No bail was applied for, nor would it have been granted in the circumstances, as the police had had to search half the jungle to find the accused. The magistrate referred the case to the Supreme Court and I was bailed to appear as a witness again and would be duly notified of the date. It appeared I had flown 6000 miles only to say not a lot more than a couple of words in something akin to a tropical beach hut. I went out for a few beers.

Two days later, just before my scheduled flight home, a message came through from the clerk of the Supreme Court via the RMP. It had been decided that as I had travelled so far to reach Belize, and to save my return at a later date, the prosecutor would bring the case forward and it would be heard within a week. In the interim I occupied myself by lounging in a hammock which I had bought, and then going for a few days adventure training on St George's Caye. I did a bit of snorkelling, scuba diving and ocean kayaking, and utterly failed to manage an Eskimo roll in a canoe. In fact, the instructor said that I was the most determined pupil he had ever had who failed every time to surface from the depths of the lagoon still inside the canoe.

When I returned to Airport Camp, I was informed that the court case had been postponed. The Creole prisoner had escaped and the police were out hunting for him again. I had been in the country for about two weeks by this stage, with just a week's worth of clothing, so I had to go into town to buy some more.

Whilst walking along I saw that the sailing ship I had wanted (but got Rosie instead) was no longer in the shabby little shop where I had first spotted it. I felt an ominous rumble in my abdomen with severe cramps and it became quite clear that I was about to have an attack of "Belize belly" or "bad belly". This was worrying, as public toilets were few and far between in downtown Belize City, but fortunately I was not that far from the Belle Vue Hotel. I fast walked, as running would have been too dangerous. I needed to concentrate as much energy as I could on maintaining the high strength integrity of my 32-year-old anal sphincter, to put it crudely. Fortunately, it was up to the task and I shot into the men's loos in the hotel to find every booth was either occupied or out of order. I dived into the ladies', startling a couple of women who were rebuilding their makeup in front of the mirrors above the wash basins. I reckon that if there was a male world record for the fastest, most explosive bowel action in a ladies' toilet in Central America, I would have broken it that day. Why am I writing this? Well, the simple answer is that it was because of this gastrointestinal near disaster that I met the public prosecutor who would be dealing with our case.

I walked into the hotel bar, pale sweaty and tight arsed, for several medicinal pints of draught San Miguel as I had lost a Sweetwater Canal's worth of fluid. There were two Belizeans at the bar, both smartly dressed. They looked at me and one of them wandered over and said, "You dat doctor fellow, do dat soldier dat got done in de Big C?" How on earth did he know? I said that indeed I was, and he introduced himself as the prosecuting council for the Department of Justice and his colleague, as his assistant. They were both barristers. He opened a case discussion in the bar area.

"I's goin' to do dat Creole boy, he goin' away for more dan 10 years. Dat's what I is goin' a do. I is workin' on it". That was the start and finish of the case discussion.

There had been several witnesses to the stabbing in the Big C. Billingham, though drunk at the time, could not have accidentally stumbled onto an unsheathed, unattended machete, standing unsupported at a 45-degree angle. How hard could it be to prosecute the case? I got back to Airport Camp, scrounged some loperamide for my gut from the Station Hospital and lay down in my hammock whilst it did its work concreting my insides.

Luckily, a few days later they recaptured Billingham's assailant, who gave himself up when he heard the tracker dogs. The trial date was set for the following Monday, thus allowing me to go to the Cayes again on the Sunday, top up the tan and enjoy quality relaxation time on a paradise island, in the company of about a million sand-flies.

The day of the trial arrived and Billingham, the RMP and I turned up at the appointed time of 1000hrs outside the Supreme Courts. They were impressive buildings, and our courtroom was on the ground floor next to the open-air market. It was a stinking hot day and there was quite a crowd of locals milling around the place, some of whom I recognised from Belmopan and San Ignacio. I asked them why they were there, and they told me that they were all on the jury for our case, which was apparently the talk of the town. What, all 200 of them, I thought? I guess they meant jury selection, as they had all been given a number.

The Court, bottom left next to the orange truck and the market, Belize 1981

We were all called into court, except the 200 potential jurors, and I was shown where to sit. The courtroom was stifling in the heat and the court officials were sweating profusely in their legal regalia of wigs and gowns. The room consisted of the dock for the accused, the unoccupied seats for the jurors, the witness box and stalls for the general public. The judge's dais and seat were raised about three feet above the rest of us. I was seated near the prosecution council, who held his head in his hands, either in deep thought or deep hangover.

Suddenly the door to the judge's chambers opened and the clerk came out and shouted, "All rise for de judge". We all dutifully shuffled to our feet and then bowed. A very large black judge entered the court, resplendent in a red and black robe with a most magnificent wig perched precariously on top of his head. He was carrying a large loose bundle of paperwork under his arm. He bowed to the Court and took his seat, carefully placing his bundle of papers on the corner of his desk, at which point his clerk turned on the judge's personal electric fan and the whole bundle went flying through the air like confetti being thrown at a wedding. Some of the legal documents fluttered out of the open windows.

The proceedings were immediately adjourned and we all filed outside while the documents in the bundle were retrieved from where they had been blown to. With the bundle restored, we all filed back into the courtroom, and the clerk stood up and shouted "All rise for de judge" again. We all rose and back came the judge.

The defendant was brought in still handcuffed and sat in the dock, surrounded by a small army of Belizean police officers. He was not going to escape justice this time. The cases for the prosecution and defence were very briefly outlined by the respective lawyers for the benefit of the judge, presumably to reassure him he was in the correct court, hearing the correct case, on the correct day.

The open windows enabled the vendors from the market to lean their elbows on the windowsills and observe the proceedings in between selling their wares. Though ordered to be quiet, the deliberations of the court were frequently interrupted by the noise of high-pitched squabbles and at one point, when a scrawny cockerel would not stop crowing, the judge ordered that it either be removed or strangled.

Jury selection played out like a game of bingo, with numbered balls that corresponded to the potential jurors being extracted from a bag. These numbers were called out and then relayed to those waiting outside. The owner of the relevant numbered ball then shouted out his presence "dat's me, yessir dat's me," (they all seemed to be male), swaggered into court, answered questions from the lawyers in turn and was either accepted or rejected for service. At around 1200hrs the court adjourned for lunch, at which stage two out of the required 12 jurors had been selected. It would be a long day.

Two fat old dogs exited the courthouse in advance of those attending, having been sleeping beneath the benches in the shade. I went for lunch at the Belle Vue Hotel, the usual haunt of the prosecution council. The prosecutor came over to me just as I was ordering, so I bought him a beer. "How you tink I'se doin' der?" he asked me.

I wasn't sure what the correct answer should be in terms of Belizean jurisprudence, so hedged my bets by suggesting he was doing just fine.

He said that I would be called to the witness stand as soon as possible in view of the fact that I had already been in Belize for a week (three actually), and I obviously had other "t'ings to do, back in dee U S of A". "UK" I corrected him. "I'm from England, the mother country, I'm British". "Dat Corpel Billham, he British too?" My heart sank.

I will digress for a minute. The British troops rather derisively referred to the locals as "chimps" as in, for example, "the bar is full of chimps" i.e. avoid it, or, "get one of the camp chimps to do it". This demeaning practice had to stop, so an order went out from HQ forbidding the use of the word "chimps" to describe the local population, with the threat of dire punishment for those who continued to offend. On my return to Belize I noticed that the soldiers were now referring to the locals as 'stills' and asked why. "Because they're still chimps, sir." I suppose I could have worked that one out for myself.

The court reassembled at 1400hrs and jury selection continued. If the truth be told, I really did not need to be in the sweltering courthouse whilst this was in progress and so I asked if I could be excused, which I was. Cpl Billingham, the star of the show as it were, stayed to try and get the measure of the jurors he would need to give his evidence to and I went outside for a cigarette and sat halfway up the courthouse steps, where there was a slight breeze and I could enjoy the sights, sounds and smells of the surrounding poverty.

Within five minutes a local policeman appeared and told me that if I did not get off the steps, one of the judges in the 1st floor courthouse would have me jailed as I was right in his line of sight and distracting him. As I was not in uniform, I rather haughtily explained that I was a British Army Officer and a witness in an ongoing trial. The policeman digested this information and for a second, looked as if he might well be impressed. "Move, or dee jail" he said simply. I moved and sat on an old bench instead. I had nothing to do, but I needed to remain in range of the courthouse, so I did what all good soldiers do under these circumstances, I went to sleep underneath a white Panama hat that I had purchased a couple of days previously (this had been an example of man shopping, as I had actually been looking to buy underwear) and was awoken by a court official sometime later, who informed me that the court would reconvene the next day at 1000hrs. Had the jury now been selected I asked? "Yes" he replied.

Next day when I arrived back at the courthouse I was pretty anxious to give my evidence and get back to Birmingham, which in itself is a surprising statement considering my views on the latter, but if the Caribbean had an anus (or shithole as Donald Trump would put it), then the Belize of the 1980s was not far from it. I needed to get on with my Higher Surgical Training.

However the judge was hearing some sort of legal argument which would be protracted and highly uninteresting, and in any event, I was excluded. I found my bench, lit a cigarette, tipped my hat and dozed. I was slowly going native; I was just slightly better dressed than all the other Belizeans who tired themselves out sleeping all day.

There were further intractable delays before I was able to give my evidence, but eventually I was called. I proceeded into the witness box and swore 'to tell de trut' de 'hole trut' and nuttin' but de trut'. I confirmed my name, address, rank and occupation and the prosecutor stood up and described me as a top British Army surgeon. Even I thought this description of me was unlikely. I put on a modest face and effected a slight shrug of the shoulders as an acknowledgement of his description, which, with a bit of mental agility, was perfectly true. Add the word "only" to the word surgeon and define the British Army, as that part of the army that happened to be in Belize at the time and he was spot on. He then outlined to the jury what I was going to say. The judge said "Lettim say it den".

I faced the jury and led by the prosecution I described what happened to Corporal Billingham on that fateful night. I explained his injuries, the surgical resuscitation and repair of the extensive damage, which was consistent with the weapon, Exhibit A, a machete owned by the accused, or stolen by the accused, or provided by the police on behalf of the prosecution from their store of weaponry evidence, for use in legal procedures when they could not actually find any weapon – or evidence.

I have précised about four hours here. There was no court stenographer, or even a secretary. All my evidence was recorded in longhand, with me spelling out the difficult words for them. 'Liver' was particularly problematic for some reason, which the Court wished to spell 'liber'. To help them cope with my pronunciation and accent, I tried using the phonetic alphabet. "Lima, India, Victor, Echo, Romeo". For all the good that it did in court, I might just as well have broken into 'Klingon', as I surveyed the sea of blank faces. Then, as if things couldn't get any worse, I was asked, "Lima? How you spell dat?"

Court was adjourned and I would resume giving my evidence in the afternoon. Again, I went to the Belle Vue for lunch and sat on my own, as I was still under oath. I was not allowed to discuss anything about the case with anybody. The prosecution team entered the bar and upon seeing me, strolled over to where I was sitting. They said they were happy with my evidence but wanted more blood and guts for effect. They had had the guts quite literally, 'Corpel Billam's' small bowel had been hanging out. His 'Sierra', 'Mike', 'Alpha', 'Lima', 'Lima', 'Bravo', 'Oscar', 'Whisky', 'Echo', 'Lima', and the knife wound was in his fucking "liber". I had made the mistake of using the word laceration once, and never repeated it for obvious reasons. I was going quietly insane. They should not have even been talking to me, and certainly should not have suggested some sort of dramatic upscale of my evidence to impress the seriousness of Corporal Billingham's wounds upon the jury, who seemed largely uninterested anyway. But that was the way it was, so I elaborated on the detail of my evidence in the afternoon. The defence team did not ask any questions. They just accepted my medical evidence as it was and when I left the witness box the prosecutor had a grin from ear to ear.

I was released to fly back to the UK on the next VC10. However, I still had one thing left to do. I had promised Aldo Moro, who had provided us with the lamb's liver BBQ on my previous tour, that if ever I returned to Belize I would visit Little Rock farm and say hello, and so the next day I signed out a Land Rover from the pool, and drove to San Ignacio along the Western Highway to Aldo's farm. Though the farm itself had not been immaculate on previous visits, it was positively run down on this occasion. There was a solitary dog remaining, sleeping under the house. It raised an eyelid pointlessly, as both of its eyes had large opaque cataracts. There were a couple of chickens scratching around in the dirt but no other livestock to speak of. I parked the Land Rover by Aldo's house and yelled up the steps. "Aldo, are you there?"

Initially there was no response, but then slowly his face appeared in the doorway. He looked puzzled and then gradually recognition arrived. He grinned at me. "Hi Doc. Wha' you doin' 'ere?"

I told him I was making good my promise to see him if I was ever back in Belize and explained about the court case.

"I know. Dam' fella get off. Too many Creoles on da jury." he said.

"The trial isn't over yet" I pointed out, "there hasn't been a verdict".

"Da verdic' came 'long when dey picked dat jury" he replied "jus' a matta o' time".

I asked him how he was generally. I could see he hadn't laid off the booze as his belly was even bigger than before and the whites of his eyes still had a yellowish tinge to them.

"I is livin'", he said.

"How are your boys?"

"Dead" he said. "Wife not long for dis earth neither". I had never seen his wife and had assumed that she was already dead.

"What happened to the boys then?" I asked.

"Youngest shot 'isself. Got love troubles. He buried next to 'is brodder".

"What happened to his brother?"

"He got plenty drunk and drove 'is car in da river an' drown 'isself". This was the son who had survived the Fer de Lance snake bite. He told me to follow him and led me to the far end of the field where there were two neat crosses marking two graves. "Dis where dey are" he said with a sigh and an air of finality. We then went back to the house and after climbing up the steps he returned with a picture of the son who had shot himself. He was lying in a coffin wearing his white shirt, heavily stained with blood, marking the spot where he had shot himself through the heart for love.

"Aldo, why didn't you change his shirt before you buried him?" I asked.

"He don' need no clean shirt where 'e is at now" he replied. I acknowledged the logic in that. I took another look at Aldo.

"What the hell. Let's go for a beer" I said.

"You payin'?" he asked, "I ain't got no money".

"Don't worry" I assured him, and we trudged to a local shack where they were selling Belikin beer and we had several drinks together with Aldo on the beer and then the rum.

The time came for me to leave, so we walked back to his farm and I got in the Land Rover, took out my wallet and gave Aldo all the Belize dollars I had left, as I wouldn't need them in view of my imminent flight back to England. I shook his hand. "T'anks Doc" he said and then added pragmatically, "Gotta shoot dat dam' dog sometime, 'e blin' and I sure ain't got no use feedin' no blin' dog".

I drove back to camp and when I got there, I was informed

Aldo Moro and I sharing a drink. Belize 1981

that the jury in the trial had found the defendant not guilty of causing Corporal Billingham grievous harm. They opined that he had brought the injury upon himself and the accused had acted in self-defence. Billingham was inconsolable and understandably went off the rails for quite some time afterwards. I marvelled at the Belize judicial system and Aldo's correct prediction.

I arrived back at my cottage in Woking with my backpack and a well-worn hammock. After the generally low-quality accommodation, toilets, showers and bathrooms I had endured in Belize, it was an absolute luxury to order a Chinese takeaway, gorge myself on it and then proceed to soak the Caribbean grime off my skin in a bath for a couple of hours. With the addition of a bottle of whisky, I relived the memories and experiences I had accumulated as a result of my first tour to Belize and then the subsequent one for the court case, when the predicted week had turned into over a month instead.

When I phoned the surgical department of the General Hospital and said that I would be back to work in a few days, starting the following

Monday, I had to give my name twice and repeat who I was supposed to be working for. So, back to earth at the General, where, with the passing of 6000 miles by air, I had reverted from the dizzying height of top British Army surgeon in Belize back to a mere senior registrar.

My clinical judgement was improving as I gained more experience and I was also quite handy around the abdomen, even when the normal anatomy had been distorted by disease processes or rearranged by previous surgery. However, at this stage of my training there was one organ that always worried me, and I suspect generations of surgeons before and after me, and that was the pancreas. When afflicted with malignancy it was a fatal disease, with a lifetime expectation of about two years. Carcinoma of the head of the pancreas would present in similar fashion to other causes of increasing jaundice, for instance a gallstone in the bile ducts. There were aphorisms to try and distinguish between the two main causes of jaundice, for example Courvoisier's Law, which has been explained, learnt and recited by thousands of surgeons as a mantra, a sacred text of diagnostic assistance.

When faced with this fatal disease I invariably performed a symptom relieving procedure to relieve the jaundice and hopefully prevent upper bowel obstruction, with three hand sewn joins of bowel and bile ducts. The survival time was not increased, but distressing symptoms were palliated. However, I had a co-senior registrar colleague in the last year of his training before a consultant appointment who was impervious to the boundaries of inoperability, and he would regularly give a patient what he considered the maximum opportunity for survival by performing the standard procedure, a Whipple's operation. This was generally frowned upon by our consultant supervisors, though in those days case selection was arbitrary, but nonetheless his results did demonstrate improved post-operative survival over the year, from about three hours to 3-5 days. Professor Christiaan Barnard's first heart transplant patients did not survive for very long either, so surgical progress necessarily incurs 'collateral damage' which of course cannot be put on a death certificate. I did everything I could in my surgical career to avoid the pancreas, not always successfully I might add.

I learned a huge amount on this firm, especially about the conservative surgery of chronic inflammatory bowel disease and the effectiveness of combined medical and surgical management. In addition, I was to get up close and personal with the large bowel, mainly the cancers under Mike Keighley's guidance. This experience stood me in good stead when I metamorphosed into a colorectal surgeon later in my career, having been trained in just about everything else in the surgical fields, though not neurosurgery (apart from drilling holes in patients' heads, which for some extraordinary reason was a general surgical procedure), ENT (except the odd tracheotomy or removing beads from infants auditory canals), or ophthalmology.

Slowly but surely, I was becoming the complete surgeon I wanted to be. I intended to be reliable and confident even in the wilderness, both surgically and geographically. With a good team, and an operative textbook to hand, I reckoned I would be okay.

One night I was asked to attend A & E urgently and was directed to a cubicle where a Jamaican Rastafarian had collapsed after he had been stabbed. The weapon was a carving knife, the entrance wound was at the top of his right thigh and the wound track seemed to suggest that the knife had somehow entered his pelvis. The knife was supposed to be about 10 inches long and according to the patient had been buried to the hilt, but he had pulled it out himself. He would not say who had stabbed him, but I later found out it was one of his several unofficial wives, the mother of a couple of his unofficial children, when they were having an argument, both of them high on ganja (cannabis) about his other women and children. She was aiming for his groin, but he had turned in the nick of time.

There was no blood in his bowel nor his bladder, but when he had been resuscitated I opened him up and found his abdomen full of blood. The source of the bleeding seemed to be somewhere in the pelvis, as the blood had broken through the thin lining (pelvic peritoneum). All the pelvic and abdominal organs as well as the major pelvic vessels seemed intact.

I just could not find the source of what was a profuse and continuing haemorrhage, even after probing, then exploring the entrance wound. I stuffed his pelvis tightly with large abdominal packs, closed him up and sent him off to ICU for further resuscitation while I had a word with Mr Keighley.

The next day we re-opened him. There was still a profuse haemorrhage on removing the packs and Mr Keighley suggested ligating both internal iliac arteries. This was an accepted method of reducing uncontrolled bleeding in the pelvis. I argued that we stood a good chance of making the young man impotent, infertile, or both. I think that Mr Keighley had to go and catch an aeroplane to a meeting, so he told me I would just have to do my best and reminded me that he had already suggested a course of action. I had another think and concluded that the bleeding originated (in the pararectal tissues) deep in the pelvis on the right-hand side. I got hold of a registrar colleague to keep an eye on the abdomen, then went down to the patient's tail end and started to mobilize his anus and lower rectum on the right. I then asked for a long straight needle and thread and passed it up and round the tissues I suspected of being the source of the bleeding, back to my colleague guarding the abdomen, and he then passed it back to me. I did an instrumental tie, enclosing all the rectal supporting tissue in the ligature, and the bleeding stopped. Why it had continued after packing the pelvis I do not know. Perhaps the pressure was in the wrong place. In any event the bleeding had ceased and provided he could shit in a straight line after his anus and rectum had healed, I had done a good job, but not as far as the police were concerned. I sat down with two detectives as they interviewed me as part of their investigation a day or so later.

"First of all," one of them asked, "How is he?"

"He's OK," I said. "He'll live, should make a full recovery".

"Hmm. That's a pity," said the other detective. "You really shouldn't have bothered, doc. He's a real bad bastard, not just your average Yardie. Drugs, burglary, theft, fraud, prostitution, GBH, gang crimes, you name it he's into it. Not surprising someone tried to do him. The world would have been a better place without him". I'm glad he got that off his chest. Unfortunately, patients are not admitted to hospital with their criminal history available and in any event, we had to save people so that they could go to prison or, in some countries, to their execution in a healthy physical state. I therefore regarded my actions as a surgical triumph as opposed to a societal triumph.

The patient had discharged himself as soon as he could with a limp, a bit of a leaky tail end and his dreadlocks in a bun. He did thank me, but realistically, he had no idea how much for. I explained that his anal seepage would recover in time, explained the (perineal) exercises he should do to help it resolve and told him to rest awhile before he returned to his life of crime. He smiled, adjusted the sanitary pad in his boxer shorts, or whatever underwear he had on, and waddled off. I explained my triumph to Mike Keighley when he returned from his learned meeting. Quite honestly, he wasn't that interested, and I don't blame him. Perhaps the police had told him what they had told me. Perhaps we should have tied his arteries to reduce his procreative and other proclivities, his nefarious activities and his standing in his community (or not standing as it were). I would imagine the police response to that outcome would have been a lot more positive.

Mrs Wrigley was in her late 80s and was diagnosed with a rectal cancer. Bearing in mind what Mr Oates had said to me about contributing patients to clinical trials, (Birmingham being one of the centres in a multi-centred investigation), I mentioned to Mike Keighley that she would be eligible for entry into a large bowel cancer trial following randomisation, as the diagnosis had been confirmed by biopsy. Mike Keighley asked me to undertake the procedure and as I would need to do a low stapled anastomosis of the residual bowel ends, he wanted to check the integrity of the join, as the stapling instruments we were using at the time were still in their infancy and could be problematic.

Mike agreed that Mrs Wrigley could be entered in the large bowel cancer trial and following a telephone call to the trial office to have her treatment randomised, she was allocated the treatment arm of a 5 Fluorouracil and heparin infusion directly into a portal vein tributary (a gastro-epiploic vein) and into the liver. This was to test the effect on survival of the cancer by trying to prevent liver secondaries from developing, using chemotherapy. In any event the operation was uncomplicated, Mike Keighley expressed his satisfaction with the anastomoses (join of the bowel ends) and I closed the wound, ensuring that the liver infusion was running satisfactorily. In those days these patients did not go to a specialist nursing area like a high dependency unit (HDU) or intensive care unit (ICU), just back to the general ward with experienced, but often overworked, surgical nursing staff.

From this point on everything went horribly wrong. It had nothing to do with the nursing staff, but everything to do with the medical staff. Next day Mrs Wrigley was stable, with no cause for concern on the Friday of a Bank Holiday weekend. I took the house surgeon to one side, a bright young girl who would be working the whole weekend, and explained the trial and the strict protocol of postoperative investigations that were mandatory to ensure that the toxic effects of the chemotherapy that Mrs Wrigley was receiving into her liver were carefully monitored. I left her with a copy of the trial information. I spoke to the research registrar who would be middle grade surgical cover for this weekend and fully informed him too. Having done all that I considered necessary, I left the General at lunchtime for a long weekend in Woking, as I was not on duty until the following Tuesday.

Nowadays chemotherapy can be more targeted, but it is still blunderbuss treatment and will not only affect the rapidly dividing cancer cells but normal cells too, especially the bone marrow. Thus, an excess of chemotherapy will result in a drastic reduction in a patient's red blood cells, white blood cells and blood clotting factors to say the least, leading to anaemia, a high risk of infection and bleeding in addition to poor wound healing.

I returned to the General on the Tuesday morning and immediately checked on Mrs Wrigley, who was by this stage deathly pale, semiconscious, breathless and bleeding from her mouth, nose and into her urine, effectively in extremis.

Few of the routine blood investigations had been performed and those that had showed a progressive deterioration. Her wound had given way and had been re-sutured and her chemotherapy infusion had been stopped, but the situation was irretrievable, especially when the laboratory refused my request for fresh frozen plasma on the grounds of the patient's age, diagnosis and a realistic appraisal of her prognosis. We had failed to adhere to the trial protocol and Mrs Wrigley died later in the day. I felt gutted.

Mike Keighley had also been away for that weekend. I informed him of the sad event on his return and he insisted on a post-mortem.

Mrs Wrigley, it transpired, had no known relatives. Things were going from bad to worse, as events like these often do. The cause of death was essentially bone marrow failure, secondary to chemotherapy in a patient who had recently been operated on for bowel cancer. The only bit of good news was that my stapled anastomosis was still intact, with no leakage. Basically, Mrs Wrigley had gone to meet her maker with a continuous large bowel and no bone marrow. Out with the trial, or in the non-treatment arm, she could easily have survived.

This had to be reported to the coroner for his determination and recommendations, not an altogether enticing prospect. I spoke to the coroner's officer who would inform the coroner and the coroner subsequently decided to investigate. Next a phone call to my Medical Defence Union was in order, always sooner rather than later in these situations. One of their advisers was dispatched to chat to me about the case and determine whether I would need advice at the inquest. I had presumed that I was blameless as I wasn't anywhere near the General Hospital when this all took place, but he said that there was an "issue".

One could argue that the house surgeon was at fault for not taking the appropriate action as a result of the blood tests, but coroners do not like downshifting of the blame to inexperienced young doctors, and also Mike Keighley had suggested that his being away and essentially un-contactable meant that his part in the patient's management had devolved to the consultant on-call for the weekend and in any event, I had done the operation and randomised Mrs Wrigley into the trial. I had this distinct feeling that shit was going uphill from the house surgeon to me and downhill from Mr Keighley. I was in the middle and receiving it from both ends. My adviser said, "Give a truthful succinct account of the case to the coroner".

At the inquest, the house surgeon agreed that I had given her all the information and instructions with regard to Mrs Wrigley, but that she didn't really understand much of what I had said, and as the sole junior doctor covering both the surgical wards and emergency admissions on a busy bank holiday weekend, she was rushed off her feet, which was fair enough. I went into the witness box and simply stated that our failures (note the use of "our") were to incompletely follow the trial protocols and to fail to respond to the blood results in an adequate manner which led to the patient's death. The coroner thanked me for being honest. Mike Keighley was next, and he eventually agreed with the coroner that even though he was somewhere in Europe at the time, he was the consultant in charge of Mrs Wrigley.

The coroner recorded a verdict of death by misadventure, but he had hit on something else. Mrs Wrigley had not given consent to her entry in the trial and informed consent had not been obtained. This was the headline seized upon by the press and as I was to find out, it became a very hot potato in the medical world. We all ran out of the coroner's court to the relative safety of the General, hotly pursued by journalists who correctly smelt a good story.

I did learn some valuable things as a result. Bank holidays and weekends represented an increase risk to patients, surgical trials should be better supervised by a dedicated team of medical and nursing staff and when I became a consultant, my duty of care to my patients did not stop, ever, until they were discharged from my care, or permanently transferred to another consultant's care, no matter where in the world I was. It goes with the territory.

CHAPTER 14

Crossing Paths with Gerry

Nepal, 1981

I left Birmingham with few regrets, but certainly with grateful thanks for what I had learned, both the good and the bad. I was now off on leave to visit Kathy in Nepal. She was going to be there for 12 months following her Hong Kong posting, which was the usual order of things. We would meet up in Kathmandu for a couple of days and then fly down to Dhahran in south-east Nepal, where the British cantonment was situated, for a day or so whilst preparing for a 10 – 12-day trek through the foothills of the Himalayas. I couldn't wait. I had missed Kathy dreadfully and our separation had been hard going. As Nepal is a repository of horrible diseases, hepatitis, malaria and Japanese encephalitis, just to mention a few, I had ensured that I had an armful of vaccinations at the CMH.

A couple of days later I was on the plane to Kathmandu, and I was soon reunited with Kathy, who had booked us in to a local hotel. We talked and talked, and then sat in a hot bath eating buffalo meat sandwiches and drinking beer from room service. Cows are sacred animals amongst the Hindus, and nothing untoward can happen to them. They are free to run around wherever they wish and if for example a cow eats a whole load of produce from a market store, then the owner of that store has been blessed. Cows were everywhere and significantly interfered with everything, especially the road traffic. Run over a cow and you risked being lynched, it was as simple as that, especially if you were a foreigner. It is the same in India. However, the domestic buffalo is not so blessed and can be slaughtered and eaten with impunity. The meat is a lot tougher.

Kathmandu was another complete shithole. It was hot during the day and filthy and the whole city and its bustling population seemed to be covered in flies. Feral dogs were in abundance, both alive and dead, and the latter were a trip hazard, as I found out in a moment of inattention. There were taxis of a sort, but we travelled by rickshaw, or walked. We explored as much of the city as we could; lots of temples, markets and Johnny Gurkha, a guesthouse and pub where the history of the service of the Gurkha Regiments could be found. It was very well known, and we ate a goat curry there which was not bad, except in my portion I seemed to have the teeth and hooves.

Whilst wandering around, I went into a local shop and bought a hat made of lynx fur and a thick pullover weaved out of yak wool. It was the warmest thing I had ever worn (the evenings were very cold) but the smell of it was appalling, and it was greasy to the touch. However, if yaks can survive the cold of the Himalayas as beasts of burden, I should be all right in one of their coats and my head and ears would be protected by the lynx fur, which from the shape of it, could have been made out of the animal's backside. It fitted perfectly. What I seem to be saying, is that my head is the same size and configuration as a lynx's arse.

We visited the Buddhist temples in Patan just outside Kathmandu. Ten percent of Nepalese are Buddhists and their temples are beautiful and intricately carved and decorated. In those days the monks made carved brass decorations and figurines, but the one I bought had a surprisingly sexual theme and certainly could not be placed on the mantelpiece of any respectable household; but it was okay in mine.

The flight from Kathmandu to Biratnagar is 150 miles and takes 40 minutes give or take. If you are ever tempted to fly with local airlines in Nepal, then I wouldn't recommend it. They have appalling safety records. At the time none of the planes were equipped with radar, and the pilots flew by Visual Flight Rules (VFR) only. If they couldn't see well, it wouldn't end well. On 19th November 1981 a Royal Nepal plane had crashed near Biratnagar with 10 fatalities; it was rumoured to be overloaded. As a result, all the passengers and luggage on our flight were weighed, before the plane was allowed to take off. I was petrified as we prepared for take-off. The engine of the plane kept coughing and spluttering, and I never thought the plane would get into the air. When it eventually did get airborne I spent the whole 40 minutes preparing myself for death on landing and clutching one of the frayed ends of my seatbelt, not being entirely sure where the other end was.

The hospital cantonment is in Dharan, East Nepal, about 40 kms from Biratnagar, and was established in 1960 to provide medical aid to the British Army, Gurkha recruits, Gurkha pensioners and their families as well as providing a service to the local population when possible. The main recruitment to the Brigade of Gurkhas takes place in Pokhara in Central/West Nepal, near to the village of Gorkha from which the Gurkhas get their names. The hospital persists in its other functions and provides an unparalleled experience for military doctors.

However, I was going trekking on this occasion, assuming the plane landed without breaking into a million pieces and bursting into a fireball. I did manage to summon up the courage to look out of a window and with the cloudless sky, the sight of the Himalayas was awesome. Everest and Kanchenjunga were easily identifiable, with a little help from those who knew where to look. I was to see this all again from ground level on the trek, the height at which I prefer to be.

Soon the pilot started the descent onto the short runway. Biratnagar airport consisted of a few huts beneath us. I closed my eyes and contacted the Almighty, whom I had neglected for quite some time, and prayed for a good outcome to this travel experience. There are two places where atheists do not exist. One is the battlefield, where all participants in the fray have a god on their side, and the other is in an ancient light aircraft, with unreliable engines, when coming in to land in the poorest country in the world which has the worst airline safety record in the history of aviation.

I waited for impact with the ground and after bouncing a few times on contact with the pitted tarmac that passed for a runway, I was relieved to find as we ground to a halt that I had been neither incontinent, nor was I on fire. At last the aircraft ground to a halt somewhere near Arrivals and Customs. It would take me a day or two to get over the flight and settle my nerves with a reliable treatment called alcohol. Army transport was waiting for us and took us to Dharan and the BMH cantonment.

That night Kathy and I, with some of the other hospital staff, went to a local hostelry to drink an alcoholic Nepalese beverage called Raksi, a distillation of kodo millet. For whatever it's worth CNN cable TV station (for whatever they are worth) had placed Raksi as number 41 in the world's 50 most delicious drinks. I beg to differ. We were served the drinks in individual wooden churns using a straw and the churn would be regularly topped up with boiling water. This is better described as Tongba, made in the same way using the fermented millet and served as a speciality of the Eastern Hills, which was where we were. The wooden vessels are greased with yak butter when not in use.

However, on the other side of the coin, I was pleasantly pissed after a few churns, at which point the recent flight and landing at Biratnagar disappeared into a bleary memory. Of course, there was the prospect of the return flight to Kathmandu, where most of the airline carnage and passenger massacres occurred, but I put that disturbing thought firmly on the back burner. I had some serious trekking to do first.

In those days retired Gurkha soldiers received their pensions at payment points scattered throughout Nepal. The level of payment was according to their rank on retirement and scaled down to suit the Nepalese economy. Retired Gurkhas were well off compared to their fellow civilians, but not as rich as Croesus, which they would have been if their pensions had been paid at UK rates. Nepal at that time was the third poorest country in the world. The average age reached by a hillman or farmer was 42 years and his wife probably needed renewing at 26 years old, as her job was to get married, have male children, do all the domestic housework, cook all the meals and work from dawn to dusk in the fields.

The pensions were paid by junior Army officers from the Brigade of Gurkhas trekking to these payment points. They could only be reached on foot by the pension payers and the payees, some of whom had to trek for several days to receive their payments. There were no roads in the foothills of the Himalayas, just narrow precipitous paths, and distance between villages for example, was expressed in terms of walking time rather than miles, in that two villages may have been five miles apart as the crow flies in Western units of distance, but three days' trek (and a knackering one at that) in Nepalese units of distance.

In addition to the pension treks, porters and equipment could be hired out for unofficial, or adventure treks by service personnel and this is what Kathy had arranged. We needed four porters to carry our equipment. They were small men, but very tough and hardy, each of them carrying about 20-25 kilos in their baskets or *dhokos*, with the straps of the baskets or *namlos* around their foreheads.

As we had to carry virtually all our provisions – mainly rice, lentils and spices – food would account for much of the weight, in addition to a two-man tent, ground sheets, sleeping bags, cooking utensils etc.

The start of the trek in Dhankuta Nepal 1981. L-R. Me, Kathy, Jagan Bahadur
with Prem Bahadur on far right.

This is because I elected to feed the porters in addition to paying them the rupee equivalent of £1 per day. Meat, goat or chicken, we could acquire along the way. I had brought out a sturdy pair of trainers with me, the recommended trekker's footwear, rather than hiking boots, and with a copious supply of cigarettes, whiskey, a rudimentary first aid kit and other essentials, we were given a lift to Dhankuta, where we would start walking.

The road to Dhankuta was an illustration of the poverty of Nepal, and on the trek we were going to encounter the poorest of the poor, all with the most welcoming of smiles, for the Nepalese are the most delightful of people, as anyone who has been there will tell you. They endure their hardships and the worst that nature can throw at them with an unbelievable tolerance. Nepal was a male-dominated society, but this is gradually changing. In 2015 Nepal elected its first female Head of State, Bidhya Devi Bhandari. In 2020 the British Army will recruit women to the Brigade of Gurkhas, having recruited only men for the last 200 years or so. Nepal was still a Kingdom in 1981, although in 2006 the monarchy was ousted and the Federal Democratic Republic of Nepal was born.

I hefted up one of the dhokos to see how much each porter would be carrying. I was 6 feet 1 in, weighed just under 100 kg and would have struggled to carry this weight over a prolonged period in the manner that the 5 ft 2" tall 50 kg porters do, using their backs and foreheads. The strain on their cervical spines must have been enormous, and I noticed that with heavy loads they applied counter traction on their necks, using their arms. Dhokos are hand woven from bamboo into a conical shape, and are also used by the women, who work as labourers on construction projects in addition to everything else they had to do. Kathy and I were burdened too; we had to carry our own water flasks.

One of the porters, Jagan Bahadur Gurung, was the head porter, who took the orders, planned the route and made himself solely at the Sahib's (me) disposal. Prem Bahadur Gurung was the most junior porter and he did the washing up and the other menial tasks around camp. The cooking was done on open fires and we would eat twice a day, with the odd break for a cup of chai or tea.

We would wake at around 6 am and Jagan Bahadur would bring two cups of tea and a bowl of warm water for me to wash and shave in. When the memsahib (Kathy) asked where her bowl of water was, she was told to use the sahib's water when he had finished, which unsurprisingly did not go down well. In the interests of fairness, I occasionally let Kathy use the water first, but obviously not in front of the porters.

In the cool morning air we would load up, the porters with their heavy dhokos, Kathy and I with our water bottles and we would start walking through the foothills. I had a vague idea of the route, but we were led by Jagan Bahadur who had trekked it many times before. He was as nimble as a goat over the difficult terrain as were the other porters, but as Kathy was tall, slim and fit, we had no trouble keeping up with them. Periodically we would stop to admire the views, particularly when the impressive peaks of Everest and Kanchenjunga were in view.

Our midmorning meal was dal bhat, a concoction of boiled rice and lentils and the staple in Nepal. As the time approached, Jagan Bahadur would race ahead with one of the other porters, build a fire to cook on, and start making the chai and the meal, so that when Kathy and I arrived, the camp chairs were out and we were presented with a cup

I had to carry my own water bottle. Nepal 1981

The Himalayas from a much safer viewpoint to my mind. Nepal 1981

of chai, soon to be followed by bhat. We always ate first, and when we had finished and had refused second helpings, all four porters ate together and believe me, they could eat a lot. In the evenings they would eat themselves to a standstill, rubbing their bloated rice-filled bellies and groaning, waiting until they had decompressed. Then they would begin the clearing up, with Prem Bahadur dispatched to wash up the plates, cutlery and utensils in a nearby mountain stream. We drank the icy cold and pure water from them without concern of deadly impurities and washed in them too. However, as the water was so cold, I would rather have stayed dirty. Loos en route consisted of convenient bushes or village 'amenities' if one happened to be near, but in all honesty, bushes were safer. We had to be wary of snakes, bears and 'dacoits', the Hindi name for bandits; we did not come across any of them.

We trekked up hill and down dale. We passed through the villages of Pakhribas, Taple Jung, and finally Sukhepokari, if memory serves me correctly. We were always greeted politely by the villagers and the children would smile shyly. We bought some provisions en route and most nights I would buy some *raksi* for the porters, to fight off the night chills, as they slept all together for warmth, wrapped in blankets and a tarpaulin. I had Kathy to keep me warm. During the day the weather was quite hot, but at night, particularly if we had climbed a couple of thousand feet, the temperature dropped as soon as the sun had set. In most villager's huts and houses, a central fire was kept burning for warmth and cooking.

High enough to be quite cold. The porters are still in tee shirts. Nepal 1981

This was without doubt one of the most enjoyable times of my life, and I relished the physical exercise, the beautiful fresh air, the scenic views, the food and the company I kept. It could not have been better, but something unexpected happened, in a very nice way, that made my jaw hit the floor, or rather the path. Briefly I need to go back to medical school. During our three clinical years, students were divided into firms of six and attended all the ward rounds, clinics and the op-theatre together as approximately 100 students are less unwieldy grouped in this manner. One girl on my firm was called Gerry Locket, very bright and attractive with a homely attitude to life. She and I graduated in 1973 and I had not seen her since. She got married during her house year.

Ninety percent of global tuberculosis (TB) exists in developing third world countries and TB was rife throughout the Kingdom of Nepal, an absolute scourge with a high morbidity and mortality. It was estimated that 45% of the total population were infected, and there were huge difficulties with diagnosis and treatment compliance (i.e. patients bothering to take the medication). Up to 80% of the population lived in inaccessible rural areas and delays in diagnoses were averaged at 60 days. Thus, eradication of the disease was fraught with problems and still is to a certain extent. Many charities and non-governmental organisations (NGOs) were doing their best to assist in trying to overcome the disease, which has been effectively wiped out in developed nations.

Some organisations sent TB doctors trekking through the foothills to reach remote villages and settlements to identify sufferers, distribute the medications and ensure that they were taken. In other circumstances, patients were expected to trek to their nearest distribution centre and pick up the treatment themselves. Being a TB doctor in Nepal was rewarding but tough and certainly required a degree of courage, single mindedness and an ability to sleep in the most godawful conditions. On our trek Kathy and I once slept huddled together in the TB doctor's accommodation in one village. We lay side by side on a wide plank, freezing in our sleeping bags with just a candle, and a primus stove, that did not work – no fuel.

One day, early in our trek, high up in the foothills and on a narrow path with a sheer drop on one side, I noticed another trekking party coming towards us, a single trekker and two porters. It was not unusual to come across the locals, but this person was too tall to be a Nepali. The pace was slow due to the terrain and the rocks which were always in the way and so the gap between us narrowed very slowly. I kept looking at them as they approached, in between keeping a close eye on where I put my feet, as I did not want to plunge into the ravine alongside us. Crossing paths with the other group would present a problem when we reached them, as the trail was quite narrow.

As the other trekkers got nearer, I realised that the tall person was in fact a girl, or woman rather. I was staggered at the coincidence, as it slowly dawned on me that I recognised her. It was Gerry Locket. Her marriage had been very unhappy and after her divorce, she had decided to go to Nepal and do something totally different. We hadn't much time to talk as dusk was approaching, so we parted after I directed her to the BMH where I said, if she mentioned my name and gave them a note

Soon we were above the snowline. Nepal 1981

I quickly scribbled, she might be able to have a bath, some good food on my mess bill and a comfortable night's sleep. I never saw her again. I was full of admiration for her and what she was doing there.

In the Western world, if a child or an adult falls over onto an outstretched hand, there are well recognised sequelae in the fracture world. These include fractures of the wrist (Colles and Smiths), the elbow (or supracondylar fracture) and fracture/dislocations of the shoulder joint, to name but a few. The most taxing to deal with can be the supracondylar fracture, commonest in young children. This would typically follow a fall in a playground, an accident at home or at school, or early sports events. Dealt with inadequately, even with the remodelling of bone alignment that occurs naturally in children but not adults, can leave the casualty with a marked elbow malformation, very poor function and early arthritis.

In Nepal things were no different, except that the commonest cause of this fracture seemed to be a fall from a water buffalo, and this was also the opinion of one of my Army surgical colleagues. Frequently, these enormous beasts, belonging to each family, were entrusted to the care of a child aged just 10 or 12 (yet only the size of a 6-7-year-old Western child if that) during the day, for grazing in the pastures and scrubland. The children would ride these tame and patient buffalos, merrily beating them ineffectually with a bamboo stick, to join others to form a small herd. They would then play on the backs of the animals, jumping from one to the other until inevitably they fell off, usually several days away from medical help. On our trek, amongst a gaggle of children who rushed out to stare at us, I noticed two deformed elbows and the cause of them both was exactly as outlined above.

Nepalese boy on a water buffalo Nepal 1980

The rest of our trek passed off uneventfully. We had to cross some ravines and rivers by what appeared to be the most fragile of rope bridges, venturing across one at a time, but we made it without incident. All too soon we reached our destination, weary but exhilarated and transport took us all back to the Cantonment with spectacular views once again of the Himalayas on one side and the Terai, the flat mosquito and therefore malaria-riddled plains on the other.

Kathy came to see me off at Biratnagar airport for my flight back to Kathmandu, but take off was delayed. Kathmandu airport located in the valley was covered in cloud, and a visual only landing would be too dangerous. So, we had to wait and wait. Fortunately, my scheduled flight back to UK was next day. Eventually we did get in the air after a fashion and though a bit bumpy, the flight was without incident. I could have kissed the ground when we landed, but I suppose that activity is reserved for popes.

CHAPTER 15

A Trophy in the Making

QEMH Woolwich, 1981

I got back to Old Woking and readied myself for the start of my second year of Higher Surgical Training, which would be in the Queen Elizabeth Military Hospital (QEMH) in Woolwich, London. I would be working for Colonel Noel Peters and Lt Col Peter Craig. QEMH's role was as the Army base hospital and servicemen and women and their dependents would be referred there for more specialised treatment. For example, most of the patients we dealt with had developed malignancies (cancers) requiring further definitive or ablative surgery and chemotherapy, radiotherapy or both. The latter treatments were arranged through the Westminster Hospital. Otherwise there were the routine general and orthopaedic cases supplied from the local garrison.

The military population of servicemen, women and dependent families are inevitably young, and in many cases the contraction of a malignant disease is an utterly heart-breaking tragedy, and in those days would, in many cases lead to death, the outcome unaltered, just delayed, by the application of the adjuvant treatment. Cancers in the young are more aggressive. Some success was being had with leukaemias, but overall, the prognoses for all these young people was grim; just a matter of time. However, hope springs eternal, and this was true for many of my young patients. I was inwardly very saddened because of what I knew, but outwardly cheerful and I projected a degree of confidence which I really did not have when treating them.

How does one deal with an 18-year-old infantry soldier, who presented with a painful knee after a training run, was treated initially with exercises and physiotherapy, then referred for an X-ray when these measures did not improve his symptoms, which revealed the typical findings of an osteosarcoma (bone cancer) which, on further investigation was found to have metastasised (spread) to his chest? Beyond treatment and deadly. How, as a doctor, do you tell this previously fit young man, full of the joys of life, that he is shortly going to die, not in combat, bravely on the battlefield, but fighting a battle he never signed up for that cannot be won, in a hospital bed and gradually wasting away by the day? A one-sided contest where the medical ammunition was not good enough. How do you start that conversation? How do you end it? Should you be totally honest or spare him the complete truth, just to leave a little hope, optimism, or something to grab onto? What about his family, wife, girlfriend? I found it all very difficult.

It was similar with the breast cancers found in the young servicewomen and wives. There is a thread that links many of these cases that may have made little difference. Early diagnosis and treatment were and still are, the only way to get a successful outcome, and in the management of these cases this was often lacking, as it still is today.

At QEMH I met a girl called Angela Peck at a hospital mess party around Christmas in 1981. I was on duty that night, otherwise I would have been back at home in my cottage for the weekend. I used to commute to Woolwich, leaving at 6 am and returning around 7 pm but stayed in the Mess when on call. Angela was twenty-two, she was attractive, but certainly not extraordinarily so, and she was not my usual type. She was short, with her hair worn in a dyed blonde bob and her nails bitten to the quick, and she had a pronounced Yorkshire accent. She was 'vivacious', a word Angela frequently used to describe herself, but my first impression of her was that she was a bit too self-satisfied. Several years later her ordinariness would be summed up quite succinctly. 'I was unmoved when I first saw her. My thoughts were 'so this is her? She's just Mrs Average'[13]'.

One of the first things Angela told me was that Yorkshire was the best place in the world. It certainly seemed that Yorkshire was the centre of her universe and that she had very little experience of life beyond it. She had finished a degree in Theology at Leeds University and was currently in Eltham, London, working at a school doing a Diploma in Education, prior to becoming a teacher. We chatted, we danced, it was all very pleasant, but I wasn't particularly interested in her, because I was committed to my long-term girlfriend Kathy, who was still working in Nepal.

After the party, I thought no more about it, but within a couple of days I got a letter from her which was to be my ensnarement, as at the end of the letter she wrote, that if I did not go out with her, I "might just miss a once in a lifetime opportunity" and "regret it for the rest of (my) life". Those words would forever haunt me. It was marrying her that I would later regret for the rest of my life, notwithstanding the children who were a product of that union. After I received Angela's letter, of course intrigue got the better of me and I contacted her, followed by a few dates and she soon wormed her way into my bed with the subtlety of a brick. "Well, if I'm going to sleep with anyone I might as well get on with it," she said.

---

13. News of the World, 21 Aug 94

CHAPTER 16

Aim for the Ocean

The Falklands War, 1982

'He who wishes to be a surgeon should go to war'
(Hippocrates)

Every soldier must have a degree of readiness to be sent away on duty, in my case 48 hours standby and in the event of a National Emergency, part of a second wave response. I was nominally attached to 2 Field Hospital, in Aldershot, as part of their surgical strength, although I was working at the QEMH in Woolwich at the time. I have mentioned that a Field Hospital is generally well behind the confrontation line. The lines of evacuation and treatment of the injured in battle are as follows: Buddy buddy (looked after and first aid applied by fellow soldiers), Regimental Aid Post (RAP), first contact with a doctor, (the Regimental Medical Officer), Field Ambulance (further medical aid and transport to pick up casualties from the RAP and take them to the Field Hospital). Other casualties would be transported by helicopter.

The Field Hospital is a 50-bedded tented unit for life and limb-saving surgery, similar to the American Mobile Army Surgical Hospital Units, but without the drama – where I would be.

On 2 April 1982, troops from Argentina invaded the Falkland Islands (FI) which they claimed as a part of their sovereign territory and called Las Malvinas, as well as South Georgia and the South Sandwich Islands, all British Overseas Dependent Territories. The Argentine military junta headed by General Galtieri wanted to deflect the economic chaos affecting Argentina with a patriotic reclamation of the Islands. However, the FI had been a British Crown colony since 1841 and the islanders were of British descent and wished to remain that way. The FI are 8000 miles away, in the South Atlantic. A task force sent to drive the Argentines out would face enormous difficulties.

Margaret Thatcher, the Prime Minister at the time, however, wanted the islands back and so on the 9th April 1982 a Royal Navy Task Force was sent on its way. 3 Commando Brigade was the strike force element, consisting of commandos, paratroopers, Special Forces and support units, ready for an amphibious assault, and they were aboard the cruise liner *Canberra*, which had been requisitioned into service. Much has been written about the Falklands War. There are several versions of the campaign, from the different points of view of those who took part in this massive exercise, only differing in minor, but important detail. I needn't reiterate them here. I shall just relate my participation in the war and only touch on some of the related, relevant facts that I know to be true. I have hundreds of photographs to jog my memory, as I was advised to take a good, reliable camera by the Director of Army Surgery at the time.

Operation Corporate had commenced. The Falkland Islands would be retaken and returned to the Crown and I would have a part to play in it. The Task Force was lucky the Royal Navy did not lose a critical number of ships and I was lucky I did not get myself killed, luckier than the 255 British Service personnel, 649 Argentine Service personnel and the 3 Falkland Islanders who did.

However, because of predicted transport difficulties of casualties over the hostile terrain it was decided, quite rightly to advance the surgical facilities one echelon nearer the frontline. I commanded Field Surgical Team 1 (FST 1) and my friend and colleague, Major (then) Jim Ryan commanded FST 2. There are nine personnel in an FST, and both teams were grafted on to 16 Field Ambulance with all their operating equipment and enough supplies to carry out around 50 major operations. Extra tentage was also supplied, and each of us were issued with cold weather clothing and a personal weapon, mine being the usual 9mm semiautomatic Browning sidearm, holster and a full clip of ammunition.

The second wave of the Task Force left on the 12th May 1982. The teeth arms were the 1st Battalion Welsh Guards, 2nd Battalion Scots Guards and 1/7th Gurkha Rifles, with Artillery and support units including 16 Field Ambulance as the medical/surgical cover. We sailed on the other liner requisitioned into service (the acronym for this is STUFT, Ship Taken Up From Trade) the *Queen Elizabeth 2* (QE 2) from Southampton, to a tremendous send off. Public opinion was on the side of Maggie Thatcher's government. We would give Galtieri and Argentina a bloody nose, a jolly good spanking for daring to annexe some British islands that nobody had ever heard of, or had any idea of their location, even if they had.

Most, if not all, the Gurkhas had never seen the sea before. Nepal is completely landlocked, so severe sea sickness was anticipated, and they were accommodated on the lowest decks of the liner, where in rough weather the effects of the sea are minimised. We very rarely saw them, but these tough, courageous and fearsome little soldiers have such a reputation on the battlefield that the Argentine soldiers certainly did not want to face them.

The cruise, for want of a better word, involved a massive amount of drills and fitness training, to hone the battle readiness of the embarked troops. One deck was used for running and the newly installed helicopter pad (over the stern swimming pool) was used for physical training. General Purpose Machine Guns appeared, mounted and welded to the deck railings. The civilian Cunard crew had volunteered to remain with the boat (including the two civilian doctors and some nursing staff) on the long journey to the South Atlantic, and this reflected a degree of courage and patriotism. I spent a lot of time fitness training and I just couldn't even estimate how many times I ran around the promenade deck. Fitness was and is a key to survival, not only in the atrocious weather, but also in the case of wounding.

Gash (rubbish) was thrown overboard and used for target practice by the Guards and Gurkhas, when they were allowed up on deck to see the sea. My FST's target practice took place at the stern, but there were no targets. Puzzled, I asked the senior rank where our targets were. He just said, "Aim for the ocean Sir. See if you can hit it". I did, nine times.

I spent a lot of my time giving first aid lectures to the troops. It was essential that I drilled into them the absolute necessity of the steps they should take if they, or their buddy were injured. They also practiced putting up drips on each other, as prompt fluid replacement would save lives. I found that my company was cultivated, and I heard no comments about the medics being on holiday as I had heard in Belize.

The food was good, the company was good, and the accommodation was crowded but good. There was however one slight problem. The QE 2 with some 3000 troops on board was a pretty high value target for Argentina and would be on the ocean for nearly three weeks.

The sinking of the Argentine cruiser, the *General Belgrano* on the 2nd May 1982 with the loss of over 300 lives, by the nuclear-powered submarine HMS *Conqueror*, had concentrated the minds of the Argentine Navy, who did not want to participate any more. They returned all their vessels to port in Argentina except the *San Luis*, a diesel electric submarine, and nobody knew where it was. The other Argentine submarine, the *Santa Fe*, had been damaged and captured in Grytviken in South Georgia on 25th April 1982 and was no longer a threat. Though the two naval carrier ships, *Invincible* and *Hermes*, would have been priority targets for the *San Luis*, there was a significant risk of an attack on the QE 2, which of course did not carry any antisubmarine equipment, so the ship zigzagged along at high speed with frequent changes of course.

We stopped off at Freetown in Sierra Leone to refuel and quickly sailed on. The QE 2 Captain was a darn sight better at docking his boat than I am at parking my SUV. I observed that as both FSTs were situated at the stern of the ship, a torpedo hit could completely erase the Brigade surgical cover. I discussed the situation with my colleague Jim Ryan and with his agreement we approached the Commanding Officer of the Field Ambulance, Lt Col John Roberts, who decided that the FSTs should be separated, and I took my team and equipment to the bow of the ship where I was delighted to find my accommodation had improved from a 4-berth cabin to a 2-berth inside suite, which I would share with my anaesthetist, Major Amit Bannergee. This tactical decision to keep the FSTs separated whenever and wherever possible could well have saved my life.

The weather was balmy until we crossed the equator, but when we hit the South Atlantic, it was awful. Even on one of the finest cruise ships in the world, the journey became a nightmare. Fee-paying passengers would have demanded their money back.

The British Government became increasingly nervous about the nation's grandest liner being in this war zone. It was felt that if it was sunk by enemy attack, then it would be a significant blow to the nation's morale (and I would add mine too) and the nearer we got to the Falklands, the greater was the possibility of this happening. The Argentine Air Force would come into play and they had already wrought havoc on the task force ships, with the loss of HMS *Sheffield*, HMS *Antelope* and the SS *Atlantic Conveyer* to name just a few, by dropping old iron bombs (British made, 1000 lbs) and also employing the weapon most feared, the Exocet missile.

We took on some supplies and one of the senior task force commanders at Ascension Island, which was a stores depot and staging post for the Task Force. We still had 3300 miles to go and it was several days later, 27th May 1982, that the QE 2 braked to a halt in Cumberland Bay, near Grytviken in South Georgia, which was covered in snow. It was not only the weather however that degraded our cruise, as the good civilian food had run out, we were on ration packs and the water, which seemed to taste of diesel, was virtually undrinkable; 3000 fit and hungry men eat and drink an awful lot in three weeks.

This was as far as the QE 2 would go and so South Georgia, 800 nautical miles from the FI and out of range of the Argentine Air Force was where the second leg of our journey began. We transhipped (a relatively short word for a very long, uncomfortable and cold process) to the MV *Norland*, by trawler cum minesweepers, or whatever they were. On 28th May the *Norland* departed for San Carlos.

The *Norland* was a roll on/roll off (RORO) ferry and she heaved around all over the place, even in the relative calm of the harbour. I had a cabin where I dumped all my kit and then went to find the emergency muster point, for when we inevitably took a hit, and if I did not happen to end up in several pieces, it would be where I would have to understand the instructions for launching the life boats. They were written in Navalese and were totally incomprehensible to anyone who lives their life on land.

The list of British ships damaged beyond repair, or at the bottom of the ocean, was getting longer every day. The Argentine Air Force pilots were that good, and the losses would have been even greater if the fuses of their bombs had been correctly primed for their skilful low-level attacks.

The journey from Grytviken to San Carlos waters and the Falklands Sound (Bomb Alley) required a stable digestive system, and it was so rough and so cold that virtually no one ventured onto the decks, with the pitching and rolling of the *Norland* and the hull crashing down with jarring thuds and ominous creaks. The temperature was below freezing and there was a significant wind chill. We were on the bloody boat for four days, double the normal two days, due to the inclement weather. If one considers the voyage on the QE 2, *Norland*, *Sir Galahad* and the MV *Fort Toronto*, the last two of which I will relate further on, I think I was seafaring more than I was soldiering.

On the 31st May I disembarked from the *Norland* into an LCVP (Landing Craft Vehicle and Personnel) with the rest of the Field Ambulance and we were ferried across San Carlos water to Blue beach opposite Ajax Bay on Red beach, where the red and green life machine (Field Hospital) was situated in the old mutton refrigeration plant, on East Falklands. There we were told to set up our equipment and be a reserve unit for the surgical teams in Ajax Bay. We also started to 'dig in', the aim being to build a deep sangar into the ground, covered with heavy wood and turf, for protection against enemy attack. That is hard work with the Army issue entrenching tool, but my sangar was never completed. Halfway through my efforts, "Air Raid Red" was called by whistle and we all had to pile into any sangar already constructed. I leapt in to one which was unoccupied and found out why. It was under about 18 inches of water. Nothing came of the air raid and I squelched out of the sangar with the problem of drying out and changing my socks before they iced up. Trench foot was to be a significant medical problem.

The weather totally sucked. I got back to digging, but events had moved on. We were now on the wrong beach and there were rumours (good rumours are always false, bad rumours are always true) that we would be advancing to Fitzroy inlet where forward elements of 16 Field Ambulance had been sent to set up an advanced dressing station. My warrant officer and chief Operating Theatre Technician, WO2 Les Viner MBE, had gone with them. A telephone call had apparently established that there were no Argentinians around, not on the ground anyway.

Communications throughout the war always seemed bad. Maybe this was because of the fluid nature of events, but though we had frequent briefings from Lt Col Roberts, it would seem that the information he had imparted was old news by the time the 'O' (Orders) group finished. On the 7th June we were ferried back across San Carlos waters with the remainder of our equipment and embarked on the RFA (Royal Fleet Auxiliary) LSL (Landing Ship Logistic) *Sir Galahad*, with half the Battalion of Welsh Guards, the other half having already gone to Bluff Cove, on HMS *Fearless*.

We would connect with the Advanced Dressing Station of the Field Ambulance in Fitzroy and set up our Advanced Surgical Centre. We were all aboard by dusk and I was in the Mess, ready to bunk down on the floor, when the Captain or First Officer of the *Sir Galahad* informed us that it was unlikely that the ship would be sailing that night, as it would arrive in the early morning. He consequently requested a postponement, which was refused, and we sailed south, around Lafonia and then back up the east coast to Fitzroy Inlet, where the other LSL, *Sir Tristram*, carrying ammunition, was already berthed. It was six o'clock in the morning of the 8th June. It was the clearest day so far in the campaign.

Sir Galahad had already been hit once on the 24th May, strafed by Argentine fighter aircraft, and a 1000-pound bomb had struck the ship but had not detonated. It was not a good omen.

There then ensued the most monumental cock up. I do not need to go into details, except to say that we were on board for several hours feeling extremely nervous. Neither LSL had any protection. However this is where I got lucky, because in keeping with the principle of separate FSTs, one team had to get off the boat, regardless of the argument that seemed to involve the Welsh Guards and the amphibious landing specialist officer regarding disembarkation. I directed my team to accompany the HQ of the Field Ambulance onto the LCVP and just after half my team had transferred, the ramp of the LSL failed. We got ashore as fast as we could, when I heard jet aircraft and the most almighty explosions. I refer to this source, the Daily History Blog. It was around 1400hrs.

Predictably, the ships were spotted by Argentine observers, and a Skyhawks attack was launched from the mainland. 5 Skyhawks and 5 Daggers approached the Falklands. The Daggers attacked HMS Plymouth in Falkland Sound, slightly damaging her. The Sea Harrier Combat Air Patrol over the Islands was vectored onto the Daggers, leaving Fitzroy defenceless. The Skyhawks pressed on to Fitzroy, three of them putting bombs into Sir Galahad, while two managed to bomb Sir Tristram. Fire ripped through both ships and they were abandoned. 48 men were killed on Sir Galahad – five RFA crew, 32 Welsh Guards, and 11 other Army personnel. Hundreds were horrifically wounded, including Simon Weston, who would later become famous for his charity work[14].

I had been minutes away from potential incineration. The Field Ambulance lost three dead, including the second in command, Major Roger Nutbeem. My FST clerk was casevacced with facial burns.

Now of course, we were faced with dealing with multiple casualties. Almost all the Field Ambulance's equipment, including my mobile FST operating theatre complex, table lights, instruments, surgical

---

14. The Daily History Blog 7 Jun 2012

packs, the lot, were on the *Sir Galahad* and we only had the medical resources brought forward with the Dressing Station. Nonetheless we gave aid to all the survivors, who were subsequently evacuated to ships and Ajax Bay. The flash burns to hands and faces suffered by many of the soldiers were so painful, and they so needed cooling down, that they were tearing intravenous fluid bottles apart. We hosed the wounded down as well as providing large doses of pain relief.

It was here I first came across Simon Weston, who was very badly burned, I estimated around 40%, and he was screaming with pain. I fixed up a fast-flowing drip, asked my anaesthetist to give him a hypnotic dose of ketamine, watched him for a while as I was dealing with other patients, (one doesn't have to protect the airway with ketamine) and as soon as he was settled I wrote a note with his name, the treatment and the dose of ketamine he had received and my estimate of his burnt area. He was put in a helicopter and either went to Ajax Bay or to the SS *Uganda*, the mother hospital ship. I met Simon many years later and filled in that slight void in his war for him.

Eventually all the casualties were dealt with. The evacuation chain by helicopter was remarkable and I take my hat off to the pilots, who not only evacuated the *Sir Galahad* but the injured that came to the Field Ambulance. Contemporary accounts number the casualties that came through the Field Ambulance at around 150, and the Army system of triage was used to distinguish those who required urgent treatment from those that did not. We were pretty much exhausted. Most people don't know that the Skyhawks had performed a low fly-past, presumably on their way back to Argentina, and they were met with a hail of small arms fire. I was looking at them and they only seemed about 50 feet above the ground. Fortunately they had expended all their bombs, so they did not pose a threat. I have later learned that the Skyhawks flew in formation over Bluff Cove where the Scots Guards were dug in, and the aircraft received another hail of small arms, GPMG and heavy machine gun fire.

This was the worst event of the war, with so much loss of life as well as dreadful injuries to the survivors. I had come off the boat in 'battle order' and my backpack, spare clothes and sleeping bag were merrily burning away on the *Sir Galahad* along with all the rest of my possessions, packed separately for the campaign. I had my DPM parka, my lynx fur hat (which always sent the Regimental Sergeant Majors apoplectic when they saw me wearing this item of clothing), and that was about it apart from the contents of my pouches. Fortunately, the Field Ambulance Quartermaster managed to find some extra sleeping bags, but not the socks and underwear I would need in due course.

At dusk the order came to dig in. The incentive to dig as deep and as quickly as possible was the *Sir Galahad* and the *Sir Tristram*, which were visible as smoky, glowing wrecks, reminders in the near distance of the disaster that had befallen 5 Infantry Brigade. I cracked on digging but unfortunately, at about nine inches into the ground, I came across a slab of concrete. I could not face starting again as the ground was frozen, so I hollowed out what I had dug into a 'shell scrape' and after a makeshift meal from the rations I carried, and a drink from my water bottle, I tried to settle down and get some sleep.

I remember it was a beautiful starry night, but as cold as the grave. Even fully clothed, boots on and in a sleeping bag, my teeth were chattering almost uncontrollably and my steel helmet, which I used for a pillow, definitely did not help. These were the conditions that the infantry would have to endure and still fight the battles. I told myself to get a grip and rest, if nothing else.

I did not sleep a wink, tired as I was, and if the cold wasn't bad enough, the memories of the young soldiers screaming, with the skin peeling off their hands and faces, and any nylon clothing melting into their burnt areas, haunted me that terrible night and for many nights to come. Initially the adrenaline and the training had kicked in, but when everything had subsided in the aftermath, I found myself dwelling on the whole nightmare and mourning the dead youths, for that is what they were, and the grief of their families to come, when in spite of fervent hope and prayers they would find out that their beloved sons, brothers, or husbands would not be coming home, or if they did, they would not be as they were before they left for war. Some would physically be the same but mentally the toll would be huge; for some, too much. I wondered how my mother would have reacted, and I couldn't bear that thought. With my sister away in Malawi and my brother having suffered from a difficult birth, she would be so lonely without the frequent contact of her youngest son.

If only the Argentine Air force pilots had not been so brave and skilful; if only their bombs had remained incorrectly fused; if only the Argentine observation point (OP) 12 miles away on Mount Harriet had not spotted the unprotected LSLs languishing in Fitzroy Inlet; if only the Harrier Combat Air Patrol had been vectored to neutralise the Sky Hawks. If only, if only, if only.

Events had conspired, in the fog of war, to jeopardise the safety of the embarked troops. There are many accounts of why this happened, and I would suggest the reader does their own research from the articles written about this tragic event. There was a Ministry of Defence Board of Inquiry.

The *Sir Galahad* was the last of the six ships destroyed by the Argentines and probably together these six made up for their loss of the *Belgrano*. The *Sir Galahad* could not be salvaged and the burnt-out hulk was eventually towed out to sea and scuttled by the Royal Navy on 25th June 1982. It is now an official war grave under the Protection of Military Remains Act. The *Sir Tristram* was eventually repaired.

Passage of 1000lb UXB by gangway on *Sir Galahad*, Falkland Islands War, 1982

During the sailing aboard the *Sir Galahad* from San Carlos Waters I had wandered around the ship, taking some photographs. I recorded where earlier the unexploded iron bomb had crashed through a gangway without detonating.

I photographed the beautiful Fitzroy Inlet before the carnage was unleashed, but most poignant of all, I took some pictures of the *Galahad's* tank deck, of the embarked personnel chatting, playing cards, cleaning their kit or sleeping. One of the 500-pound bombs went through the forward hatch and exploded in the tank deck. When I can bring myself to look at the photo below, and it has not been often, I do so knowing that none of the pictured soldiers are alive. I have to cling to the hope that their deaths were instantaneous, as their agonies in the white heat of the explosion would have been indescribable. Sometimes, even now, I can't get it out of my mind, as often when one tries to eliminate a memory, an incident from conscious thought, the mind rejects the attempt and refreshes the details of the event.

The tank deck of the *Sir Galahad*. Falkland Islands War 1982

Next morning, we attended the CO's 'O' group. We had managed the mass casualty situation well and thanks to the evacuation lines, all survivors were being treated effectively. However, the Field Ambulance needed resupply, my FST needed complete surgical re-equipping and we also needed some hot food and sleep. The plan was that my team and I would be transported to Ajax Bay to try and bastardise a spare Naval Ships Surgical Team's (SST) equipment for our own use as an Army FST.

We were transported by helicopter back to San Carlos next day and into what we felt was the security of the refrigeration plant, where the Naval SSTs and the Parachute Clearing Troop (PCT) of 16 Field Ambulance (which had been seconded to 3 Brigade) were operating. It seemed tranquil and warm compared to our situation at Fitzroy and what we had been through, but I was told that they had had their moments too; Lt Commander Rick Jolly RNR in charge of the medical squadron of the Commando Logistics Regiment insisted on showing me the unexploded bomb in the building. For me, at the time, it was a bit counterproductive. I was dog tired, starving hungry and more than a bit, shall we say, combat stressed.

His motives were based on kindness and an appreciation of the difficulties of operating right at the front line and how it had affected me and others in the Field Ambulance. I was grateful for his efforts, but what I needed was some hot food and a good night's sleep, which I then got. Next day I was much better and helped my team, led by WO2 Viner, in going through the spare medical equipment available and constructing an FST. We managed to find everything we would need except an operating light, but this took all night. Each item of equipment had to be packed in sturdy Lacon boxes, except the 'McVicar' operating table, which was in bits ready for assembly on site.

Both Rick Jolly and Les Viner have recently died. Rick Jolly should be remembered for his organisational and administrative skills in providing the means for the surgical teams to do their job in Ajax Bay, saving many lives. He should also be remembered for his support of the South Atlantic Medal Association. I will personally remember Les Viner as my mainstay, my go-to senior rank to get things done and the man who stood beside me during almost all the surgery we undertook in Fitzroy during the final push for Port Stanley, the capital of the Falklands. In addition to WO2 Les Viner and Major Amit Bannergee my team consisted of Lt Col Kenny Watts, Sgt Pierre Naya, Cpl Cliff Forshaw, Pte Ian Macmillan, Lance Cpl Richard Gramson and Pte Richards. Exceptional men; I pay tribute to each and every one of them. Our encompassing operational name including No 2 FST was 55 FST the surgical strength of 2 Field Hospital.

Sergeant Pierre Naya MM RAMC was my senior Operating Theatre Technician. The following extract was written by his brother Michael Naya in a book about his life, *'War Medic Hero, A portrait of Sergeant Pierre Naya'*:

While at anchor in Fitzroy Sound on June 8, 1982, RFA Sir Galahad was bombed and set on fire by enemy aircraft. Embarked troops included two companies of infantry and the main body of 16 Field Ambulance, men and equipment. At the time of the attack most of the troops were positioned in the tank deck, where substantial quantities of ammunition soon began to explode as the fire worked through the ship. Over the course of some two hours 135 casualties, the majority with burns and amputations, were evacuated to the Advanced Dressing Station already ashore at Fitzroy settlement. Sergeant Naya, Royal Army Medical Corp, was standing in the tank deck when he was thrown against a bulkhead by the first explosion and partially stunned. The lights went out and the tank deck began to fill with dense black smoke. A second explosion killed two men behind him, set his large pack alight and scorched the back of his head. Shrugging off the burning material, he managed to lead a third soldier by hand up two flights of stairs to daylight. There he paused to cut burning clothing from other soldiers with his scissors before mounting a third flight to the upper deck. He then helped to carry a man who had lost a leg up to the forecastle, having first administered first aid and set up intravenous infusion. He treated many more casualties, including another amputee, and set up several more infusions, until all casualties had been evacuated; he left the ship on the last helicopter, later to be evacuated as a casualty himself. After only three days he returned to duty in the Advance Surgical Centre of the field ambulance, where he worked steadfastly through the most intense period of military activity and the passage of many battle casualties. He acted in the highest tradition of the Royal Army Medical Corps.

I have recently been in contact with Pierre's wife Nina. She told me that her husband was never the same after his return to the UK and he died too young aged 67 years in 2012. I was privileged to have had him in my team.

Next morning, we were ready to return to Fitzroy. Jim Ryan's team, FST 2, would remain in Ajax bay and replace Lt Col W McGregor's team from the PCT which would move forward with us. I was more than pleased with this because I knew Bill McGregor well. He was an experienced general surgeon who could advise me in any difficult surgery I might encounter. Bill McGregor OBE is now dead too, and he should be remembered for his sterling service in the Falklands as well as other theatres of operation, as a member of the Parachute Regiment. Major C Batty RAMC leading the other surgical team in the PCT would be advanced to Teal Inlet to provide surgical cover to the west of Stanley.

It was the 10th of June. My FST, equipment and personnel, was designed to be air portable in one helicopter lift and we all packed into a Puma or Sea King, I can't remember which. All I can remember was how absolutely stuffed the aircraft was, such that I could not move. The pilot lifted off and almost immediately started contour flying at an insane speed to avoid enemy detection. One of the aircrew was behind the machine gun, scanning the terrain as we flew over it. The flight was short, but I was glad to get off and back to terra firma. I had suffered from Belize flashbacks during the whole flight.

We set up our equipment alongside the PCT in the village hall, and we designated a resuscitation/triage area. The post-operative recovery area was outside in tentage which, to say the least, was inadequately heated. We were the advanced surgical facility for the battle for Port Stanley, covering the southern approach, the ridge of mountains comprising Mount William, Mount Harriet, Sapper Hill and Tumbledown.

The government and senior commanders were pushing for the final battle for Port Stanley to take place as soon as possible, the former because the naval losses were unsustainable and they needed a political fillip and the latter because they wanted to achieve victory before winter really set in, when logistic problems would become almost insurmountable. Could the weather get any worse, I asked myself?

Yes it could. The temperature remained firmly fixed at 0 degrees C. I was persistently cold and hungry, and as I had only one mess tin, the other having melted on the *Sir Galahad*, all my meals were taken in this one container. Rations had been centralised, with an Army Catering Corps chef doing his best. We had two meals a day. The men were fed first, followed by the officers, and if you weren't there you didn't get it. I like chicken curry (even the MOD ration pack version), but not more than once a day. I dislike rice pudding at any time of the day, but I would have to have them both together at the same time, in my one remaining mess tin, just to abate the hunger: chicken curry, savoury rice, sweet milk rice pudding and jam. I needed the calories. Heavy smoking was at least an appetite suppressant; I had lost a lot of weight and was back to being a lean, mean machine.

The village hall we occupied was in Fitzroy settlement and accommodation was limited. I went to a nearby house and asked if we could bunk down in two bedrooms on their first floor, to which they readily agreed, and I moved the FST in. We were much more comfortable, but it was cold, and we once again slept fully dressed except for boots, which I cuddled in my sleeping bag to keep them warm, and keep them mine.

The battle for Port Stanley lasted from 11th – 14th June and was fierce and uncompromising. The Gurkhas took Mount William. The Scots Guards were engaged in hand to hand fighting on Mount Tumbledown. When all the high ground had been secured by the British Forces, the Argentines in Port Stanley surrendered at 2100 hrs on the 14th of June and the Falkland Islands had been returned to the Crown. I was still operating at the time and would be for several hours, but I felt a bit more relaxed about the whole thing. When, on 20th June, British Forces retook the South Sandwich Islands, code-named Operation Paraquet, all hostilities were finally over.

The surgical facility we provided was basic but effective. The military surgical principle of leaving wounds open where appropriate did much to prevent the onset of serious infections. My job was to save life and limb. The only problem was, as I have already outlined, I did not have an operating light. This was partially solved by using three forty-watt bulbs separated by a spacer. The settlement had a big diesel generator which coped well with our needs. I had made an attempt to sleep in the shed it was housed in, because it was warm, but the continuous clatter was too much, too intrusive, even in my sleep-deprived state.

My dim light was augmented by an electric Dar Ray lamp which could be mounted on part of the operating table, but this did not really solve the problem, as the focus of the beam was everywhere except where I wanted it to be. WO2 Viner arranged for the Operating Theatre Technicians (OTT) to hold the lamp in relays and direct it on the area of the casualty's body that I was working on. Directly opposite me was a dartboard, which was still there when I did another tour of the islands in 1990.

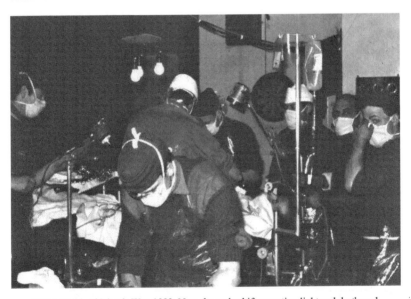

FST 1. Falkland Islands War, 1982. Note the makeshift operating light and dartboard.

The terrible human price of war will always filter through to the medical echelons. The medics, from Regimental Medical Assistants and Combat Medical Technicians to consultant surgeons, will all have to deal with the concentrated carnage as best they can. Heads, torsos and limbs mutilated or burnt in a flash of gun fire, artillery or mortar. Body parts are missing, or beyond salvage. Many wounds are untreatable, and those casualties may have to be put to one side to take their chances, whilst those that are treatable are worked on by priority.

The toll on the doctors can be horrific, not just at the time, but in later years, when the fear and the nightmares return with a vengeance and disrupt a settled way of life, career or family. The 2 Para Regimental Medical Officer at Goose Green was severely affected, and my heart goes out to him for the bravery he showed doing his job and the price he paid for some years afterwards. Even working in a busy accident and emergency department cannot prepare one for these experiences. The only preparation for being a war medic is war.

The injured I operated on were brought in by helicopter, sometimes in casualty pods. On landing they were assessed by the triage team, prioritised and then transferred to the resuscitation bay in the village hall. If resuscitation was failing, generally because of bleeding from the abdomen or pelvis, then I would be called. If I was operating, say, on a broken leg due to a fragment injury, then I would abandon that case if necessary to open up the new arrival. I could continue it later during a lull in the fighting. The teams were good, and all the training and drills paid off. Water was short, so instruments were just washed in hot soapy water. I operated in uniform, shirt sleeve order, with a cap, mask, gloves and a plastic apron. In between cases I would just change gloves, unless my arms were bloodied.

Occasionally we took a break for some food and liquids and I remember being offered a cup of "wet", which was the only word that would accurately describe the fluid I was given. It was indeed tea but had been kept in a flask that had been unwashed after its previous contents; thick pea soup. It was delicious.

For now, I am only going to mention three more of the casualties I operated on.

3 Para had been attacking Mount Longdon and intelligence had confirmed there were no minefields, yet right at the start of the battle, Cpl Brian M wandered into the middle of one and stepped on a mine. I had to do an above knee amputation of his injured leg as most of it had disappeared. His other leg was fine. He recovered well, but the point of relating his injury and treatment is because about 18 months later, when I was doing a clinic at the CMH Aldershot, he was on my out-patient list. He walked in, and had I not known that he was an amputee caused by an Argentine mine and then tidied up by me, I would never

have guessed. His gait was only slightly abnormal, and he had the new, at the time, suction prosthesis with a knee hinge. He could stand one-legged on his prosthesis and swing his remaining leg outwards.

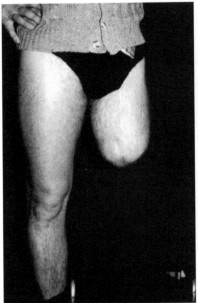 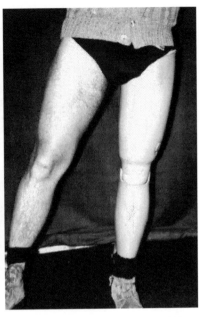

Loss of leg to anti-personnel mine. Falkland Islands War 1982

Prosthetic replacement of left leg. 1982

Paratrooper Dago D 3 Para, (nicknamed Dago, as a result of his pointed looks and Mexican style moustache) was a young lad who had sustained what we called then a High velocity (HV) fragment wound from either a grenade or mortar, so he must have been pretty close to the detonation, or a gunshot wound (GSW). The causative missile had taken off a finger from either hand, then entered his left shoulder and impacted on the head of the humerus (long arm bone) and fractured it. The outer half of this part of his bone, which forms the contour of the shoulder, became a secondary missile and exited his shoulder joint at 90 degrees to the direction of the wound. The last words he said to me before I operated on him were, "Don't cut my fucking arm off sir". I didn't.

I tidied up his damaged fingers and excised his shoulder wound. Interestingly I met him too, again in Aldershot, and he was in rude health, though of course his profile had changed somewhat. I did hear that the specialist surgeons were considering introducing one of the new shoulder joint prostheses that had come to the market, but I heard no more.

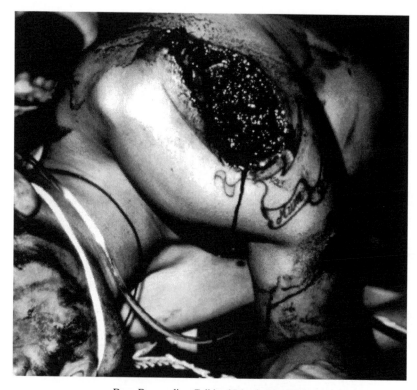

Dago D wounding. Falkland Islands War 1982

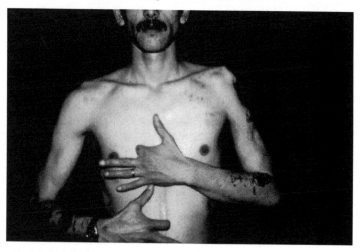

Dago D after the Falkland Islands War

This is the citation accompanying the award of the Military Medal to Guardsman Andrew P., 2 Scots Guards:

On the night of 13th/14th June 1982, on the Island of East Falklands, the 2nd Battalion Scots Guards were attacking well entrenched enemy positions on the craggy ridge feature of Tumbledown Mountain, 7 kilometres to the west of Port Stanley. During the assault, leading elements came under fire from a sniper hidden high up in nearby rocky crags. Guardsman Andrew Samuel P. reacted immediately: abandoning his machine gun and armed with grenades, he climbed up the wet and slippery rocks towards the enemy position. Reaching the top, he hurled a grenade and killed the sniper. As he threw the grenade he was hit and badly wounded by enemy mortar fire. His courageous action was a significant individual contribution to the success of the battle[15].

He had a penetrating wound of the abdomen, was leaking small bowel contents through the entrance wound, and had been bleeding heavily. This was the longest procedure I undertook, dealing with the holes in his small and large, bowel, excising and reanastamosing (joining by suture) the former, and excising (removing) part of the latter, with the formation of a colostomy and mucous fistula (large bowel brought out to the skin). He recovered well but I was to meet him again too, when I returned to duties in the QEMH at the end of the war.

Guardsman P had developed a delayed urinary fistula (leakage of urine out through the abdominal wall in his case). The wall of the ureter (the tube that takes urine from the kidney to the bladder) had no doubt been weakened at his original injury and had given way. Lt Col Nick Chetti RAMC was the Army urologist looking after him and he contacted me to ask what I had done in his abdomen.

I explained the nature of the surgery I had undertaken and volunteered to assist at the exploration of his abdomen which had been scheduled in a couple of days to try and sort out the general surgical organs, so that Lt Col Chetti could have a reasonable chance of dealing with the fistula, but I was of no help. The patient's abdomen was full of dense fibrous adhesions (scar tissue) and after a two-

---

15. https://stevecocksfalklands.blogspot.com/2007/10/

Guardsman Andrew S. P with his belly open. I was to re-open him in QEMH with Lt Col Nick Chetti. Bit of a "rabbit in the headlights" look here. Falkland Islands War 1982.

man consultation over the table, Guardsman P's right kidney was sacrificed. He had already had his colostomy closed. Ten days later I said goodbye to him as he left the QEMH in excellent health, for a prolonged period of sick leave. I never saw him again.

The strain of operating with inadequate lighting is enormous, as I had found in Belize, never mind the other conditions. What had been particularly nerve-racking was the occasional Air Raid Red alert, when everybody but the operating team, if in action, disappeared down a hole in the ground. Nothing came of them, but it did concentrate my mind.

The paper *The Falklands War: Army Field Surgical Experience*[16], written after the war, mainly by Jim Ryan, (the scholar amongst us if the truth be told), and me, gives a more detailed and perhaps more scientific account of the Army Surgical Experience during the War

Some mention must be made of the anaesthetists in the FSTs. Often overlooked in surgical anecdotes, they are the backbone of the team. They had to get the injured fit for surgery (a systolic blood pressure of 100mm Hg), hand 'bag' them (no field ventilators, nor oxygen for that matter), throughout the operation and recovery, and keep them alive and stable in spite of the surgery, using basic but robust equipment.

16. Jackson D S, Batty C G, Ryan J M, McGreggor WSP. Ann R Coll Surg Engl 1983;65:281-5.

There were no X-ray facilities and no other blood tests other than blood grouping for transfusion. They were Lt Col W Knight, Lt Col Jim Anderson, Major Malcolm Jowett and Major Amit Bannergee. I take my hat off to them.

On a surgical note, we surgeons in the FST had no diathermy equipment to assist with haemostasis (stopping the bleeding during the operation), so each troublesome vessel had to be tied off whereas smaller vessels were controlled by pressure, or left to coagulate naturally. For ligating these vessels, I had a long spool of linen in a chrome dispenser. I used the same one from one casualty to the next, with no ill effect.

There was not much for us to do by this point. We kept one surgical table set up for any emergency and then just awaited our next move. I wandered around taking photos. Some photos are too dark because my camera light meter battery was flat. It had been that way pretty much since I got to Fitzroy. My spare batteries were on the *Sir Galahad* with the rest of my kit. I also made sure that, even though I would eat last, I was always around at mealtimes.

No 1 FST after cessation of hostilities. The *Sir Galahad* is still burning away in the background

There were some amusing moments. One was the attempt by some of the soldiers to capture an Upland Goose for the pot. This bird is protected, but it did not stop the soldiers who tried to sneak up on one with their bayonets for the kill, as obviously they could not shoot it as everyone would hear the sound of the gunfire. They were unsuccessful of course, but their efforts were sterling. This had come to the attention of the Staff Officers, and dire punishment would follow any attempt to eat a goose.

The weather was so cold most of the time that slaughtered cattle would be skinned, gutted and hung up in gallows outside. It also became a severe offence for anyone to cut off a piece of beef for themselves; if they were caught, that is.

We had not had a proper drink for what seemed like years, and a good celebration was certainly on the cards. One source of alcohol was on the hospital ship the SS *Uganda*, so I asked my CO if I could hitch a ride on a chopper to the *Uganda*, just to check up on a few of our patients. He agreed and sometime later I found myself being tossed about in the back of a Gazelle flown by an Army Air Corps pilot who was fighting to keep the aircraft under control in the high winds, especially on the approach to the helipad on the boat. I closed my eyes and awaited the crash landing into either the SS *Uganda* or the South Atlantic. Of course it didn't happen, or I wouldn't be writing this. I was amazed at the relative gentleness of the touchdown, so I put on my most nonchalant, devil-may-care face and stumbled along the writhing decks. The time on land had wiped out my sea legs.

I had an hour before the return to Fitzroy. I went to the wards and introduced myself to the nursing staff, who were discussing their off duty. I was a bit muddy, smelly, unkempt, and unshaven and it took some time for them to realise who I was, where I had been and what I had been doing. They had no idea that two surgical facilities were so far forward. They thought they had received most of their casualties from Ajax Bay. As soon as I had explained, they were very helpful in filling in some of the details I wanted; I think by then Simon Weston had been airlifted to the UK.

However, time was running short and I had the other mission. I found the Officers' Mess, which was pretty much empty except for the steward, and I ordered a considerable amount of bottled booze, rum, whisky and brandy, and signed the chit with my name, rank and number. With the cargo under my arm I got back to the helipad where the pilots were waiting for me, and we air bumped our way back to Fitzroy, with my stomach travelling either 20 feet above or 20 feet below the fuselage of the aircraft. I had been prepared to travel in a helicopter in pursuit of alcohol.

Back at Fitzroy I gave most of the booze away to the Field Ambulance, except for a couple of bottles of rum and a bottle of whisky, which I took to the house I had commandeered. Negotiations with the family who were living downstairs were swift. The lady of the house agreed to cook my FST a huge mutton curry with rice pudding to follow in exchange for a bottle of rum. I had been outvoted on the detested rice pudding, but so what. By the time we got to that part of the meal, I would be as drunk as a skunk.

We also had an Artillery Officer with us and as he had presented me with the brass of an artillery shell (105mm) that had been fired upon Port Stanley, he was invited. It was a memorable occasion and that is all I am going to say, apart from a thank you to the family we stayed with and the lady who cooked the meal.

Mail drops were infrequent, but welcome. Unfortunately, Kathy did not know that I was in the Falklands until quite late in the day, but once she did, we corresponded. Angela did write to me and often enclosed the *Daily Telegraph* cryptic crossword, which she knew I enjoyed solving. A stack of these is something I would take to a desert island, with pencils too. (*Desert Island Discs* on BBC Radio 4 would not have me very high on their list of personalities, not because I wouldn't be interesting, of course, but because I am fairly right wing politically).

We were still twiddling our thumbs. We heard that 2 Field Hospital were on their way to take over the King Edward VII hospital in Port Stanley. They had a number of QA nurses on their strength, which should have brightened things up a bit. Thousands of Argentine POWs were being returned to Argentina. Port Stanley was crowded out, and some sort of post conflict planning was coming into effect.

You will remember that Major Jim Ryan and I were nominally on the strength of 2 Field Hospital with our FSTs before being grafted on to the Field Ambulance. One FST would have to stay to provide 2 Field Hospital with a surgical asset and Jim Ryan volunteered along with Les Viner and others including Sgt Naya.

I needed, once again, to get back to my surgical training. I had 2½ years to go and I had just turned 33 years old.

The PCT were departing. They would join the rest of 3 Brigade for a cruise back to the UK on the SS *Canberra* and I said goodbye to my old friends Bill McGregor, Malcolm Jowett and the rest of their team. The naval SSTs were all getting back onto the ocean where they belonged, and Jim Ryan had already moved into the King Edward VII Hospital at Port Stanley.

I decided that I would fly to Port Stanley and find out was happening. It was all happening – clearing up after the conflict, that is. We had no role now, so I asked if there were any plans for us. "Not yet" came the reply from the CO of 2 Field Hospital. I flew back to Fitzroy and the miserable cold, none the wiser.

Eventually we had to move. We were running out of rations apart from anything else and we needed some relief from the hard conditions. My FST flew to Port Stanley and were almost immediately transferred by boat to what seemed like a floating laundrette, where we could wash, dry, clean our kit, get showered and relax for a night. I peeled the remains of my underwear off and threw them away. From then on, I went 'commando'.

The ship (I can't remember its name) was warm and there was a dining mess with hot food. I felt totally recharged when next day

Climbing up a rope ladder onto the *Fort Toronto*,
Falkland Islands War, 1982

we trans-shipped to a tanker, carrying water supplies instead of the usual cargo. It was yet another STUFT. The water demands of Port Stanley, with about 10,000 extra personnel, had completely overwhelmed their usual water supply, which was now being supplemented by this tanker, by means of dracones moored offshore. I remember having to climb up the side of the boat, enmeshed in some sort of rigging or rope ladder best suited to our evolutionary predecessors and with a swing of my leg, whilst someone relieved me of my backpack, I was on board the *Fort Toronto* and my fortunes took a turn for the better.

I was greeted by the Captain, whose name I had unfortunately forgotten, but members of a Merchant Navy forum have informed me that he was Captain Robert Kinnear (Kinnier). However, I do remember Frank Smurthwaite, the Chief Engineer, with whom I bunked down. Both officers were extremely kind and their words to me, which really cheered me up were, "We are carrying water and as soon as it's gone, we can get out of here. Use as much as you want". I immediately had a bath in Frank's suite, with the water almost overflowing. I would sleep on the floor in his lounge area. The rest of my team were dispersed with the crew. The ship's mess provided plenty of good food. The bar was closed during the day, but the evenings and nights were fairly alcoholically-charged events.

The Fort Toronto was a chemical tanker on its maiden voyage when it was taken up by the M.O.D. and was fitted with RAS (replenishment at sea) gear. She was the water supply vessel as the Army needed water for its troops as they feared that the Argentine's may have poisoned the island water. She was down there for around 2 years acting as a water supply vessel and also providing R & R to the successful soldiers and airmen who were living in pretty awful conditions for a long time after the hostilities ended[17].

I assume the crews were rotated, as two years is a long time to hang around Port Stanley unless you are an Islander.

After we had been aboard the *Fort Toronto* for a few days wind down, WO2 Viner said he wanted to see everybody in the seamen's mess. There he had a good few things to say in praise of the FST, but added that the men were untidy and unruly. He ordered a clean-up of everything, the mess, the quarters, bodies and uniforms. His parting words to me were, "I expect you'll be setting an example won't you sir?" That wasn't really a proposal with any element of choice, so I

---

17. British Merchant Navy Old Friends Plus by John Arton, 5th March 2017.

did as he had suggested and turned up to the parade he had called next evening, shaved, ironed, creased and bulled. He looked me up and down and nodded his approval and then had a look at the men. The respect they had for this fine Warrant Officer showed in the way they had turned out. They were as immaculate as they could be under the circumstances.

I was getting restless. There are only so many baths you can have in one day. I frequented the bridge and chatted to the crew on watch and generally wandered around the ship and being moored in the harbour, I spent a lot of time looking over the side at Port Stanley about a mile away and at the constant movement on the water. In the evenings we would eat and often adjourn to the Captain's cabin for a few drinks and war stories.

The Captain's cabin of the *Fort Toronto*. (L-R) Frank Smurthwaite, me, Major Bannergee, Captain Kinnear and Lt Col Kenny Watts. Falkland Islands war 1982

I slept on the carpeted floor of the Chief Engineer's lounge and at the end of one evening, after a few gins, I crashed out, being rocked quickly to sleep by the gentle heaving of the boat. A couple of hours later I awoke to find that the heaving of the boat was anything but gentle. Still in my sleeping bag, I started to slide from one side of the lounge to the other, gently at first, then more quickly, until eventually I hit the wall with my feet. A few seconds later I slid in the reverse direction and crashed my head at the place where I had started this journey. I was lying head down at an angle of 45 degrees.

Befuddled, I tried to get out of my sleeping bag, but instead I shot off to the other side of the cabin, again coming to a halt with a resounding thud. The Chief Engineer, Frank, then bounded out of his bunk, yelling that they had started up the engines and the *Fort Toronto* was putting out to sea. HMS *Minerva*, a Royal Navy Frigate parked some distance away, had slipped her anchor in what was now a Force 10 (at least) gale, and there was a collision risk. I eventually managed to get out of my sleeping bag and tried to get upright, which was impossible. I was listing all over the place. I had to more or less crawl out of the cabin, and then hang on to a handrail to try and see what was happening outside.

I have never experienced such atrocious weather, several times worse than we encountered on the *Norland*. The wind was howling, the rain came down in sheets, the temperature was freezing and the sea was wild, tossing the *Fort Toronto* around like a cork. As we moved further out of the harbour it got worse, and very soon I had that awful feeling that even my stomach was not made for this sort of activity and I threw up, fortunately in an area that was getting systematically hosed down by the South Atlantic Ocean crashing over the sides.

We endured this for about two days. I was as sick as a dog. I could drink water, but I could not eat. That was the first time I have been totally incapacitated by sea sickness, made worse by my poor balance in the dark. The Captain and the crew of the ship didn't seem that bothered, whilst I was certain that the ship would just roll over and sink into the arms of Neptune, who had obviously been seriously pissed off by something or other and needed a sacrificial appeasement. Eventually the storm passed and slowly and thankfully, I regained my equilibrium as the *Fort Toronto* steamed back to its berth in the harbour.

I must express my heartfelt thanks to the Captain, Chief Engineer and all the crew of the MV *Fort Toronto*. Their kindness and hospitality were second to none, and just what we needed to get back to some degree of normality. I don't think the contributions of the men of the Merchant Navy during the Falklands War have received the public recognition they deserve. Many died for their country.

After a few more days I got word that I would be travelling back to the UK imminently, by C130 Hercules. The journey that took three weeks by sea would take just over 24 hours by plane. It would require in-flight refuelling mid-way from the Falkland Islands to Ascension Island and a refuelling stop at Freetown, Sierra Leone, before finally arriving at Brize Norton. It was absolutely freezing when I left Port Stanley and it wasn't much warmer in the aircraft.

Me awaiting transport to the Airfield.
Falkland Islands War 1982

We could only smoke on the flight deck, so I spent quite a lot of time up there chatting to the pilots. One had a fine handlebar moustache in keeping with RAF tradition. I watched the in-flight refuelling and the precision flying that was necessary to get the Hercules probe locked onto the drogue of the tanker. It all seemed very calm. Eventually I went back to my seat and fell asleep. I must have been tired, as nobody can sleep in a Hercules going at full pelt, with the accompanying and persistent turbulence we encountered. I was getting to be a good soldier – I could sleep anywhere. There is not much more to relate about the flight back. We had to remain on the runway in Freetown, but we could stretch our legs and get some food and drink.

When we touched down in Brize Norton I got onto the Army bus that would take me back to Old Woking. I was dropped off at my cottage, the last to disembark, and having thanked the driver, I opened the door and went inside to my sanctuary. I dumped my kit, poured a large scotch and set about phoning the wives and relatives of the men in my FST to let them know that they were safe. Then I turned on my TV and collapsed into an armchair.

It was just after 6 pm and I managed to catch the news, after which Sue Lawley, the BBC presenter, appeared and said, "And now we are going to discuss the death of Mrs Wrigley, who underwent major surgery and then chemotherapy without consent, at a hospital in Birmingham, from which she died. She was entered into a clinical trial without her knowledge and here to discuss the case are..."

I poured another whisky and listened to the opinions of the experts. This was when and where the whole issue of informed consent started, and the responsibility of the doctors very firmly outlined, in making absolutely sure that no patient underwent a procedure without being fully aware of everything that could go wrong. The fact that they were discussing a case I had operated on added a little twist to the story, as did the letter from my medical defence union regretting that I had not replied to their previous letter a month before, when they proposed to make an ex-gratia payment of £1000 to a relative of Mrs Wrigley.

I wrote back that if they had addressed their letter to me in the South Atlantic, BFPO 677, I could have replied, if only by way of a "bluey". I also wrote that I was quite happy for the ex-gratia payment to be made, but that when I had spoken to Mrs Wrigley, she had told me that she had no known relatives left at all. They wrote back by return and apologised.

I was granted a week's leave before going back to QEMH. I craved female company, which is a polite way of putting it. However as Kathy was still in the Far East, I arranged for Angela to come down from Leeds to spend a few days with me, which she did. I said little about my recent war experiences to her, and she certainly showed little interest. Instead I listened patiently to her telling me all about the subject she liked most, herself and what she had been up to.

I started back at the QEMH and it seemed very quiet. As the base Army hospital, elective cases had been kept to a minimum and beds were conserved for the war injured, many of whom were still in-patients.

Simon Weston, whom I frequently went to see in the Burns and Plastics Unit, was one of them. He was still in terrible pain and was racking up a large number of operative procedures to get him functional, as it were. Of course, he did not recognise me. Since his eventual recovery I have admired him for getting into the public domain. I have spent some time with him, contributed to his charity and listened to his motivational speaking. He is a national figure. In contrast, it has appeared to have been the policy of British governments to acknowledge and care for the wounded, but shy away from an open display of broken bodies and minds, which even as a result of a just war, might prick the national conscience.

To illustrate this point, I am briefly returning to Fitzroy Inlet during the Falklands War. Lt (now Captain) Robert Lawrence MC 2 Scots Guards was shot by a sniper in the battle for Mount Tumbledown. When Lt Lawrence was eventually brought into Fitzroy, I was informed that he had a severe head wound with brain loss and was clinically unresponsive. (In modern clinical parlance he had a Glasgow Coma Scale of 3). In triage terms he was a P3 and the P1s and P2s had priority. Later, when I examined him, there was very little I could do other than clean up his wound under light anaesthetic, excise any devitalised brain and surrounding tissues, remove the usual foreign bodies and dress the wound to prevent any further injury or infection. He was then treated solely with IV fluids and antibiotics and left to take his chances. Somehow he recovered.

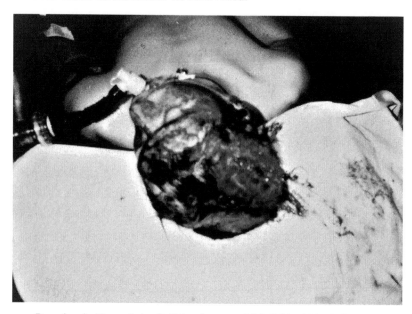

Reproduced with permission. Lt Robert Lawrence 1 SG. Falkland Islands War 1982

He gave an account of his part in the battle, on television, in newspaper articles and in the film "Tumbledown", when his experiences were portrayed by the actor Colin Firth. When I spoke to Robert Lawrence recently he told me that he also had a full recollection of the events in the Advanced Surgical Centre when paralysed, immobile and we thought pretty much brain dead.

In his own description of his wounding and then treatment, Lt Lawrence relates that he was 'put to one side' when he was evacuated to Fitzroy due to the severity of his injury and the very poor chance of his survival. This precise recall seems extraordinary, but then I must consider that when he had regained his power of speech he provided an accurate description of the battle, his hand-to-hand fighting and the sniper shot that wounded him. Thus, he had very little in the way of post-traumatic amnesia.

Capt Lawrence has no complaints, other than that on his return, he felt he was an embarrassing reminder of the perils of war. He also felt that unless it was to the advantage of the MOD or government, he was confined to the back streets of the ceremonies, church services and parades. He won the MC. He should have been celebrated at the time as one of the nation's finest, a warrior prepared to give all when required, and the UK government should have reciprocated publicly and in kind.

Robert Lawrence now, 2019[18]

Robert Lawrence is twice married with four children and lives with his wife in a château in France. He has organised adventure pursuits for injured servicemen and others. I am so glad he survived and has made a success of his life. He demonstrates indomitable strength as do Simon Weston and many others of whom the nation should be proud.

---

18. Image lifted from his Face Book page, with his permission

Finally, I must mention the MOD (and the government's) response to Post Traumatic Stress Disorder (PTSD). Initially and for many years, it was muted. The recognition of a common but diverse constellation of psychological symptoms was acknowledged as an immediate reaction, occurring after battlefield exposure, but the long-term effects were hotly disputed and rejected. Now, 38 years on, it is accepted as a severe and disabling psychological consequence of warfare and other causes, which can strike at any time with particularly unpredictable and disabling flashbacks lasting a lifetime.

When I was to serve in Bosnia-Herzegovina 11 years later, immediate psychiatric debriefing was provided at the base of operations by a uniformed Community Psychiatric Nurse, to try and prevent adverse sequelae following exposure to any potential conflict stressor. Whether this strategy reduced the incidence of PTSD, I do not know. Cognitive Behavioural Therapy (CBT) can assist in the management of those severely afflicted with PTSD, but my own view, and no doubt the view of many servicemen who have since taken their own lives, is that there is only one certain cure.

On a personal note, I was troubled 28 years after an incident in Bosnia. I shall come to this later, but I will say that I was somewhat surprised at this event, because I thought, having seen and dealt with so much human misery, I would be relatively immune to this effect. This was not so. Time and circumstances conspire to resurrect buried memories which have never been truly forgotten, but are just lurking in one's subconscious. In this case, it was not just what I had been exposed to that was the problem.

At the QEMH none of my fellow soldiers or officers asked about my experience in the Falklands. This was understandable. Someone said I was lucky to have gone, to which I replied, "I was lucky I came back". I was at the beginning of becoming a soldier surgeon; I had been blooded, but thankfully not literally.

CHAPTER 17

A Trained Fucking Monkey

Cambridge Military Hospital, Aldershot, 1982

After my year at the QEMH, I went back to the CMH for the third year of my four-year training rotation. I appreciated this, as I needed to get more experience in orthopaedics and trauma surgery, especially in the Operative Reduction and Internal Fixation of fractures, (ORIF). The AO (Arbeitsgemeinschaft für Osteosynthesefragen) system of fracture management was originally developed by the Swiss in 1958 and the principles and methods are used throughout the world. I have been on two AO courses, one in the Medizinische Hochschule (Medical School) in Hannover, in West Germany and the other in Aldershot, and I was well versed in the technique.

The lecture in Hanover regarding this system of rigid fracture fixation followed by early mobilisation was given by the Professor of Orthopaedic/Trauma surgery, Professor Harald Tscherne MD. German professors of surgery are highly intelligent, dominant and autocratic (the same as Chinese professors of surgery in my experience). No

225

surgeon, trainee or trained, in their immediate arc of influence would dare to question them, without risking their employment prospects being confined in those days, to one mile west of the Berlin Wall. I was told this by a German doctor, an oberarzt or senior doctor, when his guard had alcoholically slipped one evening in the Officers' Mess in BMH Hanover.

Professor Tscherne's lecture was excellent, but no contrary views were accepted in the discussions afterwards regarding the operative management he advocated. There was Tscherne's way, or the wrong way. He would only allow colleagues of the rank of oberarzt or above to change his lecture slides. I was to meet two other German professors of surgery when I was in Munster. One was equally formidable, if more diminutive than Prof Tscherne.

I needed access to patients with skeletal trauma, and this would not happen when I worked as a senior registrar in general surgery in a civilian hospital, but in the CMH, I was expected to cope with fracture management in addition to all the subspecialties of general surgery. I was halfway to being complete in my surgical ambition, though it is true to say that in difficult, isolated situations, I often had the appropriate textbook open and to hand when I was confident enough to undertake a procedure that I had never seen before. In addition, in those days as a general surgeon, I was expected to manage and operate on children, commonly those with undescended testicles and hernias. The Louise Margaret maternity hospital was next door to the CMH and catered for service wives and children. Infrequently a neonate with congenital pyloric stenosis (a stomach outlook obstruction) would present and I got used to operating on humans not much bigger than a rugby ball and performing a Ramstedt procedure. This is the standard operation described for this condition and is named after Dr Wilhelm Conrad Ramstedt, who performed the first operation on the 28th July 1911.

Or did he? No. According to medical history and archives, the first surgeon to perform this procedure was British, Sir Harold Stiles, and he did so on 3rd February 1910, seven months earlier[19]. You've got to keep an eye on these Germans.

---

19. en.wikipedia.org/wiki/Harold Stiles

Kathy's Far Eastern posting came to an end and she was posted back to the UK. I was originally intending to discontinue my attachment to Angela, as I was so fond of Kathy, but Angela's mirroring of my needs, particularly regarding the prospect of children which she had said she wanted, whereas Kathy did not, persuaded me not to and led me to pursue a more serious relationship with Angela in the hope of starting the family which I very much wanted.

As a doctor, I am trained to recognise the overt medical symptoms of underlying problems, so I feel that I should have been able to see the warning signs of a very flawed character in Angela, but as a surgeon, rather than a GP, my expertise did not include any in-depth knowledge of psychology or psychiatry, more's the pity. The peculiar characteristics that I noted about Angela's behaviour did not overly concern me in the early years of our relationship. I certainly regarded some of the things she said as, shall we say, 'quirky', but other pronouncements were so extreme that I incorrectly assumed that she must surely be joking and that it was just her odd sense of humour. I could never have believed that she meant what she said, especially regarding her loathing of men, or need for control and possession of money. It wasn't quirkiness, she was deadly serious.

Angela was to become my nemesis. She applied for a short-service commission as a qualified teacher in the Army Education Corps and was accepted by the Commissioning Board. She said she had applied in order to be with me. Looking back, those on the Army Board were as stupid and short sighted as I was, as she should never have been a commissioned officer (nor even recruited to the ranks for that matter).

Whilst I was at the CMH, I was given another responsibility. The CMH was the base training hospital for the operating theatre technicians and I was put in charge of their school, assisted by a commissioned OTT, Captain Peter Starling and Major Barry Gisborne. We had to oversee the change from the traditional Army instruction in this trade, to National Vocational Qualifications (NVQs), which were the recognised civilian equivalents. In truth, I was pretty much a figurehead, a go-to 'Rupert' (the slang for an officer) if a decision needed rubber stamping. I was now the Head of their Career

Employment Group (CEG) and would participate in resolving the usual disciplinary issues and attend promotion boards.

I was on call every second night and weekend. Sometimes if I had a good registrar or senior house officer I would do my on call, from the comfort of my cottage. Also on call, for obstetrics and gynaecology, was a Dubliner, Major Richard Myles, a true Army man and bon vivant. We became very good colleagues and friends and would while away several evenings in the Mess, having a couple of beers and playing penny-a-point snooker. Of those officers who lived in the mess, another OBGYN doctor, Lt Col Dennis Brennan, would join us in the bar. He liked his whiskey and would often fall asleep with half a glass of the nectar fluid clutched to his chest. The first time I saw this I thought about removing the glass in his hand for safety, but the duty steward told me not to bother. He said that in all the years he had seen Lt Col Brennan fall asleep at the bar, he had never spilt a drop of his whiskey. He would wake in an hour, drain his glass, wish everybody goodnight and retire to bed. That is exactly what happened a few minutes later.

Richard Myles and I chatted about everything. We put the army, the country and the world to rights, sharing very similar views, and I enjoyed his company immensely. He was very broadly educated and well-spoken and even when he employed the "F" word he made it sound emphatic, but completely inoffensive. Perhaps this is because his father had been a clergyman. He drawled as he spoke and was immune to the effects of alcohol.

We frequently discussed our speciality choices and it came up that in time of total war, obstetricians become general surgeons to assist in the predicted workload. From my point of view and his, this was essentially a 'hope for the best' scenario. However, opening and closing an abdomen, through a long incision and having some idea of what was inside, aside from OBGYN bits, would certainly help, and I agreed that he should assist me and then perform the procedure himself and do a couple of appendicectomies, which he did. In return I asked that he teach me how to do a lower uterine segment caesarean section (LUSCS) as in Nepal, where it was likely I would be posted at some stage, the surgeon is also the OBGYN provider.

This experience in my life I remember as if it was yesterday. Richard decided to perform a semi-elective LUSCS on a young primagravid (first pregnancy) whose labour had failed to progress during the day and who was now quite exhausted. In the early evening I went with him to the Louise Margaret operating theatre. Midwives are a law unto themselves and they were aghast that I was going to do the section, but Richard went into Major Myles mode and that was that, though mutterings could still be heard. I went through the various different instruments that are used in the procedure with the scrub midwife, and was surprised by their agricultural nature. They used a shovel when I would have used a trowel, would perhaps be a good comparison. The duty paediatrician was on hand, the epidural anaesthetic administered and soon I was off. I had seen a few sections before, so I was fairly familiar with the operative steps. Richard's reassurance that a 'trained fucking monkey' could do a section was encouraging to say the least.

The first thing I learnt was to ignore the heavy bleeding though, when the temptation was too overwhelming, I asked for a clamp. This was refused on the grounds that it was not necessary. The incision I was told to make seemed quite small through which to haul a baby out, but reassuringly Richard said, "It'll stretch". Once in the lower part of the abdomen, the first thing to do is dissect off the bladder from the front of the uterus. The bladder had already been emptied by a catheter, but I could see why pregnancy incurs urinary frequency. With the bladder out of the way, I tentatively transversely incised the lower segment of the uterus, being careful not to go too deep and lacerate the foetus, whose head was engaged in the pelvis. So far so good. When I was in the uterine cavity a gallon or more of liquor, amniotic fluid, gushed out and I was soaked, gown, underwear, everything. It was then that Richard, chortling, told me I should be wearing a plastic apron.

I then had to grab the baby's head and pull it out – well, not just the head, I don't want to alarm the reader, but the whole baby, whilst Richard applied fundal pressure (to the top of the uterus). This baby, this new life, this little boy, this miracle, popped out like a champagne cork. The midwife cut the cord and I handed the already screaming bundle to the paediatrician, who sucked its airway, whilst other midwives cleaned all the goo off it, buffed it up and handed it to the mother, who clutched it to her breasts. After a few minutes the placenta separated, and I pulled it out and made sure it was complete. A quick finger round the inside of the uterus to ensure sure it was empty and the drug (oxytocin) was given that would cause it to involute (contract), which it did. The bleeding had almost completely stopped.

Richard told me how to close the womb and promptly left the theatre for another beer in the Officers' Mess. I finished off as he had instructed and marvelled at what I had just done. I had started with one patient and ended up with two. What could be better than that? After I had cleaned up and joined my friend in the bar, he handed me a pint and said, "Congratulations, you are now a trained fucking monkey", another thrilling accolade to go along with being an undescended testicle as a house officer. My career was going well. I would work with Richard again many years later, though in very different circumstances.

Angela continued to "love bomb" me, I think the expression is, according to the many books I have since read on the subject, and I found myself more and more attracted to what she appeared to be offering, as was her intention. She then began to dog me relentlessly to marry her.

Kathy and I did go on a final holiday together to the Greek Island of Corfu and had a wonderful time, but we knew we were parting. She was everything that Angela was not, but children were the problem. I wanted children to coincide with the end of my training when I would have time to help them grow up, to guide them, to love them, to be a part of their lives, a participating dad as much as I could be.

After six months or so of Angela's persistence, I was hooked, played and landed. I agreed that we should get married, even though by that time, she would be in the Army too, and we would have to apply to be co-located. Anyway, Angela kept claiming how much she adored me, so what did I have to lose? I was on a high.

CHAPTER 18

Double L

Cambridge Military Hospital, 1982

During a morning ward round at the CMH, my SHO asked me, "Did you hear what happened to Double L?" "No" I said. My SHO enlightened me. "Apparently he did the same thing again and had to have his leg amputated in Guildford".

'Double L' was a civilian drug addict, and normally would not have been admitted to a military hospital, but he had turned up at our Accident and Emergency Dept. in absolute agony and could not be ignored. Hooked on drugs and seeking his next high, his next fix, the poor lad had mis-injected a precipitated solution of temazepam (mild sleeping tablet). He had bought the capsules, extracted the drug, heated it up in a spoon and in an effort to find a vein in his left arm, inadvertently shot the lot into his brachial artery (main arm artery). He had an immediate and pretty devastating reaction, as the artery responded to the drug by going into prolonged spasm, drastically reducing the blood flow into his hand and fingers. His skin was a very unhealthy mottled blue. In most previous cases such as this, fingers and even the whole arm have required amputation.

We treated him very aggressively with nerve blocks in the armpit to reduce the pain, and my anaesthetic colleagues also started a pretty hefty infusion of a drug to relax the muscles in the heart and blood vessels and reduce the spasm, but it would take time to work. I opened up his cubital fossa (front of the elbow) to try and expose his brachial (main) artery, which I eventually found. It was about half its normal diameter and pulsating, but very little blood was getting through. With a long length of the artery exposed and following the advice of colleagues, I emptied a couple of ampoules of papaveratum directly on to the vessel, which should hopefully reduce the intense spasm. Whilst waiting for a response, I decompressed the muscles in the forearm (fasciotomies) to reduce the damaging effects of swelling, in a response to the lack of blood flow. Very slowly the brachial artery started to pulsate more purposefully, and the oxygenation of his fingers started to improve. His wounds were closed, and he was sent to the ward.

Over the ensuing days he recovered. The superficial layers of the skin of his forearm and fingers sloughed away, but were replaced with healthy skin. Function and sensation were normal, and we were very pleased with ourselves. Double L was pleased too, but not particularly grateful, as this episode had forced him to go cold turkey with his addictions, and he was continuously clamouring to be discharged and then threatening self-discharge, which of course was no threat at all. We tried to get a psychiatric opinion but received a very lukewarm response. Double L left the hospital with dire warnings from me and just about everybody else.

A few days later, according to my SHO, he repeated the mis-injection, this time into the femoral artery of his left leg and was not so lucky. He will probably continue until he is limbless. Double L stood for "Low Life", but that was the rather derisive Army vernacular, fashionable at the time.

CHAPTER 19

Well Done Boy

St Peter's Hospital, Chertsey, 1983

I finished at the CMH having been well taught by Colonels John Carter and Brian Mayes. My final year of training would take place at St Peter's Hospital, just down the road from Woking, in Chertsey. I would be under the tutelage of Mr Arnold Ely and Mr Chris Anders and it was a very busy DGH.

All my consultants while I was in training left their mark on me, and I am grateful for their mentorship and their imparted wisdom, but Arnold Ely stands out a bit. He was indefatigable, monumentally experienced and not far away from an early retirement. He was very glad to have Army trainees, because we were experienced, amenable and used to doing what we were told. He always gave me good advice, but first he said that I would never be a proper consultant surgeon until "you have been married three times". Well I would tick that box on the 9th September 1995, having already been a consultant for 10 years, but obviously, not what Arnold would consider a bona fide one. He also advised me never to do an operation "that takes more out of you than the patient".

He had his pet hates, one of which was the midline abdominal incision. This approach to the abdomen had the advantage of speed and access, but in those days was prone to giving way over time, causing a hernia (bulge). If a trainee ignored one of his sacred cows, then a letter would be sent to them to make his displeasure known. Suffice it to say that I was soon to be in a very difficult circumstance when speed was of the essence and I had to employ the incision that Arnold detested.

It was during this year that I surgically came of age and I felt that I could cope with most of what I might be required to do. I occasionally phoned Mr Ely at night to discuss a patient, but he would never come into the hospital. He would expect me to deal with the problem. The phone call would end with him saying, "Let me know how you got on, in the morning" and that's exactly what he said to me when I phoned him halfway through the following case.

I was called urgently to A & E. A male patient had been admitted with a penetrating injury to the upper left quadrant of the abdomen. He had had a lot to drink and had sustained his injury during a mock sword fight with a friend who was equally drunk. He was around 40 years old. He had told the A & E staff that his name was Mr Mann.

An X-ray had shown a large opaque collection in his abdomen around where the spleen was, which would have been in the direct line of the presumptive wound track. On his return to his cubicle in A & E from the X-ray department, he suffered a vascular collapse. Fortunately, the casualty officer had already inserted an IV infusion, but it was the usual thin cannula which would not cope with the amount of fluid and blood we would need to get into Mr Mann to resuscitate him.

I put out a crash call and inserted a couple of very large cannulas and got a couple of A & E staff to squeeze the bags of fluid into him, then yelled for a porter to run to the blood bank and get the emergency O negative blood – all of it, which ridiculously was only two units. I sent a sample of Mr Mann's blood to the lab for grouping and emergency cross-matching. The crash team arrived, and the anaesthetists took over the resuscitation duties while I got the theatre staff to prepare for an immediate abdominal exploration. I had not said one word to Mr Mann, who was now looking a bit better, but anaesthetised. This was Cpl Billingham all over again and a bit more.

The anaesthetists were out in force for this case because the situation was dire, so immediately we prepped and gowned the patient and without any thought for the consequences (from Mr Ely), I was in his abdomen in seconds through a midline incision.

Most of Mr Mann's blood volume was in his abdomen, so I removed the clots, sucked out the blood and stuffed his abdomen tightly with large abdominal packs, while my colleagues at the top end carried on with the resuscitation and put in their lines with the usual incantations and mumbo jumbo that accompany these rituals. I waited and waited and after about 20 minutes I slowly removed the packs and Mr Mann's abdomen refilled. I saw that his spleen was damaged and his stomach had a hole in it, as did the diaphragm, but there was too much blood. I had a think. I had assumed that the wound track would be straight, but if the weapon had been a foil or epee, then these are quite flexible, and the track could have deviated.

I removed Mr Mann's spleen and repaired the holes in his stomach and diaphragm and the situation was temporised for a time. Then came another large rush of blood and I was pretty sure it came from above, not where I had been operating in the abdomen. I had no option; I was going to have to open his chest. That caused a bit of consternation amongst my anaesthetic colleagues, who had thought it was all over and were mentally preparing themselves to watch *Match of The Day*. They had to change the tube in Mr Mann's throat and make a few other adjustments, before he was turned on his right side. The scrub team opened up the thoracotomy instrument packs, and I meanwhile, enlisted more junior help to assist at the operation.

I thought a quick call to Mr Ely would be in order, just to keep him informed. I spoke to him on a phone held to my ear by one of the theatre orderlies and after the usual pleasantries I outlined Mr Mann's case. Arnold listened for a minute and then said, "Jackson, you should be in his chest by now, instead of passing the time of day with me". He finished with his usual note of encouragement, "Let me know how you got on in the morning", and the line went dead. I had been well trained in thoracotomy, the opening of a chest, with John Jackson in Harefield, but not so well trained with what to do when I got there. In this emergency I only vaguely marked the divided muscles for accurate wound closure, put my hand under Mr Mann's left scapula (shoulder blade) which was now floating around, counted down the ribs (the second rib is the highest that can be reached) and opened up the chest through the 6/7th interspace. There was blood everywhere. I inserted the rib spreader, a medieval-looking instrument, and cranked the wound open as far as I could, but I needed more access, so I divided the ribs above and below at their necks. Further cranking accompanied by the ominous sounds of tissues being stretched, and I had achieved my aim.

Once again, I cleaned out the wound and was just about to methodically examine the organs in the chest, pending the facilitated collapse of the left lung by my anaesthetists, when a jet of blood almost hit the operating lights. I then saw the hole in the pericardium, the sac that surrounds the heart, and I was pretty sure I was dealing with a penetrating wound of the heart. I opened up the pericardium, (for those of you with a surgical interest, I identified and avoided the phrenic nerve), and was hit in the face with another geyser of arterial blood from Mr Mann's left ventricle. I put a finger over the hole and felt his beating heart underneath. I managed to occlude the defect, like the little Dutch boy with his finger in the dyke, whilst a nurse wiped my face and eyes, and then of course I had to work out how to safely deal with it. I could easily over-sew it, but I would have to be very careful that I did not ensnare a coronary artery in the suture (stitch) as I swept away the fat and other coverings of Mr Mann's heart. I had forgotten the exact anatomy of the coronary arteries a long time ago. I could only just about recall their names.

With my finger still in the dyke and with the anaesthetic consultant watching the ECG heart trace, I closed the hole with a couple of strong bites of cardiac muscle. It was a heart-stopping moment for me, but fortunately not for Mr Mann. The ECG trace did not waver. There was nothing to suggest I had tied in a coronary artery, which would have caused an immediate heart attack and all the bleeding stopped. Mr Mann's heart was beating strongly, and mine eventually restarted.

I again packed both the abdominal and chest cavities. Having made the operative field safe, I delegated the care of Mr Mann to the scrub nurse (reliable) and the house officer (unreliable) and went to the rest room for a coffee and a cigarette. Pessimistically I expected to be called back as soon as I sat down, but it didn't happen. Mr Mann was no longer bleeding and was now stable. After a short break I returned to the table, dismissed with thanks the extra surgical assistant I had called on and I removed all the packs. Both wounds were dry, and I started on the long process of closing up with chest drains, pericardial drains and abdominal drains. This took more than two hours and I was tired out at the end.

The anaesthetists re-inflated Mr Mann's left lung, pronounced themselves satisfied and whisked him off to their hallowed Intensive Care Unit, settling him on a ventilator. He was pretty much unconscious whilst they started their post-operative rituals, prayer sessions, or whatever else they do there.

I could not have done what I did and kept a steady nerve without their expertise. It is all teamwork, always has been, and the anaesthetists are the unsung heroes, whilst the surgeons get all the glory. Few anaesthetists get congratulated on the quality of the anaesthetics they administer, but they should be. T'was ever thus.

I got back to the cottage late, had a large whiskey, a slice of toast and went to bed. Two hours later I was in the ward office awaiting Mr Ely's ward round. Consultants were treated properly in those days and the silver tea service was set out. Mr Ely arrived and sat down.

"How did you get on?" he asked.

I decided to be a bit nonchalant. "Oh the weapon had gone through his spleen, stomach, diaphragm and into his left ventricle" I said, as if this was the sort of case I dealt with most days on call.

"Is he still alive?" he asked.

"Yes" I replied. "He's pretty much stable in ICU."

"Well done boy" said Mr Ely.

Boy? I was a 35-year-old. In six months, I would be a consultant.

Arnold himself picked up the teapot. "I expect you'd like a nice cup of tea."

About a week later I got the letter about midline abdominal incisions. Mr Ely's ire at my use of an incision he heartily disapproved of was ameliorated by the need for speed, and therefore the salutation typed by his secretary in a letter sent to me, beginning, 'Dear Mr Jackson FRCS' was scrubbed through only once by Mr Ely himself, and 'Jackson' was scrawled in its place, in his own hand. If he had been really pissed with me, my name would have been scrubbed out completely. I treasured the letter for years, but I have now lost it, more's the pity.

With the combined efforts of all the relevant hospital departments, Mr Mann recovered. I used to see him every day on my early morning ward round and after about 10 days I had a listen to his chest. His lungs were clear, but his heart sounds were not right. He had what we call a murmur, and I referred him to the physicians, specifically the cardiologists; those with ears that can pick up a sparrow fart at 100 yards. They suspected that Mr Mann had a 'hole in the heart'. I told them he already had one, which I had repaired. Frowns and silence; their sense of humour was out to lunch.

He could have been born with it, or it could have been as a consequence, I suppose, of the penetrating injury, but he was duly sent to St George's Hospital for further studies. These confirmed the findings of a small defect in his ventricular septum (the tissue that separates the ventricles and prevents the admixing of high-pressure arterial and low-pressure venous blood). They would monitor it, as it needed nothing done for now.

The day came for Mr Mann's discharge to convalesce at home. He asked to see me before he left and we met in an outside ward area notable for its cigarette dog ends, to which I added one or two. He thanked me for what I had done, and I noticed that his now normal voice had quite a bit of the East End of London about it.

"My name's not Mann", he said.

That took me by surprise. "Why did you tell us it was then?" I asked.

"Um, there were a couple of coppers in A & E when I was brought in, and it was the only name I could think of," he offered by way of explanation.

"Apart from your own name of course?" I added.

"Yes" he said, "and the address I gave, I haven't lived there for years. It's an old girlfriend's."

"You do realise" I told him, "that some poor little medical records clerk will have to change all your medical records and investigation results, and," I added, "what about follow up at St George's for your heart murmur? We are going to have to give them your true details".

"That's all right Doc" he said, "my mother told me I had it when I was born. I doubt if it will give me any bother". He went on his way; I suspect being picked up by the same man who had caused his injury.

I did an awful lot of surgery in St Peter's Hospital. Arnold Ely would give me whole lists of things to do. He operated in an adjacent theatre, doing some major procedure with the assistance of a nurse, whilst I hogged the rest of the junior staff doing cases that would give me a very broad experience in general surgery. I could not have thanked Arnold Ely enough. He had just the right attitude to his trainees to get the absolute best out of them.

On 9th April 1984 I married Angela and the union was blessed at the Garrison Church in Aldershot. Angela's mother, who was stricken with multiple sclerosis, did not attend and nor did her father, who upon hearing that his daughter was to marry me had said that he would not pay for her wedding to me, but he would pay for the divorce. I should have taken more notice of that little gem at the time. We honeymooned in the Gambia, which was hot, unspoilt and beautiful in an African sort of way.

Angela and I started married life and I was very happy. We were getting on well and apart from her little foibles, I thought she was happy too. We were in a good honeymoon period, following our trip to the Gambia and my cottage was just right for the two of us. I was 10 years older than her and had certainly knocked around, whereas she was extremely naive about the world and had very little experience of anything. She couldn't even ride a bicycle. I hoped to rectify all this as we grew together. She had said she wanted someone experienced and capable and I was that man. I would have to protect her on the start of our journey through life.

CHAPTER 20

Leatherless

Cambridge Military Hospital, 1982

A young man was admitted through A & E. He was either in his late teens or early twenties and his name was Watson S. It had been a hot summer day and Watson had been riding his new motorcycle at a reasonable speed along a main road, enjoying the start of his motoring journey through life. He was not wearing any protective clothing, just a crash helmet, with his T-shirt and shorts on. An articulated lorry pulled out in front of him and as he emergency braked, he lost control of the bike, came off and slid 40-50 metres along the rough tarmac and potholes, de-sloughing the skin on his thighs, buttocks and lower back, down to muscle. His wound was massive, infection soon set in and he succumbed after a few days. He died for the want of a set of leathers, which would have saved his life.

In the summer when it is hot, I often see young people riding their machines in similar fashion. It will happen to one of them, and I wish the police had the power to stop them. After all, riding without a helmet is illegal, but it is not just a crack on the head that can kill.

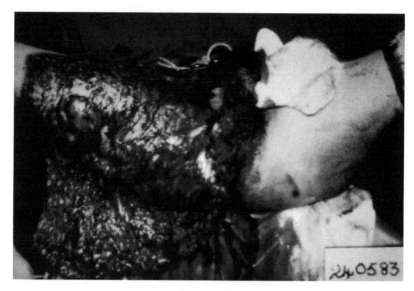

Watson S, 1983

Riding without suitable protection should be a no-brainer and against the law. In medical circles, motorcycles are known as 'donorcycles'. That should say something. In Watson's case it would have been better for him to be just a little hot, sweaty and bruised on landing, rather than have the cooling breeze, being flayed and then dead. Pictures of his injuries should be on display in every motorcycle shop in the world.

CHAPTER 21

The Missing Legs

Musgrave Park, N. Ireland, 1984

In September/ October 1984 I finished my training and expected to be posted back to Belfast for a year as the consultant in the Military Wing, Musgrave Park, which I was.

Northern Island was still very dangerous. Attacks on security force personnel and their families by the Provisional Irish Republican Army (PIRA) and the Irish National Republican Army (INLA) were frequent, ruthless and deadly. One had to check one's car for bombs, avoid certain areas (for example, the Royal Victoria Hospital in Belfast was out of bounds) and generally be alert to the likelihood of attack. Angela and I discussed the situation, and whereas I would be mainly within the confines of a guarded hospital, she would need to travel around the Province to teach the soldiers their basic education and the married quarters were, to my mind, relatively insecure.

We agreed that I would serve unaccompanied, but with return visits to see her every three weeks. She could fly out for a long weekend, and of course we would have our annual leave together. I really did not like the thought of something happening to her and after all, we had the rest of our lives to share, or so I thought; the year would pass quickly. This is a feature of Army life; it comes with the pay and we were both in the Army. The reward would be a two-year posting to the Far East, Hong Kong and then Nepal.

The terrorist war in Northern Ireland (NI) was unremitting during my tour. There were a few light-hearted moments, but overall, it was a sad, though perhaps surgically rewarding time of my life, as I look back. I have to remember that the surgical experience I gained was always at the expense of somebody who had been grievously injured, but I was in a better frame of mind than during the Falkland Islands War, where I was apprehensive about what I would have to do. I was used to the injuries of warfare and I would cope with a little help from my friends, and these included the orthopaedic consultants in Musgrave Park Hospital and on one occasion my last mentor, Arnold Ely.

I appeared before the Army Services Consultant Appointments Board in early 1985 and my position was confirmed. I have to say that even though I had satisfied the Board that I was fit, proper and trained to consultant standard, this was just the beginning. There is no substitute for clinical experience, or to my mind, operative experience, and even though I had plenty of the latter, it would actually take me another 10 years to feel that I had finally achieved my personal goal and knew exactly what to do under any given circumstance.

I had no hesitation in discussing cases with my colleagues, bouncing ideas and taking advice when necessary. Good communication, discussion and joint management are a must for a successful career as a consultant surgeon. I always taught my juniors to "never be afraid to pick up the telephone". A difficult decision is always easier to make if you have the agreement or backing of a colleague. There is no excuse for being precious in trying situations. The patient always comes first.

I packed my car which, as it was primrose yellow would hardly melt into the background, and drove to Liverpool to catch the ferry to Belfast and the Military Wing of Musgrave Park Hospital.

The war in NI was between those who fought for a united Ireland independent from Great Britain and those who wished for the Province to remain a part of the United Kingdom. It was also religiously divided, and each side had its own different factions and breakaway groups. Bombings using fuel oil and fertilizer mixes were frequent, and often these were hidden in culverts under roads. Homemade mortars and pipe bombs were also employed and of course the usual handguns and automatic rifles, the Kalashnikov being the favourite.

Arms were smuggled into Ireland from Libya for example and the Republicans, PIRA and the Irish National Liberation Army (INLA) were supported in America with funds raised by NORAID (Northern Irish Aid Committee). Bank robberies and extortion were committed by both sides which aided the Loyalists as well, who were the Ulster Volunteer Force (UVF) and the Ulster Defence Association (UDA). Punishment beatings and kneecapping were the usual way of keeping discipline, and torture and executions for collaborators and informants were rife. I used to give a lecture about the background to the conflict and my experiences over 1984/85, but this is not the place. I lived in the Mess, close to the resident Battalion's HQ (Kings Own Scottish Borderers). They were on their 'OP Banner' tour, which would last two years. Operation banner saw the continuous deployment of the British Army for 38 years, the longest in British history. In addition, the Ulster Defence Regiment (UDR) was raised to assist in 'the Troubles' and of course the Royal Ulster Constabulary was the incumbent police force.

All members of the Security Forces were regarded as a legitimate target by PIRA and INLA, and it was for this reason that I admitted any of them who needed to be operated on and/or recover in a secure area, to my care. One such patient was Pte M, who was shot in the left leg by a PIRA sniper. His femur was completely shattered into small bone fragments. He required a very wide excision of the wound with removal of bone fragments that were devitalised. I packed his wound and closed it seven days later when it was clean. He was shipped off to QEMH for more specialised orthopaedic care and bone grafting.

A Captain in 7/10 UDR was also shot in the leg. His femur was disrupted, but not so badly as Pte M's. This had happened in Magherafelt, near Londonderry whilst he was in his car. A gunman shot him through his car door.

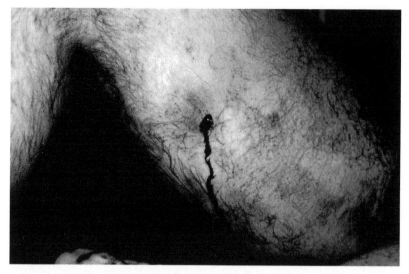

Captain 7/10 UDR. High Velocity Gunshot entrance wound, NI 1984-5

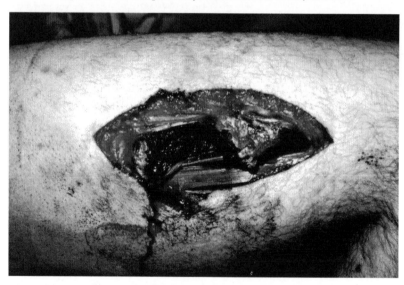

Captain 7/10 UDR. High Velocity Gunshot exit wound, NI 1984-5

His wound was large, though the damage did not seem too bad, until I discovered he had developed a 'foot drop'. I suspected an injury to the sciatic nerve, one of the two main nerves in the leg and on exploration and excision of his wound, I managed to isolate the nerve, which had been partially divided. The way to manage this situation is to mark the nerve with a sterile but non-absorbable stitch and allow for an elective repair under optimal conditions, when the wound and bone had healed. The UDR officer was also shipped off to QEMH and underwent a sural nerve interposition graft of the missing segment of his sciatic nerve. I reviewed him several months later, when he had returned to Belfast, and found he was walking well with a stick and a special splint to keep his foot up. It would take at least a year, if not two, to see if the graft had been successful. If not, then various muscle transplant procedures could help his disability. Mind you, these Ulstermen are tough and he was already back on patrol in a Land Rover.

Many of the soldiers in the UDR were part time, working evening and weekends. One of them was a Private D. He had already been blown up once and recovered, except for some hearing loss, and he was going to be blown up again. He was due out on patrol, but his Land Rover was still in REME being serviced or repaired. Pte D was told he could have the vehicle straightaway or wait until the blast deflectors were refitted, and his decision to wait no doubt saved his life. He drove over a culvert bomb which was detonated by a command wire and the vehicle flew into the air and landed in the bomb crater, with its chassis broken.

Pte D's Land Rover, NI 1984-5

The blast deflector serves to channel the high pressure of the explosive away from the occupants of the vehicle, and the fact that Pte D came into the Military Wing alive is a testament to its effectiveness. He sustained a broken jaw, a lumbar vertebral crush fracture with no neurological deficit (no nerve damage), several broken ribs and a large haemopneumothorax (blood and air in the pleural cavity) on one side of his chest, and a smaller one on the other making his breathing very difficult. He was in considerable pain.

He was resuscitated and given plenty of oxygen and I inserted drainage tubes in both sides of his chest. Once the blood and air had drained out, he was much more comfortable and could talk about what happened to him, which he did, likening this explosive injury to the last one a few years before. He had his jaw wired up by my colleague, consultant faciomaxillary surgeon Colonel Lionel Kessel. After a couple of days I pulled the drain out of his chest that had drained the small haemopneumothorax, but the lung on the other side resolutely refused to fully expand, in spite of intensive breathing exercises. The underwater seal drain persistently bubbled away. Pte D had a significant lung leak. I attached a low-pressure high-volume pump to his drain, and this did not improve matters much, even though good volumes of air were being removed.

I thought I would have to transfer Pte D to a specialist chest unit in the Royal Victoria, so I spoke to the Senior Registrar. His advice was quite simple; attach another pump for a couple of days. I did, it worked and the lung re-expanded. After 48 hours, I removed the drain and Pte D had two good lungs again, even if his first request, when sitting out in the fresh air, was for a cigarette. He needed three months for his back to heal and then he went out on patrol again. I thought he was pushing his luck.

First day on the job, a young RUC policeman opened the gates to Newry police station. A terrorist drove up on a motorcycle and shot him in the face, hitting his left cheek bone. The Officer put his hands up to protect himself and received a round through each forearm. The gunman then rode off. These were the low velocity injuries from a handgun, which are survivable, provided vital organs are not struck. The round that hit his cheek, the strong zygomatic arch, was deflected downward into the root of his neck, confirmed by X-ray, and would be very difficult to find and dangerous to extract. This put my heart rate up a bit. The young officer was perfectly fine on admission. I excised and tidied up his wounds and did not find much damage. I did an informal exploration of his neck, but I thought it unwise to over dissect the area, as there is a lot of important clockwork concentrated there.

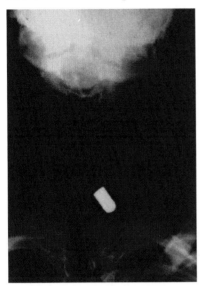

RUC Officer Neck X-ray NI 1984-5

I then packed the wounds as usual, had a couple of cans of alcohol-free beer and went to bed. In the early hours of the morning my phone rang. The RUC officer's neck wound was bleeding extensively. I had a quick look at the anatomy of the neck in one of my textbooks, took him back to theatre, and opened his neck again. He seemed to be bleeding from the side of one of his cervical (neck) vertebrae.

And then I found the source. The bullet had knocked a bit of

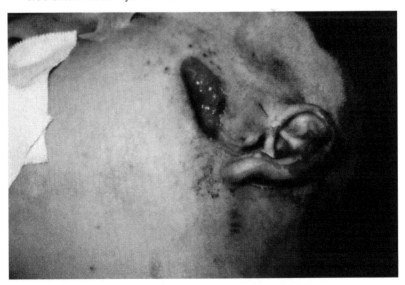

RUC Officer. Low Velocity GSW to left cheek. NI 1984-5

vertebra clean off, damaging the bony tunnel and the vertebral artery which passed through it. The artery had retracted into this tunnel and I could not get at it. I had two options. Either I could find its origin and tie it off – not for the faint hearted – or use bone wax to occlude the tunnel it was in. I opted for the latter and packed the wax tightly. This had the effect of completely stopping the bleeding, and I waited for a good half hour, during which I smoked a couple of cigarettes and drank some coffee. It was still dry, so I closed the wound and went back to my room to learn about surgical approaches to the subclavian artery, of which the vertebral artery is a branch, should the bone wax fail. Fortunately, the RUC officer did the decent thing and stopped bleeding. A few days later he was discharged. I re-examined the X-ray and realised that if I had been more observant in the first place, I would have noticed the bony damage to his neck vertebra, where the transverse process had been disrupted. The round was still somewhere in his neck.

I went home every three weeks, flying out of Belfast to Heathrow and then travelling to Woking. These reunions with my wife were too short, but nonetheless I cherished them. She visited me in Belfast when I was on call and it was on one of these occasions that she made an extraordinary comment which left me struggling for words.

Angela asked if she could come to the operating theatre to see what I did, how I earned my pay, so I agreed, subject to no objections from colleagues and the theatre staff. The patient's consent was obtained. She was allocated a "minder" to guide her as to where she could stand to observe the procedure and what she could and could not touch. I was due to explore the elbow of a soldier who had fallen and dislocated one of his forearm bones, the head of the radius, which resisted all attempts to reduce it. These injuries are quite rare, and I had rehearsed the operative steps and the anatomy, having only seen one case before.

The dissection took some time, as there are important nerves and vessels around, and I eventually found the cause of the problem. Somehow the head of the radius had button-holed through its retaining ligament. I was able to rectify this with a lot of difficulty, but fortune favoured the brave. I sutured the defect and reinforced the repair using strong fascial tissue harvested from the patient's thigh, which was the old way of doing it. I put in a small drain and closed the wound. The procedure had taken a couple of hours.

I went over to my wife, and the first thing she said to me was, "I could have done that". I remember to this day how completely flabbergasted I was, such that I just could not speak to reply. Surely, she was being facetious; surely it was a tongue in cheek remark? Yet she had not spoken in a tone that would imply that that was the case. I gently chided her for teasing me, for pulling my leg and just shook my head in disbelief. Who was this woman I had married? I had taken 17 years to be able to do 'that' and I still had to have my anatomy book illustrating the complexities of the elbow joint, opened at the relevant page and resting on the diathermy machine if I needed it.

I went away with the impression that she actually believed it herself when she said that she 'could have done that', but the remark was just so inappropriate and so outrageous that I just could not take her seriously. I should have.

There was a squash court in the compound, and I played every day against some good opposition from the resident Battalion. As usual there was a circuit for battle fitness training, so keeping fit was not a problem. Also, the British Forces were given access to Malone Golf Course, just a few miles out from Belfast city centre, and because of the security situation, we just turned up to play when the course was free. It was on the 12th hole, 193 yards par 3, that I achieved my one and only 'hole in one', using a 5 iron. Normally the player would buy club members a drink to celebrate and witnesses would confirm the fact. My only witness was Lionel Kessel, and we were not allowed to socialise in the clubhouse.

One day I nipped to the golf course for a round with the Battalion second in command. He had an army radio and his personal weapon in his golf bag. We started off and soon reached the second hole, adjacent to some fields, a par five. My competitor was lodged in a fairway bunker, and as he was addressing his ball with a sand wedge, a shot rang out. He dived into the bunker, motioned for me to join him and got on the radio, just as another shot rang out. He called in and reported the gunfire. There was no reported activity where we were, according to HQ. We hunkered down and scanned the fields, and just then another 'shot' went off. As the marauding birds in the adjacent fields took flight we realised it was a crow-scarer. We got up, brushing the damp sand off us as casually as we could, and carried on with our round.

I was very keen to record the patients I had taken care of in photographs, and I also wanted to take some pictures around Belfast, particularly of the murals and pavements which demarcated a Loyalist or Republican area. This I did wearing a loud pair of trousers, a shirt and a baseball cap, trying to pass myself off as an American at first glance. I don't think anybody was fooled, but they probably thought that the idiot in the loud trousers that was me could not possibly be part of the security forces either.

The Rossville flats were in a tower block in The Bogside in Londonderry. In March 1985 a commotion was reported to the security forces and a patrol commanded by a young subaltern was dispatched to investigate. It was a booby trap. A bomb went off, one soldier was killed and the officer had one of his legs almost completely blown off. He was treated initially at a local hospital, with completion of the amputation and then immediately transferred to my care.

He had been severely injured, but what concerned me was the damage to his remaining leg, with extensive skin and tissue loss. I phoned the Irish hospital as I wanted his missing leg. It would be a good source of skin if any remained, for the extensive grafting this soldier would have to undergo. Too late, I was told, it had already been disposed of. This young officer endured several skin grafts and his leg was in good shape by the time I had finished. I had to harvest the skin from his back and abdomen, it all healed, and he could mobilise. The rest of his recuperation took place in the UK. He was medically discharged, and I was told that he took up mountain climbing afterwards. He had been an adopted child and while he was still in our Intensive Care Unit his adoptive parents came to visit him. Their love and care for him was both uplifting and heartrending.

Dealing with the relatives of loved ones who are grievously injured, as he was, is difficult. I had to be objective and sympathetic. I had to be upbeat when possible, but suitably truthful. I saw the relief, sorrow and often anger in their eyes, then acceptance, then hope, then a plan

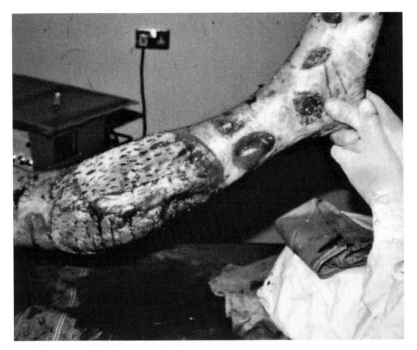

The young officer's remaining leg with fenestrated split skin grafts, NI 1984-5

for the future. I saw relatives whose lives would be forever changed. I spoke to relatives when there was little hope for the survival of their loved ones and yet they would survive, and others when there was every hope of survival, but they would not. Sometimes it just seemed so depressing, but this young officer and his determination gave me a much-needed fillip.

I am generally a modest man. Very few people know what I got up to or what I did, or know about my surgical exploits. However, I am going to lay claim to be the world expert on penetrating injuries of the ano-rectum caused by the barrel of the Belgian FN self-loading rifle (SLR), the standard British Army infantry weapon at the time. I had two cases, and as the weapon has now been withdrawn from use, no more can occur.

The first case occurred in a soldier on foot patrol in Crossmaglen. He was crossing a barbed wire fence and had leaned his rifle against the fence. It collapsed as he climbed across it and he managed to impale himself on the barrel. The second case occurred in Aldershot, where recruit soldiers were practising an anti-ambush drill from the back of a 4-tonner and one of them jumped onto the barrel of another recruit's SLR. Both recovered well after surgery with pelvic explorations, closure of the rectum and defunctioning colostomies, where the large bowel is brought to the skin surface, to divert faecal flow. It was the prostate that seemed to limit the damage and one of the soldiers had left a sliver of prostate on the foresight of his weapon. I wrote a paper on the management of these injuries, but it has probably not been widely read.

Impalement has been a method of execution over centuries. I will relate a story later of impalement on a battlefield in Bosnia during my tour in 1993/4. Fortunately, the victim, a Croatian, was already dead and a lot of him was missing by the time he was impaled.

Professor John Gibbons, who I have mentioned earlier, was my locum cover and he and I enjoyed many evenings in each other's company when he would drop into the Mess for a couple of pints on his way home. He recounted his experiences as a young surgeon and in a way, they reflected my own. He was a very accomplished and unassuming man and I liked and respected him, as did almost everybody throughout the Province. He had a rite of passage with the terrorist groups, as his surgical reputation preceded him, along with his willingness to operate and save the life of anyone, regardless of which side they were on. Soldier surgeon? I was getting there, and I had a good role model.

John Gibbons was always reliable, if a little tardy at times. I was in the habit of making sure he was at least around somewhere in Northern Ireland before I flew back to UK for a long weekend. He did take me by surprise one time, when I received a phone call from him just as I was on my way to the airport saying he was held up, but I should catch the flight anyway. I asked him where he was and he said "Berlin, but don't worry I'll be back in Belfast in the morning and my senior registrar can cover till I get there".

Even when I got back to Woking, I would still be a lot nearer to Musgrave Park than John, so I left my home phone number for advice if necessary and went on with my flight to see my wife. Fortunately, nothing untoward happened.

There are many legendary stories about John Gibbons, but my favourite is the one about when he was acting as 7/10 UDR medical officer and a potential recruit was seen by him in the Mess bar. As there was no examination couch available, no physical examination took place. After the usual questions, the recruit was passed fit. He said "Thank you, sir" and then limped out of the bar towards the door. Upon noticing this, John asked him, "Why are you limping?"

The recruit replied, "It's my leg, sir".

"What's the matter with your leg?" John asked.

"It's not there sir. I'm missing it, so I am."

"Where is it?"

"Not sure sir. Could still be underneath the tractor."

"How long ago did this happen?"

"About two years ago."

"That'll be all" said John.

"Thank you sir," said the lad and off he went.

Some years later I would meet a Col Roger Brookes who was an RAMC anaesthetist and John Gibbon's brother-in-law. He told me that John had died of a perforated colon, a rare complication following heart surgery. When his condition deteriorated and he was in the Intensive Care Unit, he wrote 'My colon has perforated' on a piece of paper and handed it to his puzzled doctors. They anaesthetised him for remedial surgery and he never recovered. Post mortem confirmed that John's diagnosis of the cause of his decline and subsequent demise was correct. I lost a colleague, friend, drinking partner and senior surgical referee. I sincerely hope that since his departure he has been in surgical heaven, with unlimited wild women and whisky, and I look forward to joining him one day and going down memory lane.

I worked with a lot of good people in Northern Ireland and the surgical ward was always full. We took in the British soldiers, the UDR, the RUC, prison officers and civil servants, and the surgery was varied and interesting. I had one patient in the UDR, if I remember rightly, and he presented a difficult conundrum with a large chronic duodenal ulcer, which had been bleeding. I had the choice of two operations. and there were good reasons to do either. As a young consultant I knew I would have a few wobbles (well more than a few actually), so I phoned Arnold Ely up. He patiently listened to my dilemma and then said "If you are not sure which operation to do, do the one you do best. Let me know how you get on". I chose the procedure that I was more practised at and the patient did well, his ulcer healed, and he was restored to sufficient health, such that he could reassume the bad habits that had got him his ulcer in the first place. I let Arnold know.

CHAPTER 22

The Jolls Retractor

BMH Hong Kong 1985-1987

My posting was coming to an end and two years in Hong Kong were next, followed by one year in Nepal. I couldn't wait. Angela was posted out a couple of weeks before me and she would have to take over the married quarter, which was next to BMH Hong Kong, in Worcester Heights, Wylie Road, King's Park, Hong Kong.

We were taking furnished accommodation, so we did not have to transport a whole load of possessions, and when I arrived in Kai Tak airport, I was travelling pretty light. I don't suppose many people will remember that airport, but I landed there a few times and the plane literally had to fly between skyscrapers. Angela met me at the airport, and we drove to the quarter. It had been recently vacated by Jim Ryan and his wife Paula – yes, I was still following him around the globe, except he did not go to Northern Ireland, I suppose because he was Irish. Jim was off to Nepal for a year.

My co-consultant colleague in Hong Kong was Major John Lovegrove, whom I succeeded in Belize and who was now married to Julie, a physiotherapist. For junior staff, we each had SHOs but no house officers.

Angela, in the Royal Army Educational Corps, would work in Osborn barracks, in the Local Education Centre teaching soldiers EPC (Education for Promotion Course) and ACW (Army in the Contemporary World) courses.

The quarters in the tower blocks were very spacious and ours gave a fantastic view of Kowloon (mainland) from our balcony. Hong Kong is terrifically crowded, noisy and never sleeps. The climate is fairly temperate, but heavy rain and the odd typhoon put in an appearance from time to time. The Star Ferry crosses the harbour to Hong Kong Island and is a delight. I would return there 20 years later in 2007 with my third wife, to show her where I had once lived and worked.

My first night on call was awful. I was asked to go to A & E. A Hong Kong Military Service Corps (HKMSC) sergeant had been involved in a road traffic accident on Stonecutter Island, which was their base. The HSMSC are a British Army Unit raised locally. He had been travelling in a vehicle which overturned; he was not wearing a seat belt and had broken his neck.

He was quadriplegic (all four limbs paralysed) and the X-ray of his cervical spine showed the fracture/dislocation. There was little hope of recovery. I put surgical tongs on him under local anaesthetic to immobilise the neck injury with some counter traction and enquired about a special Stryker nursing bed. We had to borrow one. This dignified NCO asked me if I thought he would be left with any disability and I chickened out of telling him. "Not sure yet", I said. "It will be a matter of time".

I hated these injuries, so absolutely life-changing in a split second after a moment's inattention or an act of fate. It is not possible for me to feel anything but dreadful sorrow, even though I had seen and dealt with other terrible injuries. There was not a mark on him to suggest that he had been so grievously disabled and in those days, even with 24-hour care, his life span would be considerably shortened. What about his wife and family?

Sometimes, as I have mentioned before, it is so difficult to remain unemotional. My excitement at working in Hong Kong had taken a severe knock on the first day. I would always be exposed to the tragic consequences of serious disease or injury and have to deal with them, but it didn't mean I was immune to the effects that they had on me. I am a compassionate man and my inner emotions have been ignited countless times over my career. I could and would get into a sort of robot mode and always strive to do my best, suppressing these feelings in the patients' interests, looking at things dispassionately and logically. But in the quiet hours, these thoughts can be a killer, when the mind loses the cold control necessary for the day job. It is possible to compartmentalise them, but inevitably some will resurface (as I have already described) and will keep on doing so. I don't think this is a weakness. I like to think that my admission of emotional fallibility kept me grounded and determined to fulfil my vocation as best I could, whilst retaining my humanity. It helped paint a fuller picture for me of what the patients needed, not just physical recovery, but the mental strength to cope with what had befallen them, and I too needed the mental strength to cope with that. Over the years it was inevitable that I would become desensitised to a degree and this helped me get by, but I was determined not to completely sacrifice my compassion.

Angela seemed to be very happy in Hong Kong. We bought an old Honda estate car so she could travel to her Education Centre, and we also used it for trips around the New Territories and outlying villages. I was happy too. I had managed to resurrect my tennis and a bit of golf, the former well, the latter badly. We had membership of the United Services Recreation Club with all the facilities at our disposal, including a swimming pool and tennis courts. I played first pair for the Army team and matches were arranged against the local Chinese clubs, which were highly competitive.

One day I was asked to see a Gurkha soldier. His was a strange story, though not that uncommon. It was difficult to get to the truth of the matter, but it appeared that he had an upper partial denture, fitted to carry a couple of missing teeth, which had split in half. He continued to use it in two halves but had not taken it out whilst sleeping and had swallowed one half of it two or three days before I saw him. He could feel it in his gullet, but as he could drink without too much obstruction, he had delayed reporting sick. He told me it certainly had not passed through his gut. We got some X-rays and I identified the dental plate. This soldier was anaesthetised and having been taught how to do so by John Jackson and with much trepidation, I intubated him with a rigid oesophagoscope, the flexible fibre optic ones not yet being available in this far flung place.

The oesophagus is not to be messed with, as it has a poor muscular wall even though bolus (a lump) food and drink are transmitted along it by peristalsis (intermittent wave-like contractions, like an earthworm), which requires some effort. Halfway down the oesophagus at the narrowest point, behind the branching of the trachea (windpipe), I saw the plate. I could not see the teeth and on tentatively trying to push the denture into the stomach I caused a lot of bleeding. It was stuck rigid and the teeth had impacted into the oesophageal wall. More, muscular attempts to dislodge it would no doubt cause a perforation. It had been stuck too long, so I had no choice but to perform an oesphagotomy (opening in the gullet) and retrieve the denture under controlled conditions.

My anaesthetist at the time was a Colonel Helen Hannah, a doughty, frequently irascible spinster, who no one crossed without a suit of armour. However, she was one of the best to have around at times like these. When I explained my plan to her, she just called for the special tube she needed and within a couple of minutes the Gurkha soldier was on his side. I was about to do almost exactly what I did to Mr Mann, but in a more controlled way, marking with sutures the muscles of the chest wall for later repair and in this case in search of the oesophagus, rather than stumbling on the heart. Helen Hannah deflated the left lung. I divided the inferior pulmonary ligaments and had my assistant push the lung (which was like a collapsed balloon) forward. Just above the level of the branching of the trachea, I saw a small greyish object stretching the wall of the oesophagus, one of the denture mounted teeth that had perforated the inner muscle layer and was about to breach the flimsy outer layer into the pleural (chest) cavity.

There was quite a bit of bleeding as I opened the oesophagus and took the denture out, I suppose in the nick of time, as an uncontrolled perforation of the oesophagus in those days was frequently fatal. I closed my incision; the lung was reinflated, and I did an accurate closure of the chest walls, leaving two large drains as usual. Helen reversed the anaesthetic after performing a whole load of intercostal blocks (local anaesthetic), and the Gurkha breathed away with both drains bubbling normally. He was dispatched to ITU, where he made an uneventful recovery. I was glad Angela wasn't there to witness the operation, as no doubt she would have said that she could have done that too.

Helen Hannah was a class anaesthetist. She had two rules which she never broke in all the years I worked with her (when occasionally I would get on the wrong side of her tongue). If knife to skin was at 0830hrs, then the patient would be asleep and ready exactly then. Her other rule was that she would stand up by her patient without refreshment or a seat, if the surgeon had to do the same. She had my utmost respect.

We had fairly close ties with the Hong Kong Chinese medical service and occasionally relied on their help and resources. I used to attend the weekly grand rounds at the Queen Elizabeth Hospital, where they discussed the various orthopaedic managements of the new admissions. The panel of consultants were ferocious, and the professors took no prisoners. Brutal lessons were learned. Most of the scathing comments did not need translating, even if made in Cantonese.

I was appointed an honorary Senior Lecturer in Surgery at the Medical Faculty of the Chinese University of Shatin up in the Northern Territories and every couple of months I was sent six medical students for a first surgical attachment (as in my day I was attached to Helsby and Brewer in the old Royal Infirmary in Liverpool). I had linked up with the surgical professor, Arthur Li, who was very keen to get his students into a "British" hospital for a time.

I was happy to take them, because I have always liked teaching and these students were la crème de la crème. They worked very hard at the books, but were sadly lacking in practical skills as, within their own training scheme they rarely encountered real patients, even though there were millions of them. I would send them off to take short histories of the patients on the wards or on the operating list and then make them interpret the investigations, demonstrate the clinical findings where appropriate, and then all of them would come to theatre, scrub up and see or assist at the operation. I tried to filter out the minutiae they would frequently come up with in answer to a question, as each of them seemed capable of memorising huge volumes of text, without the necessary understanding that should accompany what they had learnt. I had a lot of fun and they did too, because they could laugh, and I never taught by humiliation, or ferocious, scathing comments for that matter.

Once they realised that I wanted them to ask questions no matter how ridiculous they may have seemed in order to get an understanding of what they were trying to study, they relaxed. I said to them at the beginning of their attachment, "Never be afraid to ask a question if you are not sure. If you were blind and I could see, you would be sensible to ask me if it was safe to cross a road". They wanted to learn, and I wanted to teach them. After that I was almost continuously bombarded with questions.

A Senior Non-Commissioned Officer (SNCO) was brought into the hospital from the New Territories, by helicopter. He was a big fit man and had fallen very awkwardly and injured his ankle. I rushed to see him after my SHO had called in an emergency and this soldier was white, sweating and sick with pain. He had an obvious fracture dislocation of the ankle, which is a very serious injury requiring a large precipitating force. His foot was becoming mottled and the joint needed reducing as soon as possible because of the vascular impairment.

I tentatively considered whether I could reduce it without anaesthetic, but the muscle spasm induced by the pain would be too great. We called the anaesthetist Lt Col Ivan Houghton and after a few necessary preliminary questions he anaesthetised the patient by crash induction. As soon as he signalled for me to proceed, I pulled the foot and relocated the ankle in its mortise. It was very unstable, so I secured it with a loose plaster of Paris backslab with toes visible, to keep a check on the circulation, which I hoped would recover; it did after a few minutes. Complete loss of circulation is rare, thank heavens. The X-ray revealed the damage and I elected to send him back to the UK for ankle reconstruction, as the internal fixation he would require to get this ankle up and running was a bit complicated for me, and also he would have to endure weeks of physiotherapy.

Before I went to Hong Kong I had met an American Army surgeon called Major Bill Fallon USMC. He had trained in the military, had done his internship of four years and in their system was a qualified 'consultant' (hmm). I liked him a lot, especially for his wry condemnation of the medical bullshit he had had to put up with, which he said was rife in the US Military. I expect it still is.

The short of it was that he wanted to invite me (and my wife, I insisted) to America to talk about my Falkland experiences. I agreed that I would do it, subject to permission being granted by the MOD. They can be very cagy regarding what their consultants lecture about and want to make sure that it is always on stream, as it were, so all talks to outside agencies were vetted, even those to our American allies.

We flew to El Paso in Texas, the site of Fort Bliss, and on to the William Beaumont Army Medical Centre, where I would give my first talk. We would then fly up to Jacksonville in Florida, where I would repeat the Falklands talk and also lecture on the incidence of sepsis (infection) in soft tissue battle injuries of the limbs, a paper which I published in the RAMC journal. Lastly, we would fly up to Washington DC for another talk and a look around the Uniformed Services University of the Health Sciences (USUHS) and the Walter Reed Military Hospital in Bethesda that used to be called the National Naval Medical Centre. It was here that President Reagan had a bowel cancer removed in 1985, by the operation of right hemicolectomy, a procedure I was to do many times when I became a large bowel cancer surgeon, though none of my patients were quite so prestigious.

There is a surgical paper entitled 'President Reagan's Life Saving Colectomy and Subsequent Historical Implications'[20] which postulates that the timely and successful surgical intervention on President Reagan ensured that he could continue as President of the USA and achieve all he did to improve relations with the Russians

---

20. President Reagan's Life Saving Colectomy and Subsequent Historical Implications 2d Lt Robert H. Sorensen, USAF MC; 2d Lt G. Strider Farnsworth, USAF MC; 2d Lt Jared E. Roberts, USAF MC; Col David R. Welling, USAF MC (Ret.); COL Norman M. Rich, MC USA (Ret.)

Published in MILITARY MEDICINE, 179, 7:704, 2014 (United States)

led by President Gorbachev, resulting in the fall of Communism, the destruction of the Berlin Wall, the reunification of Germany and the end of the Cold War. In summary, the successful surgeons saved the Western world by saving Reagan. I've got to hand it to my American surgical colleagues; they made a lot of capital out of those two hours and 52 minutes operating time.

My claim to fame is a bit more modest. I saved Sir Simon Jenkins FSA FRSL. He had peritonitis, and when I eventually managed to separate him from the book, magazine, paper or article he was currently editing, correcting or writing, I took him to theatre and dealt with the problem. It only took me an hour or so, about as long as I could go at a stretch without a cigarette in those days. Sir Simon recovered in record time and took himself off to carry on being a journalist, author, panellist and some would say, a National Treasure. Amongst his many other achievements he subsequently chaired the National Trust, another National Treasure by the way, which spends its time saving most of the United Kingdom. As a result of my saving Simon Jenkins, he was able to make it one of his missions to save the UK (or most of it, for six years). Applying the same logic as my American colleagues, surely I indirectly saved the UK?

Having recovered uncomplainingly, Simon (a mere commoner at the time) was subsequently conferred with the honour of Knight Bachelor. The now Sir Simon is one of very few of my patients who have been honoured for surviving my surgery and making an exemplary recovery, though I think that his contribution to journalism may have played a small part.

On the subject of American presidents, when in office all have begun their State of the Union address with the words 'My fellow Americans', almost conferring the title of fellow as an award for being just... well, American. In the UK fellowship is not a birthright, it is an academic award, which has to be earned, and the word Fellow has a leading capital. Sir Simon Jenkins is a Fellow of the Society of Antiquities, founded in 1707 before America was invented and a Fellow of the Royal Society of Literature, which was founded 40 years before the Americans had their internecine squabble known as the Civil War. I could have legitimately addressed Sir Simon as my

'Fellow Brit" as I am a Fellow too, of the Royal College of Surgeons of Edinburgh, incorporated in 1505, preceding the Royal College of Surgeons of England by at least 35 years and the voyage of the Pilgrims on the *Mayflower* by some 115 years.

Sir Simon and I are Fellows by virtue of more than nationality, and we have history. 'My fella Americans' would be a more appropriate salutation, and the White House speech writers should take note.

The last author named on that surgical paper was Norman Rich, who was recently honoured as an icon of surgery. I had the privilege of meeting him a couple of times and benefited from his advice and encouragement in everything he said to me. He was the first Chair of the Department of Surgery in USUHS and he was renowned in vascular surgical circles for keeping the Vietnam Vascular Registry for 50 years. He instilled in me the belief that veins can be just as important as arteries.

Getting to El Paso involved changing planes a few times, and by this stage of my life I was an unwilling and nervous air traveller. After a night in a hotel, I met up with my hosts in the William Beaumont Army Medical Centre. This was named after William Beaumont, a United States Army Surgeon whom every medical student should remember with regard to his observations and publications of the physiology of the stomach using a Canadian named Alexis St Martin, whom he operated on in 1822 after he was wounded in the abdomen by a shotgun blast and had developed a fistula (connection to the skin) from his stomach. Amongst other things, Beaumont discovered that alcohol causes gastritis (inflammation of the lining membrane of the stomach)[21]. I could have told him that from personal experience.

I had a look around the Centre after breakfast, an impressive building about the size of one of our District General Hospitals. I noticed that the lecture theatre, where I would give my talk, could seat half the population on the planet. Next, we were taken for a drive to see the local county – Texas, or a tiny chunk of it. Bill Fallon told me that it taken him three days to drive across the county from east to west, about 800 miles, which is almost the whole length of Britain.

I am not sure how much of this trip Angela was enjoying, as a lot

---

21. https://www.britannica.com/biography/William-Beaumont

of our interactions centred on surgery. I don't think she coped well in what she regarded as the inferior position of 'wife of', as she preferred the limelight, as a teacher, which she likened to being on stage, putting on a performance. She was, in her own words the "best actress in the world", as I would find out. Anyway, suffice to say, Angela was not in the least bit interested in the activities arranged for the wives concerned, whom I think she regarded rather disdainfully.

My talk went down well. I was introduced as a Visiting Professor, which I thought was an inflated view of my qualifications and experience, but I graciously accepted the nomination. I outlined the medical response to the war, and I think that the Americans were truly incredulous as to how we managed to work without the usual paraphernalia of a full-blown modern hospital. The surgery I described was the standard Royal Army Medical Corps fare.

Afterwards I was asked a few questions, but nothing particularly contentious was raised. When the audience went off to do other things, like have a beer or two, I started to pack up and check the order of my illustrative slides. I was approached by a middle-aged man with horn-rimmed glasses and a twinkle in his eye. He introduced himself as Norman Rich, congratulated me on the talk and then referring to a patient I had treated with a gunshot wound to the left upper arm he said, "I would have tied off that axillary vein too". That comment

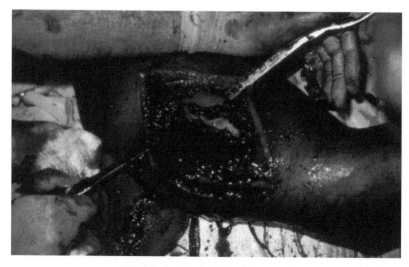

GSW left arm. Falkland Islands War, 1982

coming from a man of such stature and experience in the world of vascular surgery, going all the way back to the Vietnam War in 1965, when I was just 16, made my day. It was just the sort of reassurance I needed, because though this soldier would have a swollen arm, at least he would have a useful arm, as I had managed to repair his axillary artery.

The rest of my tour went well. I had been to one more war than most of those in the audience, which gave me gravitas. I could not help feeling, however, that if the Americans had been in Fitzroy, then there would have been a movie theatre, a commissary, a gym and a McDonald's, as well as a fully equipped District General Hospital and 400 helicopters. Some of my American colleagues would be part of the US military force that invaded the Island of Grenada in 1983, an action that lasted six days; probably best forgotten. The code name of their operation was "Operation Urgent Fury" which is suitably gung ho. By comparison, "Operation Corporate" to recapture the Falkland Islands seemed more appropriate for a Stock Market take-over bid.

I returned to Hong Kong elated. I had got my BTA (Been to America) medical qualification. Angela had said very little, but I am sure she was proud of me. Or had she resented being eclipsed by me? I was worried that she had been a fish in my pond, where her understanding and knowledge were very limited, but as I said, she had been reluctant to partake in the other activities.

Life was very good in Hong Kong, but I had a couple of setbacks. Firstly, I volunteered (never volunteer) to represent the RAMC in a competition called Exercise Sharpshooter and consequently I went into serious training mode. Whilst fully kitted up, I fell when practising on an assault course. I could not break my fall and landed straight legged and with the extra kit, weighing about 30 kg more than I usually did. As a result, I damaged my right sacroiliac joint (SI) and thoracic spine. My SI joint has caused me a lot of problems over the years and eventually I had to give up tennis and squash due to the pain. Towards the end of my career, I often operated standing on one leg, like a stork. When I left the Army my injuries were acknowledged, and I was awarded a small monthly war pension.

Secondly, I contracted a severe inflammation of my duodenum, a duodenitis, which required a couple of days in the hospital and an endoscopy. It was caused by a bug called helicobacter pylori, but in those days the treatment was unsophisticated, not like the regimes we have nowadays as the illness is better understood.

As I was due promotion, or rather had been promoted to Lt Col, I was ordered to return to the UK for my senior officer's course, where I met up with quite a few of my colleagues. This lasted just under a month, but I was still feeling a bit rough, so I took it easy. For a time, it felt as if my stomach was on fire and this was going to have consequences for my posting after Hong Kong, to Dharan in Nepal, as I was still recovering.

The routine work in the hospital kept me busy, but I was curious to find out what the surgery was like in the Chinese sector, and sure enough the opportunity came along. I had been offered admission rights to the Mathilda Hospital, somewhere up on the Peak, which was almost exclusively for the expatriate civilian population. It would be a lucrative private practice (subject to the CO's permission, which was not a problem, as he was working there already) but as I have already said, I am not particularly money orientated, though I am a careful saver and financial planner. I was more interested in the way the local population got their surgical treatment.

I was not keen on working in Shatin with their massive outpatient commitments, which was public, but I managed get into the private Chinese sector via a GP called Dr Henri Li. He wanted an orthopaedic consultant in his set-up, and as I had done a lot of orthopaedic work, he took me on. He was going to get himself into a bit of trouble with the authorities as he had approached the large corporations in Hong Kong like HSBC, Hutchinson Whampoa and Jardine Matheson, and in exchange for a massive retainer he would guarantee excellent private care for their employees at a cost much lower than the well-known private health providers. He essentially became an unregulated provider of health insurance. I was mentioned as a British orthopaedic consultant as part of his health care team, which was stretching the truth. Anyway, I obtained admission rights to the Baptist, a private hospital in Kowloon Tong, and I started doing orthopaedic clinics for

Henri Li on Saturday mornings and operated in the Baptist Hospital on Wednesday afternoons.

My first orthopaedic patient had a large goitre (swelling in the neck due to enlargement of the thyroid gland) and needed to have her thyroid partially removed, about as far away from orthopaedic surgery as you can get. I spoke to Henri Li and he said that he would have to send some of these cases my way as the general surgeon was overwhelmed. He also asked me to provide my prices for the three classes of patient. For example, if a patient wanted first class treatment – single room, food and newspapers provided – I could charge a lot more for my services. Third class was a bed in a very crowded ward with no food provided except by relatives, access to the toilets quite limited and a good chance of not surviving well, or at all. I had absolutely no idea what to charge. When I suggested 3000 dollars, about £300 for a first-class thyroidectomy, he shouted "No, no, no, 10,000 dollars, or they think you not do good operation".

I needed to do my clinics with a good nurse who could translate Cantonese to English. The nurse in question was called Claudia and her English was, um, approximate. Patients were often 'walk ins' and I found that despite my training and qualifications in Western medicine, I was pretty much the last choice for the Chinese in their quest for treatment. It was only when suction cups, acupuncture, herbal diets, massage and other methods of traditional Chinese medicine failed that they decided to give me a go.

A youngish man came into the clinic, and I said to Claudia, "Ask him what's wrong". She gabbled away in Cantonese and having received his reply, she said, "He got pain".

"Where?" I asked.

Further gabbling, then she said, "Or ova".

Fortunately I had noticed the patient had hobbled into the clinic. The problem was his left knee. Why he couldn't have told Claudia that I don't know. He had obviously twisted it badly, ruptured his medial meniscus (cartilage) and could not straighten the joint. It was locked and unstable. Employed as a labourer, he had continued to work, putting abnormal stresses on his pelvis, back and his other knee, which I suppose accounted for his pain 'or ova'. He needed this cartilage out, so I booked him on my next Wednesday list in the Baptist Hospital, with the thyroidectomy. There was no point in attempting any explanation. Both patients were third class.

Next was a man with a trigger finger whom I also put on the list, then a middle-aged woman who was jaundiced (yellow). As the commonest cause of jaundice in the population of South East Asia was due to the liver fluke parasite *Clonorchis sinensis*, I sent her off for further investigations at the Queen Elizabeth Hospital. If she simply had gallstones, I would deal with it. Henri Li paid me a flat rate of 500 HK Dollars (£50) per clinic, but surgical fees were mine to keep.

I arranged for an anaesthetist, Lt Col Roger Tamlyn, to do the list with me. Roger was old school, very correct and quite rightly he wanted to see the patients preoperatively. I took him up to the Baptist Hospital and we eventually found them on the third-class ward. Roger had dressed to impress, with cavalry twills, highly-polished shoes, blazer and regimental tie. I don't think he appreciated that the patients he would deal with had no real understanding of modern medicine. Orthopaedic and general surgical cases were not separated and the ward was very crowded, with only about two feet between beds. The nursing staff did their best in an impossible situation and everybody including the visitors were shouting in Cantonese.

I found the sister in charge and she said we could see the patients. I pointed out the man for the menisectomy and before I could say anything, Roger was off.

"Good morning, my name is Lt Col Tamlyn and I am a consultant anaesthetist working for the British Army in Hong Kong. I shall be putting you to sleep for your operation and..."

"Roger" I said, to try and get his attention.

"Now have you had any previous anaesthetics?" he went on asking the patient.

"Er, Roger" I said even louder.

"Any previous illnesses, allergic to anything?" he carried on.

"ROGER!" I tried again. At last, I had managed to get his attention.

"What, old boy?" he asked me.

"This patient is a Chinese labourer," I said. "He has no understanding of English, Western medicine, or much else. It took some persuading to get him here in the first place. I have his thumb mark on the consent form. I would just listen to his heart and lungs and give up with getting much out of him. He just wants to be able to walk and work again".

We saw the other two patients in record time.

Food for the third-class patients had to be provided by their family members, who also helped with basic nursing duties, like emptying urine bottles, helping their relatives get up and move, making their beds when necessary. The ward was the scene of continuous activity and very, very noisy. How anybody survived was a mystery.

In the afternoon Roger and I did the list. He had a female anaesthetic assistant and I had a scrub nurse and an assistant, also female. Some cases were being done in other operating theatres with several nurse anaesthetists being supervised by a doctor who flitted from theatre to theatre, or so it seemed. I did the trigger finger first and reshaped the origin of the flexor tendon sheath so that the tendon no longer got stuck and after that the menisectomy. In those days it was an open procedure into the knee joint and the medial (inside) meniscus had the usual 'bucket handle' tear. Very carefully I resected the handle of the tear and checked the knee could be straightened.

The thyroidectomy was ready, but there was a slight problem. I needed a special instrument, a Jolls retractor to keep the wound in the neck open, whilst I did a subtotal thyroid gland removal. It was pretty standard equipment for this operation. However, I could not seem to get through to my scrub nurse. I just received a blank stare in response to my request, followed by a shake of the head. I asked to see the theatre supervisor and repeated my request.

"I need a Jolls retractor" I said. I received another blank stare. Then as realisation dawned, she said "O, you wan' Yolls letlactor. It on instlument tway alledy".

There are a few difficulties operating in a Chinese hospital. My scrub nurse denied having a 'Jolls retractor' yet hidden away on the 'instlument tway' was a 'Yolls letlactor' which is the same thing, except phonetically.

CHAPTER 23

Chinese Firecracker

BMH Hong Kong

I had a patient, a young male soldier, who had been transferred in from a hospital in the People's Republic of China, just the other side of the Northern Territories of Hong Kong. He was in a very sorry state, in fact, an eye-wateringly sorry state. I asked what had happened to him and he replied that he had been given permission by his commanding officer, along with several other soldiers, to answer the call for extras in the mass armies, required to make the film "Taipan". British soldiers were ideal as they were disciplined and could march in step.

Special effects included the use of Chinese firecrackers and as a joke, one of his colleagues had put one in his pocket and lit the fuse. The result was no joke. The soldier had managed to get the firecracker out of his pocket, but not before a couple of explosions had taken place. His trousers caught fire in his groin area, but this was quickly extinguished. He was rushed to the local Chinese hospital and treated for burns to his groin and penis. They dressed the wounds and catheterised him (put a tube through the penis into the bladder).

He had lain there for a couple of days before being transferred to my care. A drop of morphine at some stage in the Chinese Hospital would have done him a lot of good, as well as IV fluids. The wound dressings were firmly stuck, so I decided that the only humane way to proceed was to examine this young man under a general anaesthetic.

When he was asleep, I removed the dressings. The first thing I saw was that the tube that had been used to catheterise him was made of red rubber and was retained in his bladder by means of a safety pin through his glans penis, the bell end, which is very sensitive. This was very crude, though urine had been prevented from contaminating his burns. I immediately changed the Chinese catheter for the standard soft rubber Fogarty catheter with an inflatable balloon.

The soldier had been burnt quite extensively in both groin areas, and the shaft of his penis and his right testicle was almost completely exposed. The wounds however were reasonably clean in some places though necrotic (dead) in other areas and worryingly, the skin over the shaft of his penis was thickened, black and contracted and if it impeded the blood supply to his member, it would basically shrivel and drop off. I wasn't too worried about the exposed testicle. God arranged for these organs to be particularly hardy and they can survive quite significant trauma.

The first thing to do was to thoroughly clean the wounds and then perform what is known as an escharotomy (incision of scarred and dead tissue) of the shaft of the penis. I debrided (surgically cleaned) the wound and harvested some split skin from his upper thighs which I would need for grafting the burns at a later date. This skin would survive for about a week, stored in saline in a fridge. I dressed his wounds with a silver-based antibiotic solution and checked that the penis was still pink, which it was. The soldier was woken up and sent to the ward for copious intravenous fluids and pain relief.

Next day he was much more comfortable. I was going to have to wait for a few days to allow the wounds to demarcate into viable or non-viable tissue. The young lad was naturally worried about his best friend and I was upbeat, having by that stage consulted the books. A few days later I had another look at his wounds under anaesthetic. The testicle was fine, granulating nicely and healthily and I would leave the rest to nature. His penis and groin areas were clean, so I harvested more split skin, got the stored skin out of the fridge and grafted his groin areas and penile shaft, fixing the grafts in place using very fine absorbable stitches.

The patient's wounds were dressed and time would tell how things would go. I prescribed regular sedatives to prevent spontaneous erections and therefore graft slippage, as I had done in Belize. Every day I smelt the wound. This young lad must have thought I was very strange, sniffing his groin, but I have taught hundreds of young surgeons that it is an integral part of surgical follow-up. If a wound smells clean, it is clean and if it smells bad it is bad.

After a week or so the dressings were soaked off and by God (who probably had a minor part to play in it) the graft take was 100%. I was over the moon, but the soldier was not so elated. His member looked as though someone had played noughts and crosses on it. His wounds were left open, and in another week under any other circumstances he was fit for discharge back to his barracks, but I kept him in. I did not want temptation to get the better of him. These grafts take a good six weeks to consolidate and at least 12-24 months for the final appearance to manifest itself. Those of a delicate disposition should skip the next couple of images.

He recovered, and a few months later I reviewed him in the clinic. I asked him how he was, and he said fine. He had however contracted a 'dose 'whilst in the Philippines on R and R (Rest and Recuperation) and was now being treated by the Genito-Urinary Department. I was delighted. It was an unusual biomarker of surgical success and I think, as yet, undescribed.

I was asked by someone I knew in the Hong Kong police (a British officer serving with them) if I would be willing to act as a consultant surgeon to the regular force and their Special Duties Unit (SDU), because of my experience with battle trauma and gunshot wounds, and I agreed. Fortunately, though on standby, I did not have to deal with or advise on any casualties or injuries throughout my tour, but I did gain some knowledge and insight into the SDU training and performance. Much of it was based on SAS techniques, particularly in counter-terrorism warfare.

The SDU selection process was tough and prolonged. As far as I am aware at the time of writing, there has never been a woman in their ranks. These men are fit, highly proficient, brave, inscrutable and utterly ruthless. They neither smoke nor drink and are well paid. I was to get a measure of their abilities when I was asked if I wanted to attend

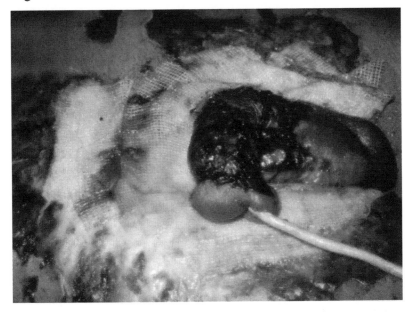

Firecracker burn. Hong Kong 1986

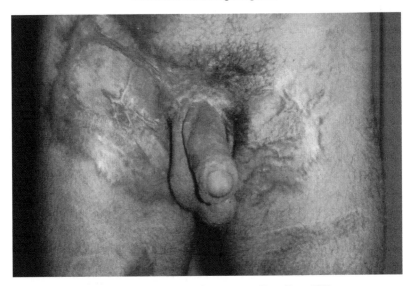

Firecracker burn 6 months after treatment. Hong Kong 1986

a demonstration of the release of a hostage, captured by terrorists, in their kill house. I agreed and was led into the building and then into a small room where there were a couple of dummy terrorists and a hostage. I was made to stand behind a rickety old screen and wait. "You stay here. No move muscle" I was instructed.

I stayed duly motionless and just when I thought nothing was going to happen, the stun grenade went off. Seconds later two SDU operatives smashed their way in, double-tapped (killed with two shots) both terrorists and left with the hostage. It was all over in about five seconds. I left the kill house somewhat dazed, and resolved never to take anyone hostage in Hong Kong, no matter what the temptation.

On the home front, I was a little concerned about Angela's attitude towards the management of the Education Centre. She was continually disparaging her Officer Commanding (OC), declaring that everybody knew that it was she who actually ran the Centre, that she was the backbone of the staff and only she was able to teach the soldiers, who adored her. I cautioned her about undermining her boss, but my words had absolutely no effect. In fact she got worse.

CHAPTER 24

Hard Graft

BMH Hong Kong

British Forces have been present in Brunei since they helped suppress an uprising in 1962. They provide security for the Kingdom and the incumbent Sultan (one of the richest men in the world) contributes towards the cost. The Army runs Imprest accounting systems which are regularly audited, and would explain our reception of a patient, a middle-aged civil service accountant, casevacced in from the Panaga Hospital in Brunei.

He had been posted to Hong Kong and flown to Brunei to do an audit but had been involved in a serious road traffic accident. He had injured, amongst other things, his back and ribs and had been treated with bed rest, pain relief and a urinary catheter because he could not pass urine. He also had not opened his bowels for five days. We were told in the clinical transfer letter that this was because he was in too much pain. He had sustained a fracture of his first lumbar vertebra, seen on their X-rays. My registrar, Major Graham Groom, examined him first and being the good clinician that he was, suspected spinal nerve, or cauda equina, damage and so he 'tickled' the patient's anus. He was looking for the integrity of the anal reflex. In other words, if something comes near your anus, the reflex reaction for the muscle guarding the entrance is to increase its tone and clamp shut.

Fortunately, most people do not have to remember to keep their anuses tightly closed because normally the resting muscle tone of the sphincter is sufficient. Of course, contraction of the sphincter can be augmented, for example in preventing a bowel mishap (as nearly happened to me in Belize) or overruled, by the brain for various reasons.

There was no reflex reaction and the muscle resting tone was absent. This gentleman had a spinal cord injury (SCI) which had damaged the autonomic nerve supply to his bowel and bladder, and that was the reason he was constipated and could not pee, though he retained full control of his legs whilst lying on the bed, where he had to remain until we knew the true extent of his lumbar spinal fracture and if it was stable or not.

CT scanners were not widely available at the time, but it was the investigation of choice. Back then the images took a long time to compute, whereas nowadays they are done in minutes. The nearest scanner we could have access to was in the Chinese University of Shatin and as an honorary lecturer, I popped over to pull some rank. I was ushered into the office of Professor Leung of the Orthopaedic and Trauma department of the hospital and discussed the case with him. He was charming and immediately authorised an emergency scan which was carried out next day.

The radiologist reported a severe burst fracture of the first lumbar vertebra. These spinal injuries are serious and unstable and the patient's spine would have to be rigidly fixed by strong metal plates augmented with bone graft. I had another discussion with Prof Leung, and he agreed to undertake the procedure in Shatin with me as his first assistant. I need not go into too much operative detail, but it was something I had never seen before and I was riveted. I took the graft from the patient's pelvis, the iliac crest, harvesting both cortical (hard) and cancellous (soft) bone which were packed around the fractured vertebra following the insertion of the plate. The patient was returned to the ward in Shatin and carefully nursed on his back until he could be fitted with a plaster jacket. Attention had to be paid to his bowels and bladder and he was going to need a lot of nursing care, physiotherapy and then training with regard to self-management of his disabilities.

I visited him on the ward in the Chinese hospital. I gave him a detailed explanation of his operation and warned him that his bowel and bladder function would take a long time to recover, if at all. Unfortunately, he seemed very reluctant to take it all in and as I visited him quite frequently in the Chinese Hospital to check on his progress and see if there was anything I could do for him, he became withdrawn and rude. This was not an unnatural psychological response to a life-changing injury, and I hoped it would dissipate with his acceptance of the consequences of the accident, but in the meantime he also became entirely dismissive of my role in deciding his future clinical management. He informed me that in the Civil Service career structure, he was a Senior Executive Officer, the equivalent of a senior Lt Colonel, or even full Colonel, and therefore outranked me. He indicated that he moved in the circles of the medical command in Hong Kong and that if there was any decision to be made about him, for example his return to the UK for the specialist management of his injury, a subject which I had already broached, it would not be up to me to make it. He had only recently arrived in the Far East with his young wife and child and he fully intended to continue in post. He was quite content to remain in the Chinese Hospital for as long as it took, and any further treatment could be arranged locally.

Regardless of what he wanted, I was going to make the decision as to whether his return to the UK was advisable on medical grounds in consultation with Professor Leung and my Commanding Officer, who would inform the medical command. The financial outlay would also have to be taken into account, because if the patient was to remain in Hong Kong, all his medical requirements would have to be paid for privately, in addition to the cost of the operation he had undergone and his stay in Shatin. It would run to many thousands of pounds and could not be justified, since the corresponding treatment would be free of charge in the UK.

He would require a lot of physiotherapy, rehabilitation and constant reviews by specialists in this type of injury. We did not have the expertise, or the facilities within the BMH. He was sent back to the UK, as it was the only sensible option, and he blamed me entirely.

Several months later I was walking beside the United Services Recreational Club swimming pool and I noticed that he was in the pool with his child. I stopped and asked him how he was. He said he was fine and that I should never had sent him back to the UK and he had nothing more to say to me. I wanted to ask him if he had had any neurological recovery, but he pointedly and rudely ignored me. I walked off, muttering to myself that he should have been wearing incontinence pants in the pool. You can't win them all.

CHAPTER 25

No Fun and Games

BMH Hong Kong

I had tried to involve Angela as much as possible in my activities in Hong Kong, but she was inept at anything sporting, despite her claims to be brilliant at everything she did, usually after having tried something all of once, or even not at all. However, as it will become abundantly clear, any activity involving rackets, clubs, or anything requiring a degree of physical skill were clearly not her forte. Even when I suggested that we go for a run together, she refused for fear of getting a 'dropped womb'.

One day she complained that though she was very good at tennis I never wanted to play with her, so I booked a court and tried to just have a gentle knock up. Predictably she was completely useless and in spite of what she had said, it looked like she had never picked up a tennis racquet before, let alone hit a ball with one. Even with a racquet the size of a satellite dish and a ball the size of Mars, any contact between the two would be pure serendipity, as her coordination was that of a five-year-old. However I persevered and gradually she improved, propelling every sixth ball that I threw over the net either vertically up in the air, horizontally straight back into the net, or out of the court altogether. When I picked up my racquet for the first time and gently dollied a ball over the net to land just in front of her, which she then missed entirely, I was accused of playing to win, not for fun and that wasn't acceptable. I tried to help her set up for a forehand stroke, but this was rejected on the grounds that she knew how to play tennis, didn't need to be shown, and if I did so, I was demonstrating my control over her. I just resigned myself to throwing balls over the net and then collecting them from inside and outside the court while she giggled away to conceal her hopelessness. We were now playing tennis for fun, though she had not actually noticed that I wasn't playing at all.

I suggested that she ought to practise a bit, get used to running around the court and learn how to keep the balls in the court. My suggestions were rebuffed on the grounds that she already knew how to do all that. The total mismatch between what she claimed to be able to do and what she was actually capable of doing was jaw dropping. I was beginning to realise that Angela's inflated opinion of her abilities ran in tandem with the inflated opinion she had of herself as in 'of course I must be wonderful at everything I do, because I am wonderful'. She really could be very odd at times and her attitude was beginning to alarm me, but as usual I ignored my misgivings.

It was pretty much the same scenario playing snooker. One evening, I suggested we went to the Mess for drinks with friends. I wanted to see Major Brian Heap, who was a consultant physician in the BMH, to discuss a problem I had with one of my patients. Angela could chat with Brian's wife whilst he and I talked over a game of snooker. Well that suggestion did not go down too well. Angela had no interest in Brian's wife. For a start they had two young children and any conversation that Angela had with her would inevitably drift onto domestic topics, which Angela found utterly boring. No, she wanted to play snooker with the men. Did she know how to play snooker? I asked. "Yes," she asserted.

Had she ever played before? "Yes", she said again, indignantly. Would I ever learn in these situations? Just as with playing tennis, she reasoned in her own unique way that because she wanted to play snooker, she obviously knew how to play snooker and if she knew how to play snooker, then obviously she must have played it before. She would play with me against Brian, who, to make matters worse, was a very good snooker player. The balls were set up on the table, the baize immaculately cared for by the Mess steward. We won the toss and I asked Angela if she wanted to break. She looked at me blankly, so I 'reminded' her, "You know, put the cue ball in the "D" and hit the pack". She picked up her 'stick', (not knowing it was called a cue) and settled down into a pose to hit the cue ball. I had an enormous feeling of foreboding. Not only was she lining up to hit the green ball but it was plain to everybody in the Mess who happened to be watching that she had absolutely no idea how to hold or use a snooker cue.

"Err, don't forget to chalk your cue" I said and then added good-naturedly "I'll break while you do that, okay?" I broke the pack of reds.

Brian's eyebrows, which had shot up to the ceiling when Angela had positioned herself for the break, were only just returning to their correct anatomical position when he took his own shot, potting a red, but missing the colour he had lined up. This left the white cue ball close to the cushion and now it was Angela's turn to play.

What happened next is difficult to comprehend. Instead of making a bridge with her left hand to support and steady the cue that she was holding, and, instead of holding the butt end of the cue with her right hand, whilst she lined up the shot, she held the cue, cupped in the palms of both her hands and made an underarm attempt to hit the cue ball, with a sort of stabbing motion, missing the ball entirely and scoring a line of chalk from the end of her cue along the pristine baize, but miraculously not ripping it. Brian Heap gave me a steely look, clearly incredulous at what he had just witnessed and almost imperceptibly shook his head from side to side in disbelief.

The meaning was obvious. Get your wife away from the table. I conceded the game and suggested to Angela that she might need a tiny bit more practice when the Mess was quieter, or preferably devoid of people. I took her to the bar for another drink; I needed one, even if she didn't. Angela, bless her, in her usual inimitable way, carried on chatting and acting as if absolutely nothing untoward had happened, impervious or simply oblivious to the fact that she had made a complete idiot of herself in her attempt to play snooker.

Every Mess guards its snooker table zealously. It is a prized possession, and Angela's antics did not go down well at all. I was asked to keep her off the snooker table until she learnt how to play. I mentioned this to her, but of course she could not see what all the fuss was about. In her mind, the members of the RAMC Mess were just a load of pompous officers, who did not know how to, you've guessed it, have fun. But it was a concerned Mess steward who had spoken to me, not one of the pompous officers.

My trouble was that I pretty much laughed off these little incidences, always preferring to take the view that she was joking or making fun. However I could not get away from the fact that even though she was an officer, she despised most of the officer class and their wives.

CHAPTER 26

A Brush with Rabies

Locum in Nepal, 1986

Jim Ryan and his wife Paula were in Nepal and in July 1986, I was going to be posted there for a month or so to do his locum, in order that they could take some leave. I was looking forward to the locum, but not the flight from Kathmandu to Biratnagar, which had frightened me to death on my trekking visit a few years earlier. I seriously doubted if there were any uncrashed planes left in Nepal, but alas there were. However, I had found out that there was an alternative. I could catch the overnight coach to Biratnagar from a bus stop just outside the city.

I went to see the Chief Clerk and asked if he could book me a seat. The coach was described as very comfortable, with air conditioning and had toilet facilities. There would also be refreshments included in the price of the ticket during the 12-hour journey.

The Chief Clerk looked at me in stunned amazement and said, "No one has ever gone overland before, sir. Are you sure you want to do this?"

"Well, yes," I reassured him. "I really don't want to fly, as the last trip terrified me".

He acknowledged that I knew best, whilst simultaneously indicating with a roll of his eyes that he knew better. "Suit yourself sir," he sighed in response. He booked me a seat on the coach, though quite how, I have no idea.

I flew from Kai Tak airport into Kathmandu on a proper aircraft with my coach ticket in my hand. On arrival I summoned a rickshaw and asked to be taken to the coach stop. The man indicated that it was too far for him to pedal with me and my luggage, so I found a taxi, which was so clapped out that it couldn't travel much faster than a rickshaw anyway. My journey had begun. The bus stop was just a field full of chattering Nepalese. I was the only European, which should have told me something. After about three attempts I found what I thought was the correct coach, and it was not because it had the destination written on the front, but because I found a Nepali policeman who could speak some English. However, before I was allowed to board the bus, he told me that my luggage had to be searched for contraband.

I explained who I was and why I was going to Biratnagar. He was unimpressed and wrestled my cases from me, dropping them on the grass in the process and demanded that I open them, which I did. He then rummaged through all my belongings, which I had neatly packed, pronounced himself satisfied with what he had seen, or rather what he had not seen, and left me to tidy up the mess he had created. All this took place under the gaze of the other travellers. I took my cases to the coach to be loaded into the luggage wells in the sides of the vehicle, but as these were full, both of my cases were unceremoniously slung up onto the roof, where they were caught by a labourer, who I hoped would lash them down. My cases would keep the goats company, who were also up on the roof, as there was no room within this 'air-conditioned luxury' vehicle to accommodate them.

I climbed aboard and found my seat. There were two aisles of paired bench seats, but each pair of seats was occupied by three people, because the Nepalese are small in stature and width. This explained why there was no room for my luggage in the coach wells, as the normal passenger quotient was 40 persons, but in fact there were 80 or thereabouts on board. The coach was aired, but not conditioned, the windows being open and mostly broken; the inside of the coach smelt like a Birmingham curry house. I had an aisle seat and on the other side of me was a young Nepalese boy of about 10 years old and beside him, in the seat by the window (from which the glass was missing) was, I assume, his mother. A tiny puppy was on the boy's lap in a small open cardboard box, tethered with some string for a collar. It whimpered continuously. Somewhere on the coach a radio was playing at full volume, the sort of monotonous Indian music that eventually induces madness.

Outside the heavens opened and torrential rain ensured that any visibility the driver might have had was reduced to zero. It would not be possible to travel in this monsoon-like downpour, as I noticed only one of the windscreen wipers of the vehicle worked, fortunately on the driver's side, but nevertheless, it was almost completely ineffective. I settled myself down to wait for the storm to pass, but just then the driver started the engine and raced out of the field at breakneck speed, all the time, looking sideways and chatting to what appeared to be the co-driver, standing next to him in the footwell. I very much wanted the driver to look ahead out of the windscreen, but as it was totally obscured by rain, there was little point. It was going to be a long 12 hours.

This was the third place I visited where atheists don't exist. I prayed on the battlefield in the Falklands, I prayed on a light aircraft crossing Nepal and here I was again, praying on a coach.

The coach climbed out of the valley and then onto the road round the mountain passes. There were no safety barriers, the storm was causing mini landslides and the traffic was hurtling along in both directions. On my side of the vehicle there was a sheer drop. My pulse rate must have been off the scale as the driver kept up his incessant chattering and sideways glances without a care in the world. I definitely wanted to get off, but that was not going to happen, so resignedly I closed my eyes and waited for the impact again.

Not much later I found myself flying through the air as the coach bounced off the side of the cliff and tumbled head over heels into the abyss. Without a seatbelt I was being thrown about all over the place,

I could not get my bearings and it seemed like an eternity as my whole life flashed before me...

I woke up with a start. We had not crashed, but the first thing I noticed was half a goat hanging outside the window. I realised that it must have slipped its tethering on the roof and fallen partway over the side. I grabbed hold of it, whilst leaning across my two fellow passengers in the process, and shouted for help. The driver, noticing the commotion, stopped the coach and some brave soul climbed onto the roof to retrieve the goat and refasten it. Apparently, it was uninjured. Just as well that goats are pretty tough creatures, cooked and otherwise.

Whilst this was happening everybody left the coach for an unscheduled comfort pause, with the women relieving themselves at the front of the vehicle and the men at the back, in the absolute darkness and rain which had turned itself into an impenetrable mist. I was about to go outside for a quick pee when the driver called all the passengers back in as though he was running late, which seemed a bit improbable considering the way he was driving. Anyway, I was not desperate and would await the next stop.

Surprisingly I fell asleep again, as did most of the rest of the passengers, including both my seat mates. However, not long afterwards I awoke to the sound of choking and gasping. It was an animal in distress. I looked down and saw that the puppy on the boy's lap had fallen out of its box and was hanging by its string collar, slowly asphyxiating between the knees of its young owner, who was fast asleep and unaware of what had befallen his pet. I grabbed the little scrap and relieved the pressure on its neck by cutting the string, but it did not look very well at all. It was unresponsive and its eyes were glazing over; that much I could see in the gloom. So I did what anyone else would do (who happened to be medically trained and slightly off their head). I gently massaged its heart, or at least where I thought the heart should be in a dog, having put its snotty little mouth and nose in my mouth, whilst exhaling gently into its lungs to expand them. After about 30 seconds I could feel the puppy struggling to breathe, just as its owner woke up.

The young boy, on seeing me with his pet's face engulfed in my mouth, looked absolutely aghast. He shouted out, waking his mother and all the other passengers for that matter in the process. I looked as though I was about to eat his dog, headfirst like a snake. The mother was mystified, but at least the puppy was alive and breathing again, or rather snuffling if the truth be told. I explained to her as best I could, by way of rudimentary sign language (not an easy feat) that I had rescued the damn thing from hanging itself and had resuscitated it. It is difficult not to look like some sort of deranged serial killer when you're trying to mime a noose going around one's neck whilst gripping one's throat to demonstrate the effect and simultaneously making gagging noises along with pulling strangled expressions. By now the puppy was recovering on my lap, where it was so overjoyed to have been saved from the brink of death that it promptly did what most stressed animals do, the most enormous wee. I could feel the warmth of it soaking through my trousers and onto my underwear. I now had a circular wet patch the size of a dinner plate covering my groin area.

If that wasn't bad enough, the coach suddenly ground to a halt in a flurry of gravel, and the interior lights went on again. It was the next comfort pause. Having missed the last stop, I was now desperate for a pee and had no option but to shuffle down the coach, looking for the entire world as though I had pissed myself. To make matters worse, in my embarrassed state, I mistakenly hurried to the front of the bus instead of the back, where several Nepalese women were squatting with their saris hooked up around their necks and I was greeted by angry shouts and hisses. I scuttled around to the back of the coach and relieved myself, the pleasure of emptying my full bladder blunted by having to put a hand through my cold damp fly after unzipping it and then searching for my member, which had rapidly diminished in size and was fiercely resisting exposure to the freezing weather. This journey was not going at all well.

The coach engine started up again. There had been a change of driver in the meantime and I was pleased to see that he was an older man, who spent a lot more time looking through the windscreen of the vehicle than the driver he took over from. Soon I found out why, because shortly after he took over the driving, he stopped the coach. After some requests in Nepali, several men got off the bus and started to clear the rocks from a landslide that had been precipitated by the rain and was now blocking enough of the road to prevent the coach from getting through. I felt obligated to help and cheerfully threw stones and rocks over the side of the road into the abyss, which was where I expected to end my days, when, not if, the coach plunged into its dark recess, with 100% fatalities, after the driver failed to negotiate a 10-mile-an-hour bend at 40. We stopped twice more for rock-clearing duties, by which time I was thoroughly soaked.

The upside was that the wet patch over my groin was now effectively camouflaged. When I regained my seat, the little boy smiled at me and offered me his puppy to cuddle and stroke. If it had another pee on me, it would not make much of a difference to the state of my trousers anyway and if it was rabid, well… I stopped in my tracks. What if it WAS rabid? The thought had only just occurred to me. Think logically, Jackson. Well then, I, I… had had my vaccinations hadn't I. Hadn't I? I did have my vaccination, didn't I? Yes, calm down, calm down, I must have done. The mind plays tricks in these sorts of situations. I had resuscitated the puppy, I had put its muzzle in my mouth, and… and, oh God, rabies is in the saliva…. Okay, I'm as good as dead. I was cold and soaked and obviously if the bus ever made it to Biratnagar and I survived the journey, I would inevitably succumb to rabies in about two weeks' time. I tentatively stroked the puppy and was horrified as it started to lick a scratch on my wrist, which I must have sustained whilst shifting the rocks. Okay I thought, resignedly; my life is officially over.

After a couple more hours, the coach stopped again. This time it was for refreshments and we were in a village, though little of it could be seen, as there were no lights. I followed the other passengers through a doorway, built for the short Nepalese, not for a six foot one inch European, and so to add to my woes, I cracked my head on what would have been the lintel in most buildings and entered the dim, smoky, candle-lit room. There was an open fire at waist height where the cooking was done, and something was bubbling away in a black pot. There was also a huge panel beaten vessel, containing about two tons of rice.

This was apparently the 'refreshments' that were included in the price of the ticket. The 'chef', for want of a better description, continuously cleared his throat and spat out the result into the corner of the room. I looked around and saw that most of the passengers were just taking drinks and eating the food that they had sensibly brought with them. I saw a diminishing stock of Coca Cola bottles, and having been warned not to drink anything that has not come from a sealed bottle, especially water, I put the palms of my hands together in front of my chest, murmured *"Namaste"* (the accepted greeting) in every direction and barged my way to the stash of Coca Cola bottles and grabbed one. It was too dark to see if it had been tampered with, but I reckoned that as I obviously hadn't got long to live, I might as well drink it and sample the food. Unappealing as the prospect was, I was ravenous.

I checked the plate for insects, parasites and vermin and held it out to the chef for a dollop of whatever was on offer. He seemed delighted that someone was brave enough to eat his fare, and he gave me a massive amount of rice, topped with the evil concoction from within the bubbling pot. I took some cutlery (at least there was some), and settled down on a stool at a table, to eat. Predictably, it was a goat curry. As usual nothing of the animal had gone to waste, I noticed as I fished out what looked to be part of the animal's jawbone before tucking in. It was fiendishly hot and in the gloom I tried to remove all visible chillies, as no European could possibly ingest them and live. Even so, I started to sweat, my nose started to drip, my scalp would not stop itching and my tongue and mouth were on fire. I tried to maintain a stiff upper lip, as everybody in the room now appeared to be watching me, but my lips felt anaesthetised and they weren't working properly. My attempt to appear relaxed simply resulted in my face adopting the rictus grin of someone about to die of tetanus (lockjaw).

I had yet to swallow what I had put into my mouth, but eventually the swallowing reflex intervened and down my gullet it went. My stomach was paralysed and resolutely refused to onwardly transmit what I had just filled it with, and yet my oesophagus refused to have it back up again, or any more of it for that matter, and went into spasm. I decided to placate my resentful digestive system by just eating the rice and drinking more Coke, in an attempt to extinguish the coals from the fires of hell that were igniting my stomach lining. Messages were sent from various nervous receptors to my brain telling me to never eat any part of that dish ever again. I complied. I tried to steady myself with a comforting cigarette, a Benson and Hedges, but my lips had been numbed by the chilli and when I tried to purse them around it, the cigarette just fell straight out of my mouth and into the curry. I wearily reopened my packet to discover that I only had two left. I had started this journey with a full packet and my cigarette consumption was indicative of my rising stress levels. I had more cigarettes, but they were in my luggage up on the roof of the coach, along with the goats, if they hadn't already been eaten.

In India and Nepal, everyone smokes Biri, or Bedi cigarettes. These are made of tobacco flakes hand-rolled in the leaves of a tendu or temburni leaf (some plant native to Asia). They are very cheap, contain much more nicotine than Western cigarettes and taste absolutely foul. For the addict, as I was, not smoking at all and suffering the discomfort of nicotine withdrawal, is the better alternative to smoking a Biri. That said, whilst leaving the dingy hut, I noticed that one of the occupants had picked up my discarded cigarette, managed to light it and was now puffing contentedly as it glowed in the dark, a curry-flavoured Benson and Hedges.

Back on the bus, the driver tried to start the engine. It spluttered once and died. Further attempts to coax it into life similarly failed. A heated discussion then followed between the driver, the co-driver and everybody else within a radius of 20 feet. I did not understand a word, but the co-driver then climbed back into the seat, turned the key and the engine immediately fired into life. He revved it mercilessly until the heavy plume of black smoke emanating from the exhaust became a lesser plume of black smoke and we were off again. How the resurrection of the engine had happened I had absolutely no idea. The only explanation I can offer is that in the Hindu religion there are tens of millions of gods and perhaps one of them was the god of ancient diesel engines, and he responded favourably in our case.

Anyway, whatever the reason, we hurtled along at the usual breakneck speed towards our destination. Soon we were out of the foothills and the road appeared relatively straight. We were into the Terai area of Nepal and my hopes of arriving in Biratnagar in one piece became slightly less gloomy as dawn began to break. The landscape was beautiful, with terraced fields on the sides of the foothills and we were heading into a sunrise that was just heart-warming.

We passed through several villages where the occupants were beginning to stir to begin another day of hardship and toil, and as time went on, the markets came to life as farming produce and other goods were offered up for sale in the stalls and shops. The smell of cooking fires became pervasive, but not unpleasant, and the drabness and the dampness of the night were gradually replaced by the brightness and warmth of the new day. I felt quite good, but my general optimism was tempered by the occasional but ominous rumbling, that was coming from my abdomen.

I lit my last cigarette, inhaled deeply and checked my watch, a cherished second-hand Rolex GMT Master, appropriate, I had reasoned, at that stage of my career. I realised that the end of my journey, if the timings were correct, would not be long and sure enough in what seemed like no time, we arrived in Biratnagar. It was around 8 am. The coach was parked up, this time on a wide expanse of gravel, and we all dismounted. I was extremely tired, my eyes were gritty and my clothes were damp, but my spirits were soaring. I had made it, but it was an experience that I was determined to never repeat under any circumstances.

The last leg of my journey was the 40 kilometres from Biratnagar to the cantonment in Dharan, and I would have to find a taxi. I retrieved my luggage and found that the corner of my case had traces of goat shit on it. Well, what the hell. Like the true nicotine addict I was, I immediately looked for and found a packet of cigarettes, then trudged to the taxi rank. There were no taxis, or to rephrase, there were taxis, but none in motion. I yelled "Taxi!" and an old man hurried over to me. I said "BMH Dharan". He motioned for me to follow him, led me to what looked like an old Morris Oxford and gestured towards it, exclaiming "Taxi". I thought that was a pretty optimistic description. It was a forlorn-looking vehicle, down on its suspension, the paintwork had faded to nothing and the springs of the rear bench seat were showing. There were the usual beads hanging from the rear-view mirror and some incense smoking away in a receptacle on the dashboard. I doubted if it could go 40 yards, let alone 40 kilometres. The old man was persistent and opened up the boot for my luggage to go in. I shrugged my agreement and got into the back seat, shifting my backside uncomfortably as the separate springs ground their way into my rear. I got out of the car again, opened the boot, and took out my combat jacket, which I folded so that I could sit on it in the rear of the car, providing a cushion between my backside and the metal springs.

I waited, but nothing happened. Then, almost imperceptibly, the car began to roll forwards, travelled about six feet and slowly came to a halt. There was a knock on the window and the old man signalled me to get out. I saw the problem; the battery was flat, probably had been for years, and they needed to bump start the car. Two Nepalese had been recruited to push, but even with the help of the old man, whom I had correctly assumed was the driver, they couldn't budge the vehicle with my weight aboard. The old man got in the driver's seat (he couldn't have weighed much more than 40 kilos) and I went to the back of the car to help push.

The car started to roll and as it picked up speed, mainly due to my efforts, the old man let the clutch out in third gear and the engine started and miraculously kept going. I hopped into the back seat again and settled down to yet another cigarette and the hour-long drive to Dharan. The drive was done at a snail's pace, all the way in third gear, which was the only one that the driver could engage, which explained why the car had been bump started in that gear in the first place. Two and a half hours later, we eventually arrived. I checked into the Mess in the BMH and had a quick handover from Jim Ryan, who was running late for his flight to Kathmandu with his wife Paula.

My ominous abdominal rumbling resulted in an attack of Nepalese goat curry belly and when I had recovered sufficiently to be away from a loo for half an hour, I went straight to the Admin Officer's office to introduce myself to Ranjit. I asked him to kindly cancel my return trip on the luxury coach when my relief stint covering Jim's leave had finished and book me on a flight back to Kathmandu instead.

BMH Dharan had around 70 beds and treated everything. The obstetric unit was entirely midwife led and they would only require my help in an emergency, and as I only ever anticipated having to do emergency caesarean sections, I was reasonably confident, having achieved my qualification of "trained monkey" from my colleague Richard Myles. I met the anaesthetist, Colonel Tony Booth, and then the physician, Colonel Guy Radcliffe, on my way to the operating theatre. The number of patients on the list was enormous, I reckoned about a week's work for three of me. It was no wonder Jim needed some leave. I still did not feel very well, being feverish and shaky, which is not a good combination for any surgeon.

CHAPTER 27

Medicinal Whisky

BMH Nepal 1986

There was the usual load of orthopaedics, mostly fractures or dislocations that were several days old, and I remember having to do an open reduction of a dislocated shoulder (a first for me), an exploration of a two-week old displaced forearm fracture with excision, reduction and external plate fixation and a patellectomy (excision of a kneecap) for an old non-union. Then we got onto the general surgery with a gall bladder or two and a couple of hernias the size of sacks of potatoes. The last patient was an elderly woman with a goitre, which would be a major undertaking. She could not rotate her head or flex her neck. Goitres are rife in Nepal. I had to cancel her as this was going to be a big job and I still did not feel very well. I have since read in a letter I sent to my mother, later that year on the 29th September 1986 that I was operating with a temperature of 103 degrees Fahrenheit. When I eventually undertook the thyroidectomy of the goitre, it was big and nodular and probably represented half the patient's bodyweight.

I ventured around the surgical wards to have a look at the in-patients. Tuberculosis (TB) was rife, as to be expected, often with joint and abdominal complications. I seem to remember Jim had done some major cancer excisions. There was one old lady whom I remember well. She had been robbed by dacoits (bandits) and to stop her running for help, they had immobilised her by cutting through both her Achilles tendons, above her heels, with their Kukri knives.

I had supper in the Mess and just as I was leaving with a shot of whisky to help me sleep, the phone rang. It was one of the midwives warning me that they had a woman in labour who was failing to progress, and they thought I might have to intervene at some stage. The foetal heartbeat was OK with no dips, or whatever they are called in obstetric language. I said "OK", looked forlornly at my glass of whisky and then decided to drain it anyway, as I did not think it would make the slightest difference to my obstetric status of trained monkey. I went to bed and crashed out.

Predictably, my phone rang in the early hours of the morning and it was the obstetric unit. "Does she need a section?" I asked, knowing full well that that was most likely the case. "No" came the reply, to my surprise. "She delivered an hour ago. It's another patient. She had a normal vaginal delivery but now has a retained placenta and she's bleeding very heavily. Be as quick as you can".

This was yet another first for me and a baptism of fire. I shot out of bed, hopped into some trousers, pulled on a shirt and ran to the obstetric ward. I went into the cubicle to find the patient on a couch, white as a sheet, with her legs still up in stirrups, and blood pouring out of her vagina. I knew what I had to do, I had to get the rest of the placenta out, but I was not quite sure how to do it. Nevertheless, a pair of gloves was thrust my way. Of course, what I needed to do was stick my hand inside the uterus and ease the contents out.

I have big hands, but I reasoned that if a baby could come out of there, then one of my hands would go in; actually, my forearm, almost up to the elbow. I felt around the uterine cavity, detected the retained portion of the placenta, managed to find or create a plane of cleavage, gently separated it from the lining of the uterus with my fingers and out it came, a great big lump of it. I felt around to make sure I had got it all, which I had, and the anaesthetist gave some oxytocin. A few minutes later, the uterus involuted (shrank) and the bleeding stopped. It was my first vaginal delivery since I had done obstetrics in medical school; a healthy partial placenta. I departed, had another shot of medicinal whisky and went back to bed.

CHAPTER 28

Burns and other cases

BMH Nepal 1986

Later next morning I was called to A & E to see a male infant of about nine months old, with severe burns. High in the foothills of the Himalayas it gets very cold (as I knew from my trek) and it was the practice of the local villagers to keep a fire going in their huts whilst they worked in the fields. This little boy was wrapped up and left in a small hammock near the fire. Somehow, he fell out of the hammock and his lower half landed in the hot coals. His screams were not heard and when his mother returned, she was horrified. She called her husband and together, having left their other children with neighbours, trekked to the nearest medical clinic. There the boy was initially treated by medical staff of the local charity that ran the clinic and they dressed the burns, understandably not appreciating their severity. The little boy was subsequently referred to the BMH.

He had sustained burns to his feet, lower legs and bottom. His feet were unsalvageable as the bones were burnt to charcoal. I was faced

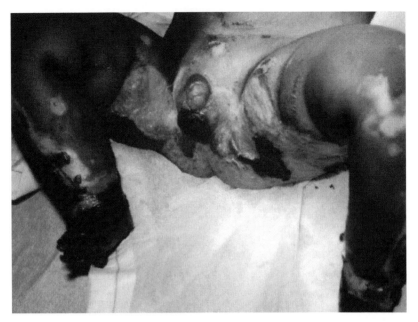

The little boy with burnt legs and feet. Nepal 1986

with a terrible quandary. If the infant was to stand any chance at all of being saved, then both lower legs would have to be amputated. With a heavy heart and a pair of heavy-duty scissors I removed both of the child's lower legs. I excised and dressed the rest of the burns and slung the little fellow up in traction. However afterwards, as usual in the dark hours, my doubts arose. His mother had come a long way, with a degree of hope, but after what I had done to her boy, albeit surgically correct in the developed world, she had no hope.

How could she look after a child with no feet? There were no wheelchairs, no orthotics, no physiotherapy, no specialised clinics, in fact nothing in the way of adequate aftercare to aid this infant and his family. I had made entirely the wrong decision. Though he developed a urinary tract infection which I did not treat, in the hope that it would be a terminal complication, the infant slowly recovered. A few days later when I went to the ward early in the morning, he had gone. The father had trekked back to the hospital to pick up his wife, as he needed her assistance on the farm, and the child was retrieved as well. I had almost ruined the entire economy of that family by applying Western medicine and expectations in a Third World country.

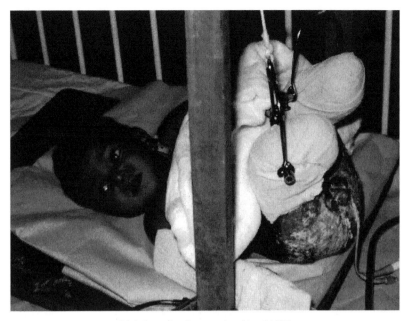

Little boy after the operation, Nepal 1986

I had created a Nepalese Oscar Pistorius. Though this little boy and Oscar Pistorius, were born at the same time, and had the same surgical procedure, though for dissimilar reasons, the outcome had to be completely different. This little boy would have had none of the advantages of the developed world to help him make the best of his disability, whereas Oscar Pistorius would. He was medically pampered, worked and trained hard and eventually became a Paralympic champion (although he is now imprisoned for shooting his beautiful girlfriend dead, which rather took the shine off his achievements).

I enquired as to the likely outcome for the little Nepalese boy and was told a quick death at the bottom of a cliff on the trek back to their farm was likely, or a burial or cremation on the family farm, when the inevitable occurred. I should have told the parents that there was nothing I could do and to take the child away. That would have been the correct decision. The Nepalese were used to the hardships they had to face, even though I was not. It was another sobering wakeup call.

I have had to deal with a lot of burns throughout my career, though with the advent of the speciality of burns and plastics, less and less as time passed, as more specialists came on stream. However not so in Nepal, which brings me to the next case. She was a young girl of about 10 years old who had suffered burns to her chest, shoulders and neck. Her airway had been compromised and she had a tracheostomy (breathing tube in the windpipe) as a temporary measure. The Nepalese are very prone to keloid scarring, especially after burns, when thick reddened skin forms and then contracts; it is both deforming and disfiguring. The skin of this little girl's burnt neck had done just that, such that her head was rotated and her neck flexed. She had to either perpetually look to the side, or walk sideways like a crab, which she did when I reviewed her.

 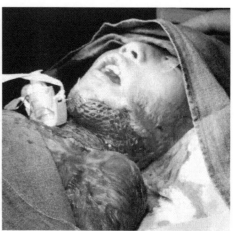

Girl with keloid scarring before the operation, Nepal 1986   Girl during the operation, Nepal, 1986

There was no option but to excise all the scar tissue, which I did, divide her neck muscles on one side and rotate her face to the front, covering her raw wounds with meshed split skin grafts. I had no doubt that with the pliable joints of youth and judicious physiotherapy in the BMH, she would keep her satisfactory facial symmetry and regain her neck movements.

I undertook three caesarean sections during my time in Nepal, delivering two little boys and a girl, all fit and healthy. The need for these procedures always arises in the middle of the night for some inexplicable reason, but the look of sheer delight on the mothers' faces more than compensates for an interrupted night's sleep. However, this joy is not always shared by the father. A baby girl is not as useful on the farm and means marriage and a dowry[22]. A boy is far preferable in times of privation. In the patriarchal society that existed then, and still does in the hills, a baby daughter is a drain on scarce resources. This leads to a debate about contraception in these places, and there was none apart from abstinence. Would there be any justification for sterilizing the young mothers at the time of caesarean section if they had too many children, or finally had the boy the father wanted? It would have been easy enough to quickly perform a Pomeroy (tie or clip the fallopian tubes) and neither she nor her husband would know. I can understand the logic of appropriate unconsented sterilisation, but I did not undertake it.

I took out a huge fibroid uterus from a Brahmin woman (one of the highest castes in the Hindu system). I must be honest here and say that due to its size, at one stage I wondered if I was mistakenly removing a pregnant uterus at term, which sent my nervous system into spasm until I re-read an ultrasound report and calmed down. I also have a feeling that I may have pranged

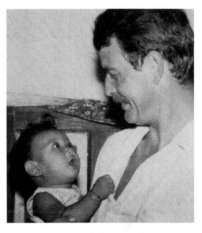

Me holding an infant, Nepal, 1986

a ureter (tube from the kidney to the bladder); it may not have been obvious at the time, but a leak can develop. The reason why I write this confession is that I recently read Jim Ryan's case load in Nepal, and he repaired a ureter!

---

22. The practice of dowry is common in Nepal, and dowry-related violence is increasingly becoming a problem. As a result, the dowry system has been banned in Nepal. Despite the laws, the violent incidents continue, under a general perception of impunity. Nepali people of the Madhesi society still freely welcome dowry as a right to the groom›s side. Even highly educated people living in the Terai of Nepal accept dowry without any second thoughts. Parents have thus started dreading the birth of daughters in the family, going as far as determining the sex of fetuses in order to abort daughters. Many deaths have also been caused by not giving dowry to the groom's side. The dowry system, however, is not practised by Non-Hindu people or indigenous people (Wikipedia).

I went out on a morning round with the senior midwife, a post-natal round, checking on the recent arrivals. I thoroughly enjoyed this opportunity and was rapt as I cuddled some of the other children. Soon Angela and I were to have a family of our own and I couldn't wait.

I left Nepal with a heavy heart. I admired and respected these indefatigable people, their toughness, their good humour, their kindness and ability to work their way through all the adversity that came their way. The average annual GDP per capita was and is around $200 - $400. A few days ago I paid nearly half of that for one meal, an Indian takeaway for the family.

If ever I think I have had a hard-working life, this photo I took serves to remind me that I haven't. This old lady from Nepal spent all her time with a circular wooden frying pan and an old hammer, converting the pile of stones on the right, to the pile of aggregate on the left. That's what she had to do to put food in her mouth, something more associated with convicts and chain gangs.

I departed Biratnagar for Kathmandu by plane. It was delayed for a few hours, because Kathmandu airport was shrouded in dense fog. I had my eyes closed from take-off to landing 40 minutes later. I returned to Hong Kong without further incident to be reunited with my wife. She had applied to have her commission

Nepalese woman breaking rocks. Nepal 1986

extended for six months, but this had been refused, so she went on a TOEFL (Teaching of English as a Foreign Language) course and gained civilian employment in a private school in Kowloon.

CHAPTER 29

Boat People, and
a Job Offer

Hong Kong, 1986

I was asked by my CO if I would do a few clinics at the Kai Tak refugee camp. This was situated in the old RAF buildings, was run by the Red Cross and housed the Vietnamese 'boat people' in pretty squalid conditions. The Red Cross usually provided the medical care, but they needed a surgeon and the cost of treatment at one of the local Hong Kong hospitals was prohibitive. It was hard for these people who fled the ethnic cleansing of the North Vietnamese following the end of the Vietnam War.

The camp held about 4000 men, women and children and some of them had been incarcerated there for many years whilst the government tried to work out what to do with them. In this clinic I was provided with two interpreters, one interpreting from English to Cantonese, the other from Cantonese to Vietnamese, but as soon as I had a rough handle on a patient's complaint I dispensed with their translations. I have mentioned having to go into vet mode when communication was just too difficult, which the following interchanges will illustrate. A Vietnamese man was brought in. He was of indeterminate age, so I asked one of the interpreters to find out how old he actually was. She translated that question into Cantonese and the other interpreter translated the Cantonese into Vietnamese. The patient answered the question and his answer was then relayed back from one interpreter to the other, then to me.

"What did he say?" I asked, "How old is he ... roughly?"

"He say yes", the interpreter replied.

"Yes what?" I asked.

"Yes, he old".

I inwardly groaned. "Ask him what the matter is" I said. Further high-pitched gabbling ensued between the three of them.

"He got pain" said the interpreter. *There's a surprise, I thought.*

"Where?" I asked, with a strong feeling of déjà vu, quite expecting the answer to be "or ova" again.

This passage of interpretation was even more prolonged, but I finally got an answer. "In gloin".

I had a look at his 'gloin' and found a very large hydrocele (water on the testis). Untreated, these can grow to an enormous size, containing litres of fluid. Normally I would drain it in the clinic to provide some temporary relief, but the room where I was working was not remotely conducive to performing any sterile procedure. I put him on an operating list for a permanent solution, but once again did not bother with the full explanation usually required by the GMC, as it was clearly pointless. I told my interpreter to tell him that the doctor would fix it, which took even more time to relay, and my patience was being sorely tested.

I found a few skin cancers during the clinic and the usual gall bladder disease, but the last patient was more interesting. He was dragged in with the support of two of his friends, or relatives. He was painfully thin and dehydrated with sunken eyes and the cachexic appearance of malignant disease. He must have been in his late twenties or early thirties, but for obvious reasons I was not going to ask.

Another interpretive nightmare began, during which I went outside for a much-needed cigarette to calm myself down and ended up giving almost a whole packet to the refugees who immediately surrounded me at the first whiff of Western tobacco.

Back in the clinic, I eventually managed to establish, through the two chattering interpreters, that the patient had been vomiting since childhood and could now no longer hold anything down, except some water. This sounded like a pyloric (outlet of the stomach) obstruction, as there was no bile in his vomit. The most likely diagnosis was a chronic duodenal ulcer. Later investigation with barium studies (X-rays) confirmed this and revealed a stomach the size of a barrage balloon.

I arranged two operating lists and cracked on with all the cases except ulcer man. He would need a couple of inpatient days being optimised before a major abdominal procedure, and I handed him over to the anaesthetists. Two or three days later he was fit enough, and I opened him up to find an obstruction the size of a tennis ball. I bypassed the obstruction and denervated (cut the nerves supplying his stomach) to reduce acid secretion. I tested the bowel joins, squeezing them to ensure that there were no leaks, and closed him up.

He recovered well over the next 48 hours, but strangely all my other Vietnamese patients self-discharged and disappeared. I was perplexed, as I would have preferred it if they had stayed for a couple more days until they were fit enough to face the rigours of the refugee camp. However, it transpired on speaking to one of the Chinese nurses that they were afraid of the duodenal ulcer man, who had been returned to the ward having been a day or two in ICU after surgery. Apparently he was a member of one of the North Vietnamese gangs in the camp. Fights and riots due to intergang rivalry frequently broke out when tensions were high, and the other patients had noticed that he was sporting a tattoo that expressed his allegiance. They were not prepared to stay in his company, nor, presumably, in the company of any of his co-gang member visitors, if there were any. In addition none of them liked the hospital food.

Ulcer man made a good recovery and could now eat, so I sent him back to the camp to carry on being a gang member, though a considerably healthier one.

Lt Col John O'Donovan was a fellow surgeon, though he had taken up the trade later in life. In theatre he was slow and methodical, which had earned him the nickname "Escargot" (French for snail) by a particularly brash RAAMC (Australian) surgical registrar on a two-year exchange with the RAMC, whom I met in the CMH. His name was Major Geoff Mummie, and he used to refer to his very good house surgeon as "Shit for brains". In spite of his rather crude and Neolithic attitude, he was well respected surgically. He did blot his copybook once when he was called into Lt Col John Carter's clinic to see a young service woman who had a small breast lump (a fibro adenoma in fact). She was standing with both breasts exposed, and Geoff walked in, looked at her and said "Christ, what a pair".

John O'Donovan had decided to leave the RAMC and set up a private GP/surgical practice in Hong Kong, and he was practising there when I was in the BMH. He phoned and asked to see me. We went out to dinner and he offered me a job as a partner in his set up, which was extremely lucrative and would easily have doubled and then tripled my salary. The offer was certainly attractive, but the prospect of the GP side of things, coupled with living in Hong Kong and all that entailed, led me to refuse his offer. He took it well but said that there would always be a job for me there if I left the Army. I was flattered, but realistically I did not think it was going to be my scene for quite some time, though the events that would later unfold caused me to seriously reconsider it.

CHAPTER 30

Doomed from the Moment...

I had already foregone my marriage to Beverley, my first wife, because my work schedule was far too frenetic to successfully factor in children at a time that coincided with her wishes to become a mother, and I had also foregone my relationship with Kathy, because she was very honest about not wanting children in the first place. I did not want to make the same mistake again, so I deliberately waited until I was at the most appropriate point in my career to eventually have children with Angela. I hoped at that stage I could devote the maximum amount of time possible to them, given the onerous nature and constraints of my work. Indeed, it is true to say that it would have been a relationship deal breaker for me if Angela had said she wasn't prepared to have children, but I guess that much she already sensed when agreeing that she would.

On the 31st August 1987, I wrote to my mother, 'Well it happened this week! (R M) Jackson appeared at 0415 hours all kicking and screaming. I was there!...So I am absolutely over the moon. It is almost the fulfilment of a dream – my own little baby daughter'. The joy would be relatively short lived.

Me with R

We had inherited a Chinese amah (maid) with the flat, whose name was Ah Ho. She would see to our day-to-day needs by doing the cleaning, washing, ironing and occasional babysitting, a luxury few new mothers who do not go out to work are afforded. She made living in Hong Kong very easy and all Angela realistically had to do was breastfeed the baby, change her nappies and tend to her own requirements.

A couple of weeks later, I had to fulfil a prior commitment to go to Singapore and play tennis on behalf of the Army for six days, a fairly high profile, inter-army match against the New Zealand army. I arranged for the obstetrician, the paediatrician and an experienced mother to be at Angela's beck and call if she needed help. It was a privileged existence as the wife of a consultant surgeon, but she showed no gratitude towards this preferential treatment and what is more, she never forgave me for participating in this competition, even though she knew I had little or no choice. I did not know it at the time, but my marriage was doomed from the moment my first child arrived and became a competing interest for my affections.

The trouble was that Angela needed to be the centre of my universe (and everyone else's), and with me being a doctor first and foremost, that could never happen. The centre of my attention had to be the hospital and my patients. Even my own life was at the end of the queue. I had signed up for that well before I ever envisioned getting married and having children.

My commitment to work did not mean that I considered my job to be any more important than my family. It merely meant that ethically and legally I had no choice but to put my patients first, but it was something Angela persistently failed to comprehend. After all, as I reasoned with her when we had our own child, she would have presumably wanted this to be the case had our daughter needed urgent hospital treatment during evening hours or on a weekend, but I soon realised that there were rules for her and by extension her children and there were rules for the rest of the population, who were generally off her radar. It would become a major problem.

My lack of availability to always meet Angela's emotional and physical demands, meant that not being the centre of my universe was more than just a simple irritation to her, it seemed to be a deep wound to her psyche, especially once she had to share my time with our dependent children. I was going to be discarded, derided and become history in quick succession. If Angela was to get her way, I would also be erased altogether as a father.

The wife of a service RADC Col. (Royal Army Dental Corps) had become an agent for a Real Estate company based in Andalucía, Spain and was trying to muster interest in the area around Mojácar. I had plans, which I had discussed with Angela, for us to retire in Spain, and this area seemed perfect, from the videos I was shown. I made as many enquiries as I could and using almost all the rest of my grandfather's small legacy, I bought a first-floor apartment in a small development which had a communal guitar-shaped swimming pool. It was called the Rio Abajo and was just outside a coastal fishing village called Garrucha. Though I was not to visit it for some time, this part of Spain would become very significant for me.

CHAPTER 31

A Matter of Life and Death

BMH Berlin, 1987

In those days, Western aircraft flying to Berlin had to cross East German air space through the designated air corridor at around 10,000 feet. This part of the atmosphere is a repository of evil turbulence and I found it a very uncomfortable journey as I made my way there for my next posting. I was going to be singlehanded in Berlin, with relief on Wednesday nights and monthly weekends provided by a local German surgical Oberarzt, pretty much like my duties in Northern Ireland. I could cope with the situation, as it would not be for much more than 18 months, but I would not have any junior support. The surgery was routine and though on call, I was not otherwise overly taxed.

Our married quarter was on the Heerstrasse, within walking distance of the military hospital. It was a beautiful tree-lined avenue. The hospital itself was small but had all the departments necessary to provide a good service. Not far from us was Spandau prison, but Rudolf Hess, the Second World War Nazi prisoner and its only occupant, had already killed himself at the ripe old age of 93 years, by the time we got there.

West Berlin was clean, tidy and well organised, in direct contrast to communist East Berlin, but of course being in the middle of East Germany, getting out of it was problematic with the Cold War still in force in 1987. Driving through East Germany to the border was strictly controlled by car registration and a strict speed limit along the only recommended route from Marienborn to Helmstedt. This highway was regularly patrolled by the East German police and hidden cameras abounded. Anyone who strayed off the road would be treated as a spy.

We could go into East Berlin in uniform, as part of one of the four occupying powers, through Checkpoint Charlie. The currency of West Berlin was the Deutschmark and of East Berlin, the Ostmark. The exchange rate was phenomenal, as the Ostmark was worthless outside East Germany, but there was very little of any value to buy in East Berlin as food and commodities were scarce. The cars were all either Trabants, which seemed to be made of compressed cardboard with foul two-stroke engines, or Ladas, the rugged Russian make of mainly 4 x 4s. The whole place was run down and depressing, so we didn't go there very often. The Berlin Wall had yet to be knocked down. (President Reagan challenged Gorbachev in 1987 to "tear down this wall" in a speech given by the Brandenburg Gate, which separated East and West Berlin. The wall came down two years later). Every so often someone would be shot or blown up trying to cross from East to West. The Wall was worth a visit as well as the imposing Reichstag building. Berlin was very much a city of two halves, the West vibrant, wealthy and opulent, the East, well, just horrible.

I was happy enough there with my new baby daughter and young wife. The work was not too onerous, but of course the on call was an anchor around some of our activities. Nonetheless we explored the city and visited Wannsee, a lake location, for beautiful walks and boat rides with a pram and all the paraphernalia required by a baby human. We had a *putzfrau*, a cleaning lady, who would help Angela out at home, rather like our Amah in Hong Kong. She was provided and paid for by the German government.

However to compound matters, Angela got pregnant again. Although an unplanned pregnancy, it was a very welcome one as far as I was concerned. Angela's reaction to the news was not as I had hoped. She was furious. There was nothing I could say to appease her, to encourage her, to look at the joys of bringing another life into the world. She began to resent me and every male on the planet who left their wives at home to get on with the child rearing. She started to argue that I should have given up my job to stay at home to look after our child, and that she should have continued to work and 'have fun'. She claimed that she had only agreed to have children for my sake and as I wanted them, I could stay at home and look after them. She constantly rebelled against the role of mother, aggrieved that she had to do things she didn't want to do for others, rather than getting on with what she wanted to do for herself.

She was eventually reconciled to having the baby, but only on the condition that after three to six months we would employ a nanny for the day-to-day care so that she could go straight back to work. She was adamant about this and also that she did not want any more children under any circumstances. I did not want a vasectomy, so she got herself sterilised.

My second child, to whom I shall refer as A, arrived in January 1989. I immediately fell in love with this new arrival, but she had two problems. She had a convergent squint which would require surgical correction and she also had marked in-toeing of her feet, undoubtedly related to her posture in the womb. This would resolve on weight bearing, as her feet could easily be manipulated into the correct anatomical position.

Unfortunately, her mother's attitude wasn't so congenial or forgiving, and I think she took these, to my mind, minor defects as a personal affront. I had had a "lazy" eye as a child and had been 'patched' for about six months, which corrected the defect. Angela knew about this and as she had considered herself a 'perfect' specimen as a child, I was therefore to blame for our daughter's squint. This of course was nonsense, but in any event, A had to be patched too. It is the good eye which is patched because the brain suppresses the image from the aberrant eye and consequently the part of the brain (occipital cortex) related to that eye will not develop. Patching the good eye forces the child to use the other eye and develop the brain, otherwise the eye will be blind. This was difficult for poor A and she used to get furious as she had to be patched for quite long periods. This task fell mainly to me, as I had been deemed responsible for her squint. I also found it very distressing, as A would twist and turn her head to avoid the patch. Anyway, persistence paid off and after a squint correction, to be repeated at a later age, she now has little evidence of it and her vision with that eye is very good.

A patched and furious.1990-1991

A and I.

Angela applied to re-enlist as she intended. Initially her application was refused as the Army Board considered that our family was too young, and they thought that she should take time out to enjoy motherhood and consider re-enlisting when the children were older. She was incensed at the idea, and it made her even more determined to escape the unpalatable child caring situation that she had found herself in. She could not tolerate becoming a member of the Army community, a 'wife-of' and mother, the role she held in such contempt. As she put it, she would not be imprisoned with her children while I had all the fun at work. It had become a matter of life or death to her and I was becoming exhausted by her attitude. She could flip like a coin, one minute flying off at me and the next appearing completely rational. Everything that went before would be totally disregarded or denied and she would resume a simmering, if temporary, even keel.

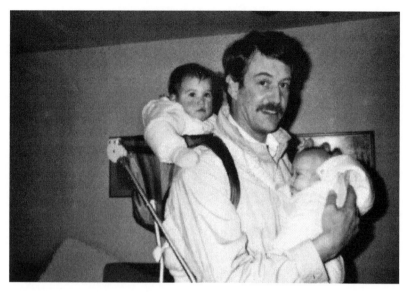

Me and my two daughters.

With such a disgruntled wife on my hands it became obvious that the only possible way to resolve the situation was to accede to her demands. Despite my reservations, I wrote a letter of support to the Executive Committee of the Army Board on Angela's behalf and they changed their minds about her re-enlistment. I hoped she would now be content and would calm down once she got back on the teaching stage and regained the admiration and attention she seemed unable to do without.

One day, Charlie, a local German gentleman who was my secretary, PA and general factotum, knocked on my office door and said that there were two German doctors who wanted to see me. I asked Charlie to send them in and met Prof. Dr. Med Ekkehard Vaubel and Dr. Med. Jurgen Hussmann. They wanted to write and publish an Illustrated Glossary of Hand and Reconstructive surgery in French, English and German. My mission, if I wished to accept it, was to translate all the relevant diseases and syndromes, texts and illustrated diagrams into English.

I could still speak passable French, but no German, and my knowledge of reconstructive and hand surgery was pretty thin. This was going to be a monumental undertaking, but a challenge I would relish, so I said I would do it for the reward of being a named collaborator. Once a week these two would turn up with a load of papers and Charlie and I would sit down and turn everything into medical English. It is a very good book and had apparently gone a long way to promote a tri-national comprehension of hand and plastic surgery before the internet and the great God, Google came along. I expect it sold at least a couple of copies.

As I look at it now I see that my address is in Munster, my next posting, so presumably I was there when the book was finally published. I have read through a couple of passages that I translated from the professor's flowery constructed German into pragmatic English. I think I did a good job.

CHAPTER 32

A Shooting

BMH Munster, 1989

Angela, with her re-enlistment confirmed, was co-posted to Munster and she would teach the soldiers their Education for Promotion courses at York Barracks. I would take up a consultant's post at the BMH. Every BMH is run on similar lines, so it is easy to slot into the routine.

We had engaged a nanny called Leila. She was excellent in her child management and relieved Angela of the burden of childcare that she so detested, as well as the label of stay-at-home mother. Angela seemed to settle down, we resumed a normal, if slightly chaotic, family life, and I breathed a sigh of relief. We had survived a difficult patch and my family was intact.

It was however a false new dawn. A couple of months later I was approached by an officer who warned me that my wife was getting a bit too familiar with the soldiers and I was advised to tell her to be careful about behaving inappropriately with the Other Ranks. My advice would fall on deaf ears. Angela would meet a Sergeant in the

Grenadier Guards who was on a course she was teaching. He was 10 years my junior, tall, fit but poorly educated, having joined the Army at 16½ as a boy soldier. He had the words 'love' and 'hate' tattooed on his knuckles. His name was Brian. Angela would find him irresistible.

The British Army of the Rhine (BAOR) was stationed throughout West Germany. I needn't go into the geography of these formations, but I need to relate that the security level was high. The Provisional Irish Republican Army (PIRA) had brought their campaign of violence into Europe and was specifically targeting British security forces with shootings and car bombs. Every day we had to check under our cars for suspicious packages and on entry to every Unit, the guards on the gates used mirrors attached to long poles to do the same.

In 1987 the PIRA had car bombed the BAOR Joint HQ in Rheindalen. On 7 September 1989 a PIRA Active Service Unit shot Heidi Hazell more than a dozen times in her car in Dortmund. They did not know she was a German citizen married to a British soldier. On 27 May 1990 they shot and killed two Australian tourists in Roermund, mistaking them for off-duty British soldiers. I was not concerned with any of these incidents, but I was involved in the surgical care of two soldiers shot and badly wounded on 1 September 1989. The soldiers, in civilian clothes, were walking in a housing area for British troops in the village of Gremmendorf, outside the 6ft perimeter wall, when a car pulled up and its occupants asked in English how to reach Munster. As soon as the soldiers answered in English one of the terrorists opened up with an AK 47 automatic assault rifle, firing approximately 25 rounds. The other weapon used was a 0.38 revolver. The latter is for administering the coup de grâce in addition to being available for use if the automatic weapon suffers a stoppage.

The standard method of killing under these circumstances is to fire the automatic burst at the victim's legs and as they collapse, they fall into the burst of fire and are killed. In this case, spaced shots were also fired from the handgun. Both soldiers were badly wounded but not dead. The PIRA assassins drove off in a black car.

First aid at the scene was administered by local troops and by a British Army medical officer who was fortuitously in the area. The German emergency services were called and having been notified of

The two soldiers were in front of this wall when they were shot. The standard AK47
magazine holds 30 rounds. 25 of them were fired, almost the whole clip.
1st September 1989 Munster. West Germany

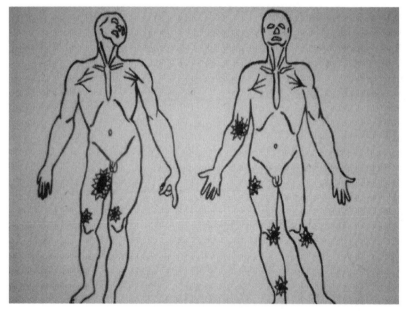

Soldier A (Left) was shot four times (once in the backside) Soldier B was shot 6 times.
1st September 1989. Munster West Germany.

the incident, I dispatched my registrar, Major David Vasallo, to assess
the situation locally. He reported back on the injuries the soldiers had
sustained and I told him to send the second soldier to a local German
Krankenhaus (hospital), as we would not have the resources to deal
with both casualties. I will call them soldier A and soldier B. Soldier
B was admitted to the Catholic St Franziskus Hospital, not far away.

Soldier A arrived at the BMH. He had sustained two high velocity gunshot wounds (HVGSW) and one low velocity wound to his lower limbs. The main problem was that one round had entered and exited his right groin, and in addition to fracturing his femur, it had taken out a long segment of his femoral artery and vein, the main vessels to his leg. Another HV round had gone through his left knee area and had exited with a very large wound at the back of the knee, but fortunately had not caused significant damage to his nerves or blood vessels.

The low-velocity round was lodged somewhere in his buttock and was visible on X-ray. This unfortunate soldier had bled out almost completely and was barely conscious when he arrived. A makeshift

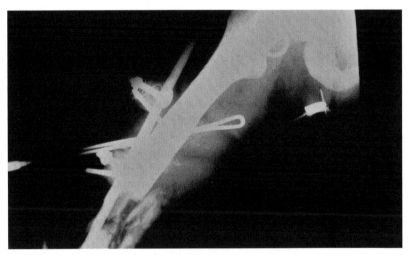

Soldier A's X-ray. Shattered femur on left, 0.38 round on right.
1st September 1989, Munster West Germany

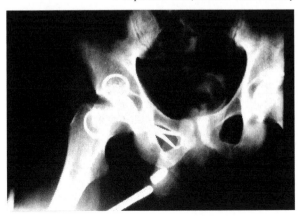

I am using the instrument as a marker to try and locate the bullet. I couldn't find it. Soldier A 1st September 1989, Munster West Germany.

tourniquet, applied to try to stem the bleeding from his femoral vessels was ineffective, but he wasn't bleeding much from this area; most of his blood was either at the scene of the shooting or in the German ambulance, as it certainly was not in him.

He was transferred to the operating theatre, where my anaesthetic colleagues, all of whom had responded to this emergency, undertook intensive resuscitation, with copious IV fluids and group compatible blood, the soldier's blood group having been ascertained from his identity card. In spite of this, soldier A's blood pressure remained unrecordable. All the blood we were putting into him just leaked out of his groin wound. I applied direct pressure and as that was also ineffective, I grabbed some instruments and packs and explored his wound. I managed to find the ends of both vessels and carefully occluded them with vascular clamps, which would not damage them. Once the haemorrhage was under control, soldier A was stabilised by further transfusion through a large central line. By then one hour had passed since the shooting.

By now I had been a consultant for around five years. It felt like five minutes. I sat down and had a think whilst the young lad was prepped for operation. I made a plan. First of all, I would have to stabilise the femur, as movement would prejudice the integrity of the repair of the main blood vessels. Major Vasallo would have to harvest a long length of (saphenous) vein to bridge the gaps. The leg had already been pretty much bloodless for nearly two hours, the maximum time which would allow recovery being around four to six hours. Anything longer could incur catastrophic vascular and kidney complications. I had to try and slow down the metabolism of that leg and in addition get some blood into it.

I asked for a thin latex rubber tube and all the ice in the hospital, even if it meant emptying both the Sergeants' and Officers' Messes. I got a lorryload of ice and a thick red rubber tube. It would have to do. I needed to temporarily bypass the arterial defect with the tube and additionally reduce the metabolism of the leg, cooling it by packing it in ice. I achieved this using the red rubber tube as an improvised shunt, and I was very pleased to find that soldier A's leg had a faint pulse as the ice was cooling it down.

I fixed the femoral fracture with an external fixation device, bringing the bone out to length and ensuring that it was completely stable. Once that was done the saphenous veins on both legs were harvested and prepared, which had to be meticulous (and is tedious). I repaired the femoral vein first and then the artery.

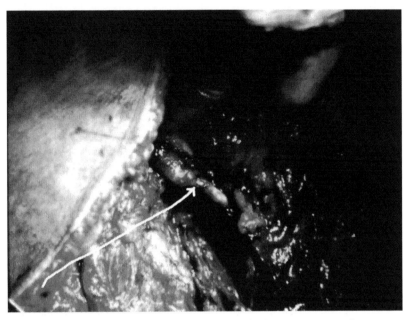

Soldier A's groin. Vascular repair in centre of the wound. Big artery to temporarily narrow vein. 1st September 1989, Munster West Germany.

I'm skipping over about five hours here. I released the vascular clamps, and nothing much happened. The blood flow was feeble. The vein (don't let anybody tell you that veins don't) had gone into spasm.

We tried warm water and at David Vasallo's suggestion I carefully incised the outer layer of the wall of the vein (the adventitia) allowing it to expand. I was just at the point of acknowledging my failure in trying to save the leg when suddenly the wound welled up with bright red arterial blood. The blood was being pumped through the venous graft and was leaking through the suture holes. I was over the moon.

I controlled the bleeding with pressure, closure of the tiny defects and the reversal of the heparin that had been given to prevent unwanted clotting. I then dealt with the other wounds and the ice was removed. I needed his blood pressure up as quickly as possible when the anaesthetic was reversed, and whilst waiting for this, I kept the grafts patent (open) by pulsed manual compression. When soldier A was extubated (tracheal tube removed) and awake, he responded appropriately to questions, which suggested that he still had a brain left and he could feel and move his right foot. I could feel his pulse, the dorsalis pedis, on the front of his foot. I never found the 0.38 bullet somewhere in his backside. That could be retrieved electively, if at all. He was casevacced to QEMH.

Eight months later he returned to his unit in Munster. He could walk with the use of a stick. He came to see me in the clinic and gave me a regimental plaque with his thanks inscribed on the back. It's up in my loft. But once again, it wasn't just me. I could not have done what I did without the help of my colleagues, dedicated medical professionals and others, each playing their part to the best of their ability to save this young man's life and limb. I just happened to lead the team.

I must not forget soldier B. He had been struck with five high-velocity rounds and one low-velocity round, but none were life or limb threatening. Unfortunately, he did have nerve damage to his right elbow and left knee. I was dispatched to report on how he was progressing and went into theatre with the German professor in charge of the surgical department and his surgical acolytes. They had done well. All the wounds had been correctly dealt with and were clean and healthy. He had about a million deutschmarks worth of shiny German surgical Meccano attached to his limbs. It was now just a matter of suturing the wounds, which we could do at the BMH, and then casevac Soldier B to the UK for further treatment. I suggested that course of action to the Herr Professor, but he was reluctant to accede to my request, saying that soldier B was not ready and that complications could ensue.

I reported this to my Commanding Officer, a dentist called Colonel David Scarborough, and quite rightly he bemoaned the cost of further treatment in the St Franziskus. A pretty hefty bill had been stacked up already, as of course it was a private hospital. Nevertheless, I really could not go above a professor of surgery, and we did not want to upset our medical allies.

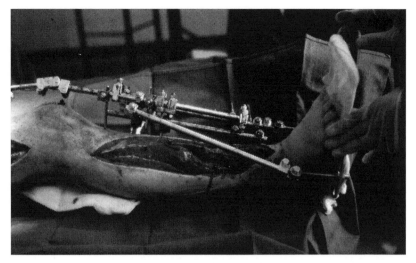

Soldier B with leg externally fixed.

Then I had an idea. Next morning, I went back to the St Franziskus, asked to see the professor urgently and spoke to him privately in his office. That afternoon soldier B was back in the bosom of the BMH.

My CO was intrigued. "How did you get a German professor of surgery to change his mind? What did you say?" he asked. I told him that our intelligence had discovered that the terrorists knew that the soldiers had survived and that they had resolved to finish them off if possible. "Soldier B would have to be under armed guard in their hospital, or we could have him back in the BMH" I said. "Er, well done", he replied, sounding rather flustered. I left my CO's office with the distinct impression that he would rather not have been a party to the explanation I had just given him.

Soldier B made a reasonable recovery. I expect that both would have been medically discharged from the Army, though I do not know for sure.

CHAPTER 33

Guten Tag,
Herr Professor

Munster Klinik

A young corporal in the Royal Engineers was admitted with a painful, rigid abdomen. He had lain in his bunk for about 36 hours with this, immobile and vomiting, instead of reporting to sick parade. He had been subject to pain around his belly button and right lower quadrant of his abdomen for quite some time. My examination of him confirmed severe dehydration and peritonitis.

I opened him up following resuscitation and found widespread peritonitis secondary to a perforated Meckel's diverticulum, which essentially mimics the symptoms of appendicitis and is just as nasty, if not worse. Though they are often found incidentally, they can cause significant problems, though perforation is rare. (The diverticulum is an embryological or developmental remnant of the vitello-intestinal duct which allows nourishment to pass from the embryonic yolk sac to the gut of the developing foetus until the umbilical cord takes over and nourishment is obtained from the maternal placenta. In 10% of the population it fails to completely obliterate and usually remains as a pouch in the small bowel.)

The whole of this lad's central abdomen was contaminated. I dealt with the Meckel's, took his appendix out for good measure and washed out his abdomen, but he did not do well. He developed a bowel obstruction with abdominal distension and vomiting. Often the cause of this is loops of bowel which stick together by flimsy, sticky adhesions which can resolve. It requires the surgeon to hold his nerve and continue with supportive treatment, because re-exploring the abdomen just risks more adhesions. The first sign of a resolving bowel obstruction, especially after the inertia following a gut resection, is the passage of wind, or flatus (medical term), or a damn good fart (colloquial term). The passage of flatus brings relief to the patient's face as his distended abdomen starts to decompress, mirrored by the relief on the surgeon's face as the problem resolves. Recovery has been signposted by a vague unpleasant smell.

However, not in this case. We would need help, and I contacted the nearby Munster Klinik of the University Hospital and asked if they would accept this young junior rank to their Intensive Care Suite, which they did. He failed to progress, so further surgery was inevitable and the duty oberarzt and I reopened him. I had to assist, as I was not on the staff and therefore did not have operating rights in the German Hospital, besides which the oberarzt had received exact instructions as to what to do by his Herr Professor of Surgery.

After the abdominal findings were communicated to the Herr Professor, the young lad required quite an extensive bowel resection, similar to President Reagan's operation, but infinitely more difficult. The bowel ends were sutured together. The join looked okay, but I wanted a large bore drain connecting this area to the skin. The bowel was very fragile due to the inflammation, and if there was a leak then a drain would channel dangerous bowel contents out of the abdominal cavity. Now I know abdominal drainage can be controversial, but in this case, I felt it was mandatory. However, I was up against a brick wall. The Herr Professor did not allow the use of abdominal drains, and that was that. To use a drain would be career end for the oberarzt, and if I kept insisting, then World War Three would no doubt break out.

Back in the Munster Klinik Intensive Care Unit, this young corporal initially did well, but at about 72 hours post-op he took a distinct turn for the worse. This is when an anastomosis or join may first leak, and is generally indicated by a spike in temperature, which he had. I consulted with the German surgical staff. I was informed that the Herr Professor was returning early from a boar hunt and that nothing was to be done until he arrived in the afternoon of the next day, Sunday. And that was that – again.

On Sunday afternoon I presented myself in the Klinik to meet the Professor and take his advice on the next stage of surgical management. Almost every junior and senior surgeon in the German hospital had turned out for this occasion. I was told that the Professor would not take notice of who was there but would certainly take notice of who wasn't. A muted whisper went around. He had arrived and appeared on the ward to a refrain of "Guten Tag, Herr Professor", not quite exactly at the same time, but near enough. Then everybody started bowing and to my astonishment, so did I. I was following the herd instinct as Herr Professor walked into the ICU. I have already alluded to the awesomeness of these characters, but I could not take this particular one seriously. He was about 60 years old, very short with little knobbly knees. He was wearing lederhosen, a Tyrolean type hat with a feather in it, and his leather shoes squeaked as he walked. He looked like a German version of my first surgical consultant, Mr Marcus. I had to look away.

After all the bowing and scraping we sycophants shuffled around my patient's bed and following a brief reminder of the history, the Herr Professor examined his abdomen in a way I had never seen before. Instead of gently feeling (palpating is the medical word) this lad's abdomen, the professor closed his eyes and plunged his fingers downwards and around, rather like a concert pianist ending his musical recital with a clipped crescendo. The Professor then crossed his hands, palms downwards, an unmistakeable gesture of termination, said something in German, coughed and squeaked his way out of the ICU.

I asked one of the German doctors what the professor had said and what the next move would be. I was pretty sure what his conclusion was. "This patient will die (it sounded like an order) and must immediately be removed from the Intensive Care Unit".

My patient was unaware of the Herr Professor's instruction that he should go ahead and die, so he didn't. On return to BMH Munster he had a massive discharge of intestinal contents and other gubbins through his abdominal surgical wound (it would have been through the drain I had wanted to insert), and he recovered with a high fistula, which is an opening between the gut and the skin. He was returned to the QEMH, where he was treated with a system of TPN (Total Parenteral Nutrition), providing all the nutrients he would need through a major vein, in short resting the gut and allowing it to heal. Six weeks later he was discharged on sick leave and he made a complete recovery.

More to the point he was the only person I had heard of who had dared to defy a German Professor of Surgery by not succumbing as instructed.

CHAPTER 34

Squid, Line Breaks, Olga and Peoles

BMH Falklands 1990 (4-month tour)

Whilst still in Munster I was posted back to the Falkland Islands for four months, eight years on from the war. I would miss Angela and the kids, but I would have some relief from Angela's misandrist tirades, which had resumed; she was once again holding me accountable for all things that men apparently did to women. On occasion, when an increasingly rare spark of normality fired up from the hidden depths of her conscience, she would excuse me from blame, as she realised the effects of what she was saying had on me, our relationship and the children. She would appear contrite, but never apologetic, and just at the point when she seemed to have calmed down and I would breathe a sigh of relief, she would reiterate her opinions and finish off with the words, "I'm sorry darling but it's true", just so that I could be absolutely sure that she had completely abandoned her moment of reasonableness. What she considered was true related to how she felt. How she felt then became fact.

Even though she had resumed her career, with my help, I was now to blame for the fact that 'forcing her' to have children had caused her to be behind her cohorts. Her career was lagging, and in her opinion, she should have been at least a Lt Col like me. I'm sure she loved me in her own weird way, but I was getting tired of being a whipping boy, though occasionally and much to my relief, her Officer Commanding would take my place as the person subjected to a monologue of vilification, in just the same way that she had disparaged the OC of the Education Centre in Hong Kong.

I was a little apprehensive about returning to the Falklands, which for me had been a war zone, but initially I need not have worried. I had no adverse effects, no disquieting thoughts. I just felt sadness for those whose lives had ended in those isolated and bleak islands. One of the first things I did on arrival was to get a Land Rover and guide to take me to the battlefield memorial sites. I started in Port Stanley, visited Goose Green, Tumbledown Mountain and Fitzroy Inlet.

I went to see the house I had been billeted in and revisited the village hall where I had operated with my FST. The dartboard was still

Memorial Cross on Tumbledown Mountain, Falkland Islands, 1990

Memorial to the Welsh Guards. Fitzroy Inlet. Falkland Islands, 1990

there. Prior to getting on board the aged VC10 at RAF Brize Norton for the flight to the Falklands via Ascension Island, I had been asked to bring some golf balls and tees with me, which I duly did.

As I have already pointed out, the worst golf course in the world is on Ascension Island, but the golf course in Port Stanley, which has only nine holes, comes a close second. As a result of the war, some of the fairways now run parallel to an uncleared minefield and only the completely foolhardy would even think of retrieving a wayward ball. As a matter of fact, after the war it was discovered that mines had been indiscriminately scattered over wide areas by the Argentinians and these areas were simply fenced off and marked appropriately, as clearing them was too dangerous. All minefields should have been mapped for clearance when hostilities ended. The penguins that inhabited the islands were not heavy enough to set off an antitank mine and would only be able to set off an antipersonnel mine if they jumped onto one from a grass hillock, disappearing in a puff of feathers.

I had the opportunity to see the Islands in their summer months, during which the average temperature of 9 degrees C could soar to 25 degrees C, and they truly are beautiful – in places; the rugged mountains, clear green seawater strewn with kelp and the beaches riddled with mines.

I would stay in the Officers' Mess in Stanley and work at the King Edward VII Memorial Hospital, or BMH Falklands. A ward had been renamed Nutbeem Ward in memory of the second in command of 16 Field Ambulance, Major Roger Nutbeem, who had been killed aboard the *Sir Galahad*. I would have a full surgical team as usual and having introduced myself to them, I tried to get some idea of my main surgical responsibilities. Of course, I would be required to look after the Garrison, entitled civilians, tourists and now the Islanders themselves. Before the war they had to be airlifted to Buenos Aires in Argentina, but this option had been removed, so all necessary surgery would be performed by me during my tour.

There was another group of patients to whom I would provide a surgical service (and almost everything else) and they were the foreign nationals of the deep-sea fishing fleets, who were paying very heavily for licences to fish the waters around the Islands. These waters were teeming with fin fish and squid and provided a very large boost to the Islands' economy. Fishing licences were issued for a short specified period within an allocated zone and the fleets were policed by a light aircraft patrolling over the whole area, which was vast. These fishermen would provide me with an interesting array of injuries and conditions to deal with, sustained on their trawlers and jiggers (for the squid). One patient, which I will describe later, was difficult to deal with, but ingenuity won the day.

Spanish Trawler, Falkland Islands 1990

Several nationalities were represented, including Spanish, Russian, South Korean and Japanese. Each patient would be accompanied by a local agent representing their companies who would ensure that all necessary care was given and accept the bill for my services, payable to either the British or Falkland Island governments of course, but certainly not to me. They would also act as interpreters.

Deep sea fishing under these circumstances was dangerous. There were no health and safety rules to get in the way, the ships were repositories for every hazard known to man, the weather was frequently awful and freezing cold and every second of the allocated fishing permit period had to be utilised. The captains were usually on catch bonuses and they would only stop fishing if they had to transfer their catch to a mother ship, or their ship had sunk. A sick or injured crewman would be dealt with on the boat and dispatched for treatment at the end of the licence period, when the boat would moor in the harbour. There were no survival kits on board and the cold seawater would snuff out a human life within a few minutes of 'man overboard'. It was rumoured that a severely injured crewman would be sent to Davy Jones' locker, rather than have a lucrative trawl interrupted. This of course was anecdotal, but it made me think.

Having outlined the golf available, I was playing as a singleton one morning and not enjoying it. It was cold and dry but a gusting wind accentuated my fade. I had just sent one of my diminishing supply of golf balls into the minefield and was about to send another to the same place when I received a message on the radio I was carrying. Could I come urgently back to the hospital? There was a Korean sailor who had a badly-crushed hand which was going necrotic (dead) and black in places. The injury had occurred about five days before. I got in the Land Rover that I had filched and drove back to the King Edward Hospital.

This Korean had been working on the processing deck of the boat. Squid and finfish were prepared and then frozen on this deck for the long journey back to Korea. If you ever go on the processing deck of a trawler, as I was to do later, take a strong stomach with you. Frozen squid will still be edible for nine months by the way. In any event the seas were strong, and this patient's hand had been crushed by a dislodged block of frozen squid. Yet another first for me.

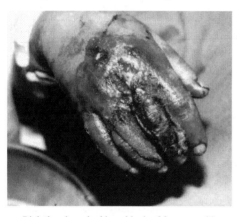

Right hand crushed by a block of frozen squid.
Falkland Islands, 1990

One of the operating theatre technicians, also a golfer, took me aside. The Korean spoke no English, but the agent who did, though very poorly, told my OTT that the injured crew member was doing his National Service. In Korea, the requirement at the age of 18 years was either two years' deep sea fishing or three years in their Armed Forces. According to the agent, this lad's father was very wealthy and owned a couple of golf courses in their homeland, but he had not been able to buy his son's way out of serving his nation. His son was a very gifted golfer who was playing from scratch when he was 16 years old and he planned to turn professional.

When the father heard that his son had a serious hand injury, he informed the agent that if I managed to save his son's hand, then I could expect to be rewarded handsomely financially, with a complimentary golfing holiday in Korea thrown in. That certainly concentrated my mind as I examined the crewman's hand.

I would have to remove a lot of dead tissue and amputate his middle finger – a ray amputation. This would result in a three-fingered palm, but he would still be able to grip a golf club. I tried to ascertain if he was left or right-handed, but soon gave up with that enquiry. Though I am sure that he was despairing at the loss of his future golfing career, this young Korean remained inscrutable. I needed to reassure him that his career was not over.

I found a nearby walking stick and holding it as I would a golf club, I showed him as best I could, a three-fingered (as opposed to four) Vardon interlocking golf grip, with the middle finger of my right hand twisted behind my ring finger. I addressed a phantom golf ball and swung the walking stick, fortunately missing the side of the agent's head, as he had approached to try and understand the finer points of what I was demonstrating. I did this a few times, giving a completely superfluous commentary. Still holding the walking stick, as my fingers were locked in spasm, I put on a (Korean holiday inspired) reassuring face and asked the agent to tell the young lad not to worry. He would be an even better golfer when I had finished with him.

The nursing staff and my OTTs demonstrated their approval of my surgical plans by nodding and smiling. The shipping agent looked baffled. He obviously wasn't a golfer, but nonetheless he seemed to do his best to soothe the lad's concerns in Korean-speak. I limbered up with a couple more swings of the walking stick and then went to the operating theatre. There was a lot of Korean prattling going on as I left the room, which seemed to be getting quite heated, but I took no notice. I was on a mission to Korea. Whilst no one else was around, I looked up and tried to memorise the finer details of an operation I had never seen or performed before.

With the arrival of the theatre team the patient was sent for. I expected a delay as he was rank with the smell of fish and had to be thoroughly cleaned before his operation. The consent form in English would be signed off by the agent. Thirty minutes later he had still not arrived and I was beginning to get impatient. After 45 minutes I sent someone to find out what the delay was, as I had already scrubbed up and had been sitting on a stool in greens twiddling my thumbs.

Word came back. The patient was refusing to come to theatre. "What do you mean the patient is refusing to come to theatre?" I asked. This was ridiculous. What was going on? I looked at the theatre clock. The Mess bar would be open in an hour.

"Why is he refusing to have his operation?" I demanded, somewhat tetchily.

"You won't shoot the messenger, sir?" inquired the Sergeant tentatively.

"No, of course not," I said sharply, more than a little irked. "Now what is the bloody problem?"

Hesitantly, he replied, "Um, he doesn't want you to operate on him, sir".

"What do you mean he doesn't want me to operate on him?" I questioned. "Who else does he think is going to do it? Who else is going to operate on his hand?"

"No offence sir, but he thinks you're mad" was the reply.

"Why on earth would he think I'm mad, for Christ's sake? I'm going to save his bloody golfing career for him".

"Err, it was the way you were waving that walking stick around and twitching your fingers at him, sir".

"What do you mean waving that stick around? I was demonstrating a perfect golf swing." I hesitated, "and, er, the...grip". I trailed off somewhat deflated as the penny slowly began to drop.

"He's not a golfer, is he?"

"No sir, he's not," said the Sergeant.

"No rich father, no golfing holiday in Korea?" I asked, as all hope faded.

"No, 'fraid not sir. He's just some poxy village peasant. He's never even heard of golf'.

At which point, the whole place erupted with laughter. I had been well and truly stitched up and the story would no doubt be related through generations of RAMC personnel. I had been completely taken in.

The following photo was taken just before I reconstructed the

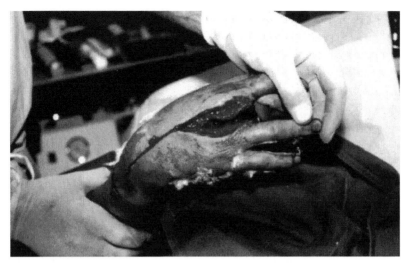

7 days after ray amputation of right middle finger. Falkland Islands 1990

Korean sailor's hand. It healed well with excellent function. He could grip anything he wanted, including a bloody golf club.

A couple of days later I received a similar call to attend A & E. "Come quick, sir. We've got a Spaniard who has had his arm de-sloughed by a fish skinner."

"Yeah, right" I said. "Pull the other one Sarge, I'm not falling for that".

"No, honest sir, it's not a wind-up".

"If you say so," I said nonchalantly.

"I swear on my father's bollocks that this is not a wind-up" he said insistently.

Five minutes later I was having a look at a partially-denuded forearm and hand. The missing human skin, mixed in with squid skin, fish skin and Christ knows what else had been thrown overboard. This fisherman was supposed to have been wearing protective gloves.

"He's not a golfer, I take it?" I asked, as I looked closer at the damage.

"Er, no sir".

The denuded limb still stank of rotten fish and it made me gag as I grafted it a couple of days later.

A few days later I was asked by the Port Authority if I wanted to go out to the Japanese jigger, as shown on the next page. The ship needed

Squid or fish skinner. Protective gloves
should be worn on both hands.
Falkland Islands, 1990

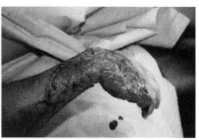

Fish/squid skinner injury.
Falkland Islands 1990

Japanese Jigger squid ship. Note the squid ink staining the sides. Falkland Islands 1990

to be inspected for cleanliness, lack of rats and other vermin and given a clean bill of health before it could berth. I think the correct parlance is the issue of a Ship's Sanitation Certificate. All I would be involved in was to wander around looking for rat droppings, an ignominious task, and report any findings to the Environmental Health team. A qualification in rat shit detection would be a useful addition to my CV. I would be accompanied by a young lady dentist who was doing a locum in the Islands and fancied a trip out to the ship. She was pleasant enough, but not to look at.

We got aboard the pilot's boat and thundered out to the jigger, where we boarded without problems. There was a lot of bowing and ritual Japanese greetings, and we were certainly treated with respect by the Master, though it seemed that he was not keen on having the lady dentist on board.

Jiggers are fully automated, using fluorescent barbless squid jigs, which are jerked up and down below the surface of the sea. Squid, for some extraordinary reason, find fluorescence irresistible and wrap themselves around the jigs. The squid are hauled up, fall off the hooks into a gutter in the gantry and are washed to the processing deck for immediate blast freezing. They fish day and night using high-powered lamps to illuminate the squid jigs in the dark, catching up to 140 tons in 24 hours.

I was told that the ship, being Japanese, would be immaculate and it was. I noticed a sign on the main deck that said, 'No Spitting or Urination'. I had to ask why the lady dentist and I were showered with salvos of salt when on the open decks of the ship. The explanation when it came was quite simple. The Japanese crews, whilst at sea, regard the ship as the only female in their lives, essentially their mother who would take care of them and see to all their needs, not in the biblical sense of course, provided she was not angered by the presence of another female. The purpose of the salt was to ward off the evil spirit represented by the totally innocent lady dentist and purify the ship in much the same way that sumo wrestlers throw salt into the ring before they commence fighting.

Having failed to spot any vermin droppings, I returned to port, a salt-free zone, and when I looked in the mirror, I found that my hair looked distinctly grey.

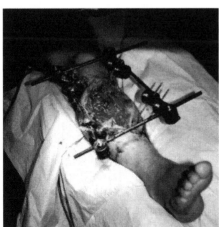

Injury to right lower leg due to a hawser break,
Immobilised with the Field External Fixator.
Falkland Islands 1990

Another call to A & E reconfirmed, in my mind, that the only deep-sea fishing I would ever do would be nothing more dangerous than a fishing trip on holiday, swanning around in a crystal-clear sea with the heat of the sun bearing down on me. When the catch in the nets of a stern trawler is hauled in by their powerful winches, the strain on the metal hawsers attached to the trawl can be astronomical. They can and do break. When this happens, the end of the line nearest the winch will whip back and damage everything in its path. When the human body gets in the way, the destructive effects can be devastating.

A Spaniard's lower leg was caught in the whiplash and the picture shows his limb after I had operated on it and fixed the (comminuted) fracture. The blood supply beyond the fracture was good, so with a secondary wound closure followed by bone grafting he should have a useful limb. He was casevacced in good nick with a warm foot and wiggling his toes back to wherever he came from, via Ascension Island and Brize Norton of course, as there was no other way by air. A few more shekels for whichever government was putting in the bills.

One evening I was invited to dinner at the Governor's abode in Port Stanley, with other senior members of the garrison. He was away, but Mrs W H Fullerton CMG (Mrs Governor), would be hosting the event. It was a very pleasant evening with polite, almost muted conversation. The hostess was charming and there was little mention of the War, which I found surprising. However, I do remember that there was a button under the dining table, which, when Mrs Governor pushed it, must have rung a bell in the kitchen to summon a member of the staff to come and attend to our needs, refreshing drinks or serving the next course of the meal.

I was halfway through a bluey (airmail letter) to Angela, when there was a knock on my door and the Mess steward said I was needed on the phone. I remember having had a few pints at the bar that evening, so I spent a bit of time composing myself into a coherent and attentive mode, in order to answer the phone without slurring. I knew it would be urgent, because I would not be getting a non-urgent summons late in the evening. However, it was a warning order. The hospital had received a message from the Port Authorities, who were relaying a message from another Korean fishing boat asking for medical assistance to be on standby, as one of their crewmen had been hit in the face by the whip back of another hawser break. I assumed his head was still on his body but thought better than to ask.

The boat was steaming in from the allocated fishing ground and the patient's ETA was early morning. "So why are you telling me this now?" I asked, slightly irritably. "Because I was told to sir". The warning I had been given was clear, I had to be around in the morning in a reasonably sober condition and not off out shooting golf balls into minefields.

I was all there when the Korean arrived with the same agent as the previous one. The agent eyed me suspiciously, no doubt half expecting me to start waving a walking stick around again. I had learned my lesson, and in any event, I was far too worried about the crewman. The Korean's face had only been slightly rearranged, which I found difficult to understand in view of the history I had received. It was nothing that I couldn't handle, as I was sure he was no oil painting to start with, but his breathing was very laboured. His upper airway was gradually being compromised, no doubt because of inflammatory oedema (swelling). What really worried me was that he could not move his neck. The muscles supporting that part of his spine were rigid and I suspected that he had a very severe injury. Things did not look good. If we gave anything to relieve his pain and his neck muscles relaxed, he could be well on the way to a serious spinal cord injury.

I was happy with his neurology at the time, because he had walked in and could squeeze my fingers with both hands. We fitted him with a cervical collar, gently supported him and helped him to lie down on his back in a hospital bed. I was sure of my diagnosis and sent for the anaesthetist whilst I referred the patient to X-ray and told the agent to inform the Korean what I thought the diagnosis was and tell him not to move his neck under any circumstances. He was wheeled off to X-ray with his head firmly clamped between the hands of a trusted member of my team.

On his return I looked at the X-rays. He had pneumonia, but more to the point he also had a fracture dislocation of his cervical spine. In medical terminology he had fractured his C2 odontoid peg and suffered an anterolisthesis (forward slip of his head and C1 vertebra on the C2 vertebra leading to a rather disturbing-looking X-ray (for the Korean that is). There is

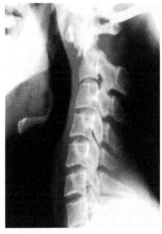

Korean seaman's cervical spine
X-ray. Falkland Islands, 1990

341

another routine X-ray that is taken through the mouth, just to look at the odontoid peg (dens is another name for it) and this confirmed that it was broken and that the strong ligament complex which keeps this peg in place had therefore also gone for six. In layman's terms he had a similar injury to criminals executed by hanging.

I was obviously not up to speed with these neck injuries, as treating them in those who are still alive is a specialised area of orthopaedic surgery. What I therefore had to do was cervical spine first aid with immobilisation by traction, tracheostomy and catheterisation. It was difficult to get through to the agent that I would be stretching this sailor's neck with metal tongs screwed into the outer table of his skull, doing a tracheostomy (putting a breathing tube in his neck), and sticking a catheter into his bladder through his winkle, as well as giving him a whole lot of drugs and sedation.

I had to assume that not a lot of what I had said was relayed with any degree of accuracy to the sailor, and judging by the expression on his face, not inscrutable this time, he was very unhappy, probably at the thought of the winkle bit. Suddenly he started speaking to the agent.

"What did he say?" I asked.

"He wan' go ship" was the reply.

"Well he'll have to wait a bit and then we will get him on a bedpan" I said having clearly misheard.

The agent looked at me blankly. "No, he wan' go ship, no shit, ship," he said.

I eventually managed to accomplish my surgical plan, but there was a problem. It was essential to supply nebulised (moisturised) air to the sailor to aid his breathing and pneumonia, but we had no tube to get the nebulised air into the vicinity of the tracheostomy tube. This is where ingenuity came in. I went to the local REME detachment in Hillside Camp and asked the sergeant in charge if he had any Land Rover heater hose spares, outlining what I hoped to do. Not new hoses he said, but there was a Land Rover that was BER (Beyond Economical Repair). We could have the hoses from that, though this vehicle was very old and had started its life in Germany before being transported to the Falkland Islands where condition did not really matter (no MOTs) for the final few thousand miles of its life. I said I'd

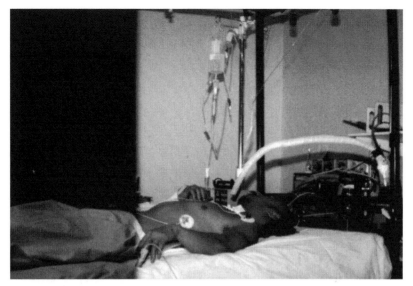

Korean sailor with neck fracture. The Land Rover heater hose connects the nebuliser on the right-hand bed upright to the tracheostomy in the patient's neck. Falkland Islands, 1990.

take them, adding "Any port in a storm". The sergeant looked puzzled, went outside and said he didn't think so. I was not communicating well that day. In any case, after a thorough washout we used the 20-year old Land Rover hoses.

After a few days the Korean was casevacced out. A special team had to be sent to collect him and I think, though I may be wrong, that his neck was stabilised in the UK before he was sent back to Korea. Anyway, he survived. I found out that this sort of damage is caused by a severe neck flexion injury, so I assume that he was hit on the back of his safety helmet and that his facial injuries, which I sorted out, were a result of hitting the deck. 25-40% of these types of injuries are fatal at the time. I hadn't saved his life, but I may have saved his spinal cord. I have also read that these injuries are not necessarily as dramatic as I have made this one out to be. This of course is not a comment coming from someone who is working 8000 miles away from home, in the middle of nowhere, bastardising Land Rover parts to get the job done.

Olga, as I'll call her, was a mountainous woman. She had thighs the size of oak trees, arms like telegraph poles and an obese abdomen that rippled like the waves of the South Atlantic as she told her tale of woe in A & E. As she cried, her face contorted in such a way that only a few of the hairs and warts on her face were visible. Her teeth were precariously loose, made of nicotine-stained plastic, and her hair was thinning. I was very surprised to learn that she was only in her late twenties, and further surprised that she was a cook aboard the mother ship of the Russian fleet. I was absolutely gobsmacked, however, when the agent told me she "vas prignant", complicated by the fact that her husband was still in the Motherland awaiting her return.

The whole thing seemed so improbable that we did a pregnancy test, which was positive, and Olga estimated about 10 weeks. That was not reliable due to translation inaccuracies and my suspicion that Russians did not necessarily use the Western calendar, for ideological reasons.

In Russia at the time, the commonest method of contraception was an abortion, a dilation and curettage, or D and C as it is known, when the cervix or neck of the womb is serially dilated until it is wide enough to admit an instrument specifically designed to scrape out the human embryo and other bits, euphemistically called the 'products of conception'. The morning-after pill, or the abortion-inducing pills and pessaries, were on their way, but not where we were. We would have to abort her instrumentally. I had seen a few done, but never done one myself, and there was the recognised complication of an inexperienced operator perforating the uterus, which in the pregnant state could generally be a bit soggy.

But salvation was at hand as we had had a change of anaesthetist, and joy of joys, my new colleague had done some gynaecology before becoming a consultant in putting patients to sleep, though not in the way that a vet would. He anaesthetised Olga and then, with me and an OTT maintaining the anaesthetic, he nipped into the nearest phone box and reappeared after a few minutes as a masked gynaecological hero, capped and gowned and wearing the requisite plastic apron and Wellington boots. As soon as I saw that he was wearing the latter two items, I relaxed. He was the real deal. He then positioned himself between Olga's legs and did the deed. The uterus was now empty of all evidence of infidelity.

We sent the Russian 'products of conception' off to the pathology lab in UK for confirmation, just in case any medico-legal issues arose, and with a sanitary pad the size of a Harrods pillow between her legs, Olga, or whatever her name really was, had the anaesthetic reversed and she was returned to the ward and then the mother ship. Her marriage had been saved. I reckoned that the Russian ship must have been at sea for several years for Olga to have become remotely shaggable.

Another Russian, this time a male, called Igor, let's say, and a jovial soul at that, had taken a tumble down an open hatch a few days earlier and had dislocated his left shoulder. He didn't seem unduly bothered by it, because, as the agent explained, what was really troubling him was his *'peoles'*. I enquired where his 'peoles' were, being unfamiliar with the Russian anatomical term he used. He pointed to his backside. Ah, piles, I thought. I had a brief look at Igor's 'peoles' and if I thought the pervasive aura of fish that inevitably accompanied these sea-folk was bad, the aroma emanating from these 'peoles' surpassed it.

What confronted me protruding from the Russian's backside, were bloody, discharging, gangrenous piles the size of grapefruits. There is nothing worse than the stink of rotting flesh and these piles were record breakers and a serious threat to life; the patient's and mine. I would have to relocate his shoulder first and then undertake a haemorrhoidectomy of gargantuan proportions. The agent spoke to Igor, and gave a limited explanation of what the problems were and I was asked if he could go back to the ship straight after the operations, no doubt wanting to reconnect with his vodka bottle, which he had been using for pain relief. My Russian language skills were improving. "Nyet" I said and then, reverting to English, "not fucking likely".

Reducing an old shoulder dislocation can be difficult. The commonest and recommended method is the Hippocratic manoeuvre. The one method that is universally decried is putting a foot in the patient's armpit and just pulling like mad until a satisfying clunk is heard. With the Russian fully paralysed, I did try the Hippocratic method but only once and nothing moved. I then put a pad in Igor's armpit, and with my size 11½ foot on top of it and someone holding me to help keep my balance, I gently leaned back, pulling on his arm until my full weight was applied. After an interminable wait, probably a couple of seconds, I heard the clunk and saw the outline of the head of his humerus relocate. I manipulated the shoulder to free it up a bit and checked the range of movement. The X-ray tech took a couple of pictures which confirmed that the joint was now correctly anatomical, and Igor's arm was put in a collar and cuff sling. That was the easy bit.

Igor was then put into the lithotomy position – legs up and bent, anus available, and I went to work on his piles. One of my technicians obtained a capsule of concentrated lemon extract and sprinkled it on the inside of a new mask, which he then put on me. This went a long way to assuage the paralysing odour I was enveloped in, at such close quarters to the Russian 'peoles'. Another technician was busily spraying some deodoriser around the theatre like a Catholic priest dispersing incense. However this did nothing to improve the atmosphere around the patient, as it just added one foul smell to another.

About an hour later, Igor was separated from his 'peoles' and I am sure that of the many procedures I have undertaken, this one provided the greatest patient satisfaction. Igor would now only smell of fish and stale vodka and he would be able to lift the bottle with a functional left arm. Perhaps he would have a chance with Olga. That thought was a bit too much for me, so I went back to the Mess for a few drinks until I was able to face dinner. I did not choose the meatballs in bolognaise sauce, for obvious reasons.

I had been writing regularly to Angela whilst I had been away and managed to get a couple of phone calls through to her and listened to the children saying how much they missed me. I had had just about enough of this tour and I needed to get back to my family. I did a few procedures on the Islanders, pretty much routine stuff, except for a small child from one of the outlying settlements who had managed to fall open-mouthed onto a tent peg; another first for me. She sustained a small laceration to her soft palate which would heal on its own. It was the bleeding which was a bit frightening for the parents, but this had stopped by the time they arrived at the hospital. I gave them a bucket load of reassurance and kept the child in overnight. With no further bleeding (children heal much quicker than adults), I prescribed soft foods and liquids for a couple of days and let her parents take her back, to the back of beyond.

Much as I saw the beauty of the Falkland Islands and I could understand how the inhabitants loved living there, it was not my cup of tea and I found that towards the end of my tour, in spite of what I had originally thought, I was getting reminders about the war, which if the truth be told I had merely succeeded in putting to one side, rather than coming to terms with it.

Apart from the mines, most of the detritus of war had been cleared up, though I did find evidence of abandoned machinery of some sort dotted around the mountains and some old Argentinian clothing and ration packs. I spent a couple of evenings with friends and colleagues in Port Stanley, mainly in the Upland Goose Hotel, which is no more. In the harbour seas of the Port there are quite a few shipwrecks colonised by seabirds and seals, gradually rusting and rotting away. The Panama Canal had eliminated the dangerous passage around Cape Horn, but these wrecks preceded it. As I write this, some of them, if still there, would be over 100 years old. I hadn't noticed any of them in 1982, though my mind had understandably been on other things.

I don't suppose I will ever go back to the Falkland Islands, but before I journeyed to Mount Pleasant to board the VC 10, I was asked by my team to sign the visitor's book in the Mess. I expect my

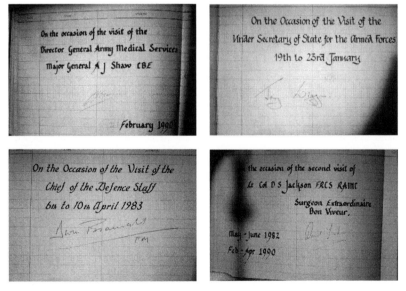

A Major General, a Field Marshall, an Under Secretary of State and me.
I keep good company. Falkland Islands, 1990.

signature against the citation they wrote for me may have caused a bit of indigestion amongst high ranking officers and civil servants.

I flew back to the UK and onwards to Munster and I was overjoyed to cuddle my two little girls when I got there. Following my return to Germany from the Falklands it was clear that another little war was looming, this time in the Middle East, the Gulf War. My role would be to maintain an experienced surgical presence in BAOR in preparation for the thousands of casualties that would be casevacced from the Gulf. I had already been to war, so it was someone else's turn.

BMH Munster was scheduled for closure and all the facilities and personnel would be transferred to the newly refurbished BMH in Iserlohn. I would have to supervise the transfer of the surgical department and for the transition period, provide surgical cover in both hospitals, which were 75 kilometres apart.

CHAPTER 35

Blackjack

BMH Iserlohn, 1991

Angela was required to attend the Junior Command and Staff course in the UK, a pre-promotion course which would last for four months. Though having her away from the family for this length of time was going to be a bit difficult for us logistically, I agreed that she should go to further her career prospects. Paula, our nanny, did not raise any objections. I would look after the children in the evenings and weekends when she was off duty or needed time off, but she would be available if I needed her. I would enjoy looking after the children; after all, I had planned to be an involved father. Paula and I would also have to pack up and move quarter to Iserlohn while Angela was away.

Every evening I would bath and play with the children until they and I were exhausted, but I was very happy. If I had to go to the hospital out of hours, then Paula would take over, though fortunately this rarely happened. At weekends I would take the children to a play park or swimming or on a mini-hike in the hills behind the BMH and I read to them most nights. R (aged 4) listened and A (aged 2) babbled away.

I had no idea that whilst I was helping Angela get her career back on track by looking after the children and everything else on the home front, I was also facilitating her having 'fun' with Brian. As often happens in these situations, the cuckolded partner seems to be the last to know, partly, I suspect, because they don't want to see the obvious warning signs. I found out what Angela had been up to when she returned to Iserlohn at the end of her course.

Surgically, apart from the two soldiers already described, I was just dealing with routine cases in Munster, with the exception of one young man who was on his Regimental boxing team. He was 23 years old. He had been attending his Medical Centre because he had noticed some bleeding from his tail end. He had been diagnosed with haemorrhoids and been given some cream and suppositories. Unfortunately his bleeding persisted, but as he had been diagnosed with piles this young soldier just continued to attribute his symptoms to them. Eventually he was referred to me for definitive treatment and I needed to return to medical school for a brief interlude and a lesson I will never forget.

In their final year before qualification each student was required to present a long clinical case, consisting of the history, clinical examination and diagnosis of one of the inpatients in the Liverpool Royal Infirmary, in front of all the other final year students. These presentations were held every Friday afternoon in a large lecture theatre and the occasion was called the 'Circus'. Attendance was compulsory and the viewing was compulsive.

Every Friday at least one, if not all, the students would be ruthlessly and ritually humiliated by the panel of supervising consultants, led by the ringmaster, Dr 'Blackjack' Roberts. He was a senior medical consultant who carried hundreds of student scalps on his belt and when my turn at the Circus came around my scalp would join his collection. It might just have well separated itself from my cranium and hopped onto Black Jack's belt of its own accord. On the appointed Friday I went to the Royal Infirmary to examine the patient I had been allocated for presentation at that afternoon's circus. I was relieved to find that the house surgeon responsible was my old friend and Percy Street co-habitee John Calam, who was to succumb to a brain tumour at an early age. Having been through the Circus himself (and now on the other side of that ritual) he was reassuring. He gave me the name of the patient and added, "Don't worry, it's perfectly straightforward".

The patient he introduced me to was an elderly man. He was in his fifties; over the age of fifty was elderly to us youthful students. He was the colour of a sunburnt lemon.

"Is he jaundiced?" I asked John Calam just before he left me to it.

"About as jaundiced as you can get without being dead" was his helpful reply.

I took the history and though not sure of the exact cause of his jaundice, on examination he had a few signs of liver failure and I could certainly occupy my time-limited slot by slowly elucidating these. John Calam came to see how I was getting on. The time for my presentation was fast approaching, but there was one thing I needed to know. "Should I do a PR?" (digital examination of the rectum) I asked. "Probably no need" he replied. I was fated from the moment I took his advice.

I went on the stage and viewed the audience, partially obscured by the lights. I was nervous, but thought I had a reasonable handle on the patient. Blackjack fixed me with a malevolent stare. I was momentarily paralysed. "Begin" he commanded.

I started on the patient's history. Long and detailed, it would use up a lot of time. But two minutes into it I was interrupted. "Summarise the presenting complaint." Flustered, I complied, missing out several bits of vital information.

"What are the clinical findings?" asked Blackjack abruptly. I was in.

"The patient is jaundiced. His sclera are yellow, he has a caput medusa (rarely seen these days with modern investigation techniques) bruising and a tremor." I said it as slowly as I could, to take up another few minutes. I was beginning to disappoint my colleagues in the audience, who were waiting for the usual ritualised embarrassment. However, like the *tricoteuses* in the French Reign of Terror when the next guillotine execution had been delayed, they didn't have long to wait.

"What are the causes of jaundice?" asked one of the other consultants. I had prepared myself for this question, but for some inexplicable reason my bloody memory, normally reliable, had gone off duty.

In medical school, many facts are remembered by the use of mnemonics, I had rehearsed a mnemonic for the causes of jaundice which I could fall back on, but try as I might, I simply could not recall it. My mind was a complete blank, and this was reflected in my face. The audience, sensing blood, leaned forward in anticipation. They did not want to miss anything. Devoid of the mnemonic, I could not think of a single cause of jaundice.

"For heaven's sake, surely after five years of medical school and the unstinting efforts of your lecturers and tutors, you must know the common causes of jaundice? Any one of them will do, to start the ball rolling as it were".

From somewhere I had a flash of inspiration, Big Kath, Queen's Head, Dock Road, dockers, heavy boozers…

"Alcohol!" I exclaimed, my thought processes now partially revitalised.

"Hmm. Another?" he asked.

"Wilson's disease?" I suggested.

There were guffaws, mixed with groans and whistles from the final year audience. I had made a legitimate suggestion, but with a disease that was as rare as rocking horse shit, the last on any diagnostic list. What was the matter with me? My brain had flipped into reverse.

The atmosphere was now unsympathetic. I was really letting the student body down.

"Have you ever heard of gallstones, perhaps a slightly more common cause?" The audience laughed at that.

"Oh yes. Those too," I said.

"Pancreatitis?" he enquired. I nodded my agreement. My mouth was dry. I licked my lips and saw Blackjack licking his too. We had very different reasons for doing so.

"Have you considered secondary carcinoma as a cause of this patient's jaundice?" I was then asked, "Perhaps secondary to a primary bowel cancer, for example?" This question had come from Blackjack through his freshly lubricated lips. He had taken back control from the other consultant.

"Yes" I agreed, "I have certainly considered that". I hadn't, and Blackjack knew it.

"Then you would have, without doubt, examined this patient's bowel, that part of which is accessible to you by the use of the educated finger, the rectum, shall we say for the sake of clarity?"

"Er…" I nervously replied.

I knew what his next question would be and so did everyone else in the audience. Their pulses were raised in anticipation, but mine was not. My heart had stopped just after the word rectum. Now the silence in the lecture theatre became deafening. The audience were witnessing Blackjack at his best and none of them wanted to miss what was to follow. I had no way out.

Blackjack did not immediately ask the question we all knew was coming. Having glanced at his watch he decided to prolong the endgame, he the cat, me the mouse

"You do of course appreciate, that a rectal examination is, um shall we say, an imperative in the elucidation of the cause of jaundice, particularly in the case of a surgical patient who presents for diagnosis for example. Surely, you could not have neglected to perform this essential examination?" he said. "You would agree with me, would you not, that it is essential?" he pressed.

"Er, yes I would," I agreed.

"And would you also agree that the omission of this procedure could be regarded as a major factor, contributing to the conclusion that should be reached that any young doctor undertaking a complete examination of a patient presenting in this manner, with the physical signs, only some of which you managed to correctly elucidate, is, um, shall we say, less than competent?"

I had some difficulty in mentally unravelling Blackjack's little homily. I understood the last three words, though. I just agreed again. My fate was sealed, but he had not quite finished.

"And of course, I am sure you would agree that there is but a fine line between simple medical incompetence and medical negligence. Which is it, is the question that must be asked and then answered; is it not?" Blackjack paused to let the effects of what he had just said sink in, and then finally asked the question that everyone had been expecting.

"You did do a rectal examination, did you not?"

"Er, um, no sir," I said feebly.

"Oh... dear..." he proclaimed, deliberately drawing out the words for maximum effect.

"What are you?" Blackjack asked.

"Incompetent," I answered dolefully.

"Yes" said Blackjack. "But when you have more experience, you will be judged more harshly. Incompetence in a young medical student translates to negligence in a qualified doctor".

The chamber erupted. There was no need for Blackjack to say anything further. I just shuffled dejectedly off the stage, head bowed and scalpless. I passed the student next in line; he was as white as a sheet.

I recalled that John Calam had said that there probably was no need to perform a PR examination, but I could not make that public. He already knew the diagnosis and so with hindsight was aware that a rectal examination was not strictly necessary, but in the context of making the diagnosis it was. However, in any event, in Black Jack's courtroom, entering a plea of mitigation, however valid, would simply lead to more scorn and a second scalping. Fuck it. I'd have to take it on the chin.

The patient had a large gallstone obstructing his bile ducts causing his jaundice, and he was also a chronic alcoholic. He did not, of course, have Wilson's disease, a rare genetic disorder that causes copper poisoning in the body which screws up the liver and other organs. It affects about 1 in 30,000 people worldwide. In 40 years of practice, I have never seen a case, nor met many colleagues who had.

It's a fact that if ever there was a conversational lull in the pub amongst medical students, then my performance at the Circus would be recounted as one of the worst ever, only to be fortunately eclipsed sometime later when Nod C's turn came (he of the psychiatric bent and seasickness already mentioned). His patient had terminal lung cancer. He managed to explain her 60-a-day smoking habit, cough, profound weight loss, fresh blood in her sputum, wheeze, breathlessness and a huge amount of fluid in her chest as a manifestation of paranoid schizophrenia. I was not there to witness this event, but apparently Blackjack was rendered speechless, never seen before or since.

I never forgot this valuable lesson. If you don't put your finger in it, you'll inevitably put your foot in it. I examined this young soldier's tail end and found he had a rectal cancer, not haemorrhoids. Rare, but not unheard of at his tender age. I surgically removed it, which unfortunately required a permanent colostomy (bowel brought to the abdominal surface) and further treatment after he had been sent back to the QEMH in Woolwich.

I found out about Angela's affair during a regimental dinner in Iserlohn in December 1991. I did not realise at the time that her lover was also in the Army, or that he was an 'Other Rank', or worse still, that he was married with two young children, and when I found out, I was at my wits end. His name was Brian Taylor, Sergeant Taylor, a Grenadier Guardsman. Angela had been behaving badly at the dinner in question, complaining that she was bored and not having 'fun' sitting with the senior officers, which included me, I might add. Whilst we were standing at the bar getting a drink, I asked what was up with her and then sensing something was off kilter I said, "You don't have anyone else do you?" to which she replied smugly, with a silly grin on her face, "As a matter of fact I have".

I was obviously taken aback and extremely upset by this admission. It was by this stage becoming quite obvious to others in the Mess that we were on the verge of having a serious row, so the Commanding Officer asked the Admin Officer to take us home. The whole hospital was going to get to know about our marital discord. That first night, I kept asking Angela why she had done it. Her replies were vague but eventually boiled down to the fact that "I had made her" and "that she had to", followed simply by, "because I wanted to". I asked her if she regretted what she had done. "No. I never regret anything that I do" she said. "I never think anything bad about myself. I did it because I wanted to. God will forgive me. God loves a sinner".

I asked her, "What about the effect on me? What about the effect on the children? Did you think about them?"

"No" she answered. "Why should I? They'll get over it".

Angela said that she intended to apply for a posting back to Aldershot in the UK. I would be required to give up our married quarter in Iserlohn and reside in the Officers Mess, whilst she lived with Brian in our house after evicting the long-term tenants. I would have to continue to pay the mortgage on it in order to provide her and the children with a home. She planned that she and Brian would continue to serve in the Army.

There was not an ounce of remorse on her face. No pity, no apology. She was completely matter of fact, cold, heartless and emotionless about the prospect of splitting up the family and the impact it would have on our children. I was dumbfounded. I did not recognise this woman, my wife, the mother of my two little girls, but this was the true Angela revealing herself. I had been completely discarded.

In early 1992 after interminable discussions and what I thought were second thoughts on her behalf, Angela convinced me that the affair was over and agreed to give our marriage another go. I wanted to go along with it for the sake of the children. I wanted to believe Angela was sincere.

CHAPTER 36

Through the Keyhole

BMH Iserlohn 1992

I had been on compassionate leave, but when things were on a more even keel, I went back to work. Whilst sitting in my office I received a phone call from the Director of Army Surgery, General R.P. Craig, who had been one of my consultants in QEMH. He wanted me to be trained in the new procedure of laparoscopic cholecystectomy. The US Medical Corps were holding an instructional course in Frankfurt and he had nominated me to take up a vacant space on the course, which had been offered to the RAMC surgeons in Germany.

Initially I was sceptical. I was used to surgery with adequate incisions. The notion of removing a gall bladder, which I had done many times, via four tiny holes in the abdomen, was a totally alien concept. It flew in the face of everything I had ever been taught. Then, after reading up about the procedure, I became intrigued.

The first thing I discovered was that although the Americans were making a lot of noise about the operation and had almost adopted it as their own, the doctor credited with the first laparoscopic cholecystectomy was Philippe Mouret, a French gynaecologist, in 1987, well ahead of the Yanks who had 'invented' the procedure in 1990[23]. I committed this fact to memory before I attended the course, just in case it was necessary to remind the American cousins that Europe had got there first, even if it had only been a Frenchman who was way outside his surgical territory. I also recalibrated my bullshit detector. I was ready to go.

I shared a hotel with a young American naval surgeon who was biding his payback time, having qualified through USUHS. He pointed out that if he continued to serve in the Navy, then every so often the American government would send him 10,000 dollars or so as a little thank you. I quite liked the thought of that. Should I perhaps transfer to the United States Military Corps? Everything they had or did was bigger and better, including their basic salaries. My bullshitometer nearly went into meltdown.

Overall, the course was excellent. We were given a potted history of the procedure and an overview of the technical aspects, told about the patient's physiological responses, the amount of air to be introduced into the abdomen and shown the specialised instruments that are used – it was all very thorough. We then watched a few videos, which were punctuated by dramatic Americanisms during the narration, for example 'Red out' (blood on the lens of the camera) 'white out' (anything else but blood on the lens of the camera), and 'mandatory conversion' (converting the keyhole procedure to the open procedure, for which all patients had to be consented).

Next day we moved to the practical side of the course and after a brief reminder of the procedure, we were let loose on nine 'patients', each of us in a surgical team of three. While we all got changed, I heard chanting and shouting outside the building from several hundred placard-bearing animal rights protesters who had somehow found out that our 'patients' were mature pigs, or in research speak we would be using the porcine model. Shouting in German and very distracting, they were the standard motley collection of men, women and indeterminates with dyed hair (usually green or mauve) scraggly

---

23. Mouret had been preceded by a German surgeon, Prof Dr Erich Mühe, who had performed the procedure two years beforehand, but he was not credited with this until 1999, mainly because nobody had believed him and his English was poor. (JSLS.2001 Jan-Mar, 5(1): 89-94)

beards, long knitted scarves and hand-rolled cigarette between their lips; those that were not shouting into megaphones, that is.

I do have some sympathy with protesters who stand up for animal rights and are antivivisection, but in truth, animal welfare is safeguarded to an enormous extent in medical research in the Western world. Another point to consider is that many of the protesters outside, given the widespread occurrence of gall bladder disease, would, in the future, reap the substantial benefit from the operation of laparoscopic gall bladder removal which we were learning. I do not think any of them would have declined the procedure on the basis that the surgeon had honed his skills on an animal model. How many desperately ill patients would refuse a lifesaving heart transplant on the grounds that quite a few chimpanzees perished before the operation was perfected?

The pigs we were using could not be returned to the food chain, as they were full of anaesthetic gases and other drugs. They would be painlessly euthanized like a family pet at the vets, rather than suffer the usual fate of being stunned, slaughtered, butchered, chilled, packaged, sold, cooked and then eaten, even down to their knuckles, especially in Germany where crispy roasted pork knuckle or Schweinshaxe is very popular in Bavaria during the Oktoberfest, when beer is very popular too. Many pig-eating countries go even further down the porcine legs and eat the trotters, which apparently are regarded as a delicacy, but that is where I would draw the line in the pig-devouring process. I do like pork belly though, and it was that part of the pig that I was going to surgically attack, unroasted of course.

The pig has a very similar bile set up to us humans and so is the ideal model. With three surgeons on each table and nine pigs dotted about, we all had a go at taking the porcine gall bladder out. I could have done with a few more pigs, but budgets were low, and the human model would have to be next. This brings me to the point that I made earlier, when I was writing about my time training at the General Hospital in Birmingham.

When I was ready and fully equipped to do my first human, Norman Dorricott, who had spent time in America learning the technique was procured by the RAMC, appointed a civilian consultant adviser and dispatched to proctor me through three cases, which he did with his usual combination of encouragement and impatience. The first case took me four hours and the second about two hours, while the third I eventually had to convert to the open procedure. I had three pig and three human gall bladders on my belt. Norman pronounced me fit to go solo and I never looked back. I had become a 'made man' in the laparoscopic brotherhood. I had status. Other surgeons would give me their respect.

Since then I have performed hundreds of lap choleys, as they are known, and taught other young surgeons just as I was taught, though with several acquired and different techniques which I had accumulated over 20 years' experience. Nowadays laparoscopic surgery has absolutely taken off and almost every branch of surgery has developed keyhole techniques, but I was there at the start line; a pioneer, in American terms.

CHAPTER 37

He's the Father

Cambridge Military Hospital, Aldershot, 1992

Eventually things seemed to settle down and Angela and I asked for, and obtained, a posting back to the UK, stressing marital difficulties. With the Army rumour service, I don't think it was news to anyone. With regard to Brian Taylor, Angela had informed me, "I just told him to go back to his wife, which he has done".

I was posted back to the Cambridge Military Hospital and Angela was posted to the Education Centre in Arborfield and we initially occupied a married quarter in Farnborough. I was still very unsure about her commitment to our marriage and her mental state, but I wanted to rescue our relationship for the sake of the children. I wanted to believe that Angela was genuine, and this clouded my judgement somewhat. I bought a house in Little Sandhurst in Surrey.

As far as I was concerned, though still unsettled, our relationship seemed to drift along and I naively thought things were progressing satisfactorily towards us salvaging our marriage. However, in June

1993, whilst Angela was adventure training in Devon with the Army, I received a phone call from a woman whom I had never spoken to previously. It was a bolt from the blue. She asked me to confirm my identity, which I did and then she tearfully asked me to 'control' my wife, whom she said had been continually phoning her husband Brian at their marital home. My heart sank, and I naively replied that I thought the affair between the two of them was over. She informed me that it had never stopped, and with that she put the phone down.

I confronted Angela on her return home from her Adventure Training. Of course she initially denied further adultery but then said that she would finally finish the affair. On a Monday morning she told me that it was over and that Brian was 'devastated', which of course Brian might well have been, had she told him anything of the sort. She was now openly manipulative, deceitful and dripping with insincerity, which reminds me of the following surgical case.

The GP's referral letter was a bit ominous.

'Thank you for seeing Mr and Mrs Smith. You undertook a vasectomy on Mr Smith some years ago when they had two healthy children, which I understand was successful. Shortly afterwards they separated for a period but have recently reconciled. Now Mrs Smith finds herself pregnant again and they both want to discuss the possibility that Mr Smith has regained his fertility and that a re-vasectomy may have to be considered as they do not wish to have any further additions to their family'.

Vasectomy is an operation to cause permanent sterility. Post-vasectomy pregnancy is very rare as a properly performed procedure is 99.9% effective. It can only occur if the operation was not undertaken correctly in the first place, or if the patient had an unnoticed dual system on one or both sides of the scrotum, or in the unlikely event that one or both of the tubes (the vasa deferens) re-joins and recannulates; this can be after a period of many years. I had performed hundreds of vasectomies and had never, to my knowledge, had a failure. The first and obvious conclusion to be reached if a pregnancy does occur after vasectomy is that the sperm came from someone or even somewhere else, which would make the outpatient discussion a trifle awkward, especially if the pregnant wife was present.

In spite of my fervent hope, both Mr and Mrs Smith came in to my consultation room. He was average, middle aged; she looked a bit shop-soiled, which is another way of saying she looked like a slapper.

"Good morning" I said, "How can I help you both?"

"He's the father" was the first thing Mrs Smith said to me. *No he isn't*, I said to myself.

"Sorry?"

"I'm pregnant and he's the father" she reiterated.

"Right…" I said. "How far gone are you?"

"About 10 weeks, give or take" she replied. *Should I bother going any further with this*, I asked myself?

"And how long have you been back together?"

I knew what the reply would be. *We got back together a fortnight before he made me pregnant.*

"Two weeks before he got me pregnant" she replied.

"Would you want to consider a termination?" I asked

Up until then Mr Smith had not said a word, but now he chimed in.

"Don't worry Doc we're not upset, it's fate and this new baby will cement our relationship; it will be the mark of our new beginning." Or of the beginning of the end, I thought. "Anyway she's a bit Catholic about the whole thing" he said, referring to his wife, "but we don't want any more". He looked lovingly at Mrs Smith as she looked away to hide her insincerity.

I opened his case sheet and noted the three negative sperm counts after his vasectomy. His chances of making his reconciled wife pregnant were about the same as my chances of winning the lottery. I could easily have solved the problem by asking him to repeat the sperm counts to see if he had regained sufficiently fertility. If by some reproductive miracle he had, then of course I would have offered him a repeat procedure. But and this is a big but, what would I say if his repeat sperm counts revealed that he could not be the father? His reconciliation would be up the Swannee as he would know that his wife was not only carrying another man's child but had also lied to him, which of course she had.

For better or for worse, I ignored the obvious solution of further sperm counts and arranged to repeat the vasectomy procedure under local anaesthetic. The histopathologist could report on the new specimens to see if there was any evidence of recanalisation. I would also diligently search for the possibility of extra tubes.

I did all this and reviewed them in the clinic a few months later. Mr Smith's new sperm counts were still negative of course. I had arranged these to complete the charade convincingly and I informed them both of the results.

"What about the other results?" they asked almost in unison.

I knew they were both hoping that there was some evidence of recanalisation. There wasn't any.

"Well, the pathologist has reported that he could not find any evidence that the first operation had failed" I replied honestly, "but there again he may not have looked very hard or maybe he looked in the wrong place because the anatomy gets distorted" I went on dishonestly. "It's difficult to tell for sure" I added, marginally less dishonestly.

They both thanked me, but before Mrs Smith left the room she turned around and winked and I breathed a sigh of relief. The truth of the matter was that Mr Smith was prepared to be the father to her child in order to get his wife and family back. She, on the other hand, preferred him to the man who had knocked her up. (The cynical me idly speculated that it probably happened on either a drunken one-night stand, or when she went dogging. It happens. The Statue of Wellington in Aldershot is apparently a hotspot).

Mrs Smith deceived Mr Smith. Mr Smith deceived himself. Both had tried to deceive me, and I had conspired to manipulate a satisfactory outcome. As I recall this case, I just hope that the child, when it arrived, looked sufficiently like Mr Smith to preserve the myth that they had concocted and was not, for example, black.

In August 1993 I went to Hong Kong for 2-3 weeks to attend the World Congress of Surgery and to speak to John O'Donovan, to see if the job he had offered me was still open, but he had retired. Whilst I was abroad, Angela installed Brian in my home with my children present. It wasn't until much later that I found out that when my new neighbours had caught sight of me on my return from Hong Kong, they had thought that Brian was my wife's husband and I was the nanny's boyfriend.

CHAPTER 38

The Black Plastic Bag and the Bluey

Bosnia, 1993

Unfortunately, in the autumn of 1993, I was the only surgeon who was sufficiently trained and available to go to Bosnia. I was to serve as the Officer Commanding (OC) Medical Support Troop in Vitez, Central Bosnia. The Director of Surgery said he had little choice but to ask me to go due to exigencies of the service. I was annoyed, not only because of the timing with regard to my marriage difficulties, but also because I was still on a 'home only' medical category due to the injury to and deterioration of my right sacro-iliac joint, following my accident on Exercise Sharpshooter in Hong Kong several years before. Nonetheless I had to go.

I told Angela that on my return at the end of January 1994 we would have to have some serious discussions about the state of our marriage and our future. Towards the end of September I left for Bosnia with a heavy heart as she waved me off from the house. However, only a couple of days after I arrived in Bosnia, I received a letter from her in loving terms, the first of many that she would write to me whilst I was away, which gave me some reassurance:

...Well my darling that's all for now, I love you very much and am missing you terribly... For you it will be different because your life has totally changed and family matters will soon seem very distant. Anyway, we will all be here safe and happy on your return[24].

I had no idea, when I received her letter, quite how significant it would be with regard to how soon she wrote it after I had left the UK. It will become apparent.

This war in the Balkans started with the dissolution of the former communist Yugoslavia, following the death of President Tito in 1980, who had managed to keep the countries and autonomous provinces together under the "iron fist". Ethnic tensions came to the fore and the Serbs were intent on annexing territory where Serbs were part of the indigenous population. The Serbs had the benefit of the JNA, the former Yugoslavian Army. By 1990 tensions had spilled into war throughout the former Yugoslavia. Slovenia declared independence in 1991 and there was a brief war with the Serbian-controlled JNA and then a peace process was brokered. Croatia had a go at proclaiming independence, also in 1991. This was to go on until 1995. Then the Republic of Bosnia and Herzegovina (B-H) followed in 1992, but this the Serbs would not allow. Though the population of B-H was mixed, the main ethnic group and the government were Muslim (44%). There were great fears of a Muslim country in the centre of Europe. The Serbs put Sarajevo, the capital, under siege for three and a half years. The death toll was 14,000.

In the initial stages of the war in B-H the Bosnian Croats fought alongside the Bosniaks (Bosnian Muslims) against the Serbs, though they also had Bosnian Serbs within Croatia who opposed them and who had been promised that any territory they occupied would become part of greater Serbia, independent of the Muslim Bosnian government. Then in January 1993, the Bosniaks fell out with the

---

24. Letter 30 Sep 1993

Bosnian Croats and the Bosnian-Croat war started. The Bosniaks only half-heartedly welcomed experienced Muslim jihadists from the Middle East, Far East and Africa, to fight for their cause. This was because the Bosniaks were not fanatical about their religion, whereas the imported jihadists were. These experienced fighters inflicted their extremist Islamic ideology on the local Muslim population.

The overall number of casualties during the Balkan Wars numbered between 130-140,000. There were episodes of murder, torture and ethnic cleansing (Ahmici, Srebrenica, and Stupni Do). Population displacement resulted in around two million refugees.

On 13 August 1992 the United Nations Security Council passed Resolution 770, the first of several, which called upon all member nations to take all necessary means to facilitate the delivery of humanitarian aid to B-H. UNPROFOR (United Nations Protection Force) was born.

BRITFOR was deployed in October 1992. Sections of the Main Supply Route (MSR) from Croatia into Bosnia, as well as other strategic areas, were allocated to various "Battalions" of those nations supplying their countries' armed forces. Thus, Canada was CANBAT and Spain was SPABAT, for example. Although UNPROFOR was subsequently given additional tasks, including the protection of six designated 'safe areas' and monitoring of Demilitarised Zones, Total Exclusion Zones and Weapons Collection Points, its responsibility for ensuring access for humanitarian supplies remained a central part of its mandate throughout the war. UNPROFOR were only responsible for the safety of humanitarian convoys crossing confrontation lines.

Between these points, convoy protection was in the hands of the local police forces, both military and civilian. By the end of 1995 there were almost 30,000 UNPROFOR troops in Bosnia. BRITBAT was allocated Routes Diamond and Triangle, subsidiary names given to lengths of the MSR, which ended at the Bosnian town of Zenica. These required much engineering work to keep open as well as a tough approach by BRITBAT because the warring factions would be intent on ignoring UNPROFOR when they wished to attack or ransack an aid convoy.

In January 1993 L/Cpl Wayne Edwards, a Warrior Infantry Vehicle driver, was shot dead by a sniper. This resulted in more robust responses by BRITBAT as the Rules of Engagement stipulated by the United Nations were pretty woolly and bureaucratic. BRITBAT was soon renamed SHOOTBAT. The Warriors they deployed had fairly formidable weapon systems and were equipped with Chobham Armour which was reassuring.

I was inserted into this incomprehensible war when I arrived in September 1993. In B-H there were Serbs, Croats, Bosniaks, Bosnian Serbs, Bosnian Croats, Mujahidin, UN agencies, third party interests, bandits and renegades with their own warlords, Non-Governmental Organisations (NGOs) and a whole load of UN observers and Military Monitoring missions.

The main protagonists however were the Bosniaks, Croats and Serbs. The Bosniaks organised into the Army of the Republic of Bosnia and Herzegovina (Armija Republike Bosne i Hercegovine, ARBiH). The Croats started organizing their military forces in late 1991. On 8 April 1992, the Croatian (Hrvatsko vijeće obrane, HVO) was founded as the "supreme body of Croatian defence in Herzeg-Bosnia". The Army of Republika Srpska (Vojska Republike Srpske, VRS) was established on 12 May 1992. It was loyal to Republika Srpska, a Serb breakaway state that sought unification with the Federal Republic of Yugoslavia. Serbia provided logistical support, money and supplies to the VRS. Bosnian Serbs had made up a substantial part of the JNA officer corps. Milošević, the President of Serbia, relied on the Bosnian Serbs to win the war themselves. Most of the command chain, weaponry, and higher-ranked military personnel, including General Ratko Mladić, were JNA[25].To say I was confused was an understatement.

The operation name was Grapple, I was part of Op Grapple 3 and was to command the Medical Support Troop, known as MST alpha, housed in ISO containers in Battalion HQ in Vitez, central Bosnia. I had an operating theatre, a small ward of about 10 beds and an office

---

25. https://en.wikipedia.org/wiki/Bosnian_War

for all the admin that could be generated if ever the hands got idle. In fact, I would find out that the facilities were perfectly adequate.

I flew out from UK to Split on the Croatian coast and was met by another Australian RAAMC major who was on an exchange scheme. The weather was beautiful, Split was an attractive city and it was hard to believe that a murderous and bloody conflict was taking place only a couple of hundred kilometres away. We stayed overnight in a barracks in Split and then climbed aboard a white liveried soft skinned Land Rover with the UN markings. The driver and the Australian were in the front. They were both armed with rifles and I had my 9mm popgun holstered on my webbing belt as we joined a convoy up through the beautiful countryside to join the MSR and then onto Vitez. We stopped for a break and a cup of wet at Camp Redoubt, an isolated fortress housing the Royal Engineers and then on via Gorni Vakuf to Vitez in the Lasva Valley, which was my final destination. It was near Gorni Vakuf that L/Cpl Edwards was killed, in his Warrior, shepherding an ambulance. He was the first of 53 British personnel to be killed and they named a bridge after him. The British base at Gorni Vakuf had suffered bomb damage and had been hit by a few sniper rounds too.

On some parts of the MSR (at pinch points, known danger points or when we crossed a confrontation line) Warriors escorted us front

This part of the route was protected by Warrior escort. Bosnia 1993-4

Houses enroute to Vitez. Bosnia 1993-4

and back, their turrets sweeping over the countryside to discourage the likelihood of an attack.

As we got nearer to central Bosnia, the signs of conflict were everywhere. Houses and whole streets were badly damaged or flattened and most buildings were pockmarked with shrapnel or small arms fire. Many were reinforced against further attack; others had been burnt to the ground.

The roads became pretty atrocious. In spite of the late summer weather everything looked dark, dismal, decayed and dangerous. Local civilians scurried around, or just stared from the doorways and windows of their damaged houses. Every so often sounds of gunfire and artillery would shatter the peace.

The Lasva Valley had been ethnically cleansed of Bosniaks by the Croats, but a pocket of a few thousand remained in Stari Vitez, which was an enclave within the town of Vitez, otherwise occupied by the Bosnian Croat HVO, which surrounded it and Kruscica, the other Muslim enclave. Outside of the Vitez pocket which included Travnik, Novi Travnik and Busovaca there was another confrontation line with the BIH Bosniak Army, who generally held the rugged high ground of the Valley around Travnik and Novi Travnik a few miles to the West stretching to Zenica, where the UN had their HQ and where humanitarian aid was stored and distributed. Thus there were pockets within pockets in Central Bosnia and concentric confrontation lines. The BIH outnumbered the HVO by about 8:1.

Sniper fire was always a danger from the BIH into the Vitez pocket and from the HVO into the Bosniak enclaves. Civilian men, women and children, Croats and Muslims were killed or injured.

Me just after my arrival. A photo opportunity requested by the Press. Bosnia 1993-4 (photographer unknown)

Battalion Headquarters was in the old school in Vitez. The battalion fulfilling the BRITBAT role when I arrived was the 1st Prince of Wales's Own, to be followed by the Coldstream Guards. Elements of the battalion were at Gorni Vakuf, Vitez and Tuzla.

I had a good bunch of lads and lasses working with me. My warrant officer was WO2 Pete King, reliable and experienced. I had some QA officers, Captains Diane Chalk (matron) and Martine Staley and other ranks and the usual FST personnel, including Cpl Rick Gramson, who was with me in the Falklands, and Private Munro, whom I shall mention in another and totally surprising capacity. We had an attached RAF nurse, Sergeant Cuthbert, and I also had a QA Community Psychiatric Nurse who was there to debrief and assist the soldiers and anyone else in UNPROFOR in dealing with contact fire, or after witnessing the evidence of atrocities.

This advanced psychiatric intervention was the step taken by the MOD to try and reduce the incidence of PTSD which I have already mentioned. Captain Paula Webster was very dedicated in this respect and popular with the troops, though I think that her slim, attractive appearance had something to do with it. In any event she was a morale booster and I have no doubt that a chat with her followed by a couple of tins of beer with their mates kept the men from dwelling on what had happened to them, what they had seen, or what they had had to do, for a while at least.

The wounds of peacekeeping are not always caused by hostile fire, land mines or accidents. They do not always leave physical scars. The mission in the former Yugoslavia was particularly difficult for those deployed there. The human atrocities perpetrated against the civilian population were horrific – witnessing human brutality on this scale has a deep impact on those who see it[26]

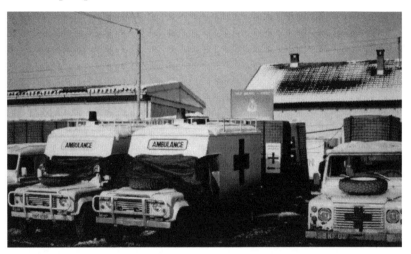

Medical Support Troop (alpha). "Rose among Thorns". Bosnia 1993-4

But what was my remit? Firstly, the MST had to provide a surgical service to all UNPROFOR personnel, entitled civilians and non-combatants associated with or attached to the UN mission. It had been emphasised that as a force we must be strictly neutral and I could not provide any surgical hands-on assistance to the enemy combatants or indigenous civilians. I would have to be completely impartial in my conduct, no matter what the surgical imperatives. I could not operate on an unentitled person, nor use any resources that may have been required by UNPROFOR. I would take part in the casualty evacuation of injured combatants, in some cases being the final arbiter in confirming that their injuries (or illnesses) were genuine, before opposing sides would allow us or the medical evacuation convoys to pass through their lines. I would also assist by giving advice to local medical personnel, in the Croat hospital which had relocated to a church in Nova Bila. We would use our personnel and ambulances to

---

26. Historical Sheet-The Canadian Armed Forces in the Balkans

evacuate Muslim casualties from the Stari Vitez enclave which could only provide first aid and get them through Croatian lines to Zenica where primary and secondary care were available.

Whilst researching the Croatian Medical Services during the War, I came across this little gem regarding the management of their casualties in their war hospitals:

On admission to war hospitals, all casualties were triaged and received antitetanus prophylaxis and initial administration of penicillin, metronidazole, and garamycin, according to the Falkland Islands experience. "[27]

All the MST officers, male and female, were billeted together in a Croatian house outside the camp perimeter. Thus, if we were required in an emergency, we could be contacted en-masse.

MST accommodation Bosnia 1993-4

The UN paid rent to the family who owned the house. They lived in their adjoining garage and I saw very little of them. I had my own room, as rank has its privileges (RHIP), which was small with a tiny bed, a desk and a single window which looked out onto a field. The water supply was variable and generally undrinkable. The house had one loo/sink downstairs and no electricity. It was freezing cold.

27. MILITARY MEDICINE, 168, 11:951, 2003 Croatian Medical Corps in Bosnia and Herzegovina during the 1992-1995 War Guarantor: Reuben Eldar, MD DPH Contributors: Ivan Bagaric, MD*; Reuben Eldar, MD DPHt

The Officers' Mess was fine, with cheap drinks, and snacks could be ordered from the cookhouse. It was warm and as an FST we would congregate there in the evenings. Meals were provided in a large mess hall, divided along the usual rank lines.

The Medical Support Troop received fresh blood supplies every four weeks and rather than discard the old blood, if it was still in date, I would take it to the hospital in Nova Bila for their use. I only had access to the medical centre in Stari Vitez if it was granted by the HVO. It was not easy.

Every so often a Bosniak artillery piece would shell the HVO in Vitez, the shell passing over the camp. If the rounds were short and getting too close, then all troops would shelter in a bomb proof sangar. Inside this sangar was an enclosed container which housed another operating theatre.

Heavily protected shelter in camp for 'close calls', Bosnia 1993-4

The MST ISO containers were located at the back of the camp, adjacent to a village house. There was no protective bastion walling between the two, hence two small arms rounds penetrated the toilet block.

At my request, some protection was constructed. To be shot on the loo was not an attractive proposition and hardly a dignified end. After only one reminder, the engineers got on with it.

Two bullet entrance holes in toilet block Bosnia 1993-4

My anaesthetist, Major Chris Taylor, was an unflappable young consultant who was a pleasure to work with. We also played together, as he had contacted me before our tour, as a result of which, we both brought our guitars for a bit of jamming and singing. With some of the girls we formed the

Constructing a bastion aggregate wall to protect the MST toilet block Bosnia 1993-4

Lasva Valley ensemble and gave a sort of Christmas concert, more filled with enthusiasm than ability.

Having met my staff, I wandered across to pay my respects and introduce myself to the CO of the Prince of Wales's Own. He was delightful and just advised me that if I left the confines of the camp, I should make sure that I was signed out in the Ops room with my destination and approximate time of return. I then met the liaison officer, a young Captain whom I could use if necessary.

The first thing I wanted to do was get some idea of the lie of the land and visit the Croat Hospital in the church in Nova Bila. We arranged to do that next day. I would travel in the liaison officer's Land Rover with an interpreter. I was given one piece of advice, which was not to assume that my blue beret or Red Cross armband would guarantee any form of safety. I found out that there was a lot of truth in what he said.

Next morning at the appointed hour, my liaison officer told me that the trip might be a little hairy as a lot of 'activity' had been reported in the areas we would have to cross. In any event he drove out of camp, then came to a halt only a few miles along the road. There were sporadic gunshots which seemed to be coming from our right flank. I was not too bothered about where the shots were coming from, just where they were going to. One round landed a little too close for comfort and as we were in a thin-skinned Land Rover, the liaison officer decided that it was too dangerous, and we returned to camp to make another attempt later on. Whatever had been happening, we were in the way.

Next day we arrived at the church bright and early. It was heavily fortified and had frequently been attacked by mortar and small arms fire. I was shown into a small common room and met most of the medical staff, whose names, if I ever did remember at the time, I do not now, though I have some photos of them. On my introduction and at any other time of the day that I visited, I found that no conversation could start, no overtures could be made, no business commenced until copious amounts of slivovitz had been offered and drunk. This was the favoured alcoholic beverage of the former Yugoslavia, brandy made from damson plums, though due to the unfavourable circumstances, it was now homemade and very strong. It was known to us as "sleep-in-the-ditch" and on more than one occasion, if I had skipped breakfast it was the first thing to hit my stomach after I got up. Nobody ever stopped at one drink.

Engaging with the medical staff took time. We represented a vast and relatively wealthy organisation and though in the same environment as them, nothing else was comparable in the way we lived. Their resources were insufficient, not just medical supplies, but also food, transport and personnel. The medical staff lived locally, and this was dangerous enough in itself.

There were no means of casualty evacuation except by negotiations brokered by the UN between the Bosniak BIH and Croatian HVO. Evacuation of injured Bosnian Croats from Nova Bila meant a long hazardous journey in the back of a four-ton lorry. BIH casualties were occasionally evacuated at the same time, with an agreed ceasefire, which was always precarious and frequently ignored. The advantage for the BIH casualties was that Zenica was only an hour away if that, where their care could be initiated or continued in the hospital there.

The church lent itself quite well to its conversion to a war hospital but had required many makeshift compromises. It was not ideal, but better than where I had operated in the Falklands. Through my interpreter I explained to the medical staff that I would do my best to help them. I could supply blood packs, IV fluids and drugs that had reached their sell-by date without compromising my impartiality. How long the blood would still be in date for would depend on when I could get it to them, if and when the replacement stocks arrived. Donated blood has a limited shelf life before the red cells start to haemolyse (dissolve) and transfusion at this stage can be hazardous, so a balanced decision, risk versus reward, had to be made. The ideal solution was to use blood extracted from healthy or recovered patients, but at first they were reluctant to consider this.

It was difficult for them. They had been thrown in at the deep end, to just manage as best they could, with no military surgical preparation. I gave them some idea of my experiences and discussed how they would have to think out of the box and recognise that in the prevailing circumstances they could not provide ideal care in every case. They had to accept an attrition rate which would be largely unacceptable before the war on the one hand, but not become blasé about poor outcomes or the loss of life on the other. I think that they appreciated my straight talking and also that I myself had been in their situation and could empathise. I gradually earned their respect, and they certainly earned mine.

There was one instance where I felt that petulance may have cost the life of a young injured combatant, though it might have been lost anyway. I knew that the doctors were war weary, and who could blame them.

My next task was to get into Stari Vitez, the Muslim enclave within Vitez, surrounded on all sides by the HVO, who were most reluctant to allow access even for humanitarian aid. The enclave was barricaded and fortified against sniper and mortar attack from the HVO, who had made many attempts to clear the Muslim population out, but they were well dug in. The only approach to the enclave was through the Croatian lines and then onto a road hidden by a large suspended tarpaulin. The road itself was mined and no attempt could be made to access it without the mines being made safe by a Croatian combat engineer. There were both anti-personnel and antitank mines.

It was a very dangerous situation, made worse by the inflexibility of the Bosnian Croats. Stari Vitez was subjected to siege and attack from April 1993 until February 1994 and there were confrontations

Mines being disarmed and moved prior to accessing Stari Vitez, Bosnia 1993-4. I was in the
Land Rover ambulance taking this picture.

of varying intensity with the use of "baby bombs", multitube rocket launchers and mortars. Snipers from both sides were always active.

Negotiations with the HVO command took place in their HQ in the Hotel Vitez and were always protracted. I only attended once, and lost patience. The HVO were not concerned with the urgency of an evacuation. What did it matter to them if an ill or injured Bosnian Muslim, either a civilian or combatant, was left to deteriorate or die? This I found difficult to cope with, but the feelings were similar amongst the BIH. A two-year-old baby was shot by a sniper in Stari

The medical centre civilian personnel in Stari Vitez. Remember the young lad in the far left of
the picture. Bosnia 1993-4

379

Vitez. The situation was critical. It took two days for the engineers to be called in to clear the mines, and by then the baby had succumbed. War has its priorities, and this child was not one of them.

I did get into the medical centre in Stari Vitez. It was set up in a pharmacy, and we took some expired antibiotics and dressings. There was no specialised medical help and in reality their only hope was UNPROFOR. I met the staff of the medical centre and also the local commander. One of his men had been shot in the leg and would need evacuation to the hospital in Zenica. We could not take him on this visit, as we did not have permission from the HVO to remove any casualties. Such was the hatred that existed that he would be shot if he was found in our ambulance without prior authorization, a threat that I took extremely seriously, as I will explain, when we went back a few weeks later to get a very ill woman out.

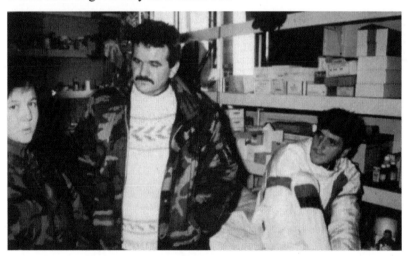

The local Bosniak Commander in Stari Vitez. The man on the couch had been shot in the left thigh. Bosnia 1993-4

One thing that was of concern to me, amongst many others, was the fact that body protection for the members of BRITBAT consisted of light flak jackets. These were designed to defend against small low velocity fragments from weapon casings or grenade and artillery projectiles, but would offer no protection against the high velocity rounds of particularly the AK 47 automatic assault rifle, the most common combatant weapon. Most of the other UN battalions, the UN observers, the European Commission Monitors, the Press Corps, and visiting politicians all seemed to wear a more robust form of upper body armour. I will come back to this later.

On the 23 October a massacre took place in the Muslim village of Stupni Do. This report from the *New York Times*:

Further ethnic cleansing in the Lasva Valley. Until about 3 p.m. on Saturday, this village in the mountains of central Bosnia, was a haven from the war that has engulfed much of this former Yugoslav republic, a cluster of houses high above a valley where the immediate concern of the Muslim inhabitants was gathering in beets, potatoes and squashes before the snows begin.

Then the brutality came up the winding dirt road from the town on the valley floor, in cars and trucks that arrived so suddenly that some of the 250 villagers had time only to pull on one sleeve of their winter jackets before rushing for the safety of the woodlands above the village. As they fled, they dropped a trail of shoes, gloves and half-emptied cigarette packs along the muddy paths. But the speed they gained from their fear was not enough to save dozens of them from the wrath of the Croatian nationalist soldiers who came to rape, to cut throats, to smash children's skulls, to machine-gun whole families.

At noon today, the funeral pyres set by the Croats in the moonlight of Saturday night were still burning, and the stench of burned bodies wafted down the hillsides, mingling with the fall scents of leaves and freshly turned sod. The only life left in the village after the massacre, a few dogs and some chickens and sheep, picked at bodies that had escaped the pyres.

"Crazy, it's all crazy," said Maj Daniel Ekberg, a 30-year-old Swedish Army officer whose persistence in trying to reach the village through three days of armed menace by Croatian troops, finally paid off on Tuesday afternoon. His persistence meant that for the first time in the 18-month Bosnian war the United Nations military command here arrived at a massacre scene soon enough, and well-enough prepared, to determine exactly what had happened and who was responsible. Gathering War-Crime Evidence[28].

---

28. New York Times (Archive) October 28, 1993:1

On the 25 October 1993 the Danish driver, Bjarne Vium Nielsen, was killed when his aid truck was caught in crossfire on the road to Zenica. A volunteer, entering a highly volatile and dangerous situation in order to bring humanitarian aid to a desperate civilian population, had been slain. Another statistic, which when reported, was a 'setback' for the United Nations High Commissioner for Refugees (UNHCR) aid program and all convoy operations were temporarily halted. That was the effect of his expiry. He was transported to the MST for confirmation of his death. I certified him in a refrigerated blood bank trailer, as we had no morgue. I closed the door of the trailer, turned my back on him and rejoined the living. I had to put him out of my mind. I didn't know him, I never would. It was impersonal. It was his bad luck, a case of wrong place, wrong time. When I had finished and confirmed the details on the paperwork, he was prepared for repatriation.

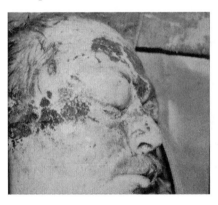

Bjarne Vium Nielsen RIP 25 Oct 1993

Well here he is. This is him. He paid the ultimate price. I had just unzipped the top half of the body bag. This 'setback' had a face, it had a life, now lost.

It was not just the warring factions and bandits that presented dangers to UNPROFOR. As well as being attacked by rocket-propelled grenades, mortars, small arms fire, mines and Improvised Explosive Devices (IEDs), the weather in winter was awful and the roads treacherous, with huge potholes and surface ice. The weather was a formidable enemy, not only of the convoys, but also the UN armed escorts.

On 29th November 1993 a Canadian Cougar, a wheeled Armoured Vehicle, was escorting a convoy from Visoko. At a road bridge in Zenica it lost traction on the ice, slid against the bridge parapet, overturned and then slithered down the bank into the freezing river Bosna.

The Cougar armoured vehicle which slid into the river Bosna near Zeneca. The casualties are being extracted through the turret. 29 Nov 1993, Bosnia.

Two of the three crew were killed: Master Cpl Stephane Langevin of the 12th Armoured Division and Cpl. David Galvin of the Sherbrooke Hussars, both aged 28 and both, reportedly in the turret of their vehicle when it crashed into the water. The third member of the crew survived and was brought to the MST. He was freezing cold and had suffered some severe facial lacerations and a broken arm. I assume that was from bouncing around inside the Cougar. I repaired his face and reduced his fractured arm. My OTTs put on a full arm backslab, to immobilise his arm, and after a couple of days he was fit enough to go to the CANBAT medical facility and then back to Canada. The loss of his mates affected him deeply; 25 Canadian soldiers serving with CANBAT lost their lives in Bosnia.

As anyone reading this might imagine, whilst I was away on tour in Bosnia, I always had the state of my marriage and my own family life at home, in the back of my mind. I had no realistic idea what Angela would be up to in my absence, but I continued to receive loving

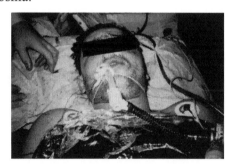

Canadian Cougar APC crew member. Bosnia 1993-4

letters from her whilst I was serving in Bosnia, and thought it must be a good sign.

The weather was extremely cold, and blustery winds deepened the chill factor to -20 degrees C, with deep snow all around. Soldiers' feet were frozen, as the standard boots (Combat Boots High), were not up to the task and Gore-Tex lined army boots were issued - eventually. These were thoroughly waterproof and insulated and were sent up from HQ in Split. I still have my pair – they were that good. But there was another item of equipment which I have mentioned previously, which needed crowbarring out of the hands of the quartermasters in Split, and that was the heavy-duty flak jackets with heart plates. The situation for UNPROFOR was getting very unsafe and the soldiers and vehicles were targeted more and more, as were the aid convoys. It took the Dutch Transport Battalion getting shot up and a piece to camera by the freelance journalist Malcolm Brabant, with a bit of inside information from me, to get them. And yes, I did mention it to the Commanding Officer. Perhaps they were on their way anyway.

The protective vest. Bosnia, 1993-4

I do not know the exact details of the following incident and despite extensive research I cannot find any reference to it. The Dutch (Belgian) Transport Battalion (DTB) were based in the Vitez pocket in Santici and their convoys provided resupply to UNPROFOR in central and northern Bosnia as well as food aid to the local populations. On this particular day, I was called to the MST as several Dutch soldiers were on their way in, having been attacked by mortar and small arms fire not far from their base.

One SNCO had multiple fragment wounds to his left upper arm and another soldier had been shot through the tip of his nose, but more importantly, one had been shot in the lower chest. If the high velocity round had not been stopped by his RBR body armour, he would have been in a body bag. As it was, he was only in for some severe bruising.

There was nothing to be done with the soldier's nose. It was a

I am holding the ceramic plate of the body armour worn by the Dutch soldier, in roughly the position it had been in when the round hit him. My finger is pointing to where the round had impacted. Bosnia 1993-4

384

through and through round which just traversed the fleshy tip. Though he too would be in for a lot of bruising, this lad was very lucky.

I had to deal with the SNCO's upper arm. His injury was due to multiple low-velocity fragments and a few days, after the usual wound excision and stabilisation of his humerus, which had been shattered, he was returned to DUTCHBAT and back to Holland land.

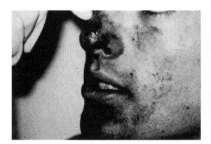

Gunshot nasal injury. Bosnia 1993-4

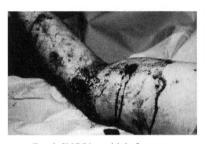

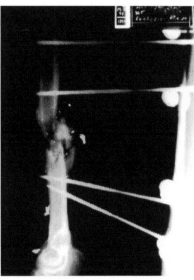

Dutch SNCO's multiple fragment
wounds of his left arm

Dutch SNCO's humerus fixed externally.
Quite a few metallic fragments remain.
Bosnia 1993-4

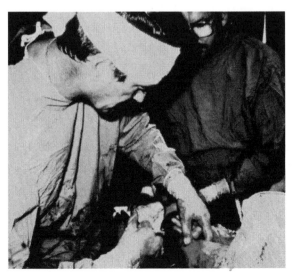

Ninja Surgeon. The operating theatre ISO containers had to be kept very warm, as patients under anaesthetic cannot maintain their body temperature well. Bosnia 1993-4

Whenever an Army goes to war and/or arms are carried by soldiers, experienced or not, there will be negligent discharges (NDs) of a weapon. This is a chargeable offence in the British Army and most others. Not long after the attack on the Dutch Transport Battalion, a young Dutch soldier went off duty. He went into his barracks but had not completely cleared his personal weapon, which was a submachine gun. He dropped it on the floor and the round in the chamber went off.

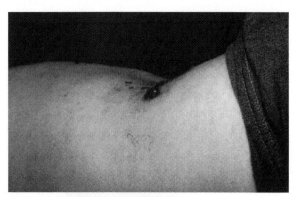

Negligent Discharge. Entrance wound in left flank. Bosnia 1993-4

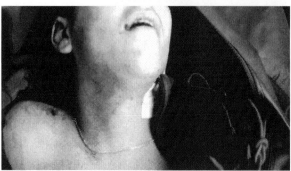

Negligent Discharge. Exit wound through right shoulder. Bosnia 1993-4

Though this unfortunate young man was brought to the MST alive, in spite of vigorous resuscitation, he died. Heart breaking, and another one for me to certify.

Another ND of a 9mm Browning side arm by one of the liaison officers working with the I PWO occurred in the Vitez School. I think it was at the handover from 1PWO to the Coldstream Guards. The round hit the floor (at least he had got that bit right) and shattered. About five or six of his fellow officers received low velocity fragment injuries, none particularly serious and only one requiring surgical exploration of his leg. The greatest injury was to this officer's pride, as he had had an exemplary tour of duty. All it takes is one moment of inattention.

I am still sticking with the DTB, because another one of their Sergeants was injured in a sniper attack on the lorry he was driving. The round went through the windscreen of the vehicle and ricocheted off the rear bulkhead. The bullet had lost its copper jacket and the mild steel core was heading straight for him. He must have turned slightly in his seat as disaster was looming. Luckily he had two pens in his sleeve (one I think was a Parker biro), and the round hit these and consequently, with considerably less velocity, was deflected into the muscles overlying his left shoulder blade and bounced off the bone.

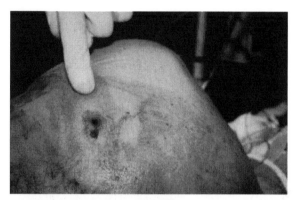

Entrance wound left shoulder blade. Dutch Sergeant convoy driver. Bosnia 1993-4

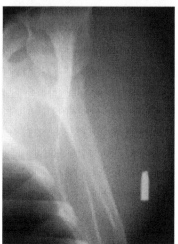

Mild steel core of the 7.62 mm round (with flattened tip), Bosnia 1993-4

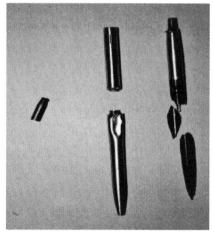

The round that I removed surgically shown alongside the two broken biros which may well have saved the owner's life. Bosnia 1993-4

I visited the Croat Hospital in the church in Nova Bila at least once a week, sometimes in a Land Rover ambulance, while at other times I would cadge a lift in an Armoured Personnel Carrier, depending on the intelligence assessment of the local activity.

Nova Bila War Hospital (Church) Bosnia 1993-4

I had become acutely aware that if I got hit, then unless there was another UNPROFOR surgical facility nearby which I did not know about, I would have had to rely on the local Croat hospital for urgent treatment, if they could spare the time and resources and of course if I was still alive.

I remember once handing over some blood packs, still usable for a few more days, some spare IV fluids and antibiotics. One of

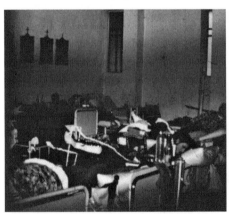

One of the wards in Nova Bila Hospital
Bosnia 1993-4

the female doctors asked me in excellent English, if I would come and see a badly-injured patient, and I accompanied her to the ward in the church. It was dark and cold, despite the efforts of what looked like a home-made wood burner. Beds were perilously close together from a cross-infection point of view, but there was nothing that could be done about that. I suppose there must have been about 30 or 40 injured.

The lad in question, for that was all he was, had lost a leg to an antipersonnel mine. He had lain injured in the cold for a considerable time and fluid and blood deficient, had gone into kidney failure, no doubt from an acute tubular necrosis (now called Acute Kidney Injury). The amputation had been surgically completed and I smelt the wound which was fine. However, the patient was soggy, sallow, drowsy and confused. I looked at his blood chemistry which was awful. His catheter bag was empty. He had no urinary output. It was obvious that he needed renal support until his kidneys recovered, which in a young man, without any other underlying pathology, may happen in a week or three. The female doctor asked me if I could get a renal dialysis machine.

"It's what we need" she said.

"No" I said, "It's not possible." Even if there was a spare one available, by the time it had been funded or requisitioned and transported through the confrontation lines with a technician and the necessary fluids, I would have retired.

"Then he's going to die," she said.

"Have you tried peritoneal dialysis?" I asked.

"No" she replied, "We don't have the catheters".

I knew that special catheters were designed for the job, but they were not going to appear either. I suggested that she use two Foley urinary catheters. "Under local anaesthetic insert a Foley, through his umbilicus, blow up the balloon and close the wound with a purse string suture" I said, "then put a second Foley into his pelvis in the same way. Then infuse a dialysate fluid [I suggested she look up what they had available that they could use] in through one tube and let it out through the other after a few hours, keeping a close eye on his blood chemistry. It may just keep him alive until his kidneys recover. Keep the catheters unobstructed with injections of saline."

I felt for this young doctor, but she was in a war zone. Her country was at war. She sighed and just said, "We need a dialysis machine".

There was nothing else I could do. I think the constant strain of working under the conditions that they found themselves in was taking its toll and I put it out of my mind. I had to remind myself, not for the first time, that it was their war, not mine. I was in it, not at it. We rejoined the other doctors, and after a couple of mugs of Slivovitz I left them to it. When I returned about a week later, I was told that the young lad had died. I did not ask if they had tried peritoneal dialysis.

Having written all that, I have just read the abstract for 'The Incidence and Outcome of Penetrating and Blunt trauma in Central Bosnia: the Nova Bila Hospital for War Wounded', in *The Journal of Trauma*:

Since February 1992, the civil war in the former Yugoslavia has left over 140,000 people dead. This study describes the injuries and outcome of patients treated at a provisional war hospital in Bosnia and compares mortality rates with war hospitals from prior armed conflicts.

This is a retrospective review of 1,703 trauma patients treated between March 1993 and October 1993 at the Nova Bila War Hospital.

In Bosnia, the overall mortality was 10.3% (5.0% dead on arrival and 5.3% in-hospital deaths). Head injuries, seen in 19.2% of patients, had a mortality of 23.8%. The odds of sustaining a gunshot wound were 2.8 times greater in Bosnia than in Vietnam (p < 0.05). The odds of sustaining a head injury were 1.1 to 1.6 times greater in Bosnia than in Lebanon and Afghanistan (p < 0.05). The overall mortality odds in Bosnia were 3.1 times greater than in Vietnam (p < 0.001) but were equal to those in Lebanon and Afghanistan.

Despite limited personnel and supplies, the in-hospital mortality rate was comparable with those found in other war hospitals. The Nova Bila Hospital represents a unique response to the great medical need brought about by the continued fighting in the former Yugoslavia.

J VanRooyen (et al) 1995 described the situation:

Despite donations from international relief organisations, the hospital remained ill-equipped to handle the large volume of patients from the nearby line of conflict (1000 metres). The single operating suite is located in the church basement, with a wood-burning autoclave and an intermittent electrical supply. Six physicians work amid frequent shelling to provide surgical and post-surgical care to – 130 inpatients and ten new trauma patients /day."

'...*Furthermore the Nova Bila Hospital lacked essential medical supplies and personnel, compared with the resources of a fully operational, mobile army surgical hospital unit and surgical personnel had no significant prior experience in the management of penetrating trauma. Surgical support from outside relief agencies was rarely available and used primarily for technical assistance. Evacuation to tertiary care facilities from the Nova Bila Hospital was inconsistent, provided only in exceptional circumstances by the United Nations Protection Force".*[29]

What they achieved under the most difficult of circumstances is remarkable. I may have had a very small part to play in it and I'm proud of that.

In their paper they mention casualty evacuation, so let's get on to that. It was quite simple in theory. A ceasefire had to be negotiated so that the Croatian injured, in the Vitez pocket, both combatants and non-combatants, could be evacuated from Nova Bila by convoy through Muslim territory back to Croatia, a journey of about 4-6 hours. The Muslim Army surrounding the Vitez pocket could get their injured to Zenica, wherein one of their main hospitals was situated, without crossing Croatian lines. From our point of view, the only Muslim evacuees needing to cross Croatian lines were those from Stari Vitez, and negotiations took place with the local commander, as I have already stated.

No, it was not simple in practice. Conditions had to be met, but more often than not each side would try and take advantage of the situation and the convoys of the wounded were frequently cancelled at the last minute as communications broke down. It was very frustrating, but the truth of the matter was that a wounded soldier needing specialised medical help became a bargaining chip. I was involved in a couple of these depressing episodes. On one occasion all the logistic preparations had been made, the date set only for the

---

29. J VanRooyen, M & Sloan, Edward & Radvany, AE & Perić, T & Kuliś, B & Tabak, V. (1995)

exercise to be cancelled. On another I had verified all the injured as best I could without taking down their dressings or removing their plaster splints. They were almost all loaded up on the marked lorries, when the evacuation was cancelled again for some reason. All the injured had to be unloaded and returned to the hospital. The Press Corps were always very interested in these activities.

When I first got into Stari Vitez at the start of my tour, there was a Bosniak who had been shot in the leg whom we could not take at the time. Eventually we were granted permission by the HVO to get him out and take him to Zenica, so back we went, a detail from the MST. I travelled in the ambulance, with my eyes shut as we crossed the confrontation line into the enclave, hoping that the Croat Combat Engineer had disabled and moved all the mines. We were shown to the house where the casualty was lodging and I helped carry him out. His leg was manky (not strictly a medical term) and he would definitely

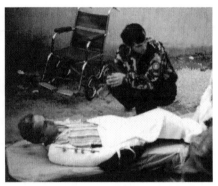

Nova Bila. The injured being taken out, Bosnia 1993-4

Nova Bila. Injured Croatian soldier settled on a stretcher, Bosnia 1993-4

Nova Bila. Casevac cancelled. Casualties return to the hospital, Bosnia 1993-4

Members of the Press Corps recording the event next to a bloody stretcher. I have no idea who these two were. Bosnia 1993-4

need some radical excisional surgery, if it was to be saved. The rest of him was all right though.

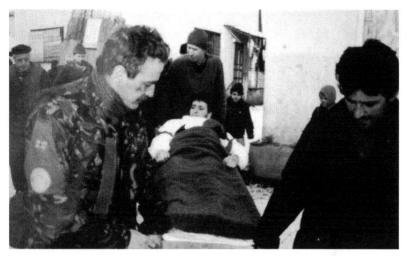

Evacuation of wounded Bosniak from Stari Vitez, Bosnia 1993-4

The remainder of my team stood guard and kept a wary eye. Though we had received permission to be there, I was always aware of the possibility of a sniper, either trigger happy or drunk. I was dropped off at the camp and the ambulance delivered the soldier to the hospital in Zenica.

Sometime later, I was informed that there was a very ill young Muslim woman in Stari Vitez. How this information got through to us, or what the lines of communication were, I had no idea. The HVO command in the Vitez hotel gave permission for us to evacuate her only if she was sufficiently sick, and only her. One casualty. Nobody else. I was firmly told that if we did not stick to that condition then any extra casualties would be returned to Stari Vitez or worse, and any further requests for access would be denied. That was pretty clear. We parked the ambulance outside the pharmacy in Stari Vitez. There were isolated gunshots ringing out, which sounded very close. We all took shelter inside as one round impacted in the wooden boarding protecting the building. It was high – deliberate, or a poor aim?

The patient in question was in the cellar of a house about 2-300 yards away. She was in constant pain, had a very swollen abdomen and was now vomiting. She had not moved her bowels, nor passed any flatus. I had to get to see her and the ambulance had to be moved to where she was, or as near as could be. This was something I was not looking forward to, but I was told that the young lad in the pharmacy whose picture I have alluded to above would lead me there. We criss-crossed the narrow alleyways and I followed in the boy's footsteps. He seemed to know which sides of the alleys were safe from sniper fire. It was not long before we reached the house in question and with some relief, I descended into the basement, which was full of women sheltering on the floor.

The atmosphere was foetid, and the women all looked at me with alarm. I pointed to the Red Cross on my arm in the hope that I could reassure them and made my way to the ill woman, whom the boy pointed out. Everywhere I looked I saw tired, gaunt, frightened faces. I briefly examined the woman. My spot diagnoses had been painfully awful as a medical student, but I had improved over the years. The patient was dehydrated and listless with a high pulse rate. Her tongue was like an old piece of leather. Her belly was very distended and she was very apprehensive when I put my ear to her swollen abdomen. I kept saying "It's OK" as I detected the tinkling bowel sounds that indicated an obstruction. She had a classical Caesarean Section scar, which I had noticed using my pen torch. I thought the most likely diagnosis was an adhesion obstruction caused by scar tissue from previous surgery and she needed urgent surgical exploration. We had to get her out.

I then noticed her son next to her, her only child, about six or seven years old. Her husband, I found out, had been killed in the war. I asked the young lad who had brought me here to go back to the pharmacy and tell them to bring the ambulance. All this was communicated in broken English with the help of some of the other women in the cellar. I signalled to the young woman that she needed her abdomen opened by drawing my finger vertically down her belly and then opening my hands as if I was opening a book. She nodded her understanding. A few minutes later my driver arrived with the ambulance, but there was a problem. She would not leave without her son, and no amount of pleading would make her change her mind. He was all she had left.

We could not take the boy. Only one casualty, that was the condition. If we left the mother, she would inevitably die a very painful death, and another family would have to take care of her boy. It would be the same if she was evacuated without him, but at least she would have a good chance of survival. I made a very difficult wartime decision, dictated by the terrible circumstances. I asked someone to tell the mother we would take her son with us and we got them both into the ambulance. Just before we reached the confrontation line, I opened the ambulance, took the boy out and handed him to one of the women who were following us. He screamed and his mother screamed. I closed the ambulance door and we drove back into the HVO held part of Vitez and on to Zenica, where the woman was treated immediately with resuscitation and surgery.

She had been in a war zone, Stari Vitez was under siege and she could not have survived her condition without surgery. In her best interests I had betrayed her trust in me and separated her from her child. She would recover from surgery and be safe in Zenica. If she and her son then both survived the war, they stood a good chance of being reunited at its end, whenever and wherever that would be. Surely I was right to have done what I did? However I cannot discount the fact that in doing what I thought would be best, I had been paternalistic. I had blatantly disregarded her expressed wishes and removed her destiny from her own hands. I had no right to take the decision I did.

That night I went to the Officers' Mess. I drank whisky alone and mulled things over in my mind. I hated being involved in this war. I wanted a bit more surgery and a little less fucking UNPROFOR. Unfortunately, I got more UNPROFOR, and it was worse, and when more surgery did come along, I really wished it hadn't.

Christmas is always a difficult time when you're away from family. We had the usual services and traditions. I had kept intermittently in touch with Angela and my two little girls by phone, but this was difficult. There was a small ISO container with four satellite phones rigged up, but connections were often unreliable and getting onto a phone involved a long wait. On the other hand, I managed to get hold of a couple of teddy bears as presents for the children, each appropriately nick named Bosnia Bear.

Me (centre), Christmas Day, Bosnia 1993[30]

The YouTube video this image is taken from encompasses the situation in Bosnia when I was there and puts some of what I have written into the correct perspective. At 5.22 minutes in, you can see me singing, as shown above, at the Christmas Service in 1993, with all the other officer out-of-tuners.

We held our concert for the Officers' Mess. The Lasva Valley ensemble belted out several well-known tunes. There was also a Christmas pantomime production, "Snow White" I think it was, bawdy and rude as to be expected. We, the officers, served the men their Christmas dinner and in the afternoon, we were entertained by the Bosniak artillery piece firing over our heads into the Vitez area, reminding the Croats that the war was not stopping for the festive season.

The war in the former Yugoslavia gave rise to genocide, ethnic cleansing and other war crimes. These were subsequently investigated by the Commission on Security and Co-operation in Europe and prosecutions were brought appropriately, after peace had been established, by the International Tribunal for the Prosecution of Persons Responsible for Serious Violations of International Humanitarian Law Committed in the Territory of the Former Yugoslavia since 1991, more commonly referred to as the International Criminal Tribunal for the former Yugoslavia (ICTY).

30. https://youtu.be/DrVLem8CPiQ John Needham Published on Oct 30, 2014

In fulfilment of its mandate, the Commission established an extensive database to compile information on individual cases, conducted studies on specific battles and instances of ethnic cleansing, and laid the groundwork for investigations of several mass grave sites in the former Yugoslavia. Testifying before the Helsinki Commission in April 1995, a Commission of Experts indicated they had identified 200,000 dead, most of them civilians, 800 prison camps and detention centres in which more than half a million people had been held, and 151 mass grave sites. Furthermore, they had investigated 1,600 cases of rape and forced impregnation of girls and women of all ages and received allegations of thousands of other cases of rape, sexual mutilation and torture. Genocide, ethnic cleansing, civilian and enemy combatant massacres were easy to ascertain, by the discovery of mass graves with the accompaniment of credible witnesses. But where did I come into all this? Despoliation of the dead, that's where.

I refer to the International Committee of the Red Cross (ICRC) with regard to the treatment of the dead: *Rule 113. Each party to the conflict must take all possible measures to prevent the dead from being despoiled. Mutilation of dead bodies is prohibited.*

This is also covered in the Geneva Convention. The obligation to take all possible measures to prevent the dead from being despoiled, or the prohibition of the despoliation of the dead, is set forth in numerous military manuals.

The prohibition of mutilating dead bodies in international armed conflicts is covered by the war crime of "committing outrages upon personal dignity[31].

The exact details of what I will now describe are hazy, so I will write in general terms. I was asked, as the highest and most experienced medical authority in the theatre of operations, if I would be able to examine some dead Croatian soldiers, killed in a recent battle (at Busovaca). The HVO command was claiming that the bodies of their soldiers had been mutilated after death by the BIH Muslim Army.

I was honest and said that all I could do was examine the bodies and see if the wounds were consistent with injuries sustained in battle.

---

31. Customary International Humanitarian Law: Volume 1, Rules By Jean-Marie Henckaerts, Louise Doswald-Beck, ICRC

Basically, I would try and advise as to whether a full investigation would be necessary.

In the evening, we drove up into the hills to a small Croatian village. I have no recollection of the name of the village or where it was. The road was very icy, the weather was absolutely freezing cold and the Land Rover was struggling to maintain traction. The liaison officer was driving, and we had a young Muslim girl to act as an interpreter. She, like all of the employed interpreters, was dressed in DPM combats and was enrolled as a member of UNPROFOR. We were met by the local priest and an HVO officer with several other soldiers hanging around. It was very dark, except in the church where I was led, which was lit with candles. The liaison officer and the young interpreter unsurprisingly chose not to accompany me. I was left with the priest and the HVO officer who spoke faltering English. I have never felt so nervous in my life.

I had brought my personal weapon, a box of surgical rubber gloves, a torch and a camera. They were not keen on me photographing their young dead, even though I stated it could be important evidence, so I took pictures of them surreptitiously.

There were about 10 young male soldiers wrapped in white sheets, each laid out in a coffin, perched on trestles with identifying crosses above them. The only illumination came from candles. Apart from a cold light breeze which whistled through the open doors of the church, causing the candles to flicker, it was deathly quiet. The main thought occupying my mind was, I do not want to be here, and I do not want to have to do this.

I opened the white sheets of each of the dead soldiers and examined them as carefully and respectfully as I could in the prevailing circumstances, changing gloves after each one. I took no notes. In spite of a running commentary on some of the dead by the HVO officer and his pointing out what he considered to be evidence of mutilation after death, all of the injuries that had been sustained were compatible, to my mind, with warfare.

On one dead soldier the HVO officer pointed to a large serrated wound overlying the sternum (breastbone), claiming he had been shot after death. I put my finger in the wound and felt a large piece of jagged metal, a fragment of some sort. He claimed another had had his throat cut after death, pointing to a small laceration in the neck. No, the wound edges were jagged, and the wound was relatively superficial. When I finished, I said that I would make my report to the authorities, but I would have to say that all the wounds could be explained by battlefield trauma. I expected some anger or disagreement with my opinion, but it didn't happen. I breathed a monumental sigh of relief as we returned to camp.

Next day we were off again to investigate another despoliation claim. I was tired from having had a sleepless night. The cost and futility of war were weighing heavily on my mind and I was getting too up close and personal in my efforts to be of assistance to the UN. In the Army there is a well-known acronym: REMF. It stands for Rear Echelon Mother Fuckers, those who never get to the sharp end of a conflict. I could have done with a bit of time as a REMF.

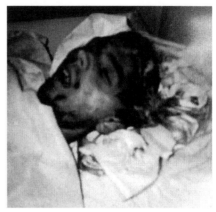

High velocity head wound in a dead Croatian soldier. Examined by me, somewhere in the Vitez pocket in Bosnia. 1993-4.

We drove into another Croatian village, just beyond Vitez. Once again, the name escapes me, if I ever knew it, and we eventually found the house, where I was expected to examine another corpse. The occupants, mainly women, were expecting us and immediately started wailing. The house itself was run down, poorly furnished and had the odd pock mark in the external plaster. Once again it was freezing. The gnawing cold just got into one's bones and stayed there. I was introduced to the householder, who looked old and worn out. He had the hangdog expression of someone who had lost too much, a look of perpetual suffering. Nothing could ever put the world right for him again, and through a nervous interpreter, I found out why. He had had four sons, but all were now dead and the last to die, his eldest, was in a coffin in one of the back rooms of the house. His was the corpse

I had come to examine. I accompanied the father, but first asked if the wailing could stop for a while, as I was having trouble collecting my thoughts and I was about a million miles away from my comfort zone. The women were spoken to and a harrowing silence ensued. On reflection, I think I preferred the wailing, because at least that represented the living.

I have forgotten the father's features, but I have not forgotten the look of absolute despair on his face. The coffin had been nailed closed, so the father picked up an axe and with the blade inserted between the body of the coffin and the lid, he levered it open, then carefully putting the lid down on the floor, he looked away. The young liaison officer and the interpreter, who was clearly very frightened, both turned away too. I was now the only one looking at the black plastic bag inside the box.

Carefully, I pulled the plastic down to reveal the face, both arms and the remaining torso of this poor man's eldest son. His lumbar spine was all that was left of him below his waist. His chest and both arms were pock marked and burnt. Rigor mortis, or the heat he had been subjected to, had caused his elbows and fingers to become contracted. There was no doubt in my mind that he had been killed by a High Explosive round, either artillery or mortar, and that the bottom half of his body had been blown away.

The father turned and drew his finger in a line along the bottom edge of his son's remaining abdominal skin, stating through the interpreter that his legs had been cut off by the enemy after death, but this could not be true, because a lot more of him other than his legs were missing; the whole of his pelvis for a start. He then added that his son had been found on the battlefield impaled on a stake and his remains had had to be lifted off the stake in order to retrieve him.

If my mind needed concentrating, then that statement did it. If what his father had said was true, then a war crime had indeed been committed, though some sort of independent verification would be needed. But there was something I could do. I had surgical gloves on. I rolled up my right sleeve and felt inside the cold torso of the dead man. Everyone looked away again. My hand and forearm disappeared along a track that does not exist in the human body, alongside the thoracic spine. It could easily have been caused by impalement. I did not say anything; indeed, I could not say anything. The old man, the liaison officer and the interpreter, were all now focusing their attention on me whilst averting their gaze from the remains in the coffin. I closed the black plastic bag and signalled to the father that he could replace the lid on the coffin of his son, as I had seen all I needed to see and this time, using the back of the axe, he hammered the nails home. I moved to a nearby sink, removed my gloves and washed up in the cold water.

I turned to the interpreter and put my hand on the father's shoulder. He did not shrink away. I said unemotionally, "Tell him that I am sorry for his loss". There were no more comforting words that I could ever say that would make him feel better, so I said no more. After she had translated that, I said, "Tell him that we have to go now but I will report my conclusions to the UN authorities".

I reported my conclusions. I never heard anything afterwards, but there again why would I? This instance of the complete disregard for International Humanitarian Law was one of thousands in this bloody conflict. Even though, during my active service, I had been witness to the most terrible deaths and dealt with the worst of injuries, the thought of this soldier, or what was left of him, being found impaled on a stake in the middle of a battlefield was hard to cope with. If I had heard about it, or read about it, I would have felt bad enough, but being so intimately confronted with the reality of it meant that the effect on me was to be much worse, not only because of what I had had to do, but because his father had been present, to watch me inspect and examine the remains of his eldest son, still recognisable as the human being he had been. His eldest son was 40 years old, five years younger than me, when he died.

I was deeply affected at the time, I know I was, but I managed to dismiss these memories from my mind until 28 years later, as I have already alluded to earlier in these memoirs. It was not so much the dreadful image of the dead soldier pictured overleaf which came back to haunt me, it was the way I had handled the situation. In my dreams, my mind, my conscience kept telling me that what I said to the son's father was not good enough. I had insufficiently expressed the empathy I had felt at the time, the fellow feeling I had as a father, for this father's loss of his four sons and the immeasurable agonies of sadness he was going through.

This is now, and my conscience in this time frame is right. I should have said more, been less cold, less impersonal, less matter of fact. But then, under the awful conditions which I have described, in truth I had no option but to accept the situation as it was, harden my heart again and move on quickly. If I was to do my job, that was the way it had to be. I was compassionate then, but I could not afford to dwell on the tragic circumstances of one soldier's death. I could not let it get to me. I kept saying to myself "it is not my war". Did that help? Yes then, but not now. Man's inhumanity to man knows no boundaries.

Dead Croatian soldier found on a stake, Bosnia 1993-4

If the image of the remains of the dead Croatian soldier in a plastic bag makes the reader uncomfortable, it should do. I make no apologies for refusing to sanitise war in the way that governments or the press often do, to make the ugly reality more palatable for the viewer and therefore easier to ignore. The price of war is grotesque; there should be no hiding from it. There is no dignity afforded for those embroiled in it. I have rarely spoken about these episodes in my life, not even to the Army psychiatrist who debriefed me at the end of my tour. It was the wrong time in any event and the human misery I had witnessed and dealt with was still locked away, besides which, as the reader will already be aware, I had other worrying things of my own on my mind.

At a body exchange, the war dead are exchanged by either side for identification and burial, closure for some I suppose, if the body of their husband or son is in the batch. It sounds civilised, but it isn't. The war dead were, once again bargaining chips, as simple as that and the preceding negotiations were long, unreasonable, tedious and conditional. Often after all the arrangements were made, with the UN present in force to supervise the exchange, the whole exercise was cancelled for a myriad of reasons just like the evacuation convoys.

I attended one exchange, the only one arranged when I was in Bosnia, ostensibly to provide immediate medical cover, but also to see if the opposing forces could act in a vaguely humane way. The well-known war reporter Martin Bell, the man in the white suit, was covering the event and I briefly met him, though he will not remember. He was damned fearless and when the sniper opened up he was unencumbered by body armour, boots or a helmet as we all ran to take cover in the ground floor of a block of empty flats. He was carrying some retained shrapnel received in Sarajevo, but it didn't slow him down. Obviously, the exchange was cancelled, but this was for a better reason than most.

Martin Bell in Bosnia 1993-4   Sheltering from sniper fire. Bosnia 1993-4

One night, Larry Hollingsworth bunked down with us in our accommodation. Based in Zenica, he was the representative of the United Nations High Commission for Refugees, and as such was responsible for the distribution of UN aid. He had served for 30 years in the Army prior to this appointment. We shared a bottle of whisky and put some of the world to rights. He said he couldn't do my job and I said I couldn't do his. He also told me that the UN was so top heavy and bureaucratic that for every one million pounds it was given by member nation states, only one pound translated into aid.

In early January I decided to hold a Port and Poetry evening for the MST and associated personnel, thus including the Coldstream Guards Regimental Medical Officer, Lt Col Kevin Cogbill, and his team of medics. This of course was greeted with howls of derision, which changed when I said that the officers would pay for the port if the senior and junior ranks could persuade the chefs in the cookhouse to donate the cheese and biscuits. Each attendee would have to compose a poem that reflected their tour here, or the war in Bosnia, or anything they thought appropriate. There would be a vote for the winner, who would be crowned MST Poet Laureate.

Well, we had a bloody good evening. Some poems were presented shyly and quietly, others were belted out confidently. This is the winning poem:

The Bluey

"Dear mother" the bluey read
"I'm fine, how are you?" her son said.
The letter sent from across the sea.
A place where most people could not imagine to be.
He was there to help and protect his kind,
A task he did not mind.
The differences he made may have been few
But with him here the people's chances grew.
His mother could never picture the everyday sight
Of killing, hunger, desperation and plight
Of the battle to survive which the people here fought.
He never wrote what he really thought.
He asked of his family and if they were well
Of himself and his feelings he could not tell.
For these new experiences were bold and frightening,
His patience and strength were everyday slightening.
He longed for the day when home he would fly.
The letter from a son to his mother ended
With a simple "GOODBYE".

The MST Poet Laureate was awarded, in January 1994, to Private M Munro RAMC one of the Operating Theatre Technicians.

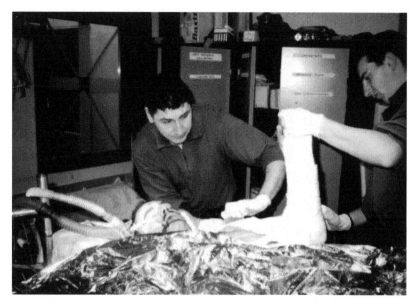

The Poet Laureate to be, Private Munro RAMC (on the right), holding up the injured Canadian soldier's broken arm. Bosnia 1993-4

On the 27th January 1994, Angela informed the Commanding Officer of the Cambridge Military Hospital that she was leaving me, and he advised her not to tell me whilst I was in still in Bosnia. Of course, this would not stop her, which she made clear, so a psychiatrist was consulted and the consensus was that she should definitely not tell me whilst I was still operational in Vitez. She should make sure that I was non-operational in Split and therefore on my way back home and no longer responsible for the welfare of the UN Protection Force. However, she did not wait until I was in Split, or bother to ask me my whereabouts and therefore, more importantly, my operational status when informing me.

I phoned my wife 48 hours before I was due to leave the theatre of operations and go to Split in Croatia for a couple of days of R and R prior to returning home. It would be the first time in four months that I would be off duty and I needed to relax in the safety of a hotel in Split, to recharge my batteries and try and put the last four months experience away in a mental box. It was not to be.

I made the call from a makeshift telephone booth, in an old (International Organisation for Standardisation) ISO container. It was very cold, very small and afforded virtually no privacy. I was surrounded by other soldiers all talking to their girlfriends and wives about the usual trivia that I had fervently wished to be talking about to my own wife. I had essentially phoned to give Angela my travel details so that the family could prepare for my arrival home. She was totally uninterested.

"Is everything all right Angela?" I asked. "You sound a bit distant, odd".

"No" she replied. My heart sank.

"Oh no, this is going to kill me,"

"Yes," she said. "It is".

"You are seeing him again, aren't you?" I pressed, already knowing the answer.

"Yes. I'm leaving you. I didn't really want to tell you now, but I've been sleeping with Brian. I want a divorce to live with him." And with that she ended the call.

Unsurprisingly, my emotions were all over the place following that news, but I was still on active duty and expected to be able to respond to any surgical emergency. There was no one else. Why did she tell me when I was still operational, I kept asking myself? Could she not have waited until I had reached Split or returned home? She had said on the phone that she didn't really want to tell me now, so why the hell had she?

She knew that I was still working, because I remember telling her that my colleague, the relief surgeon, was going to take over from me at 1700hrs the following night and that there was to be a leaving party for me which I was looking forward to, as I would finally be off duty.

Sitting in the Officer's Mess being consoled by the medical officer from the Coldstream Guards and the padre certainly helped, but consuming quite a few stiff measures of whisky was unwise. I heard the phone ring and the Mess steward called for me, fortunately before my self-control spiralled into freefall. I was notified that three aid workers had been shot in Zenica and would be extracted back to the Medical Support Troop as soon as possible. It was for exactly this reason that Angela had been instructed not to tell me she was leaving me until I was off duty.

The roads were very bad and their Estimated Time of Arrival (ETA) was in about two hours. Somehow I managed a mental backflip and put aside my personal problems. These injured men needed me in professional mode, someone who could surgically rescue them from the shit they had wandered into. I left the Officer's Mess and tried to get some rest before they arrived.

One of the aid workers had been shot dead, executed in fact, and the other two had received First Aid at the local Muslim hospital. On 29 Jan 1994 the Independent newspaper reported, *'Britons' icy escape from death: As Bosnia convoys are suspended, aid driver tells how gunmen murdered his colleague*[32]*'*.

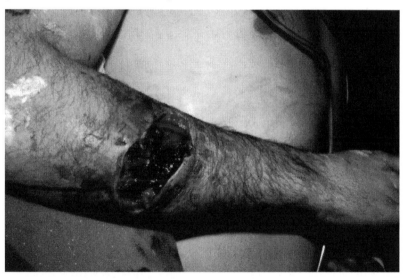

Gunshot wound to Simon King's right forearm. Bosnia 1993-4

Though I was not in a good place, one of the aid workers was in a far worse one. Paul Goodall, a father of four, had been shot three times in the back of the head. I certified him dead in the back of a Warrior armoured vehicle, after the retrieval of his body. If he had ever felt the degree of emotional pain that I was trying to ignore, then at least for him it was all over and in some of my more despairing moments, I envied him.

---

32. Christopher Bellamy, Vitez

I operated on the other two aid workers, one of whom had been shot in the back and the other in an arm and knee. I was very conscious of the fact that my mind was not on what I was doing a lot of the time, but fortunately the professionalism of my staff managed to keep me on the straight and narrow and their well-trained attitude succeeded in making me concentrate. It took all night.

After the surgery was over I was desperately tired, but sleep eluded me. I tossed and turned, my mind in turmoil as it flipped from my marriage woes to the operations I had just undertaken. Eventually I gave up the fight, got dressed and reviewed the two patients at around mid-morning on 28 January 1994.

As to be expected, there was a lot of media interest in the incident involving these three aid workers. Perhaps this was a good thing, because my mind was focused on the requirements of the injured and dealing with the press coverage, which thankfully gave me less opportunity to dwell on what I anticipated would be a very difficult next few days on a personal level. I was wrong. It would be a very difficult 25 years.

After I had operated on the two aid workers, officers and friends within the British Contingency of the United Nations, a number of the officers of the Coldstream Guards amongst them, gave me unbelievable assistance by making all the necessary arrangements to get me back to the UK earlier than one would have thought humanly possible, so I could try and salvage something from this dire situation.

The next few days were a blur. There are some things that I distinctly remember; the difficulty in acting as normally as I should have done at the party the MST held for my departure and that of my anaesthetist, Major Chris Taylor. The looks of sympathy and pity that I got from my friends and colleagues and the rather embarrassed silences that followed when we were talking together made me very angry that this should have happened to me here, in this place, in this situation. I felt that this was too much to bear. If I didn't make it back to Split, as the routes were dangerous, then perhaps it would be no bad thing. Exhausted and demoralised by my gruelling tour of duty, I did not feel as though I could face what would wait for me when I got home.

I left early next morning on transport to Split in Croatia with my mind still distracted. If things had gone wrong with the operations I had carried out following that phone call, my career could have been seriously damaged, and if there had been more casualties than we already had to deal with, I would not have been able to cope to the best of my abilities. It was unforgivable that as the only surgical asset in the middle of a war zone, I was damn near incapacitated by callous selfishness. Angela's own needs always had to come first, regardless of the consequences. I have thanked God many times for giving me the inner strength to do what I had to do at the time.

If the aid workers had died, how would their families have coped knowing that they had lost their loved ones, not from their having been caught up in a war zone, not from a lack of medical supplies, not from a lack of medical expertise, but because of a vain woman who was so wrapped up in her own needs, so engrossed in her love affair, that she could think of nothing or no one else and could not wait a second longer to impart her news when she did, even though for operational reasons, she had been expressly forbidden from doing so by her local Commanders?

I challenged Angela about this on my return home. She argued that as the patients I had operated on in Vitez hadn't died or suffered as a result of her telling me the marriage was over when she did, she had not done anything wrong. She was indifferent to the fact that her behaviour had risked jeopardising any successful surgical outcome for these two injured ex-soldiers (or anyone else under my care). As nothing untoward had happened, she considered herself totally blameless. This was not the view that would subsequently be taken by her superiors. Her failure to ever accept responsibility for the consequences of her own actions would become an enduring problem during the end of our marriage, for the army and with regard to how she subsequently dealt with the children.

When I had phoned home from Split, prior to my flight on the Sunday, my seven-year-old daughter had answered the telephone, and once she realised it was me, she said the words that I hope no other father will ever have to hear and which I will remember to my dying day: "Please Daddy, please come home Daddy, Mummy said you are not coming home, please come home Daddy". I could hardly find the words to reply, and then the phone was taken out of my daughter's hands; my call cut off.

I spent a day or so at a hotel and flew out of Croatia on an Air Croatian flight, landing in Luton airport a few hours later. I was picked up by my Commanding Officer and his driver with a view to being taken directly home to my house. He filled me in on a few more details of what had happened from his end.

CHAPTER 39

Meat Cleaver

At the end of January 1994, I arrived home sometime in the evening. Angela opened the door. Once again there was no sadness or remorse in her expression, just a silly little grin, which she told me was a sign of nervousness. My children rushed to greet me and I swept them up into my arms. I could not control the tears that came. The children assumed that I was crying tears of joy at returning, and of course it was that too, but I was also mainly crying out of self-pity. Here I should have been in the homely and safe environment of my family, when in fact there was nothing. Angela was cold and emotionless as only she could be. She simply uttered the words "Hello David". I looked at my eldest daughter and remembered when I had spoken to her on the phone from Split and had tried to ensure that Angela knew I was coming home earlier than anticipated and despite what she had tried to engineer.

Following my difficult journey back from Croatia, I was shattered. However another sleepless night followed, this time in the company of my wife, who in this respect did not wish to discuss very much beyond saying that she had thought about the situation at length and had steeled herself for two years in order to give me this news. Suffice to say that sleeping in my own bed, in my own house, with my own family around me, brought very little joy.

Keeping a diary of events after my return from Bosnia was not something that occurred to me before this happened. However a good friend and neighbour called Malcolm said to me, "I can only say one thing, keep a diary. Whatever happens it will get better, whatever happens you will survive this awful situation, whatever happens you must be able to look back and see what you went through". That, in its simplest form, is why I am writing about this particular part of my life. It is a tale which relates the survival of my surgical career, despite everything and everyone that threatened it.

I took Malcolm's advice seriously. Another neighbour, Ian, whom I also had a great affection for, told me to "remove all the alcohol from your house, because alcohol and emotion, temper and hurt don't help, and it will remove your inhibitions. With alcohol you may not be responsible for your actions". I took his advice too and threw every drop of alcohol out of the house. I only drank in the company of these very good neighbours. I was and always will be eternally grateful for those two bits of advice, but it would be remiss of me if I didn't also mention my very good friend Gerry. We shared a lot of similar views and we were extremely close regarding our backgrounds and his service connections.

With his experience of dealing with difficult sets of circumstances in his previous profession (he had served in the British South African Police) he had a remarkable ability to sense a situation and he (and his wife) saw right through Angela. Invariably his advice to me during the many difficult situations I was to face during the following months was, "Do nothing. Give her enough rope and she will hang herself".

However, I must say that when all this started, I could not have conceived that events would turn in the direction that they eventually did, but I had resolved, at that early stage, that I would fight for what I perceived to be right for me and right for the children, given my wife's conduct.

I began my diary on 2 February 1994, a couple of days after I returned from Bosnia, and what I write now is based on the details of those entries as I wrote them at the time. The entries understandably have a personal bias and it would be improper of me to suggest that this was not the case. However, as a doctor, it has always been a part of my job to record accurate, contemporaneous notes and I feel that in this regard my training has not let me down. When I read through the entries again and again, I can put my hand on my heart and say, this is what happened. It is true.

Angela had told her own Commanding Officer about her affair and was asked for her resignation. At the time she informed her CO, I had been completely unaware of her plans and believed that I would be returning to my wife back in the UK, whom I thought actually wanted me home, judging by the letters she had sent me.

Angela hadn't been the slightest bit discreet whilst I was away in Bosnia. Her boss had suspected the affair, having seen Angela at work with love bites on her neck, during the period that Brian Taylor had been back in the UK during January 1994 whilst on compassionate leave from N. Ireland.

Brian's wife had made a complaint to the Grenadier Guards Families' Officer about the affair and made it clear she intended to divorce her husband on the grounds of his affair with my wife. On my return to the UK, I too found myself forced to write to the Families Officer of the Grenadier Guards and ask him to instruct Brian Taylor to desist from phoning my wife at my family home, especially when I was on-call for the hospital. His prolonged conversations with her, often in my presence and charged at my cost by Angela, jeopardised my ability to respond promptly to emergencies and therefore to the safety of patients, which could not be ignored. The reader should bear in mind that mobile phones were in their infancy at this time, and as I did not own one, there was no alternative way for the hospital to get in touch with me.

For those who have not served in the armed forces or been married to someone in the forces, military rules might seem a little draconian, but they exist for good reason. In the 'Discipline and Standards Paper[33]', the army sets out its regulations regarding conduct, stating:

---

33. Discipline and Standards paper 21 October 1993

'The most serious cases of social misconduct involve adultery within the military community. It is essential that military personnel are not worried about the integrity of their marriages at any time, but especially when deployed away from their home base. Equally the morale of families is dependent on the knowledge that whilst the unit is deployed away from its peacetime location any extra-marital relationships will be considered unacceptable.

All incidents of misconduct which adversely affect the integrity of an officer are to be reported by the Commanding Officer to the next higher authority.'

How Angela behaved in the pursuit of her own happiness was not just a problem for me, it was a serious problem for my employers, the Army, who expected me to be able to perform the duties for which they paid me and I was commissioned to do. Surgery is an extremely challenging field of work at the best of times, even when feeling emotionally and physically buoyant. Any mistake I made, literally had the potential to curtail someone's life, not to mention end my career.

In addition, each time that seeing Brian took priority in Angela's life she unceremoniously dumped the children and left me in the position of having to find an array of volunteers, friends, neighbours, or even work colleagues, to act as short notice babysitters so that I could fulfil my commitments to the hospital. I was working full time with on-call and had effectively become a single parent overnight. Angela would flounce out of the house to be with Brian whenever she felt like it and breeze back into the lives of the children four of five days later as if everything was perfectly normal, at which point the children would just be pitifully grateful for any morsel of recognition she gave them, before she disappeared off out again with Brian.

On the occasions when Angela deigned to grace us with her presence at home, she was verbally abusive, confrontational and physically violent towards me and remained obstructive towards the hospital being able to contact me and vice-versa. She was trying to get me out of the house. Therefore it didn't take long before things began to take a sinister turn and Angela started threatening me on a regular basis. I began to think she was bordering on the brink of insanity and needed help. She warned me that if I ever brought up her conduct in court, I would be dead. I would be "killed from 300 metres away". "If I leave the house," she said, "I will take the children and if you get in my way, I will dispose of you"[34]. "Brian's friends and relatives from Hereford (alluding to the SAS) can't wait to kill a senior officer". "You will be dead when you walk out of the courtroom door". "You cut short my Army career," she claimed, "by making me have children"[35].

When the mail arrived with my divorce petition in it, citing Angela's adultery, she read it and went up in smoke[36], screwing up the papers, throwing them away and then emptying the bin all over me in the bed where I was lying. "What's your problem?" I asked her. "You've got what you wanted." Her face contorted with fury. "I HAVE NOT. IT IS NOT WHAT I WANT!" she screamed. She then proceeded to pull the bed covers off me, trying to tear them, then kicked me and hurt herself in the process. She slammed the bedroom door shut painfully on my hand before going downstairs and turning the stereo up to deafening levels, and then left the house, taking my elder child with her, leaving the younger behind, confused and upset. Angela's behaviour was getting worse by the day.

In response to my petition for divorce, Angela submitted a cross petition accusing me of unreasonable behaviour. Incredibly, she specifically denied adultery, even though she had already admitted it to the Army and to me.

Earlier I alluded to the significance of the loving letter I had received from Angela two days after I had arrived in Bosnia. When I returned home to the UK, she made a claim to Social Services that the night before I left for Bosnia I had 'savagely attacked and buggered her' and as a result she said she had lost all respect for me. However, in between sending me this letter and making this allegation, she had obviously forgotten that she had written me a further 22 loving letters, which a judge would later read. For some inexplicable reason, after she had made her complaint to Social Services about this traumatic attack, she completely forgot to include it amongst examples of my unreasonable behaviour in her divorce cross-petition seven months

---

34. Diary 6 Mar 1994
35. Diary 18 Apr 1994
36. Diary 16 Apr 1994

later, though she did not forget to complain that seven years earlier I had 'played tennis in Singapore'.

The attack was a complete invention, the product of a desperate, irrational mind going out of control. This was just the start of many allegations she would make against me. In Angela's world, the concept of truth was just that – a concept. She did not need to be bound by it; the truth was whatever she wanted it to be at any given time, as long as it suited her purposes. Why should she have to check whether her claims were even remotely plausible? I was beginning to understand how her mind worked, or rather didn't. Unsurprisingly a judge would later say that the allegation was 'unjustified' and he did not believe her evidence.[37]

The children were now becoming significant pawns in her game plan. "I shall tell the children how you have destroyed their mother," she said. "They will see what I have and what you have. I shall tell them that's what men do; they destroy women." "Don't talk such nonsense" I said to her. "Don't indoctrinate the children". "I will" she said, "They are my daughters; they are growing up just like me. They'll hate men. I'll tell them all about what you've done to their mother." And that is exactly what she did[38]. She would indoctrinate the children to hate me, to hate anyone who might be seen to 'control' or 'bully' her or them, or more accurately, challenge them and make them accountable.

I had been advised by my legal team that no matter what, I was not to leave the matrimonial home and risk being accused of abandoning the children. By this stage I was very worried about Angela's increasingly irrational and volatile behaviour. She needed help, which I had suggested many times. She agreed she did, but I knew she wouldn't seek it.

"I swear on (my eldest child's) life I will kill you," Angela told me, "You'll be dead and I won't have a problem with that... By the time they get me to the psychiatrist you'll be dead. I'll kill you with a blunt instrument. You are right to lock your door (at night in the spare room)" she warned me. "On (my eldest child's) life I'll kill you if you get the children".

---

37. Mr Justice Ewbank, 24 Feb 1995
38. Diary 12 May 1994

I told her I had a right to apply for residence of the children, especially in view of the erratic way she was behaving[39]. "The children are MINE" she spat at me. "I made them". *Sperm?* Just a thought. "I sweated agony for them. I am cloning them. They will be just like me. I am making them just like me. Already they are just like me" she screamed. "Forget it David, you'll never have them".

It was when I was trying to speak to my mother on the phone in French, as was normal for us, that Angela started to go mad. "I'm dangerous and I'm going to kill you now!" she screeched, kicking and punching me with rage. She threw the phone at the TV, breaking it in the process, and then climbed up on a stool to get the pickaxe handle from the top of the wardrobe where I kept it in case of burglars. She punched me in the mouth, pulled off my gold neck chain, breaking it as she did so, kicked me several times so hard that she hurt her own foot, and then caught me on the back with the pickaxe handle before I managed to remove it from her. My mother at this point, was still hanging on the other end of the phone and heard the commotion.

I retreated to my own bedroom and shut the door, but Angela followed me and stormed into my room after having practically broken the door down. She was wild eyed, demented and irrational. Another diatribe would follow. "I'll just tell the judge I got a buzzing in my head and everything went black. I am premenstrual and homicidal; I am going to kill you tonight. I shall come back in three hours and batter you to death". "If Brian was here, he would kill you". If I had been a woman on the receiving end of that sort of abuse, I would have been granted a restraining order.

Angela would claim that I had hit her in the mouth, but this was not true. She had hurt her mouth when she had launched herself at me, and I had held up my forearm to defend myself. I had a split upper lip, a sore neck and a scratch down my back, which was all documented in A & E at the hospital the next day. I hid the pickaxe handle.

When Angela later received a letter from my solicitors informing her that I had found photographic evidence of her adultery with Brian in my bed, she went down to the kitchen, got hold of a meat cleaver and proceeded to storm up to my room to destroy it and attack me. The

---

39. Diary 20 Jun 1994

children, just five and seven years old at the time, were at home and became distraught. Angela slashed indiscriminately at the furniture, fixtures and fittings with the meat cleaver, waving it around wildly and threatening to kill me as she chased me up and down the stairs. The children ducked out of her way. She had no concern for their safety and no insight as to the trauma it would inflict on them; I called the police.

I could not disarm her, it was too dangerous as she swung the blade in front of her; my hands were my livelihood. She then ran into the main bedroom locked the door and almost instantly became 'normal'. She unlocked the door, came out and announced that she would like to bath the children. It was quite extraordinary.

I spoke to my solicitor about Angela's mental state of health and asked whether I could get an injunction and non-molestation order, as the kids and I were being severely traumatised by events. "You'll never get the children," Angela told me, "I'll slit their throats first, then you'll have neither of us. What do you think of that?" I could not take the risk that she might do it. She was incapable of considering the consequences of what she said and did. She had by this stage admitted to a sexual relationship with Brian Taylor (which commenced in 1991) in a plea of mitigation to the Army Board and I learnt that at Angela's instigation, Brian had resigned from the Army to avoid being posted to Canada and to spare her own career.

In desperation I decided to take the children with me to book a holiday in Spain and escape their mother's madness. On my return from booking the flights, Angela became hysterical. "You'll never get the children, they are mine; I'll kill you first. You'll be dead!" she yelled. I trudged upstairs as she followed me ranting and raving and then she promptly threw two cups of hot tea over me and partially over the children as well, though fortunately neither were scalded. She was becoming totally uncontrollable. She stormed into my room and informed me that she was going to smash something, which she then proceeded to do, smashing my teacup on the windowsill and cutting her left wrist in the process.

The children were very anxious when they saw her blood, which she was deliberately dripping all over the carpet. I managed to coax her downstairs and cleaned and dressed her cuts; she was wailing and rocking herself. In hindsight I wish I'd left her where she was to bleed to death. It transpired that she had been grilled by the Army Special Investigations Branch, which had included questioning about the incident with the meat cleaver which I had been advised to report.

"I am not a danger to my children" wailed Angela, but she failed to understand that she was a very real danger to them. She then performed another extraordinary volte face. I was the one who now wanted a divorce not her, and she would no longer agree to it. "I don't want a divorce" she suddenly proclaimed. "I shall just refuse. I'll tell the judge that I just made a horrendous mistake and I want to change my mind". As simple as that.

Almost in the same breath she then announced to the children that she was joining us on holiday in Spain. Of course, I had to disappoint the children, who were mightily confused, and told them that it wasn't true. I told Angela again and again that she seriously needed help, but she replied "No, you'd only use it against me". I wouldn't need to the way she was carrying on, as she was rather making my case for me[40].

I locked myself in the spare bedroom, barricaded the door and tried to get some sleep. Next morning I noticed that my passport was missing. Angela had taken it and demanded to see the tickets and my receipt for the flights to Spain in exchange for it. "I'm just making sure that you don't take my babies away and never bring them back" she said. If I'd known then what I know now, that is exactly what I should have done.

As Brian's wife was getting an injunction to keep him away from her house, I was worried he would sleep in my house yet again whilst I was away in Spain. As it turned out, Brian Taylor sleeping in my house, in my bed, with my wife whilst I was away, was the least of my worries; my alarm bells were certainly ringing.

---

40. Diary 2 Aug 1994

CHAPTER 40

The Great Bell

Officially, the Elizabeth Tower bell in the Palace of Westminster is called the Great Bell, though it is better known by the name 'Big Ben'. Thus the words 'great' and 'bell' go together, and so it was that a young artillery soldier called Gunner Bell had the word 'great' prefixed to his name. On ward rounds he was referred to as the Great Gunner Bell. This was not appropriate, unless it referred to the stoic way in which he accepted his self-inflicted injury and the almost inevitable consequences.

When I first came across him about 30-odd years ago, he was already in deep trouble. He was not my patient, but at the time combined ward rounds were held once a week and he was reviewed fruitlessly every Friday morning by a large gaggle of military medical personnel including me. A few months before he had been posted with his Regiment to BAOR (British Army of the Rhine) and found he had little to do to occupy his time. He had also married young and regretted it. He became depressed and contemplated committing suicide.

One afternoon, alone in his quarter, with several cans of lager on board, he was watching an old black and white film during which a lovesick character who had been spurned by the girl of his dreams drank a large amount of liquid from a bottle which had 'BLEACH' written on it in capital letters. The film depicted his death, in seconds, as a result. Gunner Bell went into the kitchen to retrieve another can of lager and noticed the household bleach by the sink. In an instant he had swapped the intended lager for the bleach and drunk almost the whole bottle. He did not die instantly, although the bleach was the last thing he ever swallowed. He developed an horrendous symptom complex from this corrosive liquid which required protracted treatment in intensive care, but the cause of his demise was the irreversible damage he did to his oesophagus, which resulted in chronic and intractable inflammation, the formation of multiple thick fibrous strictures (narrowings) and the removal of unobstructed communication between his mouth and his stomach, such that the 1.5 litres of saliva that he and other humans produce daily and is normally swallowed had to be spat into a bowl by his bedside. He was nursed head up in bed to try and prevent aspiration (reflux) of this saliva into his lungs during the night.

It was impossible to try and define his oesophageal injury, and with his continuing deterioration not even the bravest of thoracic surgeons would contemplate replacing his damaged oesophagus and stomach with an alternative conduit, for example the colon. His only nourishment was by Total Parental Nutrition (liquid solutions into a main vein) and still hopeful, still jolly and still oblivious of the immense harm he had caused himself, he finally succumbed to bronchopneumonia. The flash to bang time of his successful suicide was several months.

In the literature there are differing reports about the deleterious effects of imbibing household bleach. It all rather seems to depend on the concentration, amount ingested and the length of time that the upper digestive tract is exposed to the corrosive. From time to time there are reports of this method being used to commit suicide, but believe me there are much quicker and more comfortable ways of doing it.

The Genesis 11 Church of Health and Healing was founded by Jim Humble, who is its Archbishop. A former scientologist who claims to be a billion-year-old god from the Andromeda galaxy,[41] he has discovered and promotes Miracle Mineral Supplement, which he and his church claim cures HIV, malaria and everything in between, including autism. Mix together his supplement as instructed and you have a nice dilute solution of the industrial bleach, chlorine dioxide. As of August 15th 2019 this solution could still be obtained, as MMS from Amazon and Walmart for that matter, marketed as Miracle Mineral Solution, MMS or water purification solutions. There are many testimonials on social media as to the efficacy of this treatment and Jim Humble claims that as a result of his efforts in Africa, many thousands of the indigenous populations which he treated are now malaria-free.

Is there a lesson in this? I suppose if you live in any part of the malaria belt, feel a bit ill and shivery, and good old Jim's miracle solution is not to hand, then try drinking a large amount of chlorinated swimming pool water if available and bleach yourself back to health.

---

41. https://rationalwiki.org/wiki/Miracle_Mineral_Supplement

CHAPTER 41

Sunburn

Prolonged exposure to the sun can be more harmful than most people realise, and even if it is only for a short period, the sun can cause permanent damage to one's health and future wellbeing. During the summer of 1994 I got seriously sunburnt. It was a deeply painful experience and I was scarred for many years afterwards; I still am. There was nothing that any chemist could have supplied that would have protected me.

I took my children on holiday to our villa near Mojácar, Spain, without Angela. I had flown into Alicante airport and driven to La Parata where my villa was located, just as the adjacent mountain was ablaze with a wildfire. For a short time, I had some peace and could concentrate on the needs of the children. However, it was not to last. Just a week later, on 16 August whilst still in Spain, I found myself going from hero to zero in the time that it took to print four words in a huge font on the front page of the *Sun* newspaper. 'RUMPTY IN THE RANKS!' screamed the headline, printed in bold capitals covering most of the page. 'Army Captain Angie faces sack for sex with her Sarge' - Exclusive by John Kay.

The report read: *'A married woman Captain was facing the sack last night over her passionate affair with a sergeant. Besotted blonde Angela Jackson has ignored orders to end the romance. She is expected to be the first female officer booted out for breaking the Army's strict rules on illicit sex with comrades. And she is in trouble because she fell for someone from a lower rank – frowned on by top brass as "undermining an officer's position"*[42]*'.*

With that, my world completely fell apart. Angela proceeded to denigrate both me and her employers during a spate of cringeworthy articles, recounting her life story in and out of the bedroom with me and her lover. It initially spanned two weeks, with all manner of newspapers syndicating the details. Her story was even reported in Europe, in the International Press and as far afield as Zimbabwe.

At about 9 a.m. the next morning, I answered the door to my villa to find that there were two reporters outside. My memory about this is hazy, not least because, unsurprisingly, I had a hangover. I was greeted with the headline, 'My Sarge is a sex bomb. Captain Crumpet tells of her lust for Palace guard Brian'.

Sun newspaper 17 August 1994

42. Sun newspaper 16 Aug 1994

'Col Jackson is on holiday in the family villa in Mojácar, North East Spain, with their daughters [R] six and [A] five', stated the reporter. *'He heard about his wife's revelations in yesterday's Sun when a pal rang from England. Later he battled his emotions as he read faxed copies of our exclusive story about his wife's affair with dad of two Sgt Taylor. Drawing deeply on a cigarette he said "How can she do this to me and the children?"... yesterday the surgeon went swimming with his daughters trying to carry on as usual... "I'd just like to continue the holiday with my children and try to keep some sense of normal for their sake"*[43].

The reporters asked me a few questions, but I fobbed them off and went to my neighbour's villa with the children to use their phone to speak to my solicitors. It was only then that I found out that Angela had stripped the matrimonial home of all its contents with Brian Taylor's help, rendering it uninhabitable. In my absence my solicitors had immediately taken the matter before a judge in Reading County Court. I took the children to my friend Jack's house, but the press found me there too. Jack was a cockney who had emigrated to Spain for reasons I shan't go into, but he knew of someone who could 'get rid of' my problem for £500, 'you get my drift'. I should have taken him up on the offer. Anyway, he was quite abrupt with the reporters who asked me for a short statement and a photograph to prove that the kids were okay, which I reluctantly agreed to. Eventually I found refuge with other friends who lived off-grid in the campo (countryside) where we would never be found, and I will forever be indebted to them for that kindness. We still share a friendship to this day.

On 18 August after reporters had informed me of Angela's actions back in the UK, the *Sun* reported on my reaction to the news. *'I was in Bosnia while that b****** was bedding my wife. Cheated Colonel's fury'*. *'Col Jackson is on holiday in the family villa in Mojácar, north east Spain with their daughters... "I deeply regret the actions of my wife and Colour Sgt Taylor and the dreadful effect of their revelations on four innocent children. What on earth does she think she is doing?"'*.

"For me saving lives is so important - and this is what has happened to mine. All I wanted was a happy married life. I work 100

---

43. Sun newspaper 17 Aug 1994

hours a week. I love my job and the Army. I often ask myself, what did I do to deserve this."[44].

Of course, I have the answer now; I was stupid enough to ignore the warning signs. I had married a mendacious pretender.

If Angela's position in the Army had been tenuous before, then what she did next was certainly a career end move. On 19 August she appeared on the front page of the *Sun* newspaper alongside the caption of 'Captain Crumpet Gets Her Kit Off', thus 'enraging top brass further by stripping off to her undies for a sizzling picture', without any thought as to the impact on her employer, ultimately the Queen as Head of the Armed Forces, or on me, our children, her parents, my mother, or her lover's wife and children, and she would show absolutely no remorse. *'The mum of two, nick-named "Action Jackson" by colleagues, posed for our sexy fashion shoot and declared: "I want to let the Top Brass know I'm a flesh and blood woman and not just a uniform... I'm a woman and I don't see why they should deny me my feelings any more'*. Angela added, *'The Army has forced me to go public about my love for Brian*[45]*'.

Sun newspaper 19 August 1994

44. Sun newspaper 18 Aug 1994
45. Sun newspaper, 19 Aug & 11 Nov 1994

The following day the *Sun* reported, 'Captain Crumpet fights husband for kids. Crumpet in kids battle with hubby'. A week on, the articles were still rolling off the press. On 22 August I read with incredulity the headline, 'I wanted to be a nun, says Captain Crumpet' and then, 'I realised I had a huge void in my life where love used to be', followed by, 'My husband couldn't believe I had fallen for 'cannon fodder'', and so it went on.

At the opening of the trial following 'Operation Elveden' (investigation of corrupt payments to public officials for press stories), at the Old Bailey in 2015, prosecutor Michael Parroy QC said the case was all about greed - the greed of public officials prepared to sell stories obtained through their work, and the press "greedy for stories". He said:

"Tittle tattle and gossip about the Royal Princes, William and Harry, had a special value, as did titbits involving salacious or embarrassing conduct – 'splashes' as they called them- involving the revelation of such things as affairs between serving soldiers or their civilian counterparts; a 'love triangle'... very often the only "interest" the stories had was "prurient, morbid or banal"[46].

Kelvin MacKenzie, the Sun's Editor between 1981-1994, explained the ethos of the newspaper at the time in question. He was quoted as saying, '"When I published those stories, they were not lies. They were great stories that later turned out to be untrue – and that is different. What am I supposed to feel ashamed about?"[47]'.

In 1994 Angela provided John Kay and his colleagues with the requisite salacious story for their scoop about 'Captain Angie' which kept the Sun readership glued to the story. The details more than satisfied the criteria outlined by Mr Parroy QC, 21 years later.

Though today's newspapers might well be considered tomorrow's fish and chip wrappers, in any event they end up being tossed in a rubbish bin, just like my army career after the *Sun* printed what my wife 'Captain Angie', a.k.a. 'Captain Crumpet' told them about me, having negotiated a considerable payment for her betrayal, not just for her story, but posed for photographs.

---

46. Elgot, 2015 Huffington Post
47. Andy Dangerfield (2006) https://pressgazette.co.uk/this-is-a-trial-about-greed-john-kay-ac-cused-of-paying-mod-official-100k-as-trial-of-four-sun-journalists-begins/

There was one opinion however that the tabloid press and I could agree upon. The freelance reporter Nigel Bowden, who pursued me for a follow-up to the story in Spain said, "Say nothing - your wife is a scumbag".[48]

Totally ignoring the effect of what she was saying would have on the children and indifferent if not gleeful of the effect it would have on me, their father, her cruel inventiveness went into overdrive as she ensured her paymasters got value for money for her fabrications. I was betrayed, denigrated, sold out and I had no right of reply as the Judge who later presided over my case for residence of the children would remark: 'I do not suppose that there are very many people in the country who do not remember this story about Captain Crumpet and the Sergeant. All three, the mother, Mr Taylor and the father, as well as the children, will carry that recollection with them for a very long time and behind their backs there will no doubt be winks and nudges[49]'.

The Army, when ordering Angela to resign, also had the powers to punish her with severe consequences if she defied them. She was not shame-faced or apologetic in the least but just remained insubordinate. *'The Queen may be asked to strip Captain Angela Jackson of her officers' commission if she refuses to quit over her affair, it was revealed last night. 'I'll never make it easy for the Army by quitting. If the Queen takes away my commission then so be it[50]'* she is quoted as saying. *'Last night a senior Army source said 'It is unprecedented for an officer to ignore such a direction'..... 'She was fined and severely reprimanded for disobeying orders by Col Simon Hill, Commander of the Aldershot Garrison[51]'. 'When her CO also insisted that she should leave the Army she refused and twice admitted continuing the affair against orders[52]'.*

---

48. Diary, 18 August 1994
49. Mr Justice Johnson 14 Feb 1996
50. Sun newspaper 18 August 1994
51. Sun newspaper 19 August 1994
52. Sun newspaper 19 August 1994

CHAPTER 42

Marking Time and being a bit OCD

In the operating theatre, everyone has to be meticulous and tied to a routine in order to minimise the occurrence of mishaps. For example, used swabs are counted and then packed away by the circulating nurse and the scrub sister, but they never leave the theatre until the swab count is absolutely correct, both before the surgeon starts to close a wound and also at the end of the procedure. If there is any doubt, then the surgeon is informed and there is a recount, followed by a detailed search if a swab is still missing. If there is still a disparity and the swab cannot be found, then X-rays are obtained to reveal them whilst the patient is still under anaesthetic. The same applies to all instruments and joint replacement paraphernalia.

As an example, following an abdominal procedure I had undertaken, my nurse informed me that one swab was missing before I closed. I searched the abdomen but could not find it, so I closed up and ordered an X-ray whilst the recounts were taking place. I went to the changing room for some fresh theatre greens and as I took my boots off, a blood-stained swab fell out. Embarrassingly I trudged back into theatre with the missing swab in my hand and cancelled the X-ray. A swab, instrument or anything else retained within a patient can cause devastating complications and is expensive for the Trust, as there is no defence. Thus it helps for all concerned to be fixated on getting things correct.

For my part, I was fanatical about my patients being marked preoperatively, with the proposed operation, and particularly the side of the procedure if relevant, spelled out in black indelible marker pen. Timing was important, so this had to be done on the ward before the patients were given their premedication and certainly before they were anaesthetised. I remembered the orthopaedic surgeon's mistake in Clatterbridge only too well, even though they salvaged the situation admirably, as I have already related.

My anaesthetic colleagues had their own manias too, particularly with the labelling of the contents of the syringes when they administered their pharmaceutical cocktails to induce unconsciousness and paralysis in patients. In our environment, as in many others, it is necessary to be responsible, vigilant, attentive, indeed obsessive, and those of us who have or develop these attributes are commonly referred to as being 'a bit OCD' about something which has unfortunately entered the English vernacular (and makes no sense when the expression is unabbreviated to being a bit 'Obsessive Compulsive Disorder').

Thus the term 'OCD' is mistakenly and naively bandied around by most of the population to indicate someone who is a bit of a neat freak, or someone who has a cleanliness fetish, or who has a particular way of doing things, but it is nothing of the sort in clinical terms. OCD is a devastating condition involving behaviour that is so off the normal spectrum that it impinges on an individual's life to such an extent that it blights their ability to function properly on a day-to-day basis. It is a full-blown anxiety disorder that wreaks havoc with the quality of the lives of sufferers and their families. Patients experience unpleasant, frightening and intrusive thoughts that result in the need for compelling actions or rituals to alleviate symptoms. They suffer from crippling doubt and feelings of hyper-responsibility for outcomes.

To put this into perspective, my absolute insistence on the correct marking of patients preoperatively and checking or sending someone to check that this was the case could be described as an OCD 'trait'. If I was compelled to check the patient myself time after time, if I doubted my ability to register what I saw, if I became fearful and hyper-responsible for the consequences of an incorrect patient or misoperation yet to be performed, if I recruited others time and time again, to reassure me that all was correct whilst I was swamped in a crippling adrenaline surge that made it all but impossible for me to function, then I would be suffering from OCD.

I would find out for myself just how devastating the effects of this disorder can be not only for an individual, but their family too and how adverse circumstances, or for that matter a malicious ex-wife, can tip someone who has very mild OCD traits into the full-blown disorder.

CHAPTER 43

Going for Broke

My barrister, the late Sir Gavyn Arthur QC, attended Reading County Court before District Judge Kenny on my behalf[53] whilst I was still in Spain and outlined Angela's behaviour. He explained that Angela had notified the *Sun* newspaper of my whereabouts in Spain, she had appeared on several news bulletins and had also been a guest on the Richard Littlejohn Live and Uncut Show.

"I would summarise her performance as saying she revelled in the intimate sexual details of her husband, in particular answering questions about his being a 'flop in bed' and saying that she had no regrets about what she had done," explained Mr Arthur. "She said that she had posed half-naked and sent posters to squaddies in order to enlist their support on her side".

When Angela appeared on the Richard Littlejohn show[54] on television, she was asked to explain to viewers what the publicity was about.

"Basically I'm in the news because I've chosen to fall in love with a soldier, someone who's not an officer, and er, for this reason, um,

---

53. 18 and 25 August 1994
54. Screened in August 1994

the press has found it interesting because they realise that the Army's attitude is one of severe disapproval as regards this matter" she said.

"Didn't you know that when you signed up though?" asked Richard.

"Did I know that they would not approve of me seeing a soldier?" asked Angela.

Richard expanded, "It's one of the rules when you take a commission, isn't it, really, you don't fraternise with the Other Ranks".

"Yes, it certainly is and... and I was certainly aware that that was the rule, yeah," admitted Angela.

"So why don't you now go and give up your job and go and live with your new man?" asked Richard. "You shouldn't have done it, should you?" he pressed.

"No, I shouldn't have done it, but I did," replied Angela.

"But in pursuing your own happiness was it really necessary to humiliate your husband in quite the way that you have, you, you've been saying he's terrible in bed and giving him a bucket load of unpleasantness, was that really necessary? Wasn't being cuckolded enough for him?"

"Apparently not," Angela replied, without a shred of regret.

"But why did you have to tell the world he was a flop in bed?" (audience laughs and Angela smirks). "No, actually, I don't think it's funny, I don't think it's funny, I mean he's going through a difficult enough time as it is, without him having that heaped on him surely?" said Richard.

I think there will be few men willing to take up the offer of a quickie with their partners in future, if they think that it may be used against them in a court affidavit, or newspaper article. A patient could be waiting for me in A & E or on the operating table, but in her selfish mind, Angela's need for attention and control over me would take precedence. To turn down her offer of sex was tantamount to an unforgivable rejection of her. She was incapable of comprehending how anyone or anything could take priority.

"Well if I could have followed the course I wished to," continued Angela, "it would simply have been that I divorced my husband three years ago, or he would have divorced me and that would have been the end of the matter".

"So this is revenge on him, is it?" asked Richard.

"Er, no, it's backed into a corner, rather than revenge" said Angela. "He told me at the time that if I dared to leave him, he'd find out who the man involved was, that he would ensure that I would be Court Martialled, that Brian would be dismissed from the service".

"Well" said Richard, "that's still probably likely to happen, but that's not because, that's not your husband's fault, that's because you broke the rules of military discipline. Do you think when push comes to shove and you sit back and look at the publicity and everything else, that you are going to think, my god, I've made a complete fool of myself, what have I done?"

"Er no, not really" said Angela, as usual not able to join up the dots between her behaviour and the consequences.

The MP Austin Mitchell, who was also a guest on the show, then interjected, "But what are you doing now, in posing for the *Sun*? I mean are you going for broke? Are you trying to put them in an embarrassing situation, what are you doing?"

"The problem is really Austin, I have no rich or powerful friends, um... but I'd like some support" replied Angela. "I know the quickest way of getting (soldiers') attention is to pose in the *Sun*, and what I would like is for them to be rooting for me, because I feel that I've spent my whole career rooting for them, sometimes putting my neck out for them (laughter from the audience) and I'd like them to be there rooting for me". Richard, picking up on her Freudian slip, said "I'm sure they're rooting like rabbits for you." (More audience laughter.)

Angela also appeared on the After 5 Show[55] with Brian. The interviewer introduced them, saying, 'Army bosses have reacted furiously. Yesterday Angela, who lives in Camberley, was fined £1200, the price of defying orders not to see her lover, and he's left the army so that they can stay together. Well even now Angela could become the first ever female officer to be sacked for breaking the army's strict rules on relationships with comrades'. Angela was asked what the problem was with regard to an officer having a relationship with an Other Rank.

---

55. Screened in Aug 1994

"Basically, it undermines military discipline" said Angela.

"Now we understand from, we've got military quotes here" said the interviewer "to say that if you make any more transgressions, that's like talking to the *Sun*, you could be Court Martialled, in other words simply by appearing on After 5 today, that's another transgression".

"Yes," Angela replied.

"You're going to be Court Martialled, aren't you?"

"Yes," she said.

Mr Arthur QC continued to update Judge Kenny: "It was discovered a few days ago that the mother had arranged for Col Jackson and the two little girls to be met at the airport on their return [from Spain] by the mother and by representatives of the *Sun* newspaper and photographers and there she was to remove the two little girls, take them from him in the presence of the press...If I may sum up, therefore the enormity of what it is said the wife has done, she has sold for sums of cash (*£26,000*) intimate details of the life of her family, including and perhaps most humiliating of all, intimate details of the sexual performance of her husband. She has posed in her underwear, supposedly titillating pictures, in the tabloid press. It goes rather than further with that. With the aid of the *Sun* newspaper she has arranged for a poster of herself in her underwear to be made available free to anyone sending a stamped addressed envelope to the *Sun*. Even worse, she has sent with the aid of the *Sun* newspaper copies of that poster to all other ranks or a large number of other ranks at the military base where her husband works".

"She has last week stripped the house of all except four items, a couple of beds, a computer and the husband's chair (the items taken included the dishwasher, the fridge/freezer, the microwave oven)... she has sacked the long-term nanny who looked after the children and has removed the little girl's cat[56]".

Most women seeking a divorce do not behave in this extreme manner in order to voice their dissatisfaction with their husband and their employer, so it was not surprising during court proceedings that Angela's state of mind was considered questionable and it was concluded that the children needed to be protected from the effects of

56. Sir Gavyn Arthur Aug 1994 transcript

her behaviour. Consequently, I was awarded interim custody of my two young daughters, pending a full hearing for permanent custody a few months later. Angela's demeanour in court was not helping her case either.

"I do wish you would ask her to stop making faces at me" Judge Kenny instructed Angela's counsel. "It makes my task extremely difficult, you understand. It is most distracting, and it is quite extraordinary that she should behave in this way. She is an intelligent woman. You cannot see it, but I am faced with immediately behind your left shoulder, the most appalling faces being pulled and nods, quite a lot of it, quite I think, unacceptable behaviour".

Angela's counsel attempted to mitigate the judge's criticism of her client. "Your Honour, obviously with the distress of the proceedings it is perhaps Captain Jackson's way of dealing with the emotional aspect".

However Judge Kenny was having none of it. "There is no distress demonstrated in these pin-ups which she posed for last week" he pointed out. "What sort of distress am I supposed to assume she is feeling when she poses for money for photographs of that kind which she must know would be immensely damaging for her children? My reaction to the case is that, given the public interest in these, what to my mind are rather personal details of a person of high standing in the Army, it ought to be transferred to the High Court forthwith." And that is exactly what happened; my case was transferred to the Royal Courts of Justice in London.

Angela's intentions had clearly been premeditated. She had intended to remove everything of use to her in the house including the children's possessions whilst I was away in Spain, and then take the children from me immediately on my return to the UK to live with them and Brian in Pudsey, her home town, with everything recorded and published by the *Sun*. Angela knew full well that by colluding with the *Sun* her army career was over and she intended to do as much damage to me as she could, to ensure that mine would be over too. I would suffer the same fate that has befallen many other Army personnel with otherwise unblemished armed forces service records.

'Another poster showing Captain Angela Jackson in bra and knickers was offered free to soldiers yesterday a day after she was fined £1200 over her love affair with Colour Sgt Brian Taylor. Captain Jackson has refused to resign her commission. But last night Army sources said she could face a court martial. But the love affair and sexy photos were the talk of the pubs in Aldershot, home of the British Army[57]'.

'Free Angie pin-up, lads. Quick march, lads! Here's your chance to get a free poster of sexy Captain Crumpet Angela Jackson[58]'

My concern for my career was prophetic, as it turned out. '"My career in the Army is finished,"' I was reported as saying. '"How can I take out soldiers' appendices when they've got a pin-up of my wife on the wall in the mess?"[59]'.

Angela's revelations to the *Sun* and her other media quotes were deliberately made with the intention of ruining my career. Mr Justice Johnson summed up:

"The impact on a serving Lieutenant Colonel is obvious. It was apparent from what the wife said in evidence before Mr Justice Ewbank and on television that she knew perfectly well what she was about and intended to cause damage to the husband and his career. The TV interviewers asked her 'wasn't it enough that he should be cuckolded?' and her reply was 'apparently not'. The husband was humiliated as the wife, I find, intended. The husband's position in the Army became untenable as she intended, and he was driven out of the Army, I find, as she intended... 'There is nothing that I have read in the evidence, nothing that I saw in the two television interviews which the mother gave, and nothing about her evidence before me which suggests she has any feelings of remorse or regret for what she did to the father, and more importantly for my purpose, to the children'.[60]

---

57. Bob McGowan (Daily Express & Evening Standard) 1994, *Blonde Officer could face Court Martial*
58. Sun Newspaper 19 Aug 1994
59. News of the World August 1994
60. Mr Justice Johnson, 13 June 1996

CHAPTER 44

Intersex

At the CMH I was often operating on children, and my paediatric colleagues had asked me to examine a young girl of about seven years old who had developed a small lump in her groin. There was not much about this, as for all the world it just looked like a late presentation of a childhood hernia and could easily be dealt with. However all surgeons are coloured by previous experience and thoughts can ferment and fire off in many unlikely directions, and there is always a case that sticks in one's mind.

Intersex has become highly topical in today's world, and I had my first experience of it several years before when I had absolutely no idea what I was dealing with. This previous patient who came to mind was also a young girl of similar age who had groin hernias on both sides. She seemed a normal little girl with normal female genitalia. Her phenotype (appearance) was absolutely female, and I had no reason to suspect that she might not be what she appeared to be until that is, I surgically explored her groins to find two little testicles, one on either side, at which point I had to reassure myself that I was operating on the correct patient to alleviate the heart stopping moments these situations engender.

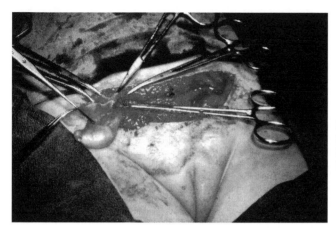

Right testicle in little girl. The left side has been dealt with.

Of course this surgical surprise was way outside my generally meagre knowledge base at the time, but after a flurry of phone calls to my consultants, ("Girls have ovaries; you sure they actually are testicles?") to the paediatricians, ("What did you just say?"), I realised that I was not the only ignorant one. I finally obtained advice from a colleague who had the decency to open a textbook and informed me that I was dealing with the now misnomered Testicular Feminisation Syndrome. Repair the hernias, biopsy the testicles and leave them in situ was the surgical plan of action, with onward referral to the paediatric eggheads.

If I fast forward 20 years or so, I can explain that the little girl in question was genetically a little boy, having XY sex chromosomes (genotype) as opposed to XX for a girl, with no uterus or ovaries amongst other things. I can also explain that the correct basis of the genotype/phenotype mismatch is because the developing foetus is insensitive to the effects of male hormones, secreted to differentiate male from female. This allows female characteristics to develop, if not completely anatomically, in the testicle bearing female, who when born, to all intents and purposes is a girl when the between the legs identification process is undertaken. They are raised as girls but will require hormone treatment and some corrective surgery at a later date, with removal of the testicles when puberty arrives.

Thus in these cases, it is not the testicles that feminise the foetus as was originally thought, and hence the misnomer. It is the complete or partial lack of response to the hormone they secrete (e.g. testosterone) caused by the absence of the appropriate cellular receptors, which results in feminisation. In other words, the cells cannot receive the message that the foetus requires masculinisation because the letterbox won't open. These phenotypic girls will grow up to be tall and beautiful, with a female psyche, but infertile. Many will marry and adopt children. Some will become actresses and even supermodels. The correct medical term is now Complete or Partial Androgen (male hormones) Insensitivity Syndrome.

There are a whole load of other intersex syndromes which are too complicated for this account. Anyway, to get back to the little girl of the moment, I decided to request an ultrasound just to confirm the hernia, if there was a testicle in it and/or another one anywhere else and check the pelvis for anatomically normal female organs.

When the request reached the Radiology Department, I received a phone call.

"Why are you looking for a testicle? The patient is a little girl, is she not? Girls have ovaries".

I explained my previous case, but I was interrupted. "What did you just say? Are you sure they were testicles?" I was asked.

The radiological receptors were unresponsive. Their letterbox was closing and I had an attack of déjà vu.

"Look, just indulge me on this occasion," I said. "Put my mind at rest".

The ultrasound was perfectly normal, with a pointed report, 'No testicles identified in this female patient'.

CHAPTER 45

After Sun

The army were very supportive of me and assisted in every way possible. Initially when I returned to the UK from Spain, I was sent on indefinite compassionate leave, so that I could sort out my life with the children and get the house back into a habitable state for them to return to. This would take me a week, whilst they stayed with my mother in Didcot. Angela had taken virtually everything from the house, even down to the light bulbs and the washing-up liquid.

However, as I have always believed, as one door closes another one opens, and unbeknown to me, the newspaper caption 'My Sarge is a sex bomb' along with the subsequent tasteless articles, was the catalyst for my third marriage. The *Sun* was the typical choice of tabloid newspaper for the Other Ranks, and would be read by thousands of military personnel each day, which was Angela's intention. They were her target audience, the people who she hoped would rally around her.

An ex-RAF airwoman called Nicki was one such person. Intrigued, she read the articles about Angela, but her sympathies did not lie with her. I had never heard of this woman before, but she would write me a letter of support, as would a lot of other newspaper readers, friends and colleagues, and she would become a significant threat to the success of Angela's crusade. Angela's need to court publicity and controversy as well as humiliate me for revenge had inadvertently brought Nicki to my attention, in the most bizarre of circumstances. The true love story was not the tawdry one printed in graphic detail in the newspapers for all to read, about Angela and Brian and their supercharged sexual antics; it was the quiet, dignified one between Nicki and me that would gently unfold in the background. Angela, with her campaign of domestic war, had inadvertently scored an outstanding own goal.

After collecting Nicki's letter of support from work on my return to the UK, I phoned to thank her. She listened to my problems and sympathised, as so many other kind friends and colleagues had done. Nicki and I seemed to share many of the same philosophies about life and family values, and we vowed to stay in touch. However, because of my need for emotional self-preservation, I was cautious in my response to her. I need not have worried.

In 1994 custody of the children of a failed marriage was almost inevitably given to their mother as presumed main carer. In our case Angela was not the main carer, our nanny was, and next in line was me. Angela had done everything she could to get out of child care. By her own admission, she could not stand it. The children bored her.

In the months that followed the words, 'mood changes', 'not in a fit state', 'unstable', 'unbalanced', 'volatile' and 'incapable' would all be used by professionals to describe Angela in court, and the words 'brainwashing', 'damage', 'emotional harm', 'abuse' and 'poisons' would be used in relation to her behaviour towards the children. I had to protect my children from their own mother. I could not forget that it was her intention to mould them in her own image, to make them grow up to be just like her and teach them to hate men for what they do to women.

Unsupported by any evidence whatsoever, Angela would repeatedly claim that the children needed 'protecting' and 'saving' in order to justify her actions and her attempts to extract them from my care. She would project her own characteristics onto me and I would become cold-hearted, dangerous and a bully. She would complain that the Court experts were 'wrong' and 'rigid thinking traditionalists', the Judges were 'outmoded dinosaurs' who 'despised' her and that the Court cases were a 'fiasco' and a 'catalogue of mismanagement'[61].

As Angela had already made the decision to sack our nanny whilst I was in Spain, I would need assistance with the children and household chores. A Mrs Sue Thwaites, the mother of my youngest daughter's friend Robyn, volunteered her services, and I will forever be indebted to her for her help. I needed to get back to work to fulfil my obligations to the army and my patients. It was initially ordered that Angela should be allowed contact with the children for only two hours a week every Friday afternoon at the former matrimonial home. Predictably she would utilise this precious time to raid my filing cabinets, steal my possessions and inspect the cleanliness of the house in order to berate Mrs Thwaites.

Then she would deliberately start to poison the children's minds. When she was later allowed to take the children away from the home for contact, she invariably returned them to me in a sobbing state whilst she stood on the doorstep completely dry eyed, smug and aggressive. She was not dry eyed because she was good at controlling her emotions for the sake of the children; she was dry eyed because she had cruelly manipulated them to perform for her benefit on their return to me and she could enjoy the dreadful drama she had orchestrated. Of course she was able to weep out of self-pity, but she generally reserved her tears for when she needed to emotionally induce a sympathetic response from the children or change their minds about something, for example when they told her they were quite happy living with me. Later a very experienced social worker would witness one such handover for herself. She reported that in her long experience with children she had never seen anything like it; 'it was quite awful'.[62]

In the meantime I met Nicki for the first time at the Highwayman pub in Ascot[63], an area I knew well, having worked there previously. Nicki had just turned 31 years old and I was 45. Despite our 14-year age gap, our children were very close in age. My two were just seven and five at the time and hers were five and nearly two. We swapped

61. 11 Mar 1997 OS report
62. Mr Justice Johnson, 14 Feb 1996
63. Oct 1994

photos of our children and stories of our lives and got on very well. I did not know that Nicki was technically still married to an Airman at this stage, though the marriage had come to an end and she was legally separated from her husband before I had opened her letter to me.

Nicki's change in circumstances did however drive her back to Fleet, Hampshire the area where she grew up and where her parents lived, a mere six miles from the Cambridge Military Hospital. When we parted on that first night, I gave her a chaste kiss on the cheek and we vowed to see each other again. When we did so, the kisses would not be so chaste. My attraction to Nicki was guarded in terms of a marriage partner, though almost immediate as a sexual partner! Gradually I came to recognise that she was genuine and I started to relax. Slowly it dawned on me that I would be a fool to pass up this opportunity to turn my life around and enjoy a relationship with someone who genuinely wanted, desired and loved me for the right reasons.

Nicki's concern for her children, my children and me was then and always has been profound. Her moral compass and desire to do the right thing in life meant that she demonstrated the virtues which I hold dear, but the flipside was that these same qualities predisposed her to an anxiety disorder which would have a devastating effect on her mental health in years to come, aggravated and ruthlessly exploited by Angela.

We doubted that our paths would have crossed at that particular point in time had it not been for the publicity in the *Sun* newspaper, though we did later establish that our meeting was far more likely than we had originally thought, especially in the early 80s when we had both worked in Aldershot military town. I was working at the Cambridge Military Hospital and was seeing Angela for my sins, and Nicki was working for the Ministry of Defence at the Army School of Physical Training and was in a long-term relationship with an Army Captain at the time. Had we but known it, we had been working less than a mile apart from each other.

We had a lot in common. Her father had been an RAF fighter pilot and her mother an RAF nursing sister in the Princess Mary's RAF

Nursing Service (PMs) and prior to that, her mother had worked as a state registered nurse (SRN) at two of the hospitals that I had worked in, the General Hospital Birmingham and Liverpool Royal Infirmary. No doubt influenced by her mother, Nicki also had a longstanding and serious fascination with all things medical and particularly surgical, so career wise, she would always be on my side and would relish the supportive role she could play in my life, rather than resent it. Fate was steadily steering us towards each other.

CHAPTER 46

On a Fag Break

I had always smoked, quite heavily at times, since my late teens, and I was addicted. The stresses in my life and occupation did not help and I was grateful for the nicotine crutch getting me through some difficult times. In those early days, smoking was socially accepted, but nowadays all that has changed and people like me became pariahs. My advice in retrospect would be, don't start. Nicotine has been likened to crack cocaine in its ability to snare the unwary or the thrill seeker, or those conforming to what they perceive as societal norms in the circle in which they are associated.

Anyway, 15 years ago I decided to give up the weed. This was not through any particular health consideration, though as a doctor it should have been. No, it was because I could not go anywhere without checking that I had a sufficient cigarette supply to get me through the day, or if on call, the night as well, and frequently I would leave my house early in the morning to buy some cigarettes from the Co-op, on my journey to the hospital or a peripheral clinic and smoke a couple on the way, often in lieu of breakfast. I was absolutely fed up with this and decided one day to go cold turkey. Other addicts had done it and though I knew it would be hard I was quite confident that with willpower and determination I would succeed.

I lasted about an hour before I felt the usual cravings, but I managed to ignore them. The trouble was that on this particular day I had nothing really taxing to occupy my mind apart from about three cigarettes' worth of administrative paper shuffling. I grabbed my coat and went outside the hospital for a walk. Unfortunately I had to traverse the area of the bus shelter where several co-addicts were indulging themselves. The smell of the cigarette smoke, which I cannot stand now, was welcome and intoxicating. Standing there nonchalantly inhaling the second-hand smoke, I could almost feel my receptors trawling through what I was absorbing into my blood stream, albeit diluted by the previous owners, to try and find any trace of residual nicotine.

After I smoked my last cigarette that morning I ceremoniously threw the rest away, though I had read that others in similar positions had kept a couple handy just in case they needed a quick fix during the withdrawal procedure. At the time I had felt that this would not be necessary, but this decision had been made on a nicotine high and directly inversely to my sinking nicotine levels was the rising regret at this course of action.

I would need help. I phoned my GP, Dr Frances Gerrard, on the pretence of my wishing to discuss a patient of hers and slipped into the conversation the fact that I had given up smoking, which she had always nagged me to do, finally taking heed of her advice. I did not mention that my smoke-free existence had lasted all of about an hour and a half. She congratulated me, and before she could ask how it was going, I casually remarked that I found my operation day stressful and would it be possible for her to give me a prescription for some nicotine replacement therapy, just in case. I thought I gave a good impression of calmness and control, even though I was climbing the walls. She was happy to do this and said she would leave a prescription for nicotine patches with the practice receptionist for me to pick up later in the day. My mind became fixated on one thing. How much later? I needed something within the next hour, minute, nanosecond. "Actually I shall be passing your practice in a couple of minutes," I lied. "I don't suppose I could pick the prescription up now, save me coming back?"

At a rate of speed which only the truly nicotine deprived can muster, I obtained the piece of precious paper, wheezed my way to the nearest chemist and minutes later I had a patch on my arm, of the highest strength allowable. I waited for the relief, but my expectations were unrealistic. The slow transdermal (across, or through the skin) absorption of the nicotine in no way relieved my immediate cravings. Having read the indications and side effects of this replacement therapy in the blurb that is churned out by the pharmaceutical companies, I decided that my needs surpassed their dire warnings, and soon, with the application of more patches, I had arms similar to those of accomplished cub scouts, with merit badges up and down the sleeves of their pullovers.

Slowly my withdrawal symptoms abated and I was happy to carry on living, but as time passed I began to notice that I was sweating, I had stomach ache and my heart rate was abnormally high. I ripped off all the patches except one. This was not going to work. I would have to set my alarm for 7 am for patch reapplication in order to be functional for work at 8.30. In addition there was no way of initiating an immediate nicotine boost when required, such as a downturn in a patient's well-being, or an act of monumental idiocy by one of my junior staff, or my car not starting, or the central heating failing, or just about anything which disordered my life.

Then I discovered nicotine gum. Crack open the packet and start chewing for a fairly immediate high and rest it by the gums during the day or on the bedside table at night until another shot was required. When I was in theatre and got into difficulties, instead of taking a fag break, I would just masticate myself back into operative karma. I had found the solution, and indeed I have not smoked any form of tobacco since.

There was only one drawback. I could not go anywhere without checking that I had a sufficient gum supply to get me through the day, or if on call, the night as well and frequently I would leave my house early in the morning to buy some gum from the Co-op on my journey to the hospital or a peripheral clinic and chew a couple on the way, often in lieu of breakfast.

CHAPTER 47

Far Too Intelligent

By 21 October Angela was back in the papers again. 'Barracks ban on Captain Crumpet', the *Sun* headlines read. 'SEXY "Captain Crumpet" Angela Jackson has been banned from every Army barracks in Britain[64]'.

On 8 November the *Sun* newspaper finally printed a piece in my defence, courtesy of my mother and concerned friends. 'Awful secret hubby found in Captain Crumpet's drawers' said the headline, accompanied by a photograph taken by Angela of Brian lying naked in my bed.

'Col Jackson is gagged by military rules from talking to the Press. But now his friends and family and fellow officers have joined forces to tell his side of the story – and set the record straight... "I've been worried about the fact that I was silently watching the character assassination of my son and the destruction of his life and career while he couldn't speak in his defence. In spite of my son's wishes, I had to do something[65]"'.

---

64. Sun newspaper 21 Oct 1994
65. Sun newspaper 8 Nov1994

By 11 November Angela's career in the Army finally looked to be over. The *Sun* printed the headline 'Captain Crumpet gets marching orders'.

'Friends expect Angela, 35, will agree reluctantly to quit so she can collect a £30,000 pay-off and pension. But they think she will protest at her treatment in a letter to the Queen. Married education officer Angela will not be allowed to call herself Captain after she goes. She was suspended from her £25,000 a year post after disobeying orders to end her romance with Colour Sergeant Brian Taylor 34. Angela enraged top brass further by stripping to her undies for a sizzling picture spread in the Sun. The Ministry of Defence said, 'Captain Jackson was asked to resign her commission because of admitted misconduct[66]*'.*

Sun newspaper 11 November 1994

The Director General Army Medical Services informed me that The Staff of the Adjutant General, was using my wife's conduct and the 'Captain Crumpet' story as an example of Conduct Unbecoming of an Officer on Commanding Officers' Designate courses. The story of

66. Sun newspaper 11 Nov 1994

Captain Crumpet was also cited by Admiral Sir Michael Boyce, GCB, CBE, Chief of Defence Staff (2001), who said that those who followed in the footsteps of Angela Jackson had 'no place in the force'.[67]

My legacy would be to be remembered as the unsatisfactory husband of Captain Crumpet, rather than the army surgeon who served Queen and country and saved the lives of soldiers during two military campaigns. For years afterwards, each time an officer had an illicit liaison that came to the attention of the press, the story of Captain Crumpet was resurrected, invariably accompanied by a picture of Angela in her red bra and knickers.

Meanwhile, due to the nature of some of the items Angela was persistently stealing from me whilst visiting the children in my house, I had to get the police to intervene. "You can't do this to me", she apparently said while in the police station when they arrested her. "I have the backing of the *Sun*". I awoke to see a photo of my children in the *Sun* newspaper on 28 December, with my eldest daughter perched on Brian Taylor's shoulders. 'Captain Crumpet is arrested in front of kids. Hubby accused her of theft[68]'.

Sun newspaper 28 December 1994

---

67. https://publications.parliament.uk/pa/cm200001/cmselect/cmdfence/298/1030107.htm.
Minutes of evidence, Select Committee on Defence 2001
68. Sun newspaper 28 Dec 1994

What was not stated was that amongst other things, Angela had stolen my Dictaphone from work with a tape in it giving the details of the patients in my last clinic, which of course are medical-in-confidence.

The situation with the children was becoming worse, not better, as time went on, and in preparation for the main residence hearing, Angela increased her emotional pressure on them, in particular my elder daughter, whom she had failed to hand over after a contact visit. She had been persuaded to write a letter to the judge claiming that I lay on top of her and held her down. The 'brainwashing process', as the judge referred to it, was well under way, and he concluded that although my daughter's views were accepted, they were 'the product of the extreme pressure put upon her by her mother'[69] and that if my daughter remained with Angela for just a matter of weeks, untold emotional harm would be done to her. He ordered that my daughter be returned home immediately.

I had expected to do battle with Angela if only to exercise my rights as the children's father, to have some regular influence in their lives and protect them from their mother's ceaseless indoctrination, but fortunately I did not have to. Angela's appalling and abusive manipulation of the children, her inability to tell the truth and her grandiose performances completely undermined her own case for Residence. "What the Judge didn't' like" Angela asserted, "was that I was far too intelligent, and I could beat David's barrister down on every question[70]". The quote often attributed to Abraham Lincoln or Mark Twain 'it is better to remain silent and be thought a fool, than to open one's mouth and remove all doubt', sprang to mind.

The judge, Mr Justice Ewbank, stated that I [the father] could 'provide the children with security, stability and a balanced life'. He concluded that Angela 'suffers from mood changes and is unstable and she places her own interest before those of the children. She lacks common sense. I have to say that in my view she has little true concern for the children[71]'.

---

69. Mr Justice Douglas Brown 25 Jan 1995
70. Telecon Angela/Nicki 14 Sept 1995
71. Mr Justice Ewbank 24 Feb 1995

Even though I was working full-time, I was awarded permanent custody of my two little girls, and that fact speaks for itself with regard to the court and the Judge's opinion of Angela. It was a huge relief, but as I suspected, it would be short lived. Angela had failed her children spectacularly, despite the advantage she had due to the prevailing bias that still existed in favour of mothers. Her emotional abuse, and her little true concern for them as stated by Mr Justice Ewbank, was also the direct cause of her contact being strictly curtailed. She would be given every possible opportunity to change her fortunes around over the years that followed, far more than any father would have been given in the same circumstances, but her disordered personality was such that she refused to be told what to do by those in a position of 'power', because she believed she was being 'controlled', 'abused' and 'victimised'.

In one respect I will be eternally grateful to Angela for continuing to behave as she did, because it gave me the opportunity to share many precious years with my daughters, of which I would otherwise have been deprived. However, it would come at a very high price. I wrote to Nicki and warned her that Angela's maliciousness would be unstinting:

'Though I have won custody of the children I am sure that this is only the commencement of my troubles; I am sure I will be plagued by an unbalanced, vitriolic and vengeful 'nearly ex-wife'. She is dangerous and this does worry me. She is still capable of causing immense emotional damage to the children and I do not think that the judgement against her and the comments made by the judge will in any way stop her. The children require emotional support, confidence and stability and a love of their present life (and stability) that will extinguish anything their mother tries to do'[72].

Nicki was on my mind more and more. I had been discarded by Angela for the final four years of our marriage, in favour of Brian. Did I not deserve another go at a happy marriage? There was another consideration though. Residence had been granted to me whilst I had

---

72. Letter to Nicki 2 Mar 1995

the assistance of Mrs Thwaites as housekeeper. Marriage to Nicki and the addition of two stepchildren would give Angela (now unemployed and legally aided) the ideal opportunity to challenge the Residence Order based on a significant change of my circumstances. If this succeeded, then all my efforts to protect the children from the tangled mind of their mother would have come to naught. I was in a quandary, which kept me awake at night.

To compound matters, I was then informed that an allegation of sexual abuse had been made against me by Angela's sister Christine Peck-Russell with regard to my eldest daughter[73]. As a result, the Child Protection Unit interviewed the children and found that the allegation originated from their mother. They concluded that there was no evidence to support it, but Angela cared not that she had needlessly subjected her own child to an intrusive interview in the process. I would just have to add it to the growing list of allegations – buggery and child abuse. What would be next I wondered? I was to find out.

Slowly but surely, Nicki and I amalgamated our two fractured families and I asked her father for her hand in marriage; he agreed, so I then asked Nicki and she also agreed, though knowing my emotional turmoil, she gave me until the following morning to change my mind. I was not going to[74]. Finding love and happiness again when I did wasn't exactly the best of timing – these things rarely are – but Angela had brought us together as a result of her own public rejection of me. My children were very much in favour of my asking Nicki to marry me, not least because Nicki liked my youngest daughter's hamster!

I needed to distance myself from the now infamous 'Captain Crumpet', both physically and emotionally. I had to get away, to find anonymity if that was at all possible, and start over again. Every expression of sympathy from well-wishers, whilst greatly appreciated, was also a constant reminder of what had happened to me and would prevent me from being able to heal. I needed to be confident in my ability to do my job, and my patients needed to have the utmost confidence in it too. Posters of Angela semi-naked were still surfacing in the forces community, and I could not enjoy the military social life

---

73. Diary 27 Jan 1995
74. Diary 22 Apr 1995

as I had once done due to the acute embarrassment. I had therefore been excused from compulsory military functions. My position in the Army had become untenable. If I left the Army, neither my employers nor I would have to be connected to the whole sorry saga, even though I had been due to command the military surgical department at Frimley Park Hospital, following the planned closure of CMH.

I resigned my commission. It was a bitter blow. 'This is a widely-read paper' remarked Mr Justice Ewbank a few months later, 'and many people would know of it to the detriment of the father, mother and children. The mother had said that she did not expect it to be printed but that her husband deserved it. The father has been deeply wounded. Of course, his pride was hurt but his career was destroyed, and his self-esteem destroyed[75]'

I needed to find a civilian surgical post back in the NHS, in a hospital somewhere off the beaten track. I had to escape, to start again, to rebuild my career and regain my confidence without being tarnished, if at all possible, by association with 'Captain Crumpet'

Mr Justice Johnson would later sum up. 'In evidence he said: "What made me leave the army was that I felt I had lost my confidence in myself"...'he had now decided to leave the army and to escape (a word I choose deliberately) to the remoteness of Aberystwyth' said the Judge. 'He had to take up a position as a general surgeon in a local hospital[76]'.

And as predicted, Angela applied to have the Residence Order overturned by Appeal based on my change of circumstances.

---

75. Mr Justice Ewbank 24 Feb 1995
76. Mr Justice Johnson 14 Feb 1996

CHAPTER 48

John Bach

Bronglais General Hospital (BGH), or Ysbyty Bronglais is located in Aberystwyth. It was small, with about 200 beds, but necessarily provided a wide generality of services due to its isolation from other hospitals in Wales. It had the biggest catchment area in the United Kingdom, but outwith the towns and villages, it was sparsely populated. The catchment area crossed three counties, Ceredigion in which the hospital was located, Powys, and Gwynedd. The nearest hospital was Glangwili, 53 miles away in Carmarthen (nearly an hour and a half in the car on single carriageway roads). This suited me well, as a broad general surgical practice was just what I had hoped for.

Bronglais General Hospital was nicknamed BMH Aberystwyth, as quite a few ex-service doctors worked there. These included Richard Myles (who had turned me into a trained monkey many years before), Peter Gardner, Graham Housam and a Mr Jones. BGH was also one of the biggest employers in the town, the other being the University of Wales, Aberystwyth, so the town was quite cosmopolitan due to the influx of foreign students and university lecturers, which made for interesting and lively times. The locals were very Welsh, often conversing preferentially in their own language. The Welsh are just nice people, fiercely loyal to their traditions and way of life and to a certain extent, exist in a time zone several years behind the rest of the UK.

This is how the job came my way. My colleague and friend John Lovegrove had left the Army two years before me and had failed to find a suitable substantive civilian consultant post. In about April/May of 1995, when I already had full permanent custody of the children, he phoned me at the CMH. After we exchanged a few pleasantries, he came to the point of his telephone call. Whilst he was doing a long-term locum at a hospital in the North of England he applied and had been appointed to a vacant and permanent post in a small hospital in Aberystwyth. Just after he had accepted the post, his employers decided to create another consultant post where he was already working and as he was a known quantity, the job was his for the taking. Thus, having failed for two years to secure a single substantive post, he now had two on offer. He and his wife Julie both expressed a preference to remain where they were, rather than move to Wales (Julie especially, really wasn't keen), but John felt guilty about accepting the BGH job and then almost immediately resiling.

When he informed the Trust, in order to assuage their feelings on the matter, he said that he knew someone who was looking for a civilian job and who would be a much better fit for the post than he was, as he was now quite specialised in his practice. John then admitted that he was referring to me and asked if I would consider it. He gave me the name and telephone of the Personnel Director, Suzanne Penny. I liked Wales, I had lived there once, camped and holidayed there and yes, I liked the Welsh. Wales also had significantly cheaper housing than the South East, which would suit my impoverished state. As soon as John was off the phone, I looked up where the hell the hospital was. Hmm; it sounded remote and it was. Perhaps it would provide the anonymity that I was looking for. Aberystwyth, or "Aber where?" as Nicki would say when I first told her of my plans, is a small seaside town on the west coast of mid-Wales. I phoned Miss Penny and told her I was going to travel to Wales to see them with a view to applying for the job in lieu of Mr Lovegrove.

In May 95, I duly drove to Aberystwyth to see the hospital and meet the Chief Executive, Paul Barnett, and the senior consultant general surgeon, a Mr John Edwards, with whom I would be staying overnight, thus giving each of us a bit of time to get to know each other. I did the rounds, taking in the fact that all the staff were excellent, but equipment levels and ancillaries were ancient, especially to my mind, the three operating theatres. Anyway, I decided that I could certainly work there and confirmed this to Peter Gardner, who was the Medical Director and Richard Myles' co-consultant. I was then told that I should meet John Edwards at the Black Lion pub (right next door to the White Lion pub) in Tal-y-Bont at around 4 pm. I would know him when I saw him. Where the hell was Tal-y-Bont? I was given directions. There are only three roads out of Aberystwyth, north, south and east, and there were no traffic lights or roundabouts at that time. It couldn't be that difficult to find. I went north for a few miles and found the pub, went into the bar and ordered a beer. It was a beautiful day (rare in Wales), so I sat outside in the sunshine, with my necktie loosened and suit jacket off and wondered what Mr John Llewellyn Edwards would look like and when he would be arriving, as it was already past 4 pm. I had been given a vague description of him, but it would not have been the least helpful in my identifying him. He was apparently about 5 feet 10 inches tall, of slim build, a bit of a ladies' man, who did not tolerate fools, especially amongst his medical and surgical colleagues.

Sitting outside, by now on my second pint, I glanced up the hill towards Aberystwyth and there I saw a male cyclist in a dayglo top and black bike shorts, steaming down the road at a maniacal speed. He swerved to a halt, dismounted from his racing bike and left it leaning against the pub wall. He took off his helmet and without so much as a glance in any direction, went straight into the pub. I was near enough to the door of the pub to hear a chorus of greetings from the regulars. "Hey John boy!", "John bach!", "how are you, you old bastard?" and other such terms of endearment. It appeared I had found John Edwards. I got up and went into the pub, approached him and asked if he was John Edwards. He turned and we shook hands. "We've had three English surgeons apply for this job, all ex-army," he said "I didn't like the first one and the second one pulled out after he was appointed, so let's see if you can do any better".

With that, he said goodbye to the occupants of the pub and gave me directions to his farmhouse nearby. I was a soldier surgeon and he was a gentleman farmer, practising surgery in between lambing seasons. Would this combination work, I wondered? I turned my car into the drive of his farm with John following some way behind on his bike and waited for him by his front door in the car, imprisoned by two angry collie dogs, who obviously suspected that I was an English sheep rustler. John arrived, whistled in the dogs and told me to wait until he had got changed. I was totally bemused.

He soon reappeared, showed me where to dump my overnight bag in one of the bedrooms and then said, "Follow me, we can talk on the way". I followed John and his two dogs on a tour of his farm – I can't remember how many acres he had. He asked about my history, my surgical preferences, sub-specialities, but I never had the chance to reply, because he then said, "We can go over all that at supper tonight. I just want to check on the well that's supplying the farmhouse". The well was fine as it turned out, as were the sheep he was due to ferry off to market. I just tramped along and admired the amazing scenery, the lush hills and valleys mixed with the black mountains.

"What are you like around the pancreas?" he suddenly asked, in spite of having decided that supper was the time to discuss all this, so that he could concentrate on his farm. Then without waiting for a reply, he said he had been called in a couple of nights before to the hospital to deal with a fractured pancreas in a young woman who had been involved in a road traffic accident. He'd had to take half the pancreas and the spleen away. I felt a little uncomfortable as I have already mentioned that the pancreas is not an organ I am entirely surgically relaxed with, so I muttered that "I would do emergencies, but pass on anything more complicated". "Nowhere for them to fucking go," he said, "most would rather die in Aber than travel to Carmarthenshire and then onto Swansea, where they might have a pancreatico-biliary surgeon".

That set the tone for most of my surgical time in Aber. It started slowly, but soon became a roller coaster. John and I went out to supper at a small restaurant in town. He had obviously dined there a few times, as he was greeted by name at the door. We sat down, ordered our drinks and food and commenced our compatibility conversation. We agreed on women, the Welsh rugby team, the poor administration of most health facilities, cars in general (he had an old Ford SUV, I had an old Mercedes estate by this time). We disagreed on the surgical management of breast cancer and the new keyhole surgery fad – he had done one laparoscopic cholecystectomy and promptly gave up the procedure.

We exchanged stories of marital discord. My details are documented, but I couldn't possibly reveal his, though I did point out that he was in league division two compared to me. We were like two schoolboys playing Top Trumps when it came to problematic ex-wives and I had smugly put the A1 card onto the table. At least I could be grateful to Angela for that; she had enabled me to 'out ex-wife' my soon to be good colleague, confidante and friend for many years. We left the restaurant in fine spirits. I was quite happy I could get on with JLE (consultants in the NHS are generally known and referred to by their initials) and he felt that I had demonstrated a tad of surgical merit, in spite of being English. I had earned his seal of approval and never looked back. We worked together for 17 years and never had a cross word.

I returned to Aberystwyth on 12 May 95 to attend the formal interview for the post, and this time Nicki accompanied me. My children stayed with Sue, my housekeeper, and Nicki's two stayed with her parents. It was another beautiful sunny day and the scenery looked fantastic with the trees and hedgerows in full leaf. We were to stay overnight with Richard Myles and his wife Alyson.

My interview went well. Dr Alan Axford, a consultant physician and a very good one at that, was also the Medical Director elect. He asked me about the recently published Calman-Hine report on cancer services provision, advising both sides in the purchaser-provider split, and the way health services were being provided at the time, in a vaguely internal capitalist market. I had heard of the report but not exactly studied it in detail. I slipped into medical student mode and managed to provide a satisfactory answer without saying anything of note, relevance or importance and Dr Axford seemed satisfied.

I was offered the job and accepted it. Later that day, Lt Col Jackson became Mr Jackson, newest employee of BGH in Wales. Richard, Alyson and I went out to celebrate and Nicki came with us to drown her sorrows; we all got outrageously drunk. Nicki was not really enamoured with Aberystwyth, as from her point of view, living in the back of beyond was not something she would look forward to, having lived in the affluent South East for most of her life, and Aberystwyth would be a five-hour drive away from her own home, family and friends. However, as she has always done, she (mainly) uncomplainingly made the best of it and took the bad with the good. We both had relatively little choice but to move, she because she wanted to be with me, and I because I needed to escape what had gone before.

I was delighted. I hoped to be able to get back on my feet financially having had to trade in my Mercedes, sell my share in a property that I had inherited and cash in a life insurance policy or two just to pay the legal bills relating to the residence of the children to date, though there would be more to come. In fact, I gave up counting how much I had parted with to protect my daughters after the total had exceeded £100,000.

I would have to work hard, which I did, but the prospect of working in a small self-reliant, isolated hospital was very appealing. I would have very good colleagues and there was an ethos of providing the best care possible that pervaded every department. Yes, it was a good day for me, because not only did I get the job that day, but my Decree Nisi was also granted. I was only six weeks away from the Decree Absolute and my release from the ignominy and embarrassment of being married to Captain Crumpet, Angela Melanie Jackson, the disgraced army officer sacked for unbecoming conduct and disobeying orders. However and almost to this day, I would never be completely free from the effects of her disordered mind.

CHAPTER 49

A Skivvy and a Housekeeper

I had wondered what would be next on Angela's list of allegations, and I was about to find out. It transpired that my eldest daughter had asked to see her head teacher after a contact weekend spent with her mother. She was very upset about things her mother was telling her. "Mum told me that dad wants to have sex with me" she told the headmistress, who then promptly reported her concerns to Social Services. Yet another false allegation by Angela that had to be investigated, then disproved, and it demonstrated the lengths that she was prepared to go to in order to gain the children's allegiance[77].

Angela also started to make her feelings about Nicki quite clear. To me she said, "She's a skivvy who looks after your kids while you're out having fun". To Nicki she said, "Look I don't want to argue with you because you are of no consequence. I want to speak to my daughter, I'm their mother, you are nothing... you mean nothing to them, you are just a skivvy and a housekeeper[78]".

---

77. Diary 10 May 1995
78. Telecon 14 Sep 1995

I had planned to bite the bullet and introduce Angela to Nicki as my fiancée when she returned the children to me after a contact visit with her, but there was an appalling scene involving Angela's predictable verbal attack on me, which soon became physical. She then fought her way into the house, where Nicki was consoling my now very upset youngest child.

"How would you like to have YOUR children taken away?" screeched Angela when she found Nicki in the utility room. She then turned on a very startled Nicki like a woman possessed, tearing her earrings out, pulling her hair, scratching her and punching her. I dragged Angela off her, but she managed to break free and attacked her again, kicking and lunging at her and knocking her toddler Kelly over in the process. Eventually I managed to eject Angela from the house, while Nicki called the police[79].

Nicki and I held a small party in my back garden to celebrate our engagement with friends and family, but Nicki's engagement ring, the symbol of my love for her, was put on hold.[80].

(L-R) Robyn, Kelly, Karl, Nicki, R, me & A. Wedding day, 9 Sep 1995

79.Diary 4 Jun 1995
80. Diary 1 Jul 1995

On 9th September 95 Nicki and I were married at Guildford Registry Office, with all four of our children present. The girls were bridesmaids along with Robyn, my housekeeper's daughter and Karl was the page boy. Our wedding reception was hosted by Nicki's parents in the garden of their home in Fleet and was attended by Brian's ex-wife and her new partner, amongst others.

I gave Nicki a simple gold wedding band with my love as we said our wedding vows together. A honeymoon was out of the question. We did manage to get one night alone without the children in my former matrimonial home and we spent it eating pizza and drinking a bottle of champagne that we had been given. Our first night as husband and wife would see us sleeping in my bed, 'the bed' in which Angela had entertained Brian. It was a less than perfect start to our married life and set the scene for what we were to expect for many years to come. At least we were getting the 'for worse' and the 'for poorer' bit of our wedding vows out of the way early on in our marriage, even if we couldn't enjoy the 'for better' or 'for richer' bit for years to come. The adverse situation tested both the strength of our relationship and our commitment. Neither would be found wanting.

Angela meanwhile had begun trying to track down Nicki's ex-husband, who was still a serving airman, in order to persuade him to give incriminatory evidence against me at the upcoming appeal hearing, which by necessity would require him to commit perjury if he was to be of any real benefit to Angela's case. She had no hesitation in upsetting Nicki's ex-husband by providing him with false and inflammatory information about the care of his two children to gain his sympathy and support. Nicki's ex-husband knew that what she wrote to him was completely untrue, but the worst part of Angela's action was enlisting my eight-year-old daughter to try and extract the information from Nicki and me that she had needed to be able to contact him.[81] She encouraged R to be devious and lie to us.

The court psychiatrist[82] noted in one of his reports: 'Mrs (Angela) Jackson has indicated that she will be relentless in her efforts to achieve residence of her children with her. Her behaviour in attempting to

---

81. Diary 24 Sep 1995
82. Dr Buglar, Psychiatrist 26 Jan 1996

achieve her goal could be described as excessive in such actions as writing a somewhat distorted letter to the former husband of Nicki'.

Nicki and I had only been married a few weeks when it became apparent that my children had been instructed by their mother to do certain unpleasant things to Nicki's children in order to make her leave me, just as they had been told to do nasty things to Robyn, my housekeeper's daughter, to make Sue leave my employment. This added another layer of stress to my fledgling marriage to Nicki, just as Angela hoped.

The Appeal Hearing was heard before Lady Justice Butler-Sloss (Head of the Family Division) and Simon Brown LJ on 10 October 95 and was adjourned generally and remitted to the High Court for a further hearing, based on the significant changes in my circumstances since the previous hearing for residence. Sir Stephen Brown (Lord Justice of Appeal and the President of the Family Division) appointed the Official Solicitor as the Guardian *ad Litem* to represent the welfare of my two children and an official was duly allocated to oversee our case. Fortunately, Social Services supported our move to Wales for the greater good of the whole family. Lady Justice Butler-Sloss warned Angela in court not to destabilise the children and pointed out that she had lost residency of the children. She told her to accept the outcome if she lost again. She was the first female Lord Justice of Appeal in the UK, the highest-ranking female judge in the United Kingdom at the time. Did Angela care? Of course not.

Despite the warning, that very same day Angela would defy Lady Justice Butler-Sloss during a telephone call to my eldest daughter.

"What happened?" asked R, already fully aware of the court proceedings, thanks to her mother.

"Oh, sweetie pie, because you're eight and you're not supposed to be interested in any of this, you're far too clever you see, you shouldn't be clever like this when you are eight" said her mother.

"Why did you win?" my daughter asked.

"Oh well" said her mother, "it's going, its going …I'll tell you this, it's going back to the High court for another judge to look at it, and (the Court Welfare Officer) will be coming round to see you and all I want you to do is tell her the absolute truth…and nobody God nor

Jesus or the angel Gabriel can fault you for telling the truth...there's nothing wrong with telling the truth[83]".

Nicki took on the full-time duties of a mother to my children once we were married, a role that she enjoyed and embraced wholeheartedly, in stark contrast to Angela, who had been resentful and bored, but it did not stop her from bombarding officials with a mountain of complaints about our care of the children over the subsequent years, citing our alleged emotional and physical neglect of them and demanding that we be investigated by Social Services. This was particularly galling, because Social Services had already put the children on the 'At Risk' register under the category of emotional abuse, to safeguard their welfare and protect them from their mother.

I have a good professional record for giving quality care to my patients, but the minute custody became an issue, I found myself being accused by Angela of being negligent where our children were concerned. Angela's incessant need to disparage me was greater than any true concern she might have had for the children and her constant demands for their unnecessary medical treatment, bordered on Munchhausen's by proxy, in other words, another form of child abuse. Moreover, once temporary custody had been awarded in my favour, Angela developed opinions about every minutia of the children's upbringing and considered herself to be some sort of renowned expert on all matters relating to paediatric health care. Where was her concern for her children, and where had she been when they had needed her presence and stability during the lead up to the separation and divorce? Where had her motherly vocation been since either of them had been born? I had been considered a fit parent to look after the children each time she disappeared for trysts with Brian, instead of spending time with them.

Anyway, Social Services completed their investigations into Angela's vexatious allegations of negligence and concluded that there had been none. They reassured her, but she promptly rejected their findings, because they did not serve her agenda.

---

83. Phone transcript 12 Oct 1995

PART 3

NHS 1995-2012

CHAPTER 50

The Great Escape

Bronglais District General Hospital,
Aberystwyth, Wales, 1995

My last day in the Army was 3 December 1995 and I started work in Bronglais Hospital in Aberystwyth the next day. Nicki and I moved to Wales with the four kids, Bevvy the dog, who was always spectacularly car sick, and two removal lorries in convoy with all our worldly belongings aboard. The weather was grim as we traversed the Welsh mountains amidst flurries of snow, travelling to a new beginning. We had arranged for the children to start school almost immediately to give them some much-needed routine and stability, and Angela was prevented by Court Order from seeing them until they had settled.

On the Monday morning, on my way to the hospital, I took the children in to their new school for their first day. I was introduced to my secretary, Carol, whom I treasured until her retirement a couple of years before my own. I also met the Associate Specialist who was allocated to my surgical firm, a man called Venkat (his actual name was considerably longer than that and difficult to pronounce). Here I had struck gold, as he had worked in the hospital, on and off, for many years and was highly respected by the medical and nursing staff and most importantly by the patients. He and I worked very well together, and I was lucky to have a doctor of his experience to help me out. I had of course already met my surgical colleague, John Edwards (JLE). I got down to work.

Nicki had only been my new wife and a step-mum for a mere three months before she found herself living in Wales, without the hired help that Angela had taken for granted, looking after four children under the age of eight (a two-year-old, two six-year-olds and an eight-year-old). I left her surrounded by a sea of packing cases that had been deposited in a beautiful old white Georgian house called The Old Vicarage in a tiny village called Capel Bangor. We intended to buy it once the Ancillary Relief hearing had taken place. The house was located about five miles short of Aberystwyth if driving in from the east and sat alongside a small stream. The fields were full of sheep and cows and we were surrounded by the rolling hills, trees and hedgerows of the Rheidol valley, an area of outstanding natural beauty. It was picture perfect.

Me, A, R, Kelly, Karl and Nicki, Nant y Arian

The village had a couple of pubs, one of which, the Tynllidiart Arms, was to become my local haunt with the dog on a Thursday evening, after my allocated day in theatre. The area offered the children an ideal, innocent, playground, an antidote to what they had had to witness in their previous home and a refuge from the emotional abuse that they would continue to be subjected to by their mother for many years to come. We all walked every weekend into the hills and mountains, took the children on picnics by the Rheidol River and beach at Ynyslas, and Nicki and the children regularly went horse riding at weekends; well, the girls did.

There was only one person who could ruin it for us and with her concentrated brand of vindictiveness, she damn near did.

CHAPTER 51

Mr Jones' Rapture

There was only one slight drawback to working in BGH. The local population cherished their hospital. Most of the adults in the town either worked there or had been treated there at some point and everyone knew everyone else – and their business. I found over the years that I was to become well known, almost common property as the time passed, but in the initial stages I was regarded with reservation as I was of course an Englishman. Even though the hospital had its fair share of immigrant doctors, I think they were more acceptable than someone who had crossed the border from England, the land of the oppressors and invaders who in 1283 AD, following the conquest by Edward 1, had annexed Wales as a Principality.

Even though I had supported the Welsh rugby team for many years, had played squash with the bravest and finest Welsh rugby fullback of all time (JPR Williams when we both worked at the Battle Hospital) and had lived in Tenby, South Wales as a youngster for a couple of years, I still had to prove myself. I did, though it took a bit of time. They have long memories, these Welsh people.

I was given a few nights off call at first, just to get established, and I was grateful for this as we got the house and children straight and settled. The children liked their new primary school, Plascrug, which was to be granted International status due to the many different countries the enrolled children had come from. The children, though taught through the medium of English, did however have to learn Welsh. In fact, within two weeks they were singing Welsh songs for a Christmas concert held in a local chapel and knew all the words, even if they didn't understand any of them. All the teachers and most of the locals were bilingual. Some of the Welsh elderly did not speak much English at all, so one of the nurses would interpret for me in outpatient clinics, in theatre or on the wards. I was used to it.

Many of them had never left their home area at all and only went into town to shop or attend the market maybe once a week. Some spent their holidays in the next town, as if it equated to going abroad. They found the later addition of roundabouts and traffic lights to their road system quite baffling, as gradually, Aberystwyth was hauled into the 21st century. I was bemused by how modern development had totally bypassed Mid-Wales, but it was geographically challenged. The hill farmers had a tough time, especially if they had to lamb their flocks twice a year. This was always a consideration if a farmer required a surgical procedure, and frequently the date of this had to be rearranged to suit the uterine contractions of his sheep.

By this time, I had undertaken an operating list on a Thursday. I reconfirmed that the operating theatres really needed updating and to my mind the operating lights were just awful, in that the focusing mechanisms on both the main light and the satellite did not work, so a stand-alone satellite had to be utilized if the operation was deep in the body cavity. Even so, the combined wattage of the three lamps would provide less illumination than a half-decent domestic bedside lamp, and I resolved to get modern lights installed, at least in the theatre that I was allocated to work in. I had spent too long working with inadequate illumination and as I got older, long-sightedness became more of an issue. I was getting to the stage when I needed more light to distinguish the fine detail.

On my first night on call, Venkat, my Associate Specialist, was around, and he could fire fight most surgical admissions, so I relaxed with Nicki in front of an open fire in the lounge of our rented house. I had been issued with a pager for contact during the day or if out at night. Later in the early evening, the phone rang and the BGH switchboard operator, Nan, who lived in our village and had worked nights in switchboard for as long as anyone could remember, asked me to urgently go to A & E. Venkat had requested my assistance.

By the time I got there, the patient he had asked me to see was having an ultrasound examination of his abdomen. I went into the department and spoke to the Radiologist performing the procedure. Her name was Mair Jones, and she had been a couple of years ahead of me at medical school in Liverpool. She confirmed that the patient, an elderly male, had a ruptured triple A (Abdominal Aortic Aneurysm) which Venkat had suspected, and he was already getting the emergency theatre on-call staff in. Soon a couple of porters came in to whisk the old boy up to the theatres on the fifth floor by way of the arthritic dedicated patient's lift, which was state of the art when originally installed in the last century, but nowadays could only just elevate the weight of itself against gravity when empty of all cargo.

The patient needed some pretty vigorous resuscitation and the duty anaesthetist made a start whilst I went to the ward to see if I could find a relative. All the anaesthetists at Bronglais were consultants who had elected not to train junior staff, so they could provide a high-quality service without the encumbrance of any untrained embryo anaesthetists. Their choice.

Ruptured Triple As carry a very high mortality rate, especially in a District General Hospital without specialist vascular surgeons on hand, especially in anyone over the age of 70 years and especially if there is free blood in the abdomen. This old boy had all three factors against him, but in those days, it seemed to be incumbent on the hospital staff to 'give it a go'.

The patient's name was Jones. Mrs Jones, his wife, had been directed to the patients' waiting room on Owain Glyndwr Ward, the main surgical ward, where I had access to 20 beds. I went into the nursing office and asked one of the nurses if she knew where Mrs

Jones was and if she had any idea of the severity of her husband's predicament. I was informed that she was next door, and I raced into the waiting room and asked for Mrs Jones. An elderly lady answered, and I took her to one side. I introduced myself and said, "I'm so sorry to tell you that your husband is extremely ill. He needs an urgent operation and we are preparing him now. He has a ruptured aneurysm, a leak of the main artery in his abdomen and I must warn you that he may not (I should have said, would not) get through it".

A masterpiece of understatement, to soften the blow. There is a consensus amongst some of my surgical colleagues that the better option in these cases is to tell the patient's nearest and dearest that death is inevitable, but you will do your best. If the patient does survive, you are a hero, and if the patient dies, then that's what you said would happen and you were proved right; a surgical win-win.

Mrs Jones looked at me quizzically. I was not sure that I had got through to her, so I elaborated a bit further.

"It's all so sudden" she said, "When I came in to see him yesterday, he was fine." Not picking up on the words 'when I came to see him' during the second half of that sentence, I went on to explain, "These things happen very suddenly, totally unpredictably" (in the days before routine Triple A screening, available now). I was amazed he had even made it into the hospital.

"Well" she said, "do your best", then added, 'it wasn't anything to do with the operation he had, is it Bach?"

My mind skidded to an abrupt halt. "Er, what operation?" I asked.

"Mr Edwards, he repaired my husband's rapture," she said. She meant rupture, the old word for an inguinal hernia.

"Er, rapture?" I said.

"Yes" she said. "You know, when the groin gives way. I came in tonight to take him home. Mr Edwards said he'd be as good as new".

Suddenly I felt slightly queasy. "Mrs Jones" I asked, already knowing the answer before I asked the question, "it isn't your husband who has just been brought in by ambulance is it?"

"No, he's been here for a week, on Owain Glyndwr ward. Mr Edwards made him stay in, because it was a very big rapture. My husband had it for over 40 years and he only agreed to have it done when he had trouble walking. He's just gone to the gentleman's toilet. Oh, there he is now." She pointed to a perfectly healthy Mr Jones walking towards us, with a slight post-'rapture' repair limp.

I apologised and said I had got the wrong Mrs Jones. My hasty and parting words were, "Forget everything I said". I rushed off to find the right Mrs Jones in the patient's waiting room. The correct Mrs Jones had not answered when I had called her name because she was almost completely deaf, and she had also never been in a hospital in her whole life before. I sighed. I had absolutely no hope of getting through to this old lady, and in any event, they were calling for me to get to theatre as the patient was on the table. I left her in the care of one of the nursing staff, who began to shout in Welsh into her ear.

I did a quick midline incision (Arnold Ely would have turned in his grave if he had got there). The idea is to cross-clamp the aorta as swiftly as possible to prevent further bleeding and then effect a repair using a Dacron graft. To cut a long story short, I managed to get the graft in, and then the patient promptly had a heart attack and died. Not a good start to my emergency surgery in Aberystwyth.

I told the correct Mrs Jones that her husband had passed on and that there was nothing more that we could have done. After I had said this loudly about four times in both ears, she asked, "Where's he gone then?"

This mix-up should never have occurred. I had worked with a Welsh regiment and those soldiers with similar surnames also recited the last 3 digits of their service number to distinguish themselves, for example, Private Jones 735. In civilian life, it was rather different and when I went to the Tynllidiart Arms for a couple of pints after walking the dog on a Thursday after theatre, I met Gareth (Jones) the Coal and Barry (Jones) the Grave; the coal merchant and the grave digger respectively. I should have also remembered my two co-consultant Joneses, Jones the Bones and Jones the Groans. I suppose the urgency of the situation just got to me.

CHAPTER 52

Baby Talk

Nicki and I agonised for many years as to whether we should have a child together. The deciding factor was not whether we wanted one, but whether to risk destabilising the precarious situation we had with my children, given the way their mother would use the addition of another child against us to create yet more rivalry.

The children were being systematically robbed by their mother of the certainty that I was a good man, a trustworthy man, that I would protect them, and that I did not present any danger to them. They were robbed of the certainty that I loved them, that I would not let them down and that I wanted them in my life. They were deprived of stability, their innocence, their childhood and their good memories of me and of the love and attention available to them from their new extended family. These people could have enriched their lives, but the children were encouraged to regard each of them with suspicion and as rivals for my love, consideration and money. Ultimately, the children were to reject us all, yet they were encouraged to thoroughly embrace everyone in their mother's new circle. Had I known that

Angela would persist until her dying day in punishing me, I would have had that theoretical child with Nicki.

I missed the opportunity of having a child who would have loved me for simply being me, a child who would not punish me for not being the father that they thought I should be, or was, a child who would not unjustifiably reject me, a child that would fill the aching void where my own children had once been, a hole in my life eroded by Angela's maliciousness, when at first she stole the children from me emotionally and then physically too. The children don't realise the extent of what they lost in terms of their relationship with me, because they were told by their mother that they never had it in the first place.

Angela hoped that if she could make Nicki leave or create enough chaos in our household, I would not be able to cope on my own and would hand the children over to her. In fact Angela was so desperate to get rid of Nicki by any means that she began to tell my confused young children that she planned to put a bullet in her head or poison her tea in order to achieve her aim. As Angela had no concept of consequence, it was a seriously worrying situation.

CHAPTER 53

Who is George?

As I have already mentioned, my patients had to come first, regardless of my own needs or those of my family. Our lives, by necessity, revolved around the requirements of the hospital, and all our activities as a family, in some way, were governed by my job, especially before consultants regularly carried mobile phones with them; thus, I was tethered to a landline and a pager. A couple of occasions come to mind which demonstrate this.

I received a call to attend A & E, this time to see a woman who had been brought in with a closed head injury following a horse-riding accident. This was something I always feared, because we lived very near to riding stables and all the kids had a chance to ride. My youngest daughter was not too enthusiastic and Karl soon found he got motion sickness when the pony was trotting, but my eldest child and Kelly were very keen and became good horsewomen. Nicki had also been taught to ride as a child and frequently went out on hacks.

I asked where the patient was, and I was directed to a cubicle and then told, "Oh, by the way, it's your wife". It is never a good idea to treat and be responsible for one's own family, but I was in a dilemma.

I was the only consultant surgeon in the hospital at the time due to the absence of my two colleagues. I pulled back the curtain and greeted Nicki, who I have to say, was not all there – at all. She had taken a tumble over the neck of her mount, which she had never ridden before, when it stopped mid-canter and she didn't. She was wearing a new riding hat, which was dented, as she had hit the ground with the back of her head. Fortunately, she and her companion had been cantering across a field rather than on the road.

Venkat joined me. He showed me Nicki's X-rays and neither of us could see a fracture, though severe head injuries can occur in the absence of bony injury, as illustrated by my A & E experience in the Battle Hospital. Nonetheless, the X-rays were immediately reported by a consultant radiologist, who confirmed our findings. My beautiful wife had sustained quite a severe neuronal (nerve) injury to her brain and her thought processes were a tad off course. I am pretty sure that she recognised me, but she was not quite sure why I was there, as I should have been at work. I told her that she had been riding George and had fallen off him.

"George is a horse", I added hastily, for the benefit of anyone who might have overheard and had formed the wrong impression. It was a mistake talking to Nicki about George and how she had fallen off him, because for the next few hours she kept asking, "Who's George?" and "did I fall off him?" regardless of any reply to the affirmative.

On neurological examination Nicki was sound, but not aware of time, place, day of the week or even the month, so we would just have to keep her observed until her concussion subsided. She was subsequently admitted to the surgical ward for hourly neurological observations with my name placed at the top of her bed as her consultant.

I saw her frequently, but being asked repeatedly about George was getting somewhat wearing. She was in a single room at the front of the hospital where there was a view of the National Library out of the window, which at least changed the text of her repetitive questioning somewhat.

"Is that the National Library?"

"Yes" I replied.

"Why can I see it out of my window?"

"Because you are in hospital. You banged your... never mind." I didn't bother continuing, it was pointless and I couldn't face going back to George again.

"Is that the National Library?" She asked again.

"Yes darling".

"But I don't understand why I can see it".

"It's because it is there".

"But why is it outside my window?"

"That's where they put it".

"But the National Library is in Wales" she exclaimed, indignantly this time.

"Yes. We live in Wales" I informed her, with as much patience as I could muster.

"Do we?" Nicki then asked what day of the week it was.

"Wednesday" I said and quickly disappeared for a cup of coffee before she could ask again. The nurses would have to deal with her instead.

She has no recollection to this day of walking back to the stables with her friend and the horse, or the journey to the hospital in her friend's car or being seen in A & E by me. The 'lost' time frame of at least an hour showed significant retrograde amnesia which indicates, to a certain extent, the severity of her brain injury. The first memory she has is of seeing the National Library out of the hospital window. She didn't even know if we had missed our annual holiday to Spain. However, she did later recall that she had intended to canter across an uphill field and the next thing she remembered was sitting on the ground with a buzzing noise in her head, and becoming distressed, because she found my hospital pager in her jacket pocket and couldn't understand why it was there. I had given Nicki my hospital pager to take with her on her ride, in case I was called to the hospital, in which case she would have to return home as quickly as she could, to look after the children. Little did she know that the pager would be to warn me of her coming in as my patient.

I decided to keep her on the ward for a couple of nights. I couldn't face being at home alone with four young children and a wife with an addled brain.

My stepdaughter, Peachy Pie, as I still call her, made the term 'accident prone' all her own. She probably had one of the thickest A & E case sheets, as her succession of injuries were serially added to the folder and a lot of the nurses in A & E knew her by name, not just from having seen her toddling around with me whilst I did the ward rounds with her at a weekend, but as in, "Hello Kelly, what have you done this time?"

It was a Thursday, my designated operating day, and I had to be changed, fired up and ready to go at 8.30am to see my patients pre-operatively. I was just about to leave the house when there was a great crash, followed by agonised wailing from Kelly's bedroom. She had been trampolining on her bed prior to school, despite this being a forbidden activity, and had crash landed on her front with her head twisted to the side, wrenching her neck, the muscles of which went into a painful spasm. She could not move herself and we could not move her an inch without her screaming with pain, so Nicki called an ambulance whilst I shot off to do my job. Fortunately, after being seen in A & E she was deemed fine and discharged without serious injury. I was reassured by a telephone message to theatre as I struggled to remove a large rectal cancer.

Kelly, bless her, really got her money's worth from the NHS, well before she made her first National Insurance contribution, having fallen and cut her hand on a plate she was carrying, had a car run over her foot ending up on crutches and in a cast, been admitted drunk as a teenager overnight after pilfering the contents of our drinks cabinet with Mari, our 'adopted' daughter (and replaced the alcohol with water), had been admitted with a refractory pneumonia, having to be stretchered away from a water park in England having crashed at the bottom of a waterslide, then returned to Wales to sustain a serious eye injury caused by an orchard apple that was thrown at her, which required 6 weeks bed rest right at the start of the summer holidays, screwing up the entire summer for all of us and also a broken nose when her boyfriend accidentally elbowed her in the face.

Karl, my stepson, also found my name at the end of his hospital bed after being admitted for an infection, and A, my youngest daughter, required my attention, though totally unaware of the fact, after being admitted one winter night when still a teenager, drunk as a skunk and somewhat hypothermic. All in a day's work.

CHAPTER 54

No Plainer Case
of Conduct

I had only been in my new job in Bronglais for a matter of weeks before
I had to go back to the Royal Courts of Justice in London[84]. There I
would read the progress reports written by the children's Guardian
ad Litem for the Official Solicitor to the Supreme Court. So as not to
destabilise the children following our move, Angela was ordered by
the court to sign certain undertakings regarding her behaviour before
she could have contact with them. Meanwhile whilst I was settling
into my new post, she made sure we were inundated with obnoxious
paperwork or verbal diktats from her or her solicitors on an almost
weekly basis.

After Christmas, I had to return to the Royal Courts of Justice yet
again[85], this time for another custody hearing based on my change
of circumstances, which was preceded by interviews with Social
Services, a Court psychiatrist and the Guardian *ad Litem*. Of Angela,
the psychiatrist wrote, 'I don't think I have ever met a person [who,

---

84. Before Lord Justice Hogg 21 Dec 1995
85. Mr Justice Johnson 14 Feb 1996

in an interview], was able to speak about someone (the father) in such contrasting extremes. One has to be concerned about that[86].

However, despite my marriage to Nicki, two stepchildren, my move to Wales and my new job, the judge, Mr Justice Johnson, again made the residence order in my favour, with full custody with Nicki looking after the children on a day to day basis.

A very rigid court order was put in place for staying contact between the children and their mother during holidays and in addition, a very restrictive telephone contact schedule was arranged which was intended to safeguard the children from their mother's emotional abuse and unceasing attempts to pressure them to reject me. The calls were to last no more than five minutes per child on a Tuesday and Thursday at 6 pm on the dot, no matter what anyone else wanted to be doing, and despite the many commitments I had at the hospital such as meetings and my allocated day in theatre on a Thursday.

The lack of flexibility caused us logistical nightmares trying to work it around my on-call commitment, which was a 1:3 rota during good times, 1:2 in bad times and every night on-call when JLE was on leave. Of course, despite what was stipulated in the order, Angela held the children captive once they were on the phone to her. The law was no barrier to her abuse.

"Why do you have to go?" Angela asked my daughter as she tried to finish the phone call.

"Because the clock says so," replied my daughter.

"Why, what will happen, will a thunderbolt come out of the sky and strike you down if you don't?[87]"

If we were so much as five minutes late making a phone call to Angela or delivering the children to her home, she would fire off scathing letters of complaint to the Official Solicitor and telephone calls to me.

"Well I know it's very difficult for you to organise the children David, because you're not used to it, but you must do your best... We don't want to be in trouble with the High Court judge, do we?... and I'm sure you can organise yourself so you can obey a High Court

86. Report to the OS Jan 1996
87. Telecon Dec 1996

Order. It doesn't take much in the organisation department… looking after children does involve some sort of organisation. Sort it out, get your diary out, if necessary, David!"

"Thank you, Angela" I said sighing.

"That's a pleasure" said Angela sarcastically. "I can always advise you on how to look after the children, if you can't cope.[88]"

She would return the children back home when she felt like it, sometimes hours late or even on a different day, despite what her solicitors had confirmed to the contrary, and no matter how inconvenient her antics were to my work schedule, the children's schooling or their social life at home.

I returned home from work especially mid-morning on one such occasion, to welcome the children back from contact with their mother at the appointed time of 11 am. I received a phone call from Angela at 12.10 p.m.

"Ah David, I will be returning the children at four o'clock" she said.

"Angela, the children are supposed to have been returned at eleven o'clock. I am here waiting for them. Where are you?" I asked.

"None of your business" she said,[89] and that was the end of the discussion as far as she was concerned.

Another lengthy trip back to the Royal Courts of Justice in London was required for my Ancillary Relief Hearing,[90] during which the judge made it clear that he would 'attach substantial weight' to Angela's conduct in respect of her deliberate attempts to damage my career and reputation.

'There can be no plainer case of conduct' he said, 'which comes within the category which parliament intended to be considered by a Court in matters such as this… I propose to take account fully of the conduct to which I have referred briefly in this judgement and more elaborately in my earlier judgement'.

He did. Angela was not awarded one penny of the marital equity, not least because she had refused to disclose any of her own assets

88. Telecon 23 Nov 1995
89. Diary 2 Jan 1996
90. Mr Justice Johnson 13 June 1996

when ordered to. She was ordered to sign over her interest in the matrimonial home, the villa and our combined life assurances. Of course she refused, but it was a pointless gesture. A district judge did it for her.

The *Sun* would publish another exclusive mere weeks later: 'Captain Crumpet marries her Sarge. Captain Crumpet Angela Jackson has tied the knot with her hunky sarge Brian Taylor two years after the affair which ended their Army careers[91]'.

The *Sun* forgot to mention that their publication of the story had also ended my career, but I don't think that either the 'journalists' or 'editorial staff' lost any sleep over that. All in the public interest. Well done.

It was the summertime and the night before our family holiday to Spain in 1996. We stayed overnight with Nicki's parents in Fleet. Spain became our sanctuary during the summer for many years and in our impecunious state we gratefully accepted the invitation to stay with the friends who had shielded me during the newspaper publicity two years before. However, we were still required, as per the court

The family in Spain

91. Sun newspaper 29 Jul 1996

order, to phone Angela each Tuesday and Thursday at 6 pm on the dot from a pay phone abroad, no matter how much fun the children were having at the beach, or in the pool. The night before we left for the airport, we had to make the duty phone call to Angela with the children from Nicki's parent's house on the appointed day. I overheard my youngest daughter discussing the need for sun protection on holiday with her mother. "No, I won't" [get burnt] I heard my daughter assure her mother, "Because David says I have to wear a T-shirt".

David, I thought? *Who is David? Who is she referring to?* Puzzled, I asked my eldest daughter and she pointed to her sister, "Ask her" she said. It transpired that the children had been instructed to call me 'David' when in the presence of their mother, and to call Brian 'Daddy'[92]. Parental alienation was well under way. I was being incrementally erased from my role as father to my daughters, even though they lived full time with me.

---

92. Diary 13 Aug 1996

CHAPTER 55

I Even Remember You Swearing

Within my work schedule I travelled widely, undertaking peripheral clinics through the catchment area. Once a month I would travel to Newtown (one hour away) Aberaeron (half an hour away) and twice a month to Tywyn (one hour away) to provide the service north of the county. Later Llanidloes would be added so I really was peripatetic, but this was a good way of delivering the surgical service by my doing the travelling to the local hospitals rather than the patients coming to me in Aberystwyth. It was however very tiring. If I was on-call for one of these excursions, then I would be covered by my colleagues.

The first time I went to Tywyn Venkat was away and as I had no idea how to find the hospital, I went by taxi. I was picked up at 1 pm as the clinic would start at 2 p.m. When I got in the car, the driver asked me a few questions regarding my work in the hospital. I explained that I was a recently appointed consultant surgeon. "Oh" he said. "That must mean you work for Mr Venkat". Of course, it was the other way around, but it just illustrates how highly regarded Venkat was in Aberystwyth. Everyone knew, liked and trusted Venkat; he was a known quantity. I said nothing.

The first patient in my clinic was a mature lady from the Birmingham area. Not infrequently, Tywyn and nearby Aberdovey were the selected retirement areas of choice for West Midlanders and I was to meet many of them amongst the local population. This lady had attended for her yearly review following a bowel cancer operation prior to her moving to Wales. Not having the information immediately to hand, I asked her when she had undergone the procedure and she replied, "About five years ago".

"Not done here then?" I asked.

"No" she replied, "I had it done in Birmingham by Mr Oates. Do you know him?"

Well, there you go I thought. Here I was in remote mid-Wales, reconnected with an old boss who on the whole had not thought much of me when I was training under him. Mr Oates should have retired by this time, though I could be convinced that he would remain in post until he collapsed and died in the operating theatre. But he had retired, after a significant heart attack. He recovered sufficiently to maintain a surgical interest, keeping the long-term results of his bowel patients.

"Yes, I do know him" I told her, "I worked with him and had a lot of respect for his, er, surgical abilities". She picked up on what I had said. "He was a good surgeon" she remarked, "No sense of humour though; not that what I had wasn't serious, but he could have smiled once".

I checked her over, arranged for the routine follow-up screening procedures and told her I would copy her results to Mr Oates as a matter of courtesy, which I did. I received a letter by return. Mr Oates wrote that he was delighted to read that I would be looking after some of his old patients, that he was reassured that they would be in competent hands and he expressed his thanks at my keeping him in the loop. Either his memory of our prickly relationship had softened over the years and he had forgiven me for what I said about Birmingham, or Alzheimer's had struck.

Travelling to these small town or cottage hospitals had the disadvantages of the miles driven and the time consumed, but these were offset by the wonderful hospitality. Each of them had their own kitchens and I was always provided with hot drinks and the latest pastries cooked (or even bought locally) to sort of keep me going and I was very conscious of the fact that these clinics were of immense value to local inhabitants to whom travel to Aberystwyth could be a major and expensive undertaking as public transport throughout Mid-Wales was scanty to say the least and frequently patients arrived by taxi. There was a railway station, but the train only went in one direction, north west towards Shrewsbury. Thus, I was always against the closing down of a peripheral clinic which was frequently considered as a cost saving measure by my employers, the newly named Ceredigion and Mid-Wales NHS Trust.

In the clinic, there were a husband and wife sitting opposite me, both very elderly. They had been married for a millennium and both had worked together in founding and running a flourishing private school in the West Country, he as the headmaster and she as the music teacher, in addition to raising their own family. They were totally inseparable, as one might expect, not only because of their devotion to each other, but also because of their interdependence. Though they were two physical adults in the clinic in actual fact, if you broke each of them down into components, the faculties and senses that they were left with, then only in combination did they add up to a more or less complete functioning human being.

I should explain. She was completely blind, but her hearing was excellent, and she was very mobile for her age. He on the other hand possessed good vision but was deaf as a post and struggled to get around, being dependent on walking aids. Together they managed very well and could even (er...safely, for want of a better word) drive their small car, Sunday drives being one of their favourite pastimes. Watching TV together also required that all their remaining faculties were coalesced, with the addition of subtitles when available.

Their tenacity in overcoming life's hurdles was heart-warming and they were fiercely independent. Thus, I had to carefully consider the wife's admission to hospital in terms of how her husband would manage alone for a few days. One of the many joys of my job was working with a dedicated group of GPs, many of whom had grown up in the area. Those who had taken employment in this isolated part of the country had done so with their eyes open and an appreciation of the extra efforts they had to make on their patients' behalves, to provide a totality of primary care.

I phoned this couple's GP and immediately all arrangements were made for the care of her husband during the absence of his wife and for a few days afterwards until she had fully recovered. I breathed a sigh of relief. All I had to do was ensure that the practice was informed of her admission date and they would take care of the rest.

I would come across similar examples throughout my practice in Wales, but there is another issue related to the interdependence of long-standing couples. I raised these concerns particularly when I specialised in large bowel cancer during the last 10 years of my career, but they could be applied whenever one partner had a long-term, life-limiting illness.

I had noticed that on at least four occasions, both husband and wife had significant symptoms indicating the probable diagnosis of a bowel cancer, but the second diagnosis was often long after the first. This was because the first of the couple to be investigated and then treated was inevitably going to be looked after by the second, who would ignore and deny their own symptoms so that they could provide the necessary care and support to their partner. Only when one was treated and fully recovered did the malignancy in the caring partner come to light, and because of the delay, it was frequently more advanced and deadly than their partner's. The carer died before the cared for. I called it 'carer cancer' and taught my colleagues in other hospitals to be aware of it at a lecture I gave when Chair of a bowel cancer network.

It was a Friday evening and a middle-aged woman had been admitted. Venkat was unhappy with her and called me to have a look. In short, she had always been in possession of a 'difficult bowel' and at the start of the week she had felt very ill with a fever, loss of appetite and general malaise. When I examined her, I found that she was very unwell with a high pulse rate, coated tongue and a tender mass in the lower left quadrant of her abdomen with signs of peritonitis. These were the typical findings of acute, severe diverticular disease (when pulsion pouches, for want of a better description, form in the wall of the bowel, usually the sigmoid colon, and become inflamed). She really should have accessed medical help much earlier on in her illness, but this was typical of a Friday admission in that without the hoped-for resolution of symptoms during the week, the onset of the weekend with the prospect of a reduced medical emergency service tipped the balance.

Venkat thought she might settle with intense resuscitation and antibiotic treatment, but I had a feeling (in my own bowel), that she was beyond that stage and may have had a localised bowel perforation, which could be catastrophic, with the onset of generalised sepsis. I decided to open her up. There is an adage in surgery that 'it is better to look and see than wait and see' and I was glad I had, as she had a huge inflammatory phlegmon of the sigmoid colon with a smell of faeces and localised pus. I scooped the foul bowel out and formed a colostomy, the safest option under the circumstances and with all the other surgical procedures complete, closed her up and went home.

At some unearthly hour, the phone woke me from a deep sleep. I could tell that Venkat, always cool under pressure, was seriously concerned. I hoped it was not about the lady I have just described. That was a forlorn hope. Our conversation at night always started with Venkat saying "Good evening, sorry to bother you", but on this occasion, there was no preamble. He explained quite simply that the patient in question was bleeding to death. He had already returned her to theatre, but the haemorrhage was widespread, and he could not staunch it. She was on the High Dependency Unit (HDU) and had developed a serious sepsis induced clotting defect known then as Disseminated Intravascular Coagulation. All her clotting factors had been hoovered up and she had run out. Donated stored blood would not solve the problem as the clotting factors are separated out with the plasma. Fresh donated cross-matched blood would certainly help, but I was no longer in the Army. What she needed, fresh frozen plasma (FFP), was only available if the consultant in charge of the case contacted the consultant haematologist on call and explained the case and the need for this quite expensive treatment.

I drove to the hospital and ran to HDU. The situation was critical and as the FFP would take at least an hour to thaw out after the authorisation process, I decided to keep her on her bed and pack her abdomen. I asked the theatre staff who were standing by to bring bowls of sterile water, packs, long forceps and strong elastic sticky bandage to the HDU ward. I unpicked her wound from top to bottom, sucked out all the uncoagulated blood and then painstakingly packed every square inch of all her abdominal surfaces, which were freely oozing. Fortunately, the patient was still under anaesthetic and on a ventilator. Using a special membrane dressing I left her abdomen open and then with help, trussed her up tight with the sticky bandage, a sort of abdominal tourniquet. The obvious, overt bleeding stopped. By then the consultant haematologist had been located and he immediately allowed us to use four packs of FFP. One problem was that the increased abdominal pressure I had created, by tightly packing her abdomen, was splinting her diaphragm and the ventilator was struggling to get oxygen into her, puffing, wheezing and squeaking as it tried to overcome the large increase in the pulmonary (lung) resistance that I had caused.

Even after many years on the job I was kept awake by my ill patients. My mind always goes back over what I had done and whether I had covered all bases to the best of my ability. It was part of the job I didn't get paid for, especially whilst on-call. This particular night, I was not on-call, but she was my patient and I could not have abrogated my responsibility under any circumstances.

Next day this lady's clotting profile was much improved. The FFP and her own bone marrow had risen to the task in hand replacing her depleted clotting factors, so I loosened her abdominal trussing, to the relief of the ventilator and my anaesthetic colleagues. A couple of days later I closed her abdominal wound, and she then made an uneventful recovery. I was several years older by this point, but nature can soften these blows and when I reviewed her in outpatients, I was delighted to see that she was full of the joys of spring. She had a bowel that worked, even if into a stoma bag. I asked if she wanted a reversal of the colostomy to re-establish gut continuity and she emphatically declined. She was booked on a two-week cruise to the Canary Islands with a friend.

"I can do it when you get back," I offered. "We'll leave it for six months if you want."

"No", she said, and I asked why.

"Because I nearly died," she said.

"I know, but that is unlikely to happen again," I said. "It was because you were very ill and septic".

"And the other reason" she said, "is that I was awake when you operated on me in Intensive Care. I felt no pain (due to the routine epidural) but I remember everything you said. I even remember you swearing."

That had to be true. My language is directly linked to my stress levels. I wished her a happy holiday and she thanked me for saving her life and almost skipped out of the clinic. I reviewed her a couple of times in outpatients. Her answer was always "No". I think she had more common sense than I did.

CHAPTER 56

The Judge Said So

Though still recovering from the legal bills, Nicki and I decided to design and build a six-bedroomed house in Aberystwyth to accommodate our amalgamated family. Even though I was mortgaged up to the hilt, I loved that house. I loved my family and I loved my job, but Angela the scourge of all our lives, was relentless, determined beyond reason, to destroy us, to blight every shred of happiness we had, with her unrelenting abuse of the children and indeed, the whole family.

Another progress report was due to be submitted by the Official Solicitor and the court-appointed psychiatrist to the judge reviewing the case. Residence was not up for discussion, but Angela insisted that it was and set about emotionally manipulating everyone in order to achieve it.

'I will never accept the decision made by the Judge to give David custody of the children' she wrote, 'and there are no sanctions that can be applied to make me change my view[93]'.

---

93. Letter to the OS 5 Dec 1996

She made it very clear what the repercussions would be for the children if she did not get her own way.

In view of Angela's continuing and worsening emotional abuse of the children, the Court psychiatrist recommended that, 'in order to protect the children from Mrs Taylor's [Angela's] unceasing coercion to reject their father[94]', the children would remain with me and Angela's contact would be reduced even more. She would be allowed to see the children four times a year for a total of three hours at a time, in Aberystwyth, with no telephone contact permitted in between. The Court directed that these visits be overseen by a court-appointed official. For several months Angela refused to participate, her logic being that if the children could only see her under stringent and protective contact arrangements they would think (or rather know) that there was something seriously 'wrong with mummy' and what she was doing to them.

With such a devastating outcome for Angela, it was hoped that she would finally be able to join up the dots and understand that as her emotional abuse of the children got worse then the Court reduced her contact with them, but she didn't, and we just couldn't comprehend why. She must have known that during the latest proceedings, the officials had considered the possibility of a 'parentectomy' for a few years[95].

In order to make sense of her absolute conviction that there was nothing wrong with her, Angela had to believe that everyone else must be wrong, Social Services, the court appointed psychiatrist, the Official Solicitor and even the judges. 'If I was a mindless idiot' she wrote, 'I might simply say "oh it must be right because all the experts and the Judge said so". Unfortunately, I can still think and more importantly, I can feel in my soul that this situation is wrong[96].'

It took a long time for us all to realise that intellect, and the fact that she could still think, was incidental to her 'problem'; it was about how her mind worked, and this eventually had to be spelt out in court.

---

94. OS report 11 Mar 1997
95. An action to prevent the effects of Parental Alienation
96. Letter to OS 3 Sep 1996

According to Mr Justice Johnson:

'However, to a degree which in my experience is fortunately highly unusual, the mother has repeatedly proved herself incapable of seeing the effect upon others, including principally her children, of her actions and her words... I say that she is incapable of foreseeing those effects rather than that she is unwilling to do so because of the persistence of her conduct in spite of repeated criticisms about it...

'In cases such as this it is usual for judges to seek to avoid making hurtful findings beyond what is necessary to sustain the decision. Usually it is left to the professional reader of a judgment to read between the lines. Here, in my view, it is necessary for me to state my conclusions clearly and unequivocally.... Nothing that has happened in these past 18 months leads me in any way to doubt the conclusion [of the social worker] that the mother's commitment to achieving what she wants for herself blinds her to the needs of others and would blind her to the needs of the children. That she has demonstrated over and over again[97]*'.*

That conclusion was a game changer in terms of understanding Angela's behaviour, but with that understanding came the daunting realisation that nothing would ever change, nothing could ever improve. We would only ever tread water. We just had to hope that we could keep the children with us for long enough to neutralise the effects of the venom she inflicted on them and to reduce the long-term damage. We also had to hope that our marriage would survive the severe beating it would take in order to do it.

On the other hand, for the best part of a year we led a normal, happy, carefree family life. There were no court appearances to endure, there were no solicitors' letters to dread, there were no abusive faxes to receive or phone calls to suffer, there were no upsetting contact handovers to witness. We breathed a much-needed sigh of relief, but of course, as we had anticipated, it was not to last. Angela suddenly decided that she would take up the offer of supervised contact and pick up exactly where she left off, only this time with more vehemence, the minute she had contact with the children again. It soon became clear

97. Mr Justice Johnson 14 Feb 1996

that being monitored by a court official wasn't going to prevent her from continuing to emotionally abuse and destabilise the children[98]. However, the aim was to progress contact for the sake of the children, if at all possible. It was acknowledged that any progress to reinstating unsupervised contact would be experimental and to the children's detriment if it all went horribly wrong, which predictably it did.

---

98. Jan 98 – Feb 99 supervised contact took place on 5 occasions

CHAPTER 57

Falklasswaractually

Gradually I was accepted into the community, not just for my job as a consultant surgeon looking after them, but for who I was. Patiently explaining that although I was not Welsh, I was not actually English either, but British through mixed parentage, may have helped.

Vocal support for the Welsh National Rugby team, memorising the names of the Welsh squad and a few trips to the Millennium Stadium in Cardiff to watch them play certainly helped, but when they were playing against England in the annual six nations, my loyalty to Wales faltered somewhat and of course I was reminded that I was an Englishman when the Welsh defeated the English bastards, the team everyone loved to hate, and received texts and phone calls from a gloating JLE especially. JLE spoke fluent Welsh and wore his nationalism with pride, but one day he let slip that he was born in London, so I had a measure of retaliation.

I was often asked to give a talk at the annual meetings of various locals groups in the area, including the Lions and the Round Table, but the most memorable event was when I agreed to talk at the AGM of Aberystwyth Golf Club, having been invited by the family dentist, Dai Turner, who unfortunately, not much later, was to die young, though he had lived very well up to that point.

When I turned up at the appointed hour, 7 pm, it was obvious that the celebrations marking another successful year for the club in avoiding repaying its rather unsustainable debts were well under way. I was driving and speaking later, so I kept off the alcohol. I was due to talk after the meal at around 9 pm for about 40 minutes following the speeches by the various officers of the club. I was set up and ready to go.

Now there is no one more verbose than an alcohol-infused Welsh golfer, and in that meeting there were at least 40 of them relating their golfing successes (few) and disasters (many) and as a golfer I listened attentively as the jokes were also related, all pretty smutty as no women were present. Some were told in Welsh, so I just laughed when everybody else did. At around 11.30 pm, I asked when they would like me to speak. "Hold your horses boyo. We need a few more drinks yet, isn't it?"

I was pleased with the boyo salutation, as it is slang for Welshman. Alcohol had altered my nationality in their eyes, if only for a while. At midnight I resignedly said I had to go. There was little point in my starting at that time, but the President of the club got up, called for order and introduced me.

"Right then lads. Settle down for the guest speaker, Mr...er... Johnson. No, Jackson. Who will... er... is tonight's guest speaker, er tonight, and is going to talk about his experiences in the... the Iraq War".

"Falklands War, actually", I whispered in his ear. The President corrected himself. "Falklasswaractually".

He sat down, his head slumped onto the table, and he went to sleep. Most of the rest of the audience were in a similar state. I gave up when I was hit by an incoming half-eaten, bread roll. I don't think anyone noticed when I left, and I'm sure that they all thought I had given a pretty good talk, even if none of them could remember it, or me for that matter.

CHAPTER 58

A Dangerous, Manipulative Child Molester

Whilst we had been in the throes of divorce proceedings, Angela had threatened to destroy my career. She had already fulfilled this in terms of my Army career, but she was now determined to do likewise to my NHS career.

"We will argue and argue forever as long as you keep my children away from me. You want to wreck my life. It's ridiculous and I tell you that I will be going into court and I will destroy you without doubt," said Angela.

"Why?" I asked.

"You will be destroyed, and I will have you struck off as well" she said.

"Struck off?"

"I promise you that David, I will carry on, I will carry on," she warned me,[99] and it was only a matter of time before I found out how she planned to do it.

---

99. Telecon Angela/David 9 Nov 1994

On holiday in Spain I had been talking to Nicki and friends about Angela's inappropriate behaviour with my eldest daughter whilst we were still married, drenching her in kisses and stroking her excessively all over her body in such a way as to make me feel extremely uncomfortable. I had asked her to stop doing it, as had my mother, who had also witnessed Angela behaving in the same way on another occasion. My mother said that it looked like they were "kissing like lovers". Angela would not stop. It was also the way she behaved towards my eldest daughter when she returned her after contact. I described these events as Angela 'making love' to my daughter. Angela would justify her actions to me with words to the effect, "Look at how much R loves me; she loves me so much". Angela was satisfying her own needs, not my daughter's. It was very odd, inappropriate.

These observations of mine and Nicki's subsequent diary entry revealing her own unease about Angela's behaviour with my eldest child, provided Angela with the perfect opportunity to extract her revenge on me and sabotage my career - again. This entry, along with other evidence which outlined the worsening contact problems, would eventually end up in a court bundle, copied to Angela. Having read this extract Angela would begin by claiming that amongst other things, she had been accused of being 'a dangerous, manipulative child molester', a huge and deliberate leap of imagination even for her, and when court officials assured her that they had not given this behaviour sufficient weight to require any investigation, even though she was insisting they did, she took matters into her own hands.

First she wrote to the Lord Chancellor, of all people, claiming that she needed to be 'arrested and/or investigated' as she was 'apparently a dangerous child molester' and stated that the allegation had been made 'by someone whose honesty and integrity are beyond question and who is perhaps reluctant because of some misplaced loyalty to have me arrested and questioned[100]'.

She then went on to write to Social Services, the Police, the General Medical Council, and the Chief Executive of Bronglais Hospital where I worked, with the help of her sister Christine, each

---

100. Letter 23 Jun 1997

time posing as the abuser of a child, whilst neglecting to state that she was the mother of the child in question. Each time she stated that I was aware that the child was being abused, that I had done nothing to protect the child by reporting the matter to Social Services and that I was actively encouraging a relationship between the abuser and the child. She deliberately omitted the fact that I was the father of the child in question, that I had permanent custody of that child, or that an enforceable High Court order existed that dictated the terms of contact between the mother and child.

I shall try to explain Angela's mind-bending logic, her mental acrobatics. Prior to these letters, Angela had spent three years informing all and sundry, including the children, that I was doing everything in my power to prevent her contact with them, despite knowing that the Official Solicitor, Court psychiatrist and Social Services were responsible for the expert recommendations to the judges, not me. The fact that Angela's own actions were the cause of her reduced contact was anathema to her. Now that it more suited her determination to discredit me and destroy my career once again, she was happy to describe herself as a 'dangerous manipulative child molester', in order to claim that I was actively encouraging children (mine) to have contact with an abuser (her) thus facilitating the abuse of my children by their own mother. She had hoped the letters would prompt the GMC to investigate and question my fitness to practice. The matter would end up going to Court – again.

Then, just to crown things off, a few more Captain Crumpet stories would make an appearance, reminding the nation of the original one, my ex-wife. *'Captain is caught in bunk with her corporal'*, *'Captain Crumpet Mk III'*, *'The first Captain Crumpet, 37-year-old Angela Jackson, was sacked in 1994 over her affair with Grenadier Guards Sergeant Brian Taylor. Two years later blonde Karen Card 30, became Captain Crumpet Mk II*[101]*'*. Yet more tittle-tattle, all in the name of serving the 'public interest'.

---

101. Sun newspaper 8 Oct 1997

CHAPTER 59

Remove his gallbladder, old boy

I have mentioned before that if a general, or abdominal, or biliary surgeon is going to get sued, then there is a high likelihood that the excision of a gall bladder, cholecystectomy, will be the procedure which will lead to this outcome. To be accused of negligence, or carrying out the procedure in a negligent fashion, or being unaware of the likely complications of it, (or being fucking useless at surgery, which is the translation of the medico-legalese), is very hurtful and debilitating, particularly for me, as I had a large experience of the procedure, both open and keyhole and I had a good experience of the complications and dealing with them over the years.

However, there is no other option but for the consultant in charge of the case to carry the can for any perceived problems, even though the Trust will pick up the tab, if and when the case is concluded in the plaintiff's (patient's) favour. Defending an accusation of negligence is expensive for any NHS Trust, as medico-legal lawyers have to be instructed, expert witnesses are called upon for medical reports and everybody from car park attendant to consultant have to take time out to write a statement. Frequently the complaint is beyond recent memory, so case sheets have to be duplicated and sent out to all and sundry.

Then there are case conferences, often with the unspoken intention of 'let's get rid of this as cheaply as possible with no admission of anything. £10,000 - £15,000 is a good start and will almost equal the cost of defending the action.' Meanwhile the 'not guilty' plea of the consultant can be ignored – 'don't be so precious, we are not going to admit liability (your cock up)', as attempts are made to reduce the cost/effect of the complaint in question, on the NHS budget. Cynically I am explaining that settling a claim without admission of liability is often the better financial option, rather than defending a case, losing the judgement and paying damages, and both sides' legal costs, which may be astronomical. While the Trust and for that matter the NHS, will usually if not always regard the proceedings in budgetary terms, scant regard may be paid to the reputation of the doctor concerned. If the Trust settles a claim then in spite of the legalese, payment equals guilt. Morality and truth are soluble in cost-effectiveness.

Some of my colleagues would give up almost from the start, at the receipt of a legal letter of complaint, as these cases can be time consuming and attract far more attention than they deserve in the grand scheme of things. Another old surgical adage, that you are remembered for the one case that went wrong rather than all the cases that went right, is also still true to this day.

The patient was middle-aged but physically, much older. If and when he worked, it was as a cleaner, and one day he was admitted under the care of Dr Aeron Davies, one of my medical colleagues, and one of the best physicians I have ever worked with. He was the specialist in diabetes as well as cardiology, gastroenterology and general medicine, and when he retired, he had to be replaced by three new appointees. This patient was an insulin-dependent diabetic who was now unstable, and the cause was acute severe inflammation of the gall bladder, leading to his widely-fluctuating insulin demands.

I was summoned to *"Remove his gall bladder old boy. I can't deal with his diabetes while it's still in situ as it were. There's a good chap!"* Did Aeron say this? No, not quite, but he was old school and did not regard the practice of surgery as a suitable employment for a doctor. The surgical barbarians were the handmaidens of the cultured, sophisticated and educated physicians. I got a phone call and he asked me to see the patient and then arrange to rid him of his bloody gall bladder, urgently, i.e. now.

When I saw the patient, he was in a lot of pain, ill and feverish, with a high pulse rate. With his unstable diabetes, his very heavy alcohol intake – he actually drank more than his doctor, so it was significant, and should have been noted somewhere – his cardiovascular system, which was on its last legs following a recent heart attack, and his ultrasound report indicating a severely thickened gall bladder, full of stones and an odd appearance to his liver, this was not a case to jump into. I detected a tinge of jaundice, unnoticeable to physicians, which was confirmed by wildly abnormal liver function blood tests and halitosis that would not have shamed one of Daenerys Targaryen's dragons in *Game of Thrones*, just to give an up to date comparator.

I needed an anaesthetic opinion, which, when it came, was suitably gloomy. We elected to treat the patient intensively, conservatively up on the HDU and I communicated this to Aeron, who swore under his breath, knowing that his future rounds of golf would be interrupted by requests for help in insulin dosages. Once more stable – less ill, that is – I could go for his gall bladder, which I did a few weeks later. Thus, he was transferred to my care and Aeron's golf improved.

The operation was very difficult. Venkat, who had started, quickly handed over to me. I removed the gall bladder and also took a liver biopsy, as the patient's liver looked very abnormal. I put a special drainage tube (a 'T' tube) in the patient's bile system for safety purposes, as I had opened it to remove a gallstone and a large bore tube drain to the gall bladder bed which was oozing blood and bile, to further be on the safe side. It has taken me two minutes to write that. It took me about four hours to do it.

Post-operatively he was a bit unstable but recovered, and was soon eating and drinking, but a couple of days later it became plain that the 'T' tube was not functioning, and further investigations revealed that it had become partially dislodged, in spite of being stitched in. This was not a problem, as I was happy that any bile collection, which can be a very serious complication, was being drained by the other tube I had inserted for safety's sake. To my mind, the best way of dealing with complication was by a procedure known as ERCP (Endoscopic Retrograde Cholangiopancreatography) whereby a drain could be inserted, through the stomach and small bowel into the main bile ducts using a special endoscope (long flexible telescope, inserted through the mouth). It could be done under sedation and would avoid surgical reoperation, which I thought would be far too hazardous. This was a standard and recognised alternative. At the time it was not available in Bronglais, but my colleagues in Carmarthen Hospital had the facilities and expertise and consequently a now relatively healthy and diabetically stable patient was transferred for this to be undertaken, though by this time the liver biopsy had been reported as showing a severe chronic hepatitis – inflammation of the liver.

So far so good, but of course everything went downhill from there, in that the ERCP failed due to a small narrowing of this part of the bile duct, and I received a phone call from a close surgical colleague, who had experience of these sorts of cases and was prepared to re-operate if I agreed. I was reluctant. The patient was perfectly safe and could be optimised and then sent to a specialist liver unit in Birmingham. I warned my colleague that the patient's liver was compromised and that he had a good chance of not surviving a major procedure – which was why I had been reluctant to re-operate in the first place. The discussion went to and fro and was eventually resolved in favour of the patient having the operation in Carmarthen. I knew my patient was in good surgical hands, but the co-morbidities involved (additional unrelated illnesses as it were) were significant. I wished my colleague good luck, but lady luck was out to lunch. A couple of weeks later I received a letter from him explaining, that although the operation had been successful, severe septic complications had set in and the patient had died.

To my mind there had been no negligence, but that was not the view of the patient's wife or her solicitor. They tried suing my colleague in Carmarthen, but this failed, so they came for me. I was aggrieved, as I had actually kept her husband alive after I had operated on him, but there was a scorpion-sized sting in the tail from her expert witness, not necessarily by what he wrote, explaining what should have been (my) the correct course of action in this case, but by who he was, an internationally known, knighted, retired professor of transplant surgery who wrote books on surgery in this area. In his view I should have re-operated and re-sited the 'T' tube, and had I done so 'it is most likely that the patient would have survived to this day' (two years on) or words to that effect. I could not comprehend this logic. I had not re-operated because the patient's chances of survival were poor, I had advised against it, and when the patient was re-operated on, he died. Surely I should be vindicated, but that is not how the system works.

Someone had to be accountable for this poor outcome and the finger of blame was now pointing in my direction. I think I was their best chance. We were a small Trust, and if intimidated by the big boys, we might just cave in. Legal services to NHS Wales are central and they have their own specialised lawyers. The lawyer assigned to us went white when she realised who the plaintiff's expert witness was, Professor Sir R. C., followed by more Fellowships than our surgical department had in total. But she was made of steely stuff and we were not a bunch of hick medical country bumpkins, as often seemed to be implied, because we did not conform to the NHS hospital stereotype. Though it may have looked inconceivable that any self-respecting doctor would ever want to work in such a remote area as mid-Wales, our employment by the Trust was not indicative of an inability to get a post in the great metropolises. My co-consultants were masters of their medical briefs, as were the rest of the hospital staff, and in fact our rate of complaints was much less than some of the other Welsh hospitals, when compared like for like. I had to defend my position, because I had acted correctly, and our lady lawyer agreed to fight the allegations and see what happened.

First, we obtained our own expert opinion from a senior consultant, well known in Cardiff (Mr Brian Rees), who reviewed the case. He not only said that he could not criticise me in any way, but that he would have followed the same path I had done. Brian Rees was awarded an OBE for his services to medicine and was later to become the High Sheriff of South Glamorgan. In addition, he had played twice as hooker for Wales, once being sent off after punching an opponent. This latter information was from my colleague JLE and may have simply been apocryphal, but it did have the ring of truth about it. A fine man to have on our side, and we lobbed his opinion into the fray, unfortunately a grenade in response to the artillery shell. Brian Rees's opinion however, bolstered our lawyer and she wrote expressing the condolences of the Trust (remember the patient had died in Carmarthen) but denying negligence.

I am going to fast forward now to the surprising outcome, as the case was discontinued and then resurrected over a period of several years. The wife and her solicitors (not the original ones) finally withdrew and completely dropped the allegation of negligence against me/the Trust. Our lady lawyer explained why, and this is the sadness of it all. It turned out that when approached for an expert witness statement Professor Sir R C deeply sympathised with the unfortunate wife, and in a fit of altruism, he wanted to help her get some degree of compensation for the loss of her husband. He had proposed his alternative surgical strategy of choice to this end, and from what I understood from our lawyer, admitted it.

Unfortunately, in law they had to prove that I was negligent and had caused harm. Once embarked upon this course of action, it was difficult for him to back down. However, he manned up and he did back down. I admire him for that and have some sympathy for his motive, but it had caused an awful amount of grief.

CHAPTER 60

The Penalty

The matter of the 'dangerous manipulative child molester' and Angela trying to get me struck off from the General Medical Council Register was dealt with in the Royal Courts of Justice, London. The fact of the matter was that a complaint of this nature on my GMC entry would have lasting repercussions. As a precaution, whilst the allegation was investigated, my employers, who had no knowledge of my ex-wife beyond the limited information I had given them, stopped me from examining or operating on children. Not only did Angela try and destroy my record of good paediatric care but she also deprived several children of the operations they could have had in Aberystwyth. Several families had to endure a 100-mile return trip in order to get the surgical treatment their children needed.

Mr Justice Johnson stated:

'My hope and expectation was that arrangements would be made for the girls to see their mother by going up to stay with her from time to time in Yorkshire. In the event this has proved impossible as the mother seemed unable to control herself when the children were with her which led as a consequence to the children being emotionally

*damaged by her… One of the symptoms of the mother's obvious distress is that she has taken to writing to professional bodies of the father, Mr Jackson to the Health Authority by whom he is presently involved, to the Government and to others. I have no doubt that in doing so, she is **intending** deliberately to harm him. As said in my judgement in Feb 1996, that was then her **intention** and everything that has happened since indicates that this remains her **intention**. She wrote to these various bodies with the **intention** to damage Mr Jackson's career and cause him distress and indirectly her actions have repercussions for the children.*

*'I wish to take this opportunity to make it plain to anyone who reads this judgement that in the course of my long involvement with this family, I have not seen a shred of evidence or slightest hint or suggestion that Mr Jackson has behaved wrongly to any child, either his own or anyone else's. In particular, there is nothing that I have seen, read or heard about him that he has ever harmed a child, physically or sexually. Moreover, I make it plain that I am entirely satisfied that there has never been any question of him having colluded in any way with anyone accused of abusing a child nor can it be said that he has shut his eyes to anything untoward happening to his own children or any other children. The suggestions made by Mrs Taylor were made falsely and maliciously with the **intent** of damaging Mr Jackson.*

To mark my considerable concern at what has been happening in this regard, I propose to order [Mrs Taylor] to pay the costs incurred by Mr Jackson in seeking this injunction and in responding to Mrs Taylor's action, to be paid by her[102] *'.*

Angela's sister, Christine Peck-Russell, was ordered to pay £1000 to me as a penalty for her involvement in writing and/or signing the letters, even though the actual content had been conjured up by Angela's malevolent imagination.

---

102. Mr Justice Johnson 16 Dec 1997

CHAPTER 61

By Jehovah

I got a call in the middle of the night to tell me that one of my patients had bled heavily into her abdomen and was now in extremis. She was a reasonably fit lady who had undergone an uncomplicated laparoscopic cholecystectomy. When I arrived, she was as white as a sheet with a distended abdomen and a haemoglobin level of 1 gram (normal range 12-14 grams). Intravenous fluids were being pumped in by a similarly white-faced consultant anaesthetist, but no blood. She was a Jehovah's Witness (JW). Fuck. I could feel the blood draining from my face and a slight loosening of my bowels.

There was no question of a transfusion of blood or blood products, so the only thing I could do was to open her up, scoop out the blood in her abdomen and use the cell salvage machine (by that I mean get the qualified OTT in to operate the machine, which in the past had only ever been used for orthopaedic cases), and recycle some of her own blood into her. This is perfectly acceptable with regard to their religious convictions. That is what I did, and got her haemoglobin level up to 3 grams, still life threatening, but a lot better than 1 gram. I found the bleeder, a small arteriole caught up in a stitch in the original trocar wound, and dealt with it.

She was managed on intensive care, fully anaesthetised, as such a fast and dramatic fall in her oxygen-carrying capacity would not allow her to survive without all the work being done by a machine. We took advice from the haematologist as to whether we could stimulate the red cell production of her bone marrow and he got hold of industrial levels of the hormone erythropoietin, which is used in chronic anaemias amongst other things. We also gave her a total infusion of iron to top up her iron stores, which had a good chance of being depleted, and waited. Fortunately, she recovered without any complications – perhaps her faith had something to do with it, and I will confess I had consulted with my neglected God. She was discharged with a haemoglobin level of 6 grams about seven days later.

I had operated on JWs before and I was au fait with the principle of bloodless surgery, but shit happens. Bleeding as a complication of a surgical procedure is always on the consent form. Of course, a few months later a letter arrived alleging negligence in the performance of the operation, but this was batted away quite swiftly. However, it did colour my attitude to operating on these patients and I asked JLE to be the designated Jehovah's Witness surgeon while I recovered from the whole episode.

Two years or so after I retired in October 2012, I received an apology from the Trust for the 'enclosed letter of complaint'. The patient concerned was a sweet mouse of a woman, loved and dominated by her husband, who ran his own business in the Tywyn/ Aberdovey area. She was troubled with gallstones and I had listed her for operation. At the end of the consultation, the husband added that they were both JWs. Remember I had sworn off treating these patients, and I suggested that I transfer the wife to JLE's care, explaining what had happened in the case described above. Unfortunately, our success in rescuing that particular patient from the brink, which they knew about, as the JW community is small, was why they wanted me to undertake the procedure. I was recommended.

Against my better judgement, I agreed, fallaciously putting my faith in the myth that lightning does not strike the same place twice.

She had an uncomplicated operation and was discharged from hospital the next day. But lightning did strike again, though not quite in the same way, and at about two weeks after her operation she became unwell. She had developed a late bile leak, almost inevitably from the tube that attaches the gallbladder to the rest of the bile duct system and is clipped off in the laparoscopic procedure, or tied or clipped off in the open procedure, to prevent such leaks. Following the usual investigations, including a CT scan, she had the bile drained from her abdomen and an ERCP was arranged to correct the problem, which was now available at the hospital, and was undertaken by a specialist gastroenterologist, the very skilful Dr Mark Narain. Unfortunately, the patient found this very uncomfortable, making the procedure difficult, and it had to be abandoned.

What I haven't mentioned yet is the trouble I had in dealing with the patient's husband, who was there all the time, asking hundreds of questions, even collaring me in the hospital corridor. I could understand his concern, but in truth it got to a stage where I was finding it very difficult to concentrate on the job in hand, the further management of his wife.

The GMC guidelines on what to do under these circumstances are clear and I contacted a surgical colleague in Swansea, a Mr Tim Brown, who specialised in this area, and explained that my interactions with the husband in this case were affecting my ability to do my best for his wife. He said that he understood perfectly and agreed to accept the patient for another ERCP, probably under general anaesthetic. This was arranged, and I explained to the husband that I was transferring his wife, not because I had lost my rapport with him but, because she might need specialist care (which of course we were quite capable of providing, but I did not tell him that either).

A 'blown cystic duct stump' is a well-known complication of gall bladder surgery and the reason why it happens is sometimes just a matter of bad luck. In this lady's case the two clips I had applied to close the duct had just slipped off. She was treated successfully and made a full, if protracted, recovery. I met her husband sometime later whilst driving to do my clinic in Tywyn and stopped to ask him how his wife was. He was very distressed and informed me that one of the doctors in Swansea had told him that their purpose was to correct other people's mistakes, obviously in this case mine. It was not my surgical colleague who imparted this information, but it was most unfortunate, because it fed into the husband's perception that he was right in believing I had cocked up his wife's operation. Hence the letter alleging negligence I received in retirement. This was easily defended. I went through the CT scan and referred them to the film, which showed that the clips were nowhere near where the cystic duct stump should be. As it was a late presentation, I suspect that the cystic duct just rotted off. It happens.

There is another adage in surgery which is, 'Never do a surgical operation if you do not know how to manage the complications'. Through my career I think I probably managed every complication described in the operation of cholecystectomy, which I would say, is a tried and tested cause of ageing prematurely.

CHAPTER 62

False Memory

While Nicki was digging in the garden one weekend she was approached by my youngest daughter, who was sobbing uncontrollably. It transpired that her sister had been taunting her during an argument, and had said she was a mistake and therefore not wanted. Whilst it was true enough that she wasn't a planned baby, it was not this fact that bothered her; it was the fact that her mother had told her during a previous contact visit that I was not her father, Brian was, and that she should call him 'Daddy'.

Although the details were investigated by court officials and Brian confirmed that it was logistically impossible for him to be the father, Angela, when questioned, then claimed my daughter had a 'false memory' about the conversation. This of course was another complete untruth, made up on the spur of the moment to shift the blame away from herself. Not one of the court officials believed her. Unfortunately her comment can never be unsaid, and deliberately planting this doubt into my youngest daughter's paternity has had the effect of robbing us of the absolute assuredness of our relationship for the rest of our lives.

Whenever my children had staying contact with their mother, Nicki and I were intensely worried, but after five years of waiting at home fretting about what Angela was saying to them we decided to distract ourselves by going away on holiday during the time that they saw her. These holidays were precious and generally worry-free times for us. The best of the lot was when we flew to the Big Island, Hawaii for a belated honeymoon, five years after we had married. It took a long time to get there, but it was worth it in every respect, especially because we had time, a special time when we could celebrate our marriage and our love for each other having never had a time to ourselves since our wedding.

The weather was beautiful as we explored the island in a hire car. We went swimming and snorkelling in the inky-blue Pacific Ocean, observing the fantastic array of sea life. We went on a "jungle trek", plunging into a leaf-strewn natural pool beneath a little waterfall in the middle of nowhere, and Nicki flew over the Kilauea volcano in a light aircraft (why, I ask myself, but she has a thing about volcanoes), and we ate outrageously well, except at an Hawaiian Luau where we tried Poi (pounded root of taro plants), the staple local dish, which after cooking, came out purple and tasted, I imagine, like wallpaper paste would taste. The accompanying suckling pig, however, was delicious.

When we returned from our belated honeymoon we collected my children from their mother's house in Leeds after their court directed staying contact. It was the first long period of contact that Angela had had with the children since the reinstatement of contact. Predictably she had not wasted a moment of the time she had to further indoctrinate the children.

CHAPTER 63

Benediction

Most hospitals run a local anaesthetic lumps-and-bumps list every week or so, and the general feeling is that this is a list of patients who can be safely operated on by the junior surgical trainees. I did not take this view as a matter of course, but with the now constant pressure to reduce waiting lists, some accommodation had to be made with the hospital management. I insisted that any local anaesthetic procedure should be supervised by either me, Venkat or another experienced specialist registrar, but circumstances were such that significant harm was done in the case I am going to describe.

He was an elderly gentleman, recently retired. He had gone to his GP with a small lump in his right forearm that had been slowly growing with little else in the way of symptoms. He was referred to my outpatients and seen by a locum registrar, who diagnosed a lipoma which is a very common benign fatty tumour. He was put on the local anaesthetic waiting list. In time he was called in for his minor operation to be undertaken by my senior house officer and in accordance with my instructions he was supervised by Venkat, who unfortunately was on emergency call at the time.

Of course predictably, sometime later Venkat was then called away to Casualty and on checking that the last patient on the list, the old gentleman in question, was a simple lipoma excision, rather than cancel him (as he had travelled from Newtown one hour away by road) he told the SHO to go ahead, which he did. I was away at another peripheral clinic at the time and knew nothing about any of this.

I met this old gentleman for the first time for follow up in my Newtown clinic. I asked him how he was and he replied that he was very pleased with the procedure and remarked how well the wound had healed. I thought I would just check this out and indeed the wound was sound. What I did not like however was the way he held the fingers of his right hand, which had assumed the classical 'sign of benediction', the position in which a priest will hold his hand to bless his congregation. In those who are not priests this is an indication of ulnar nerve damage (one of the main nerves in the arm), and the patient explained that his hand and fingers had adopted that configuration after his operation and he could not rectify it. His little and ring fingers were also numb. I always checked the histology of excised specimens and I suspected that the lump which had been removed was a benign tumour of the ulnar nerve called a schwannoma, with damage or division of the nerve. This was indeed the case.

This is another trap for the unwary as these tumours are very uncommon, but of course that is no excuse. My SHO had removed the lump. He may have known that it was not a simple lipoma, but it was unlikely that he would have known to leave it in situ, close the wound and speak to me or someone more clinically senior about it. Venkat had taken the wrong decision to instruct the SHO to continue in his absence, but it was understandable based on what he had read in the out-patient notes. The locum had misdiagnosed the lump, which due to the rarity of these lesions, is not unusual.

As the consultant I bore full responsibility for the consequences of this mishap. When the inevitable solicitor's letter arrived, the Trust had no defence and a financial settlement was in order after I had explained the deficits that the old gentleman would have to live with, particularly undertaking fine movements with his right (dominant) hand. What I did not know, which was stated in the letter of claim for damages, was that "in his retirement the patient had intended to take up clock and watch repairing, model making and painting little lead soldiers for war gaming with his grandson which now of course he cannot do.....", or words to that effect. The settlement was very generous due to these losses of amenity.

I reckon the old boy's solicitor had been round the medico-legal block a few times and had got it just about right. The more cynical side of me wondered if there actually was a grandson.

CHAPTER 64

Never Do That Again

It was a Sunday evening in October 2000 and we were having a roast dinner with the children in the dining room. They were sitting at the dining table whilst Nicki and I went into the kitchen to sort out the pudding. Nicki was absolutely stressed out about the situation with Angela, and the children were due to see her in the half-term. I was going to be on call when the children would need taking to Leeds, so in desperation, I asked Nicki to do the handover with Angela for me.

The thought of dealing with the long journey, coupled with Angela's increasingly hostile attitude, was the final straw for Nicki. She said she wanted to leave; not me, but the situation. She wanted an end to the emotional suffering. She said she felt trapped, she had no control over her own life, she wanted the drama and anxiety to stop, and wanted a life rather than just an existence that continually revolved around Angela's malicious antics week in week out, year in, year out. She was distraught.

Nicki says that she slashed at her wrist in that moment to polarise the situation, to numb her emotions with a physical distraction and vent the constant frustration and overwhelming anxiety that was plaguing her life daily. This incident of self-harm was undoubtedly a manifestation of complex post-traumatic stress disorder (C-PTSD) as a result of her prolonged and sustained exposure to Angela's abuse as opposed to straightforward PTSD caused, for example, by a one-off event. Almost immediately afterwards she was mortified by what she had done, by what she had been driven to, but worse than that, she feared that she could have bled to death and robbed her own children of a mother they needed. She was inconsolable.

The children suddenly appeared from the dining room at the sound of the commotion. My youngest child in a panic called for an ambulance, my eldest child was nearly sick at the sight of the blood and Kelly, Nicki's youngest child was totally traumatised by the event. "Mummy" she said tearfully, "promise me you'll never do that again". She was only seven years old. The ambulance arrived and the paramedics treated Nicki's wounds whilst she cried uncontrollably. "She'll never stop" sobbed Nicki repeatedly. She meant Angela of course. She would fulfil the promise she made to Nicki as soon as we were married. "I will fight like a tigress to get them (the children) and there's very little that I wouldn't do to get them" and "David knows that, he knows basically that I will carry on until I get them back", and "I shall wait as long as it takes and I will go back to court time and time again until I get them[103]".

The situation was detrimentally affecting all of us in different ways. I downed a large slug of whisky, went to bed and tried to sleep before having to work the next morning, whilst Nicki wept beside me.

Nicki has always had a reputation for being a vigilant, responsible and meticulous person. She had minor traits of obsessive-compulsive behaviour when I met her, as do many people, such as being overly cautious about removing plugs from power sockets to prevent fires and locking the front door to prevent burglaries, but her behaviour was on an entirely normal spectrum. However, Angela's unjustified and unrelenting criticism of Nicki and her parenting of my children caused her such accumulated stress over the years that it eventually tipped her normal vigilant traits into the full-blown disorder that OCD really is, causing her to slip into a deep depression. She underwent many hours

---

103. Telecon 14 Sep 1995

of cognitive behavioural therapy (CBT) over the years that followed and treatment with sertraline, a selective serotonin reuptake inhibitor, (SSRIs), which will continue for the rest of her life. SSRIs effectively increase the level of serotonin, one of the neurotransmitters required by the brain to carry signals. Nicki's OCD became so overwhelming at one point that I feared she would take her own life. It was hard and frustrating for me as a doctor, not to mention her husband, that I could not fix her problem. Angela's merciless behaviour had netted another victim.

CHAPTER 65

Know What I Mean?

I had just opened up a middle-aged man and rectified the cause of his abdominal pain. This had been a prolonged and difficult procedure and I expected a pretty stormy recovery. I was asked to speak to his relatives, who were in the waiting room. I entered and in the half-light I saw a sea of anxious men, women and children. One man, young and well-built with his chin thrust forward aggressively, stepped in front of the other relatives and demanded of me, "What 'ave you done to my granddad? We 'ope he's gonna be all right. Is he gonna be all right? Know what I mean?" I had a momentary vision of ending my days encased in concrete, as part of a motorway flyover. The conversation was going to be a difficult one anyway.

I was the focus of everybody's attention. Hundreds of eyes seemed to be boring into me and as I started to explain what had happened, the owners of the eyes surged forward. It was like being back at the Circus of my medical school days. I adopted a pose that would indicate confidence and gravitas and then squeaked,

"He's all right. I expect he will recover just fine" (wrong choice of words, as it was certainly going to be touch and go). After realising what I had just said, I added, "Of course it was a very serious operation and anything could happen".

I had corrected my squeak, but unfortunately overcompensated by going to the other end of the scale. I was now talking in an unsustainable Barry White baritone. Further questions ensued. Having recovered my equilibrium, I went into more detail about the patient, who, I was to find out, was the much-loved and appreciated family patriarch. Should I have been worried? Absolutely not. I had now met the Barkers (my patient was Tom) and the Scarrats, who, amongst other things, owned and ran the Clarach Bay Holiday Village, a couple of miles up the coast. They were two of the nicest and closest-knit families I had ever come across. Tom did recover and our friendship and his trust in me developed over the years. I was referred all members of their families who required any surgical opinion, or operation, from hernias to circumcisions. Frequently they would come into the consulting room and their opening words were "My granddad/ my dad/my uncle/Tom said I had to see you" and that was that.

Many went privately when there was no need, as our waiting lists were short, but that was their way. Tom would frequently pop in to see me for an outpatient chat and some advice, and once I went to Clarach Bay to have a couple of whiskeys with him in the holiday village pub, where he went every evening "just to check on the cashing up".

By this time I had started a charity (I will go into more detail later), and every year I would get a letter from Tom, with words to the effect that "The company has had a good 12 months and we would like to donate to the hospital". Enclosed would be a cheque for £500 or so. In addition, a bag full of fluffy toys for the children's ward would be delivered. I have found out that Tom Barker has only recently passed on, so I reckon he reached a good old age. He is survived by his wife Gladys.

As a general surgeon, I would inevitably have to face the death of a patient. I have mentioned some of the difficulties of dealing with this in my Army career. With the elderly who had lived a good life and were often 'ready to go', if not at that particular moment, it was easy to reconcile the event, as it is with those afflicted with terminal, inoperable cancer. For the incurable patients who lived a life of sustained pain and misery, it was not hard to regard the passing of life as a mercy. However, there is a category of patient who die who should not have done, and these are difficult to accept, especially in the context of a planned surgical procedure. Quite rightly as the surgeon, I carried the can for this and did my best to try and reduce the risks involved. This involved anaesthetic opinions and preoperative optimising, where the risk was obvious, but in some cases, despite every precaution being taken, and the risk being minimal, sudden death ensued.

I am referring, again, but this time in more depth, to deep vein thrombosis (DVT) followed by a fatal pulmonary embolism (PE). Here large blood clots form in the veins of the legs or pelvis, break loose and are conveyed by the blood stream to the lungs, where they may be big enough to obstruct a pulmonary (lung) artery, causing chest pain, breathlessness and death. Though the use of heparin, TED (elastic) stockings, calf-stimulating boots, chest physiotherapy, early mobilisation and all the other therapies have reduced the frequency of these tragic occurrences substantially, a fatal PE will still inevitably happen to some patients and it carries off the young, the middle-aged and the elderly in descending order of frequency.

The risk of DVT and PE is on every consent form, but that essentially means nothing. There is little point in yelling at a corpse "I told you this might happen; don't say you weren't fully informed". But explaining the sudden demise of a patient to their nearest and dearest can be very difficult.

They were a middle-aged couple, both previously fit, who were involved in a road traffic accident; a head-on collision. Both had seat belt and air bag bruising, and in addition the husband sustained a broken tibia (shin bone) which required orthopaedic fixation with a nail. His wife had little in the way of symptoms, and following routine investigations was settled on the surgical ward for close observation.

Gradually she developed abdominal pain and a CT scan demonstrated free air in her abdomen. She underwent an exploratory operation and a tiny hole in her small bowel was repaired. Next morning, she was feeling fine, no cause for concern. Mr Salami, my registrar at the time, who had performed the operation on the wife, knocked on my office door and told me what he had found and what he had done to rectify it. It was perfectly straightforward.

Then suddenly he received an emergency call from the surgical ward. The wife had complained of a pain in the chest, breathlessness and had then become unrousable. Resuscitation attempts by the on-call cardiac arrest team had failed, and she was declared dead, with the provisional diagnosis of fatal pulmonary embolism. Mr Salami was asked if I could speak to the husband, who had now been wheeled back out of the lift to the surgical ward, as his wife was undergoing resuscitation and he obviously wanted to know what had happened. I went to see him on the orthopaedic ward. He was slumped in his wheelchair and he only had to look at my face to know that bad news was on the way. "Is she all right?" he asked. The lump in my throat which had been born the size of a grape in the lift on my way to the ward was now the size of a melon.

This couple had been on holiday. They were going to visit their daughter and meet their first grandchild. He blurted this out as if God or lady luck could just reconsider the situation and transport him back in time to a point where he could have avoided the accident, which from all accounts was not his fault. No, that was not going to happen. I was deeply upset, but what I was going to say to him would always have a lasting effect, not only on how he remembered receiving the news of his wife's death, but also how he would cope with it. "I am sorry, but your wife has just died. She had recovered from her operation, but we think she developed a pulmonary embolism which was fatal. The arrest team did their best, but she could not be revived".

Did I say this? Not quite. I sat down beside him and held his hand. Over the years I had learned that warm human contact is very important when imparting bad news. I looked at him directly and said, that I would have gladly given up a lot to not be the one to have to tell him the worst news he was ever likely to get. His wife had died suddenly. She had almost inevitably succumbed to a pulmonary embolism, with no prospect of revival, and I explained the mechanics of the embolism. It had been swift, and she would have felt very little, if anything at all.

I could not imagine how he would feel when the news sank in over the next day or so, but if I could offer him any solace, the sun would rise again, life for him would go on and he could relive the happy memories that he had shared with his wife in the quiet moments. We were all there to help him get through this, and we had a dedicated support team who could take care of the mundane aspects of dealing with a death.

I then had to mention the inevitable post-mortem. His wife's death had to be referred to the Coroner for an inquest. That was the law, and we had no choice in the matter. Even though we were pretty sure of the cause of death, we needed it to be confirmed by a consultant pathologist and then the Coroner's verdict, investigating the relevant circumstances leading to his wife's cause of death.

I said "Don't dwell on these details. We will take care of everything. We have already made contact with your daughter and son-in-law. Once again, I am so sorry. If you have any questions later, please contact the nursing staff and I will come directly". Though misty eyed, he managed to thank me for my understanding and explanation. "I wouldn't have your job" he said, and he started sobbing.

Dejected, I went back to my office and sat down. It always happened to the good people. How many convicts, for example, violent robbers, rapists or murderers died of pulmonary embolisms? How many corrupt politicians, for that matter? Where was the justice in this world?

CHAPTER 66

Love, Appraisal and the Consultant's Contract

When I first met him, John Edwards (JLE) was having an affair with a cousin of his who was an actress in a well-known Welsh soap opera. This had displeased her father, who had sworn revenge, which made JLE's life a bit uncomfortable until his cousin precipitately terminated their liaison. He had divorced his wife of many years, called Margaret, but then realised that this was not a good move (not that the loss of half his pension had anything to do with it) and so they remarried in Las Vegas. "Why Las Vegas?" I asked him, to which he replied that it was the only place he knew where he could get remarried without having to get out of his car.

However, this remarriage did not last long, because JLE had met a young nurse called Sarah, who was also married with a young son. He was ahead of her by 32 years, though that did not stop him, and he courted her furiously, but not without incident. He phoned me up one evening and asked if I could cover his on call for a week or 10 days. I immediately said no problem and asked if he was taking some leave.

I was the one that did the consultant rota, and any on call alterations from the fixed rota were always taken into account for leave, meetings etc., so this request was a surprise. He needed to take some sick leave, or recovery leave, as he called it, and as I type this, I recall him asking me to keep it under my hat. However, with the close community and the rumour mill which existed in Aberystwyth and the surrounding villages, what happened soon became common knowledge.

He and Sarah's by now estranged husband had got into a fight. The husband was a strapping Welshman and JLE had his work cut out. "I managed to get him in a headlock and held on until the police arrived" he said, "but he did manage to land a few. I can't go to work with my face like this".

So I covered JLE's on call until all his facial bruising had subsided. However, this act of settling an issue of the heart in the old-fashioned way cemented Sarah's love for JLE. I was there to congratulate them on the eve of the birth of their daughter Esme.

Slowly but surely, I was becoming disillusioned with the NHS. The consultant contract was the only bright spot in a dismal succession of constructed administrative protocols and requirements, which simply served to try and diminish the role of consultants. It was designed to get them into a controlled, planned method of working, with job plans, then obviously job plan reviews, revalidation, continuous professional development and yearly appraisals. Once all boxes were ticked and everything signed off to satisfy local audits, the paperwork was duly sent to the NHS department of the Welsh government, to be filed away unread and never seen again. I also had to indulge in "reflective practice", as a part session would be written into my job plan. I had to sit down and reflect on the positives and negatives of my previous actions and benefit from it.

Nowadays this sort of activity has to be recorded in an e-portfolio and evidence of it would become part of the revalidation process, which every doctor would have to undergo every five years. It didn't work, but it did satisfy a need to vastly increase the management contingent in the system, and soon the medical staff in any given hospital became a shocking minority amongst the overall employees. Treatments were initiated and continued according to algorithms and multidisciplinary teams (MDTs) became the method of deciding a patient's fate, which only served to delay treatments when a bunch of clinicians could not agree on a course of action. Having had years of making my own decisions and judging my work/life balance in favour of my patient's needs, everything was changing. The rules of the game were now complicated, and the referees were not on the side of the consultants. I was on the verge of going rogue.

My waiting list, which had been very efficiently kept by my secretary on 'T cards' in her office, was removed without my consent. It had run very successfully, because I would see a patient, then get Carol to book them into my diary then and there. However, I was told that the list would be managed centrally by a new admin department, such that no patient breached the government's waiting list targets. My operating list would be compiled by a clerk in 'consultation' with me. She had no medical training whatsoever, so she had no idea what a named procedure meant, or what it entailed. It all led to a massive amount of frustration and I railed against this perverse system, though not against my little clerk, who I remember as always polite, enthusiastic and thoughtful. I could not shoot the messenger, but I would have liked to nuke whoever dreamed up this scheme. The reality was that the waiting list targets became more important than the needs of the patient to actually be able to attend, when considering family and work commitments. If they couldn't attend within a certain time frame, they were simply removed from the list and had to start all over again within the process.

JLE's and my appraisals were proving problematic. The Clinical Director of Surgery was miles away, several years our junior and did not relish appraising us, and the Medical Director, quite understandably, felt it would be inappropriate for a consultant physician to appraise two senior consultant surgeons. We suggested and it was agreed that in order for the boxes to be ticked, we would conduct each other's appraisals, to the best of our ability and for the benefit of the Trust.

I was sitting in the surgeons' changing room. I had just completed an exceptionally bloody case, had showered and was getting ready for my next patient. JLE wandered in and mentioned that we had to have our appraisals completed in a couple of days.

"OK" I said, "I'll come to your office at lunchtime tomorrow. Are there any special forms?"

"I expect so" he replied. "Anyway, I'm not in tomorrow. We could do it now"

"What, here?"

"Yes, why not?"

I could not think of a reason, so I went first and asked, "How do you think you have performed over the last year; professionally I mean?

"Usual" was the reply. Then he announced that he was going for a crap.

"Carry on though, this should not take long". *What, my appraisal of him, or his time on the toilet?*

"What did you mean by 'usual'?" I asked

"I performed to my usual high standard," he said.

"Any difficult management problems you need to discuss?" I went on.

"Only yours" he replied through the cubicle door.

"Anything you think you could have done better?"

"If I hadn't been so bloody impatient, I could have got a better price for my house," he informed me whilst attending to his bowel action.

"What about your CPD?" I asked. We were nearing the end.

"What the hell is CPD?" he asked.

"Continuing Professional Development. You go off and learn something on a course that will benefit your professional practice and you can bring it to the benefit of Ceredigion, indeed the whole of Wales. If it is agreed at your appraisal, then the Trust are pretty much obligated to fund it."

"I have no idea what I do not know enough about!" he exclaimed.

"Can I make a suggestion?"

"By all means."

"Well, you're a urologist. Why don't you seek to benefit all your fellow Welshmen and go on a willy extension course? When did you have yours done by the way?"

JLE was fighting to put his theatre greens back on, to get out of the cubicle and to inflict some damage on me.

"Gotta go" I said, "next patient's on the table."

He did my appraisal in the Cooper's Arms pub next evening after he had returned from wherever he had gone to. He suggested that for my CPD, I could go away on a course that would teach me how to go fuck myself. My appraisal of him had taken two minutes, his of me about eight seconds. As an hour was the allotted time for this activity, we remained in the pub and drank some Guinness. John Edwards and I were both going rogue. I wrote our appraisals up for signature and onward transmission to the Welsh Assembly. Or did I?

However, let's get back to the consultant contract, which was the biggest own goal in the history of the management of the NHS. Once again, the purpose of the new contract was to rein in the power of the consultants and subject them to better scrutiny in the way they managed their patients, their time in the hospital, and of course their time doing private practice and playing golf. This was all achieved under the pretence of reducing the hours per week (in line with the European Working Time Directive) and of course reducing pay. I always regarded my contract as it was originally – open-ended. I looked after the patients, day and night, but regulated my own time off, my own timetable, with my fixed sessions (out-patient clinics and theatre sessions) remaining unalterable.

This gave me a certain amount of flexibility. For example, if I was due to do a major bowel case on a Thursday, and there was no High Dependency Unit (HDU) bed available, then I would slip the case to Friday, or even Saturday. Thus, I could combine the hospital's need to remain within the government-dictated cancer targets and the patient's need to have their operation more or less on time, without further bowel preparation or the requirement to rearrange their lives to suit another date. I was quite happy to do this. It was all part of correct patient care.

At the start of the exercise we had to keep diaries for six months and then negotiations would begin around new job plans which I am not going to bore the reader with, but as a result of this exercise and the realisation that in order to meet the Trust's waiting list and cancer targets, I was working at least 20–40 hours per week beyond my soon-to-be new contract. In order for me to be 'reined in', I would have to give up a substantial number of my sessions, which of course would be clinically completely unacceptable. Having got all the evidence together (I was in charge of clinical audit as well as being the Post Graduate Organiser at the time), I started my job planning meeting with the words, "In order to get me down to the maximum 10 sessions a week stipulated in the New Contract, I will have to give up five or six of my present sessional commitments, so I propose to cancel all my peripheral outpatient clinics and my weekly all-day Thursday operating list. I shall also resign as Chair of Audit, which takes up a considerable amount of my time".

This of course was disastrous for the Trust. Another half a consultant or more would have to be recruited. They capitulated and agreed that they would now have to pay me for my extra sessions under the terms of the new contract, and as a result of this little administrative whipping in, I walked away with a 50% pay rise. It took me half an hour. Not bad work if you can get it, but they got their money's worth out of me, which they graciously acknowledged. But, and this is a big but, I had to stick to my fixed sessions, and so slipping a case to another day as I have described above was curtailed.

The situation became ridiculous, as on any given Thursday with a major case planned I waited for an HDU bed to become available, which often would never materialise, so I just did the *Telegraph* crossword. I got paid a lot of money for it. As of course I was on this fixed session contract, if the Trust needed me to operate on my patients out of my contracted sessions (which I could refuse to do), then this would attract an agreed extra payment of £500 or so, and of course with the rigorous monitoring of cancer targets this was very frequent. The situation had developed such that as a result of the New Contract, I was often paid to do nothing but the crossword on my operating day, and then paid a lot of extra money to operate out of session. This also applied to non-urgent waiting list patients, which were paid for under the Waiting List Initiative Scheme.

I was never money-orientated, but this total and unnecessary meddling in the consultant work pattern changed all that. I was now very handsomely paid for doing less work, whereas previously I had regularly worked beyond my contracted sessions for free. And with the award of clinical excellence payments (discretionary points), I financially recovered well from the legal costs I had incurred. The whole issue of "managing" me (and all other consultants), proved to be a very costly exercise for the Welsh NHS. The situation was not broken beforehand, but it certainly was after it had been fixed.

However, this new era of management was making me uncomfortable. I was old school. I had a very wide surgical repertoire, but attempts to curb me in, in this respect too, were looming. The numbers game appeared, and the basis of this was that if a surgeon did not do a specific, but arbitrary, number of cases a year, then these cases should be passed on to someone who "specialised" in that procedure, yet often could do nothing else.

Cancer centres were established. I was running a bowel cancer centre, but was frowned upon because a cancer centre required at least two specialist surgeons, and in this respect I was single handed, as JLE, though probably more experienced than most of our detractors, was now regarded as a urologist, his favourite speciality. I needed to be absorbed along with my cases into a centre somewhere else. However, the 53 miles that separated Bronglais from Carmarthen, where the nearest and bigger hospital was located, was a barrier to this and in any event, such was the local and colloquial nature of our patients that many publicly stated that they would rather 'take their chances' in Aberystwyth than travel miles away from their loved ones and relatives. Fortunately, all results from bowel cancer surgery were audited centrally, UK wide, and published annually as the National Large Bowel Cancer Audit. They were not analysed on a named surgeon basis, but because I was the only surgeon in Wales who was single-handed, the published results for Bronglais hospital were my results, and they were as good as everybody else's, if not better.

By this time there had been a Trust reorganisation in Wales and the overall number of Trusts was reduced by amalgamations. We were subsumed into the Hywel Dda Trust and lost our individual identity. Local decision-making disappeared, as did senior management representation. Gradually I began to realise that I was being viewed as useful, but a bit obsolete, a surgical relic. There was a new breed of surgeon on the way, young and thrusting but under-experienced for the requirements of a truly general surgical job, because truncated training schemes, in order to swell consultant numbers as promised by the government, could no longer produce surgeons like me, who were experienced enough to handle just about anything by the time they were a consultant.

I would not be needed any more. I was a throwback to the old times, but I had a large patient base, totally loyal to me and my cause, and even though I was beginning to outlive my usefulness in the new NHS, I was a difficult opponent for them to handle.

CHAPTER 67

A Bitter Pill

Nicki and her children provided Angela with the ideal tools to create jealousy, friction and instability within my family and cultivate my children's rejection of us. Getting rid of Nicki wasn't necessarily personal for Angela, she just symbolised a bothersome obstacle that needed removing just like my housekeeper before her, an unwelcome cuckoo who had invaded Angela's nest and a mother figure upon whom, she was adamant, she did not want her children imprinting. It was imperative that the children should be perfect duplicates of their mother, with the emphasis on 'perfect'.

To make matters worse, against our wishes and those of the court officials who had sought to protect the children from their mother's abuse for so long, Angela bought mobile phones for each of them and paid for their contracts to ensure their loyalty, obligation and availability to her. She would infiltrate every moment of our lives and brainwash the children daily. I was emotionally very fragile by this stage and all my funds had been depleted, so I wasn't able to return to court, which I guess Angela sensed and exploited to the full. She began a two-pronged approach, firstly to poison my teenage daughters' minds against Nicki and secondly, to wear me down and then go on a charm offensive.

Not unnaturally, by this stage, my teenage daughters were using the situation with their mother's disruptive behaviour to avoid all boundaries at home with us, in exchange for the inappropriate and seductive freedoms permitted in their mother's home. My elder child shared my home, but she lived by her mother's lax and amoral armchair parenting, which was being constantly reinforced and endorsed via the mobile phone. She did not want me to be a father; she wanted a provider and an enabler, in just the same way as her mother had. Could I halt the process? I am still trying.

When my elder daughter was nearly 15 years old, her mother arranged for her to spend a week in Leeds with her, ostensibly to do work experience, but she never returned home. It had taken Angela eight years to indoctrinate her sufficiently to extract her from us, despite the court ruling which was still in force, by convincing my daughter that she needed saving, rescuing and protecting from our cruel, dangerous and negligent care.

By the time my younger daughter was 15 she too would disappear to her mother's. Nicki and I arrived home from work one evening to find that she and Angela had removed everything from her bedroom in our absence and gone. My daughter would not speak to me or see me for almost three years.

Parental alienation was now complete. The children thought they had arrived at their decision to reject us all on their own. They wanted to believe that it was a sign of their maturity that they had formed these opinions without influence from their mother, and indeed they would have felt insulted to be told that this wasn't so. They had been primed and set on the pre-determined path of rejection, before the ink on my divorce petition was even dry. They had been oblivious to the inevitable and predictable trajectory of alienation and the long-term effects of the mistreatment. These beliefs had been foisted onto them by proxy, by their mother, a bitter pill that they had unwittingly swallowed, the slick sales patter of my ex-wife; a scam.

By the time the brainwashing reached its conclusion, the children had managed to wipe out all pleasant, happy memories of us from their minds, so that only hatred and anger remained. I persistently tried to reach out to my younger child after she left our home and eventually, after nearly two years of total silence and rejection, she wrote me an angry, hate-filled letter that demonstrated only too clearly the cumulative effects of the brainwashing she had endured – the very result the court officials had tried so hard to avoid.

When my younger daughter eventually allowed me back into her life to resume some semblance of a relationship with her after the years of silence and rejection, I had to give her photographs of herself during the years she had lived with us to prove that she had been a happy child in our home, even though she chose to deny it. Slowly but surely, I regained her trust after initially being regarded with unwarranted suspicion and fearfulness. She would need a large dose of the antidote to her mother's abuse this time.

The unilateral decision that Angela made to remove the children from my care, without leave of the court, was illegal and neither Nicki nor I, at any point, ever consented to it. We put up a gallant fight to the bitter end, but not unnaturally we saw the cessation of the emotional warfare we had endured for 10 gruelling years as a welcome and long-awaited relief. We were exhausted, and it was time to re-evaluate and reprioritise, a time to reassess what was realistically salvageable. We had two other children who had been totally monopolised, marginalised and trivialised and who still needed us, and more to the point, they wanted us to carry on parenting them.

During the custody proceedings, which had spanned more than eight years, a County Court judge, several different High Court judges, a child psychiatrist, the Official Solicitor to the Supreme Court and two separate county Social Services departments had all been involved, and none of them had had any impact on Angela's abusive behaviour towards her own children, my children.

CHAPTER 68

Tail End Woes and a Load of Bollocks

In such a small population, and I had probably operated on most of them at one time or another, I was pretty well known, particularly for being approachable and fairly down to earth. I would always go the extra nine yards and Carol, my secretary, would be ready to slot a patient or two into my clinic at 8.30 am before the nine o'clock start, if say a member of staff had a problem or concern for me to deal with. I always gave them priority – in spite of the guidelines, or more accurately, diktats. Other patients were slotted in for urgent consultations, or for conditions that were not urgent surgically, but had a severe knock-on effect for the patient's family.

One day in the late evening, I was jolted from my severalth gin by a rap on the front door. I was not on call and therefore relaxing with Nicki. On opening the door, I recognised the caller as a gentleman who was a butcher by trade, though we had rarely talked. I asked him what he wanted, trying not to slur, or to get just a bit too up close up and personal with him, with the aid of the supporting door post.

"I'm sorry to bother you at night," he said.

"That's all right. How can I help you?" I replied. Each of my words was articulated with the care and precision of the slightly (in truth very) tipsy; others would say, half pissed.

"I wouldn't come to see you if it wasn't urgent, but I can't sleep," he said.

"You can't sleep," I unnecessarily repeated back to him, as a sense of disbelief seeped into my brain.

"No" he said. "It's killing me".

"Who's killing you?"

"No, not who, it. It's killing me, isn't it?"

I was beginning to wonder if I was not the only one who had had a few. I leant forward to try and smell his breath, but couldn't without abandoning the door post, which was providing me with the necessary stability.

"Ok, what is it?" I asked.

"The pain," he replied, "that's what it is, isn't it. I'm in agony, I can't work, and I can't sleep. If I go to the toilet the pain is worse and just burns for hours, so I try not to go and then I feel terrible. My wife told me to come and see you."

I needed more information, though I had a pretty good idea, in spite of the gin, what was going on.

"Do you mean if you go for a pee it burns?"

"No," he replied, "the other way, and there's blood".

"How long has this been going on?"

"A week. I was constipated and felt something go and I've been in agony ever since. The pain is too much."

He had an acute anal fissure, essentially a tear in the skin and deeper tissue of the sphincter. Only that could cause him so much grief with his history. I told him I would fix him up. I asked him to come to my clinic next day, starved from midnight, and if the diagnosis was confirmed, then I would put him on the day case list that afternoon. Being starved would evidently not be a problem for him, as he had reasoned that if he only put a little in, then not much could come out and aggravate his pain. I asked Carol the next day to add him provisionally to the operating list and she informed my admin clerk.

She asked me for a name, and I said, "Butcher in Aberystwyth".
"Mr Butcher?" asked Carol.
"No," I replied, "he's a butcher who lives in Aberystwyth".
Somehow she traced him, and a new patient folder was inaugurated. I confirmed his fissure in the clinic and in the afternoon, under a deep general anaesthetic, I stretched his anus (the official term for which is a 'Lord's 8-finger Manual Dilation of the Anus'. Though somewhat discredited now, if performed properly it is very effective, and the pain relief is immediate). When he went home, with suitable advice, he was a very happy man and a couple of weeks later he again presented at my front door, but this time with a plastic bag full of fillet steak.

A local builder known as Truck, because he was built like one, drove up to Nicki, who was gardening at the front of our house, and asked if I was in. She said, "No but I can get him to call you when he gets home". "Nah" he said "It's all right. Give him this will you, and tell him I said thanks".

Truck handed over a bin bag and drove off. Nicki, by now slightly apprehensive, looked inside the bag to find a large salmon, fresh out of the river Rheidol, covered in grass and slime and with a bloody mouth where it had taken the hook. It was a thank you present from Truck and his wife after I had operated on his father-in-law, who had now returned to his expatriate life in sunny Spain, not far from where I am now, as I type this, cured, healed and happy. I chalked up this success with a few mouthfuls of freshly-cooked salmon.

On another occasion, I was in Halfords with Nicki getting something for our road bikes when I was approached by a young man. He looked vaguely familiar and I was to remember he was the husband of one of my nurses. He asked me if I was Mr Jackson, to which I replied "Yes".

He then said that he had a 'problem' and would I have a look at him. Nicki just rolled her eyes and wandered off to the furthest point in the shop, whilst still managing to remain in Halfords. She seemed to be getting used to these unconventional consultations that took place in small close-knit communities. It wouldn't have happened in the centre of Guildford.

"Of course," I said, "Just get your GP to refer you to my clinic".

The young man looked uncomfortable, shifting from one foot to the other.

"It's very embarrassing. They all know me in the clinic, my wife is a nurse you know, and she said I should ask you, and that you wouldn't mind."

"I don't mind, but you're not suggesting that I examine you in the middle of Halfords, are you?"

"Well there's no-one about. You could have a quick look now. I've got three testicles, when I used to have two. It's embarrassing it is, I don't want anyone to know. My wife works at the hospital and they all know me, her friends and that, so it is".

I looked up and down the aisle, confirmed that there was nobody in sight and hoping there were no security cameras, I took the risk. I asked him to drop his trousers, whilst mentally rehearsing my story to the police as to why I was fiddling with a young man's groin in the middle of a large well-known retail store. I had a quick look and told him to cough.

"Pull up your trousers" I yelled at him, as a customer turned into the aisle, fortunately looking for something in the racks, rather than in our direction.

"Does this third testicle come and go?"

"Yes" he replied, "but then when the missus and I have…"

I stopped him there.

"Okay, I don't need to know. You have a hernia, not an extra testicle. It's been present from birth and has shown itself now, which is not uncommon. It is probably your sigmoid colon you are feeling. You have what is known as a sliding hernia".

He did not look relieved. The thought of feeling his own colon, or even his wife feeling his colon, when he and the missus were having… was too much for him.

I rephrased it. "You have a hernia. Get your GP to refer you to me. Do NOT mention a consultation in Halfords. I will repair it, and everything will be fine. It is NOT an extra testicle. OK?"

Relieved, he thanked me and left. I walked out of the shop having completely forgotten what I had gone in for, staring from right to left to see if I was getting odd looks, or if anyone was on their mobile phone calling the law.

I am not a gambling man, but I would have put my mortgage on the fact that he did not have a third testicle. It is known as polyorchidism (if the patient has more than two testicles, the most common finding being three, two on one side and one on the other) and it is extremely rare. Less than 200 or so cases have been reported in the world literature and I know this because I had a case under my care in 1989 or so. An excited radiologist had phoned me to say that the lump on one side of the scrotum that we were investigating by ultrasound in a young serviceman looked like an extra testicle. This was confirmed at operation and it was removed, with biopsies of the remaining two.

Radiologists spend most of their time in the dark looking at X-rays (now mainly computerised images) or ultrasound images. They are uncomfortable in daylight. When I met Major John Donaldson for a discussion about the case as we walked to the Officers' Mess ten minutes later, he

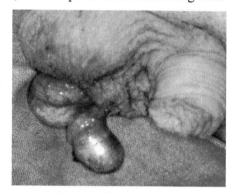

Polyorchidism. Two small testicles in the left scrotum

was still blinking and shading his eyes from the weak winter sun. John was unpublished and he asked me if I would submit this case for publication with his name attached as an author. Because the clinical findings were so rare I agreed, but insisted he write the ultrasound findings in the special language that radiologists employ, using the mysterious terminology known only to them. With his agreement, I said I would write it up and then promptly told my registrar to do it. Brian Singer would get first authorship, followed by John Donaldson, and I would be the senior author and lend clout to the paper in a Mike Keighley from Birmingham sort of way. Of course I was deluding myself. Mike Keighley was internationally renowned, whereas, if I am honest, I was not; in fact I was hardly known in BMH Munster, where I was posted at the time. In any event, the case with a bit of developmental classification and management padding was published in the journal 'Urology' in 1992. It has actually been cited 132 times[104].

It has been written that in the 14th Century, the Pope allowed a man to marry two women because he had three testicles (the man, not the Pope, because Popes are not supposed to have any testicles). Anyway, the imposition of an extra wife would seem to be a punishment for the condition, even though it has also been written that polyorchid men have superhuman fecundity (fertility) with reproduction rates that are off the charts.

There were four brothers, two of them very well known to locals, Alwyn and Aled. We were great friends and I enjoyed their company immensely, both on and off the golf course. The younger brother, Aled, was troubled, and we all arranged to meet for coffee in a small café where Aled's paramour worked (and where he could get free coffee). After a couple of minutes, as we were served our drinks and had sat down at the table, Aled excused himself and disappeared.

"Where's he going?" I asked Alwyn.

"No idea." He was reading a text message on his phone.

Aled soon returned, sat down and then took out his phone and thumbed through the pictures in his gallery. He found the one that he wanted and passed his phone for me to see.

"What do you think of that?" he asked.

I looked at the picture. I could not make head nor tail of it. "I don't know what to think. What is it?"

"You're a fucking colo-rectal surgeon Jackson, it should be obvious to you", he said.

I had a closer look. The picture was slightly out of focus and a bit grainy, but with the colo-rectal clue, I concluded that it was a tail end. It was an anus tucked between some very hairy buttocks.

"It looks like an anus," I said. "Arsehole to you. Is that what it is?"

"Yes" replied Aled, his faith in my anatomical knowledge slightly restored.

"Why are you carrying a picture of an anus around with you and anyway, who does it belong to?" were my next questions.

---

104. Singer B, Donaldson J, Jackson D, Polyorchidism: functional classification and management strategy. Urology 1992:39, 384-8

"Me. It's mine," he said

"This is a picture of your arsehole?"

"Yes. I just took it in the toilet a minute ago".

"And you just thought you would show it to me over coffee and Welsh cakes?"

"Yes. You are a friend". Christ, I thought, what did he show his enemies? And for the record, I was not that sort of friend.

"I have been very sore and it's getting worse. I've got piles, haven't I? You can see them".

He showed me another picture, this time a close up. I looked carefully, shielding the camera as someone walked past. Alwyn, who had said nothing up to this point, then remarked that he was fed up with Aled complaining and had told him to see me. Aled had resisted because he had heard that if he needed something doing, it would be very painful and Google had "frightened the shit out of him"; his words not mine.

Aled did not have piles but a very common affliction which certainly would need dealing with, following a proper consultation in the clinic, certainly not in the gents' toilet, as may have appealed to him. I explained to him what he had acquired and the possible treatments, adding that as he had consulted me, I might just as well ask him a few questions. Did he want Alwyn to leave, I asked?

"No" he said.

"First question. Do you swing both ways or just the other way?"

Aled stiffened and then swelled into indignant manspreading, mansplaining, double alpha male mode.

"Fuck off Jackson," he replied. "Bloody hell, my girlfriend's over there."

"Cover," I said.

"What?"

"It's their cover. Leads people off the track. Frequently they get married, have a couple of kids, get divorced (Aled was divorced with two children), just to maintain a veneer of heterosexuality, and then they go off to some gay bar in the middle of the night. They often say they have a 'girlfriend' hidden away. Aled, I have to know everything, and it's all medical in confidence".

"I'm not fucking queer, you bastard, and I do not go to gay bars," he growled.

"But what about these pictures you carry on your phone? I only have your word for it, that the... er... anatomical site belongs to you." I turned to Alwyn. "What do you know about your brother's peccadilloes?" I asked.

"If Aled's queer, it's the first I've heard of it," said his brother.

Aled rolled his eyes and yelled just a bit too loudly, "I am not fucking queer, Jackson!" With that the eyes of all the other customers in the café turned to see who had made this particular statement public, and their ears pricked up for any more juicy morsels.

"Shh!" I hissed, "keep your voice down. You don't want the whole of Aber to know."

"There's nothing to know."

"So they already know?"

I got a murderous look in reply. He'd had enough, so I stopped taking the piss.

I fixed Aled up and it was painful for him but there was nothing sinister, which was good news. He did phone me up after two weeks because he was still in a lot of discomfort and said would I mind having a look. I was almost tempted to ask him to send me a photo. After six weeks, which was how long I told him it would take to heal, he was fully recovered. Playing a round of golf with him some time later, he managed a straight drive off the first tee and that was a first.

"That's down to me," I told him, as those waiting nearby applauded the fact that Aled's ball was both in bounds and what's more still on the fairway.

"No, it isn't" he retorted. "I just had a lesson from the pro."

"Yes, it is," I argued. "I noticed you were more relaxed, not clenching your buttocks so much now that I've cured you. And by the way, you do have a cute little arse."

I ran ahead. I did not want to eat a nine iron.

Remaining with golf, Lindy came into the clinic. I knew her and her husband Gareth, who was a village idiot. By that, I don't mean to seem disparaging; he was the rhythm guitarist of a locally formed group of middle-aged nutcases called the Village Idiots, who performed middle-of-the-road music and songs for those who were old and hard of hearing. In other words, it was raucous and enthusiastic, to say the least. They were very capable, popular musicians, who even played at my retirement party and during the 20-odd years of their existence, contributed enormous sums to charity. Gareth was also a patient of mine. He had required emergency surgery for an uncommon large bowel problem, which had left him with a stoma (bowel brought out through the abdominal wall) and he was fine.

Lindy had had a different problem, where the whole of her large bowel had been removed, but she elected to have gastrointestinal continuity restored by the construction of a reservoir pouch from her remaining small bowel in her abdomen. Thus, in short, she continued to use her tail end. The only problem that had arisen was that with the fluid nature of the small bowel contents and recurrent bouts of what is known as "pouchitis", her bowel habit was such that she was chained to the toilet. This is a very distressing state of affairs and almost always leads to social exclusion, and in her case, also led to her having to give up her one passion – golf – as she often could not get beyond the first hole before having to rush back to the clubhouse and the loo. She had terrible urgency, which was coupled with the dread of incontinence.

Though the procedure she had undergone is usually successful and compatible with a pretty normal life, I think in her case when it had been performed in late middle age, her body found it difficult to adjust. She had seen how well her husband was coping with his stoma, indeed leading a perfectly normal life, and if that alternative still existed, she would rather go along with it. She said to me that all she wanted to do was "play nine holes of golf"; I had a lot of sympathy for her. This was an important quality of life issue.

I was not going to attempt removal of her pouch, which would have been a very major procedure. I simply defunctioned it, short-circuited it as it were, so that her gastrointestinal contents drained into a bag before getting to this troublesome pouch. She was now similar to her husband. From then on, Lindy's life was transformed. When she had fully recovered, she could manage 18 holes of golf occasionally, I assume with a quick bag-emptying exercise behind a bush when necessary. She also resumed her life as an active contributor to the social activities of the golf club, of which I was also a member. A couple of years later she was elected as Lady Captain. Not all my surgical exploits have had such a happy ending, but this one made up for a lot of them. Unfortunately, Lindy has since died, of an unrelated cause, but as I write this, I see her husband is still going strong. He was the secretary of the charity I co-founded, so let's get onto that.

CHAPTER 69

The Mid-Wales
Colo-Rectal Cancer Fund

His name was Melville and he was married to a woman called Cheryl. Melville was in trouble that was soon to become fatal, and Cheryl would follow not long after him. As I write this, recalling the details causes me a lot of sadness, not only because they were devoted to each other, but also because they were both examples of late presentation of malignant disease and the poor prognoses that this leads to. He was a librarian, or similar, and she worked as a legal secretary. Childless, they lived together in a rented council house just outside Aberaeron.

Melville had been ignoring bleeding from his tail end and a severe change of bowel habit, and when I examined him, I found a very large fixed carcinoma of the rectum, totally inoperable in its present state. In these circumstances it is possible to downstage the tumour by the use of what is called neoadjuvant therapy (radiotherapy, chemotherapy or both) in intensive doses, to try and shrink the tumour and hopefully render it operable. Melville was referred on for this, as in Bronglais we did not have a radiotherapy unit, though we could supply chemotherapy. During the course of this treatment Melville's rectum perforated, an absolute disaster, which led to a very capable colo-rectal colleague of mine operating in totally adverse conditions to salvage the situation and save Melville's life.

However, the cancer could not be removed in its entirety and with the release of faecal organisms into a pelvis full of blood and tumour, a severe and untreatable rampant infection set in, a form of necrotising fasciitis. I received the call from my colleague. He had done his best, but Melville was being returned to our care for palliation until his inevitable death. I had to inform Cheryl of these developments, which she found difficult to understand when she returned with her husband. Melville was one of the most stoic men I have ever met. The infection in his pelvis was awful, and so was the smell of the faecal organisms and the rotting flesh they caused. On several occasions I had to return him to theatre to cut away great swathes of tissue, just to render him more comfortable and the smell less appalling. He never flinched, he never bemoaned his lot, he just kept thanking me for what I was doing, futile though it was. He was fully aware of his impending demise and just accepted it. He died about two weeks later.

During this time Cheryl had slept on an old foldaway bed by Melville's side and tended to his needs as much as she could. The nursing staff on the ward were magnificent in the way they cared for him too and were much appreciated by Cheryl in their dedication to her husband's lost cause.

She asked if she could do something to repay the hospital for their care, and I suggested that she might like to help me found a charity that I had long being thinking about. Just to recap a bit, when I first started at Bronglais I said I would work to get the operating lights replaced in my theatre. This I managed by accumulating public donations to the hospital, specifically targeted to the surgical ward, and with half the cost available, then getting the Director of Finance of the Trust (Derek Jones) to agree to fund the other half. This would be the pattern of events. If I got half the money for something, then the Trust would always find the rest, probably by creative accounting.

But this enterprise was different. This charity needed to be totally independent of the Trust and devoted to reducing the hardship of those patients with colorectal cancer and their families. It was called the Mid-Wales Colo-Rectal Cancer Fund. We had enormous free help from a variety of sources in setting up the charity legally, getting a website together, publishing our enterprise and then standing in the foyer of Morrison's shaking cans for donations. I managed to clobber the Medical Director of the Trust on his way in and again on his way out. We also held charity auctions and dinner dances with the proceeds going to the charity.

It was not long before we were funding a State Registered Nurse, with a view to her becoming a colo-rectal specialist nurse, one of the new breeds, and many other varied deserving causes. Cheryl became the Chairman of the Trust and had recruited a friend of hers with impeccable credentials to be Vice Chair. His name is Owain Peckover and he also lived in Aberaeron. I was the advisor in matters of patients and donations and I took this role so that I could ensure that the decision-making process was made by the officers of the charity, not by me. As the charity was set up in 2009, it would not be long before I would be retiring.

I have mentioned carer cancer. Cheryl had it. In order to take care of Melville and further the objectives of the charity, she completely ignored the lump in her breast and the development of hard, then ulcerated swellings in her axilla (armpit), and when she told me, I was devastated. In spite of a good operative clearance procedure and intensive chemotherapy, the outcome was predictably poor.

About a year after I had retired, Nicki and I were in our villa in Spain, when I received a phone call on my English mobile phone. The caller was almost unintelligible, but I reasoned it was Cheryl, simply because I could recognise her voice. She asked if I would come and see her in hospital as she did not feel very well. A nurse then took over the phone and explained to me that Cheryl was dying and wanted to see me before she passed. I was completely choked up. I explained to the nurse that I was in Spain, but fortunately I was booked to return to the UK for a break from the hot weather very shortly and would go to the hospital as soon as I got back.

The nurse told Cheryl this, and then informed me that Cheryl had said she would try and hang on. As soon as I was back in the UK I drove to the hospital with Nicki and we raced up the familiar stairs to Meurig Ward (the chemotherapy ward). I went to the nursing station and asked if Cheryl was still alive. "Yes Mr Jackson" the duty nurse said "She has been asking for you every day. Come with me". We followed the staff nurse to a side room and went in.

"Cheryl, look who's here to see you" the nurse said. Cheryl was very weak. She could hardly turn her head, but when she did, I noticed her eyes light up with the familiar blue sparkle that I had got so used to when we worked together. She was heavily sedated, but she managed to hold out her hand for me to take, which I did after I had sat down. Trying to hold back my tears required a massive amount of self-control, and I was really not up to the task.

"Thank you both so much for coming," she slurred through her heavy sedation. "I knew you would not let me down".

There was not much more to be said; in fact she was too exhausted to speak. Her cancer had completely overwhelmed her. Cheryl lapsed into a restful if slightly laboured sleep and would not regain consciousness. I continued to hold her hand for a long time. Eventually we had to go, kindly and with understanding, but we had the urgent affairs of the living to attend to. Cheryl died early next evening.

This was not the first time I had held the hand of a dying friend. A few years earlier I had travelled to Harrogate, at the request of Sarah, the wife of my childhood friend Dog. He had contracted oesophageal cancer two years before and was now terminal. For all the deaths I had experience of, these two were the most harrowing. I knew all about the awful prognoses of oesophageal cancer and the late treatment of widespread breast cancer, but it did not make it easier to bear. I suppose it was the dying of a friend rather than a very ill patient which made the difference between my taking it in my stride or caving into grief. Dog also died on the evening of the day after I visited him. I was terribly upset.

As a rule, I never go to patients' funerals. I suppose I have to try and maintain a sort of detachment, to remain unemotional, publicly and privately, so that I can tackle the next problem with a clean diagnostic approach. However, in the case of Ms Aileen S, I made an exception and I went to her funeral. I was very glad I did.

One of the local GPs had asked me to do a domiciliary visit on her. She lived in Borth village, in a lovely cottage near the beach. She was Scottish, and an academic doctor, and she worked as a research scientist at the university. She had very severe colicky abdominal pain and could not open her bowels, except to pass a few pellets and then nothing else, not even flatus. When I opened her up, I found a nasty little constricting cancer of her sigmoid colon. It had perforated the wall of the bowel and all her draining lymph nodes appeared involved, though her liver was clear. Another late presentation with a poor prognosis, five-year survival odds of zero, in medico-statistical speak. It was all doom and gloom. However, after surgery and chemotherapy she felt well, and having had my guarded prognosis, she retired from the university, bought a brand-new convertible car and enjoyed her life as best she could, with lots of wine and her favourite tipple, malt whisky. She partnered me in mixed golf competitions.

When the inevitable recurrent disease occurred, its manifestation took everybody by surprise. She had developed headaches and a visual disturbance, and though the former was typical of brain secondary deposits, the latter was not. Further scanning advised by the multi-disciplinary team where her management was under discussion revealed a likely tumour of her pituitary gland, which was the cause of her deteriorating vision. I argued that on the balance of probability, it was a secondary from her bowel tumour. The riposte was, how many have lodged in the pituitary gland? Very few, but secondaries can travel to wherever there is a blood supply. I was outnumbered and a neurosurgical opinion was requested, delaying the whole secondary treatment process by two weeks. The opinion obtained was inconclusive, as were further scans, so a transnasal biopsy (through the back of the nose) was suggested to definitely elucidate the problem. I argued that essentially every second counted, and we should assume it was a cerebral secondary and not another primary. This was countered correctly, in that if it was a second primary cancer, then bowel cancer specific chemotherapy would be ineffective, and the situation could be rectified by stereotactic surgery. However, tempus fugit, and I have an everlasting memory of greeting Dr S at the hospital door one evening, as she was led almost blind and in incontinence nappies beneath her nightdress, to be admitted to Meurig Ward for the last time.

"Don't worry David, ya did ya bes'. Ta for everythin'".

Post-mortem revealed it was indeed a bowel cancer secondary in her pituitary gland. In truth I don't think it would have made any difference, though if her tumour had responded and shrunk, she could have regained some of her sight.

So I went to her funeral. It was not a sad event. Her life was widely celebrated by those who elected to read their own eulogies. Her work in the university had been ground-breaking and of international importance. Her sense of humour, her wit, her adventures, her successes and failures were extolled in joyous terms. This was a curtailed life, but lived to the full. No one at the funeral could have failed to be uplifted. There had been no sombre music throughout the service, and as the coffin disappeared behind the curtains en-route to the crematorium, 'Only look on the bright side of life' started blaring out of the PA system, and many of the funeral attendees started to rock and sing. I had an epiphany.

CHAPTER 70

Mia and the Man

When somebody undergoes an operation, in effect they are being injured, but in controlled circumstances. Most mammals have a similar response to this assault and healing should take place, though there can be complications, no matter the precautions. Other cases of injury, sustained whilst not under the supervision of the medically qualified, will lead to a similar response but with a greater chance of unwanted complications.

They were both injured at around the same time. She was a tiny Chihuahua bitch weighing in at 1.6 kg who was spayed at seven months old. He was a 70-year-old man, weighing in at 105 kg, who was impaled in his right calf by a cactus spine whilst chain sawing excess foliage from an adjacent palm tree, under the direction of his wife, who indeed was actually responsible for the presence of the cactus and for that matter, many others.

The dog's injury was the incision made by the vet; his was the penetrating wound of the cactus spine. Though the dog had been under anaesthetic and felt no pain, she did not whimper or show any sign of distress afterwards. She required minimal pain relief and indeed a few hours later, though groggy, was moving about quite effortlessly. On the other hand, the man hopped around in agony. Most cactus spines are not poisonous, but they can contain an alkaloid which causes a stinging sensation. He described this pain as the worst known to man. His wife seemed neither impressed nor concerned, and in any event suspected her husband had a pathetically low pain threshold. "If you want to know what real pain is like, try having a Caesarean Section" she suggested indifferently.

He limped and mooched around and taking comfort from a whisky bottle, sat down with his leg elevated so that he could examine the tiny puncture wound he had sustained. He subsequently refused to even go into their tropical garden until all the cactus plants had been destroyed with a flame thrower.

The little bitch (dog) as opposed to the unsympathetic big bitch (wife) was soon running about and playing with the other family dogs. Indeed, a brake had to be put on her activities, as she would need time to heal. Conversely, great efforts had to be made to get the man to move from his death bed, though his injury had already closed over.

Soon the dog was fit enough to gently walk around a field, accompanied by the man with his pitiful limping gait and permanently pained expression. Over the next couple of weeks the man noticed that though his wound had healed, he was left with a lump under the skin, a very prickly lump. This bit of cactus, a foreign body no less, would have to be removed at a later date before it took root and started to grow into and then out of his leg. Similarly it was noticed that the Chihuahua's wound was a little lumpy, and through the wound the absorbable stitch used to close the skin after the spaying could be seen. Both therefore had retained "foreign bodies".

The man explained to his wife that the vet had said that the stitches would resorb, but it might take a little time and was nothing to worry about. The dog would be all right, but he would gradually turn into a cactus. Fortunately, nature dealt with both problems in her own time. The bodies of both mobilised their immune forces, white cells were transformed into giant cells and eventually the cactus remnant and the stitches were removed. Munched away, they disappeared without trace.

The dog's name is Mia. The "cactus" was an *Agave angustifolia marginata (variegata),* which for the sake of accuracy is a succulent plant with spines, and I was the man.

Mia and the Man. Spain 2019

CHAPTER 71

Retiring in Stylus

The third consultant in our set up, Mr V, was not performing well, and had to be heavily supported by his very experienced Egyptian Associate Specialist, and I mentored Mr V for years. I think as a breast surgeon, for which he was mainly trained, he was fine, but the generality of the job, particularly the on call, was taking its toll. With the agreement of the Trust and the then Chief Executive, a very likeable ex-nurse, Allison Williams, he was persuaded to take early retirement.

Replacing him would be very difficult, as recruitment to that part of Wales was not easy. JLE put it to the CEO that he and I could do the job of three consultants because we were highly supported by very capable and experienced juniors, and would really only have to provide consultant direction rather than too much extra work. It was seductive for the CEO and she agreed that JLE and I would do it all and we could split Mr V's salary between us. As a result, I ended up with two associate specialists, one specialist, a senior house officer and two house officers on my firm.

I provided consultant cover for the breast work and had two full-day and two half-day operating lists a week, instead of the usual single day or even just a half day, as some surgeons are allocated these days. My patient turnover became ridiculously high for a singlehanded consultant, but it was manageable for a period of time. My salary was enormous, but my work life balance took a severe knock because of the frequency of the on call.

There was very little emergency surgery that my juniors could not handle, and therefore required my presence, but I was tied to the area and a telephone. My Army experience of long periods of being on call stood me in good stead, but in truth I needed to wind down, not wind up, as I was 60 years old. After 18 months or so I spoke to JLE and he agreed that we should discontinue our arrangement and the Trust should advertise for another consultant; my workload reduced substantially.

My father-in-law and I in my Stylus sports car

I was now considering my retirement. It had been a sort of truism, years ago, that if a consultant general surgeon retired at 60 years old, statistically he would live for a further 14 years. If he left it until he was 65 years old, he would live for 14 months. I proposed to lay down my knife at around 63 and following Nicki's advice, I found something else to do in evenings and weekends prior to my retirement. I built a kit car in my garage. It took me 18 months and I required a lot of help, but finally a Specialist Sports Car Stylus was on the road, in Ferrari red livery with two asymmetrical white stripes down the bonnet. It was fast, I mean very fast, and extremely noisy.

The Trust was still trying to transfer my bowel cancer practice and patients. However, whilst I was still in post, my reputation and the loyalty of my patients made this very difficult for them. They set up public meetings to outline the benefits of the proposed changes, which would simultaneously downgrade the status of the hospital. This was fiercely resisted by all and sundry, but I was getting very despondent. I had enough to do without firefighting the snipes from Trust HQ. At one meeting, an imported management heavyweight presented completely incorrect figures for the number of cancer patients I had operated on in the previous year. I had been pre-warned by a mole that this was on their agenda, so I extracted the correct number from my audit department and challenged the figures presented, offering to read out the hospital numbers of all the cases I had done.

I was looking at some of the persuasive literature the Trust had left scattered around the room when the Chairman of the Trust, whom I had met on a number of occasions and liked very much, approached me. He said, "Don't worry David, it's not personal".

I realised that he too was under orders to amalgamate and consolidate the administrative burdens of the organisation, and it became pretty obvious to me that notwithstanding my wishes and the wishes of the overwhelming majority of the local population, these changes would occur, certainly if and when I retired. My experience and expertise counted for nothing now, my loyal patient base could be ignored, and it would all fade into a distant past. Next day, I approached the Clinical Director of Surgery at an appointment meeting and gave him 18 months' notice. I would retire at the end of October 2012 when a large leaving gathering would be organised for me in the Welsh Belle Vue Hotel.

Postscript

Sunnier Times, Sunnier Climes

In 2001 we bought three acres of farm land in the south east of Spain, just short of the foothills of the Sierra Cabrera Mountain range; a truly stunning backdrop to wake up to in the morning. Our villa, which Nicki designed, is situated less than a mile away from my friends Rod and Wendy, the couple who so kindly shielded me and my children from the paparazzi all those years ago. It took us 11 years to build it.

On my retirement we anticipated spending more and more time in Spain, as we loved the way of life, the countryside, the people and of course the beautiful weather. With 320 days of guaranteed sunshine a year in an area designated as desert, it would, it would undoubtedly help Nicki in providing her with additional serotonin from the strong sunlight, at a time when her OCD symptoms were escalating into the full blown disorder

Though I would have happily stayed in Aberystwyth, a role reversal was in order. Nicki had prioritised my needs and supported me by moving to Aberystwyth when my own life was in crisis 17 years before. It was my time to support her in her time of need.

During my notice period pending retirement, we bought a house in Shropshire. Nicki wanted to move from Aberystwyth to be closer to the children, who as young adults had moved away from the town, and to be near to her beloved airfield on the Long Mynd which had provided her with a remote and much needed sanctuary during the difficult years we had endured. It was where she had gained her solo glider pilot's wings at the age of 40.

Unsurprisingly, Angela has not moved on. She is still full of bile and hatred to this day. I have had to include far more about her in this memoir than I wanted to, but on the other hand, far less than I could have, given the enormity of the damage she caused the whole family. To have omitted an account of her actions would not only risk trivialising them and their consequences, it would also have concealed the real reasons behind the tough decisions I had to make. Her unforgiveable behaviour made my surgical practice far more difficult than it should have been, both in the army and the NHS.

However, notwithstanding Angela's attempts to completely alienate the children from me, I still have loving contact with both to this day. Nicki has maintained regular contact with my younger daughter and despite every discouragement over the years, my younger daughter also has a very genuine and close relationship with both of her stepsiblings. However, it is still a work in progress as the indoctrination has been deeply ingrained and is on occasions, still the default opinion. I suspect some of the emotional damage is irreversible, but as usual I will bide my time and hope for the best.

My children can now know the truth of what really happened, not the fallacious version of it they were coerced to believe for so many years. Hopefully, they will now understand the steps Nicki and I took to shield and protect them from their own mother's damaging influence and the huge disservice we did ourselves in the process. Perhaps they will finally have a degree of empathy when they realise the sacrifices we had to make, both individually and as a newly-married couple, and the toll it took on us and the members of their extended family, in order to safeguard their emotional wellbeing. Maybe my children will realise that when I made the decision to prioritise protecting them, rather than myself, by refusing to surrender to their mother's demands, abuse and threats, my career in the army became irreparably damaged as a consequence and very nearly in the NHS too. In spite of all this I refused to give up on them.

Every surgeon carries a sack full of mistakes and regrets on his back from which he will learn. Each one induces feelings of remorse which soften over time, but never truly go away. Their purpose is to remind us of our fallibility in surgical uncertainty and moral dilemmas. However, as I look back on my life in print, I regard the many challenges I have faced with a degree of satisfaction, in that I have, on the whole, prevailed through adversity, through my wars, both military and domestic, and through my work in an isolated hospital of last resort. I never gave up climbing the mountain, even if I lost my footing a few times.

In the villa now as I write this, it is 8.15 am on a fantastically clear morning, still cool enough to get things done. Nicki has just informed me that the new trees she has planted need staking against the strong winds and so I will get on with that. Later in the cool of the evening, we will relax in our rocking chairs on the front porch with cheap gin martinis and not a lot of tonic. We will eat a bit of *jamón* in the company of our loyal pets, four dogs and a 17-year-old yowling, deaf cat. We will laugh, we will joke, we will get slightly tipsy and I will be conscripted into Nicki's next project. Our lives now could not be better. We have peace.